VISUAL QUICKSTART GUIDE

DHTML AND CSS

FOR THE WORLD WIDE WEB, THIRD EDITION

Jason Cranford Teague

Peachpit Press

Visual QuickStart Guide
DHTML and CSS for the World Wide Web, Third Edition
Jason Cranford Teague

Peachpit Press

1249 Eighth Street
Berkeley, CA 94710
510/524-2178
800/283-9444
510/524-2221 (fax)

Find us on the World Wide Web at: www.peachpit.com
To report errors, please send a note to errata@peachpit.com
Peachpit Press is a division of Pearson Education

Editor: Nancy Davis
Production Editor: Becky Winter
Copyeditor: Kate McKinley
Technical Editor: Thomas I. Williams II
Compositor: Danielle Foster
Proofreader: Ted Waitt
Indexer: Joy Dean Lee
Cover design: The Visual Group
Cover Production: George Mattingly / GMD

Notice of Rights

Notice of Liability

Trademarks

ISBN 0-321-19958-8

9 8 7 6 5 4 3

Printed and bound in the United States of America

Dedication:

For Jocelyn and Dashiel,
who are making my life more dynamic
every day.

Special Thanks to:

Tara, my soul mate and best critic.

Nancy, who guided this project through to the end with great patience.

Kate, who dotted my i's and made sure that everything made sense.

Thomas, who checked the code on every browser we could lay our hands on.

Molly, who pitched in and updated Chapters 19 and 20.

Mom, Dad, and Nancy, who made me who I am.

Uncle Johnny, for his unwavering support.

Pat and Red, my two biggest fans.

Neil and the good folks at Studio B, for representing my best interests.

Charles Dodgson (aka Lewis Carroll), for writing *Alice in Wonderland*.

John Tennet, for his incredible illustrations of *Alice in Wonderland*.

Judy, Boyd, Dr. G and teachers everywhere who care. Keep up the good work.

Douglas Adams, Neil Gaiman, and Carl Sagan whose writings inspire me every day.

The Cure, the The, Siouxsie and the Banshees, the ie America Radio Network, Shakespeare's Sister, Type-O Negative, Blur, Cracker, Danielle Dax, Nine Inch Nails, KMFDM, the Pogues, Ramones, New Model Army, Cocteau Twins, Cranes, the Sisters of Mercy, the Smiths, Mojo Nixon, Bauhaus, Lady Tron, Bad Religion, This Mortal Coil, Rancid, Monty Python, the Dead Milkmen, New Order, The Sex Pistols, Dead Can Dance, and ZBS Studios (for *Ruby*) whose noise helped keep me from going insane while writing this book.

TABLE OF CONTENTS

TABLE OF CONTENTS

Chapter 18: Navigation and Controls   367

Chapter 19: GoLive CS Primer   407

Chapter 20: Dreamweaver MX 2004 Primer   423

Chapter 21: Debugging Your Code   437

Appendix A: CSS Quick Reference   449

Appendix B: DHTML Quick Reference   459

Appendix C: The DHTML and CSS Browsers   465

INTRODUCTION

Once upon a time creating Web pages was no more difficult than using a word processor. You learned a few HTML tags, created a few graphics, and presto: Web page. Now, with streaming video, JavaScript, CGI, Shockwave, Flash, and Java, the design of Web pages may seem overwhelming to anyone who doesn't want to become a computer programmer.

Enter Cascading Style Sheets (CSS) and Dynamic HTML (DHTML), technologies that give you—the Web designer—the ability to add pizzazz to your Web pages as quickly and easily as HTML. With DHTML, you don't have to rely on plug-ins that the visitor might not have—or rely on complicated pro-gramming languages (except maybe a little JavaScript). For the most part, DHTML and CSS are created the same way as HTML and require no special software.

That's what this book is about: How to create attractive Web layouts and interactive Web pages as simply as possible. This book will not turn you into the ultimate Web-design guru overnight, but it will give you the foundations you need to realize your own Web-design vision.

If you are learning Web design and do not know CSS and DHTML, this is where you need to begin. Welcome.

What Is This Book About?

In the years since Netscape Navigator and Internet Explorer began supporting CSS and DHTML, the Web itself has changed significantly. The browser wars, the dot-com explosion (and subsequent crash), and the Web's enormous growth in popularity have led to a shakedown of the technologies that are regularly used to create Web sites. Both CSS and DHTML, however, remain two standards being used to create some of the best Web sites around.

In this book, I'll show you the best ways to implement CSS and DHTML so that the broadest spectrum of the Web-surfing population can view your Web sites. To help organize the information, I have split this book into three parts:

- **Part 1** details how to use CSS to control the appearance of the content on Web pages. I'll show you accurate ways to control the various aspects of how your Web page is displayed.

- **Part 2** deals with how to use the Document Object Model (DOM) with CSS and JavaScript to create basic dynamic functions. I'll show you how to use the DOM to run dynamic functions in most browsers, with as little redundant code as possible.

- **Part 3** will show you some real-world applications of DHTML and CSS, as well as how to use some of the most popular software (Adobe GoLive and Macromedia Dreamweaver) and how to troubleshoot your own code.

- **The Appendixes** include quick references for all of the information in the first two parts of the book as well as a list of the browser-safe fonts, and tools and resources for Web developers.

Who Is This Book For?

If the title of this book caught your eye, you're probably already well acquainted with the ins and outs of the Internet's most popular offshoot, the World Wide Web (or perhaps you're just a severely confused arachnophile). To understand this book, you need to be familiar with HTML (Hypertext Markup Language). You don't have to be an expert, but you should know the difference between a `<p>` tag and a `<br/>` tag. In addition, several chapters call for more than a passing knowledge of JavaScript.

That said, the more knowledge of HTML and JavaScript you bring to this book, the more you'll get out of it.

INTRODUCTION

Everyone Is a Web Designer

Forget about 15 minutes of fame: In the future, everyone will be a Web designer. As the Web continues to expand, a growing number of people are choosing this medium to get their message—whatever it may be—out to the rest of the world. Whether they are movie buffs extolling the virtues of *The Third Man* or multinational corporations extolling the virtues of their companies, individuals and companies see the Web as the way to get the message out.

The fact is, just as everyone who uses a word processor is at some level a typographer, as the Web grows in popularity, everyone who uses it to do more than passively view pages will need to know how to design for the Web.

This does not just mean designing complete Web sites. Many people are using HTML to create simple Web pages for auction sites such as eBay, their own photos albums, or their own Web logs (Blogs). So whether you are planning to redesign your corporate Web site or place your kid's graduation pictures online, learning DHTML and CSS is your next step into the larger world of Web design.

Why Standards (Still) Matter

The prime meridian and Greenwich Mean Time are standards that allow us to determine our position on earth with pinpoint accuracy. These standards can be applied anywhere at any time by anybody; they are universally accessible and understood because everybody has agreed to do it that way. They allow ships to ply the seven seas without bumping into land (usually) and airplanes to fly in friendly skies without bumping into each other. And they have opened the world to travel not necessarily because they are a superior way of doing things, but simply because everyone has agreed to do things the same way. Sounds like a pretty good idea, doesn't it?

The idea of a standard was the principle behind the creation of the World Wide Web: Information should be able to be transmitted to any computer anywhere in the world and displayed pretty much the way the author intended it to look. In the beginning, only one form of HTML existed, and everyone on the Web used it. This situation didn't present any real problem, because almost everyone used Mosaic, the first graphics-based browser, and Mosaic stuck to this standard like glue. That, as they say, was then.

Along came Netscape, and the first HTML extensions were born. These extensions worked only in Netscape, however, and anyone who didn't use that browser was out of luck. Although the Netscape extensions defied the standards of the World Wide Web Consortium (W3C), most of them— or at least some version of them—eventually became part of those very standards. According to some people, the Web has gone downhill ever since.

The Web is a very public form of discourse, the likes of which has not existed since people lived in villages and sat around the campfire telling stories every night. The problem is that without standards, not everyone in the global village can make it to the Web campfire. You can use as many bleeding-edge techniques as you like. You can include Flash, JavaScript, VBScript, QuickTime video, layers, or data binding, but if only a fraction of browsers can see your work, you're keeping a lot of fellow villagers out in the cold.

In coding for this book, I spent a good 35–45 percent of the time trying to get the code to run as smoothly as possible in Internet Explorer 5+, Netscape 6+, Opera 6+, and Safari 1. This situation holds true for most of my Web projects; much of the coding time is spent on cross-browser inconsistencies. If the browsers stuck to the standards, this time would be reduced to almost none.

Your safest bet as a designer, then, is to know the standards of the Web, try to use them as much as possible, and demand that the browser manufacturers use them as well. The Web Standards Project (www.webstandards.org) is a watchdog group working to make sure that browser manufacturers stick to the standards they helped create. Get involved.

Netscape 4: The Death of a Legend

Although I am a strong believer in coding for as broad an audience as possible, there comes a time when you have to recognize that backward compatibility has diminishing returns. That time has come and gone for Netscape 4. Current estimates place its user base at less than one percent of the browsing public. However, most importantly, Netscape 4 was not terribly standards compliant, meaning that it requires a massive effort to make your code cross-browser compatible and severely limits what can be done with Web design.

Therefore, when revising this book, I made the difficult decision not to support Netscape 4. This book still includes a few scripts to fix problems in Netscape 4, as well as a work-around for the Document Object Model, but most of the DHTML scripts will not work in Netscape 4. Doing this not only greatly simplifies the code in this book but also expands the horizons of what we can do with DHTML.

Values and Units

Throughout this book, you'll need to enter different values to define different properties. These values come in various forms, depending on the need of the property. Some values are straightforward—a number is a number—but others have special units associated with them.

Values in chevrons (<>) represent one type of value (**Table i.1**). Words that appear in the code font are literal values and should be typed exactly as shown.

Length values

Length values come in two varieties:

◆ Relative lengths, which vary depending on the computer being used (**Table i.2**).

◆ Absolute values, which remain constant regardless of the hardware and software being used (**Table i.3**).

I generally recommend using pixel sizes to describe font sizes for the greatest stability between operating systems and browsers.

Table i.1

Value Types		
VALUE TYPE	WHAT IT IS	EXAMPLE
<number>	A number	1, 2, 3
<length>	A measurement of distance	1in or size
<color>	A chromatic expression	red
<percentage>	A proportion	35%
<URL>	The absolute or relative path to a file on the Web	http:// www.mySite.net/ bob/graphics/ image1.gif

Table i.2

Relative Length Values			
NAME	TYPE OF UNIT	WHAT IT IS	EXAMPLE
em	Em dash	Width of the letter M for that font	3em
ex	x-height	Height of the lowercase x of that font	5ex
px	Pixel	Based on the monitor's resolution	125px

Table i.3

Absolute Length Values			
NAME	TYPE OF UNIT	WHAT IT IS	EXAMPLE
pt	Point (1 pt. = 1/72 in.)	Generally used to describe font size	12pt
pc	Picas (1 pc. ff 12 pt.)	Generally used to describe font size	3pc
mm	Millimeters		25mm
cm	Centimeters		5.1cm
in	Inches (1 in. = 2.54 cm)		2.25in

Table i.4

Color Values		
NAME	WHAT IT IS	EXAMPLE
#RRGGBB	Red, green, and blue hex-code value of a color (00-99,AA-FF)	#CC33FF or #C3F
rgb(R#,G#,B#)	Red, green, and blue numeric -values of a color (0–255)	rgb(204,51,255)
rgb(R%,G%,B%)	--Red, green, and blue percentage values of a color (0–100%)	rgb(81%,18%,100%)
name	The name of the color	Purple

Browser-Safe Colors

Certain colors always display properly on any monitor. These colors are called the browser-safe colors. You'll find them fairly easy to remember because their values stay consistent. In hexadecimal values, you can use any combination of 00, 33, 66, 99, CC, and FF. In numeric values, use 0, 51, 102, 153, 204, or 255. In percentages, use 0, 20, 40, 60, 80, or 100.

Color values

You can describe color on the screen in a variety of ways (**Table i.4**), but most of these descriptions are just different ways of telling the computer how much red, green, and blue are in a particular color.

Percentages

Many of the properties in this book can have a percentage as their value. The behavior of this percentage value depends on the property being used.

URLs

A Uniform Resource Locator (URL) is the unique address of something on the Web. This resource could be an HTML document, a graphic, a CSS file, a JavaScript file, a sound or video file, a CGI script, or any of a variety of other file types. URLs can be local, simply describing the location of the resource relative to the current document; or global, describing the absolute location of the resource on the Web and beginning with http://

In addition, throughout the book, I use links in the code examples. I use the number sign (#) as a placeholder in links that can be directed to any URL you want:

```
<a href="#">Link</a>
```

The number sign is shorthand that links to the top of the current page. Replace these with your own URLs as desired.

However, in some links, placing any URL in the href will interfere with the DHTML functions in the example. For those, I used the built-in JavaScript function void():

```
<a href="javascript:void('')">Link</a>
```

This function simply tells the link to do absolutely nothing.

Reading This Book

For the most part, the text, tables, figures, code, and examples should be self-explanatory. But you need to know a few things to understand this book.

CSS value tables

In Part 1, each section that explains a CSS property includes a table for quick reference with the different values the property can use, as well as the browsers and CSS levels with which those values are compatible (**Figure i.1**). The Compatibility column displays the first browser version that supported the value type. **Table i.5** lists the browser abbreviations I used. Keep in mind, though, that even if the value is available in a particular version of the browser, it may not be available for all operating systems. Appendix A shows in which operating systems values work and whether there are any problems.

Table i.5

Browser Abbreviations	
ABBREVIATION	BROWSER
IE3	Internet Explorer 3
IE4	Internet Explorer 4
IE5	Internet Explorer 5
N4	Netscape 4
N6	Netscape 6*
N7	Netscape 7**
O3.5	Opera 3.5
O4	Opera 4
O5	Opera 5
O6	Opera 6
O7	Opera 7
S1	Safari 1

* Includes Mozilla 1
** Includes Mozilla 1.3, Firebird, and Camino

Table 5.7

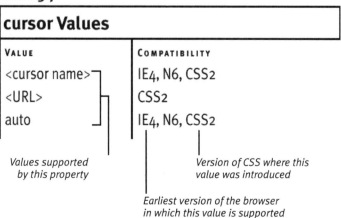

cursor Values	
VALUE	COMPATIBILITY
<cursor name>	IE4, N6, CSS2
<URL>	CSS2
auto	IE4, N6, CSS2

Values supported by this property

Version of CSS where this value was introduced

Earliest version of the browser in which this value is supported

Figure i.1 The property tables in Part 1 of this book show you the values available with a property, the earliest browser version in which the value is available, and with which version of CSS the value was introduced.

The code

For clarity and precision, I have used several layout techniques to help you see the difference between the text of the book and the code.

Code looks like this:

```
<style>

p { font-size: 12pt; }

</style>
```

All code in this book is presented in lowercase (see the sidebar "Uppercase or Lowercase Code" in Chapter 1). In addition, quotes in the code always appear as straight quotes (" or '), not curly quotes (" or '). There is a good reason for this distinction: Curly quotes (also called smart quotes) will cause the code to fail.

When you type a line of code, the computer can run the line as long as needed, but in this book, lines of code have to be broken to make them fit on the page. When that happens, I use this gray arrow → to indicate that the line of code is continued from above, like this:

```
.title { font: bold 28pt/26pt times,
→ serif; color: #FFF; background-
→ color: #000; background-image:
→ url(bg_ title.gif); }
```

I often begin a numbered step with a line of code. This is intended as a reference to help you pinpoint where that step applies in the larger code block that accompanies the task. This code will then be highlighted in red in the code listing to help you more easily identify it.

HTML or XHTML?

The Web is currently undergoing a metamorphosis behind the scenes, as the markup language used to create Web pages migrates from HTML to XHTML. Although very similar in their syntax, XHTML is much less lenient with errors.

For this book, I use XHTML as the markup language. For more details, see "Markup Languages: HTML, XHTML, and XML" in Chapter 1.

What Tools Do You Need for This Book?

The great thing about CSS and DHTML is that, like HTML, they don't require any special or expensive software. Their code is just text, and you can edit it with a program such as SimpleText (Mac OS 9), TextEdit (Mac OS X), or NotePad (Windows).

Appendix F includes a list of extremely helpful (and mostly free or cheap) utilities and tools that I recommend to anyone who creates Web sites.

In addition, a couple of programs make life with DHTML and CSS much easier by automating many of the tedious and repetitive tasks associated with Web design. I recommend using Adobe GoLive or Macromedia Dreamweaver. Part 3 of this book can help you decide which program is better for you.

Supported Browsers

Although most of the screen shots in the book were taken using the Camino browser, all of the code in this book has been carefully tested in Internet Explorer 5 and 6, Netscape 6 and 7, Mozilla 1.3, Firebird, Camino, Opera 6 and 7, and Safari. These browsers make up a good 99% of the browsers being used to surf the Web. All code should work in these browsers unless otherwise noted in the text. If you experience any problems with the code, please check the Web site (`www.webbedenvironments.com/dhtml`) first for any updates, and then write to the author (`vqs-dhtml@webbedenvironments.com`).

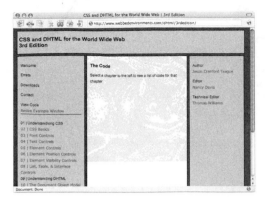

Figure i.2 The *DHTML and CSS for the World Wide Web: Visual QuickStart Guide* support Web site, open 24 hours a day.

Figure i.3 Built with DHTML. Use this logo on your Web site to link to the list of DHTML-capable browsers I have set up

Built with DHTML

In addition to the support site, I have set up a list of the most current DHTML-capable browsers at

www.webbedenvironments.com/dhtml/builtwith/

Web Sites for This Book

I hope you'll be using a lot of the code from this book in your Web pages, and you are free to use any code in this book without having to ask my permission (although a mention for the book is always appreciated). However, watch out—retyping information can lead to errors. Some books include a fancy-shmancy CD-ROM containing all the code from the book, and you can pull it off that disk. But guess who pays for that CD? You do. And CDs aren't cheap.

But if you bought this book, you already have access to the largest resource of knowledge that ever existed: the Web. And that's exactly where you can find the code from this book.

This is my support site for this Visual QuickStart Guide (**Figure i.2**):

www.webbedenvironments.com/dhtml/

You can download the code and any important updates and corrections from here. The site also includes other articles I have written about the Web.

If you do retype the examples from the book, you might find that some don't work without the support files I used to create them. No worries—at the support site, you'll find the various examples, which you can view live to compare results.

You have DHTML questions? I have DHTML answers. You can contact me at:

vqs-dhtml@webbedenvironments.com

Also, be sure to visit Peachpit Press' own support site for the book:

www.peachpit.com/vqs/DHTML3

You can use the Built with DHTML logo (**Figure i.3**) to link to this Web page from your own DHTML Web site to help visitors find the right browser.

INTRODUCTION

Part 1
Cascading
Style Sheets

1

UNDERSTANDING CSS

Let's face it: HTML is not exactly a designer's dream come true. It is imprecise, unpredictable, and not terribly versatile when it comes to presenting the diverse kinds of content that Web designers demand of it.

Then again, HTML was never intended to deliver high-concept graphic content and multimedia. In fact, it was never really intended to be anything more than a glorified universal word processing language delivered over the Internet—and a pretty limited one at that.

HTML is a markup language that was created to allow authors to define the structure of a document for distribution on a network such as the Web. That is, rather than being designed to show the style of what is being displayed, it is intended only to show how the page should be organized.

Over time, new tags and technologies have been added to HTML that allow greater control of the structure and appearance of documents—things such as tables, frames, justification controls, and JavaScript—but what Web designers can't do with fast-loading HTML, they have had to hack together using slow-loading graphics.

It's not a very elegant system.

continues on next page

So when Web developers started clamoring for the World Wide Web Consortium to add greater control of Web page design, the W3C introduced cascading style sheets (CSS) to fill the void in straight HTML (**Figure 1.1**).

Now, you're probably thinking, "Oh, great— just when I learn HTML, they go and change everything." But never fear: CSS is as easy to use as HTML. In fact, in many ways it's easier, because rather than introducing more HTML tags to learn, it works directly with existing HTML tags to tell them how to behave.

Take the humble <bold> tag, for example. In HTML, it does one thing and one thing only: It makes text darker. But using CSS, you can "redefine" the <bold> tag so that it not only makes text darker, but also displays text in all caps and in a particular font to really add emphasis. You could even make the <bold> tag *not* make text bold.

In this chapter, you'll learn how CSS works and the principles involved in creating style sheets. In subsequent chapters, you'll learn how to apply all the individual properties.

Figure 1.1 The CSS logo.

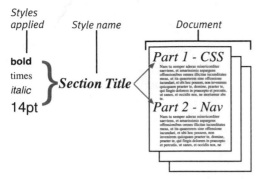

Figure 1.2 Styles being applied to section titles in a word-processing program tag.

What Is a Style?

Most word processors today include a way to make changes to text not just word by word, but throughout an entire document by means of *styles*.

Styles collect all the different attributes, such as font family, size, and color, that you want to apply to similar types of text—titles, headers, captions, and so on—and give these groups of attributes a common name. Suppose that you want all the section titles in your document to be bold, Times font, italic, red, and 14-point. You could assign all those attributes to a style called Section Title (**Figure 1.2**).

Whenever you type a section title, all you have to do is use the Section Title style, and all those attributes are applied to the text in one fell swoop—no fuss, no mess. Even better, if you decide later that you really want all those titles to be 18 point instead of 14 point, you just change the definition of Section Title. The word processor then changes the appearance of all the text marked with that style throughout the document.

What Are Cascading Style Sheets?

CSS brings to the Web the same "one-stop shopping" convenience for setting styles that's available in most word processors. You can set a CSS in one central location to affect the appearance of HTML tags on a single Web page or across an entire Web site.

Although CSS works with HTML, it is not HTML. Rather, CSS is a separate code that enhances the abilities of HTML by allowing you to redefine the way that existing HTML tags work (**Figure 1.3** and **Figure 1.4**).

For example, the header level 1 tag container, <h1>...</h1>, allows you to apply styles to a section of HTML text, turning it into a header. But the exact display of the header is determined by the viewer's browser. You cannot control how it will be styled in your layout. Using CSS, however, you (the designer) can change the nature of the header tag so that it will be displayed in the style you want—for example, bold, Times font, italic, and 14 points (**Figure 1.5**). As with word processor styles, you can also choose to change the definition of the <h1> tag and all header level 1 elements on a Web page.

Figure 1.3 An HTML page using CSS to add an image in the background, position the content down and to the right, and format the text.

Figure 1.4 The same code displayed without the benefit of CSS. The page still displays, but without the formatting of Figure 1.3.

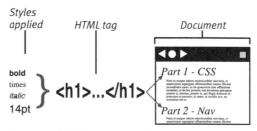

Figure 1.5 Styles being applied to an HTML tag.

Table 1.1

CSS Properties		
PROPERTY	WHAT YOU CONTROL	FOR MORE INFO
Font	Letter form, size, boldface, italic	Chapter 3
Text	Kerning, leading, alignment, case	Chapter 4
Background	Behind the page or behind a single element on the page	Chapter 5
Border & Margin	Margins, padding, borders, width, height	Chapter 5
Interface	Bullets, indentation, mouse pointer, scroll bars	Chapter 8
Color	Borders, text, bullets, rules, backgrounds	Chapters 4 and 5
Positioning	Exact placement on the screen	Chapter 6
Display & Visibility	Whether one element appears and how much of it is showing	Chapter 7

Table 1.1 shows some of the things you can do with CSS and where to find more information.

✔ Tip

- The power of CSS comes from its ability to mix and match different rules from different sources to tailor your Web pages' layout to your exact needs. In some ways, it resembles computer programming—which is not too surprising, because a lot of this stuff was created by programmers instead of designers. But once you get the hang of it, CSS will become as natural as putting together a sentence.

What's Next: CSS Level 3

Never content to rest on its laurels, the W3C is hard at work on another rendition of cascading style sheets: CSS Level 3 (www.w3.org/Style/CSS/current-work). Many of the problems that CSS2 doesn't adequately address will be resolved in this upcoming version.

Although the standard is still under construction (and has been for several years), many of the additions to CSS3 sound very exciting. Here are some highlights:

- **Columns.** The most exciting new feature proposed for CSS3 is the ability to create flexible columns for layout. CSS is complicated when used to replace tables for multiple-column layout. Ideally, CSS3 will take care of this problem.

- **Web fonts.** Although CSS2 theoretically provides downloadable-font capability, it's still too hard to use. The W3C wants to make fonts more Web-friendly in CSS3.

- **Color profiles.** One common problem with graphics is that they may be darker or lighter, depending on the computer being used. CSS3 will allow authors to include color descriptions to offset this problem.

- **User interface.** CSS3 will add more pointers, form states, and ways to use visitor-dictated color schemes.

- **Behaviors.** The most intriguing new capability uses CSS to dictate not only visual styles, but also the behavior of objects. This would provide further dynamic controls through CSS.

WHAT ARE CASCADING STYLE SHEETS?

Versions of CSS

CSS has evolved over the past several years under the guidance of the W3C (**Figure 1.6**) into its current form. Most modern browsers (Internet Explorer 6, Netscape 7, Mozilla 1, Safari 1) support CSS Level 2 (which includes CSS Level 1 and CSS-Positioning). However, CSS Level 3, which adds some accessibility functionality, has gone widely unused:

◆ **CSS Level 1 (CSS1).** The W3C released the first official version of CSS in 1996. This early version included the core capabilities associated with CSS, such as the ability to format text, set fonts, and set margins. Netscape 4 and Internet Explorer 3 and 4 support Level 1—almost.

◆ **CSS-Positioning (CSS-P).** Web designers needed a way to position elements on the screen precisely. CSS1 had already been released, and CSS Level 2 was still off in the distance, so the W3C released a stopgap solution: CSS-Positioning. This standard was intended to be a proposal that the various parties concerned could debate for a while before it became official. Netscape and Microsoft jumped on these proposals, however, and included the preliminary ideas in their version 4 browsers. Do both Netscape and Internet Explorer support CSS-P? Sort of. Although most of the basic features are supported in both of the "name-brand" browsers, several features were left out.

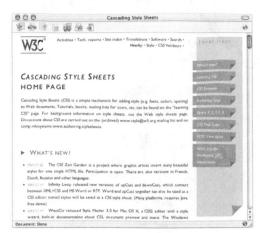

Figure 1.6 The W3C's CSS home page (www.w3.org/Style/CSS/).

◆ **CSS Level 2 (CSS2).** This version of CSS came out in 1998 and is the most widely adopted by browser-makers. Level 2 includes all the attributes of the previous two versions, plus an increased emphasis on international accessibility and the capability to specify media-specific CSS. Internet Explorer 5 and Netscape 6 support Level 2.

◆ **CSS Level 3 (CSS3).** This standard is still under development, and it usually takes a few years for browsers to support a standard once it has been released. See the sidebar "What's Next: CSS Level 3" for more details. Although this standard is still under development, some browsers (most notably Apple Safari) have started implanting some of its features.

✔ Tip

■ While knowing the differences between the CSS versions may be interesting, it isn't necessary for using styles on the Web. What you do need to know is which styles are supported by the browsers you're designing for. Although most modern browsers support most of the CSS Level 2 specification, older browsers support combinations of older versions of CSS. Appendix A details which browsers support which CSS properties.

VERSIONS OF CSS

Types of CSS Rules

The best thing about cascading style sheets is that they are amazingly simple to set up. They don't require plug-ins or fancy software—just rules. A CSS rule defines what the HTML should look like and how it should behave in the browser window.

You can set up rules to tell a specific HTML tag how to display its content, or you can create generic rules and then apply them to tags at your discretion.

There are three types of CSS rules:

◆ **HTML selector.** The text portion of an HTML tag is called the *selector*. For example, h1 is the selector for the <h1> tag. The HTML selector is used in a CSS rule to redefine how the tag displays (see "(re)Defining an HTML Tag" in Chapter 2). Example:

```
h1 { font: bold 12pt times; }
```

◆ **Class.** A *class* is a "free agent" rule that can be applied to any HTML tag at your discretion. You can name the class almost anything you want (see Appendix B for name limitations). Because it can be applied to multiple HTML tags, a class is the most versatile type of selector (see "Defining Classes to Create Your Own Tags" in Chapter 2). Example:

```
.myClass { font: bold 12pt times; }
```

◆ **ID.** Much like class selectors, *ID rules* can be applied to any HTML tag. *ID selectors*, however, are usually applied only once on a given page to a particular HTML tag, to create an object for use with a JavaScript function (see "Defining IDs to Identify an Object" in Chapter 2). Example:

```
#object1 { position: absolute;
→ top: '10px; }
```

Uppercase or Lowercase Tags?

HTML tags are not case-sensitive. That is, the browser does not care whether the selectors (the text) in the tags are uppercase or lowercase. Most people prefer to use uppercase for tags, because this makes them stand out from the surrounding content.

I counted myself in that camp until the release of the XHTML standard. One important characteristic of XHTML is that it is case-sensitive, and all selectors must be in lowercase. Therefore, to prepare for what is likely to be the next evolutionary step of HTML, I have started using lowercase selectors in all my HTML tags.

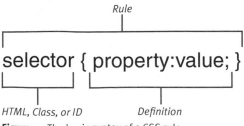

Rule

```
selector { property:value; }
```

HTML, Class, or ID   *Definition*

Figure 1.7 The basic syntax of a CSS rule.

The parts of a CSS rule

All rules, regardless of their location or type, have the following structural elements:

◆ **Selectors** are the alpha/numeric characters that identify a rule. The selector can be an HTML tag selector, a class, or an ID.

◆ **Properties** identify what is being defined. There are several dozen properties, each responsible for an aspect of the page content's behavior and appearance.

◆ **Values** are assigned to a property to define its nature. A value can be a keyword such as "yes" or "no," a number, or a percentage. The type of value used depends solely on the property to which it is assigned.

After the selector, a CSS rule consists of the properties and their values, which together I will refer to as a *definition*; a single CSS rule can have multiple definitions. **Figure 1.7** illustrates the general syntax of a rule.

What Is the World Wide Web Consortium?

The World Wide Web Consortium (W3C) is an organization that sets many of the standards that browser manufacturers eventually use to create their products.

Created in 1994, the W3C's mission is "to lead the World Wide Web to its full potential by developing common protocols that promote its evolution and ensure its interoperability."

The W3C comprises more than 400 member organizations around the world. These organizations include vendors of technology products and services, content providers, corporate users, research laboratories, standards bodies, and governments.

According to its Web site, the W3C has three goals:

◆ *Universal Access*: To make the Web accessible to all by promoting technologies that take into account the vast differences in culture, education, ability, material resources, and physical limitations of users on all continents.

◆ *Semantic Web*: To develop a software environment that permits each user to make the best use of the resources available on the Web.

◆ *Web of Trust*: To guide the Web's development with careful consideration for the novel legal, commercial, and social issues raised by this technology.

TYPES OF CSS RULES

Where to put the CSS rules

You can set up rules in three places:

◆ **In an HTML tag** within the body of your document, to affect a single tag in the document. This type of rule is often referred to as an *inline* rule (see "Adding Styles to an HTML Tag" in Chapter 2).

◆ **In the head of a document,** to affect an entire Web page. This type of rule is called an *embedded* rule (see "Adding Styles to a Web Page" in Chapter 2).

◆ **In an external document** that is then linked or imported into your HTML document(s), to affect an entire Web site. This type of rule is called an *external* rule (see "Adding Styles to a Web Site" in Chapter 2).

The position of a rule in relationship to the document and other CSS rules determines the scope of the rule's effect on the document (see "Determining the Cascade Order" in Chapter 2).

✔ Tips

■ Although you don't have to include a semicolon with the last definition in a list, experience shows that adding this semicolon can prevent headaches later. If you later decide to add a new definition to the rule and forget to put in the required semicolon before the addition, you may cause the rule to fail completely—not just that one definition, but all the definitions in the rule will fail to be used (see "Troubleshooting CSS" in Chapter 21).

■ Don't confuse the selector of an HTML tag with its attributes. In the following tag, for example, img is the selector, and src is an attribute:

```
<img src="picture.gif">
```

■ Although Netscape 4 and later and Internet Explorer 3 and later support CSS, none of these browsers supports all the CSS capabilities, and the support varies depending on the browser version. When you use CSS, check Appendix A to see whether a particular property is supported by a browser.

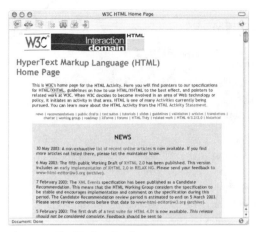

Figure 1.8 The W3C's HTML home page (www.w3.org/MarkUp/).

CSS and Markup Languages

The latest version of the Hypertext Markup Language, HTML 4.01, was released in December 1999 by the W3C. HTML 4.01 includes the style-sheet methodology (previously maintained as a separate standard) as part of the HTML specification (**Figure 1.8**).

This does not mean that CSS is HTML; it simply means that HTML now relies on the capabilities of CSS.

The W3C's thinking is this: Style sheets should be used to "relieve HTML of the responsibilities of presentation."

Translation: Don't bug us with requests for more HTML tags to do layout. Use style sheets instead.

That's probably a good idea. It means that anybody can use HTML tags, whether she is Jo Web Designer or not. But ol' Jo can use CSS to reassign standard HTML tags to do whatever she wants them to do, for more professional results.

In addition, this means that CSS can be used with other markup languages—such as XML (Extensible Markup Language), XHTML (Extensible Hypertext Markup Language), and even SVG (Scalable Vector Graphics)—just as easily as it can be used with HTML. This book will focus on the use of CSS with HTML, but virtually all of this information can equally be applied to these other markup languages.

CSS AND MARKUP LANGUAGES

What Are XML and XSL?

The Standard Generalized Markup Language (SGML) is the grandfather of most markup languages used for both print and the Internet. SGML is the international standard used to define the structure and appearance of documents. Different SGMLs have been created for a variety of document types and for different specialties, such as physics, accounting, and chemistry. HTML is the Web's version of SGML. Compared with full-blown SGML, however, HTML is lacking in several key areas.

The Extensible Markup Language—XML, for short (www.w3.org/XML)—is, like HTML, an offshoot of SGML. Unlike HTML, XML gives Web designers the ability not only to define the structure of the page, but also to define the types of information being presented. XML produces a Web page that works like a database and is convenient to search and manipulate. This is why XML is being touted as the greatest thing to happen to the Internet since HTML.

XML works a lot like HTML and CSS. It is made up of tags that describe how a browser should render the document. The document's author creates his own tags to identify explicitly the content of the document and its various pieces. Then the author creates a Document Type Definition (DTD) file to define what those tags mean. The DTD sets out what names are being used as tags, what type of information the tags contain, and in what context the tags can be used.

Suppose you have this list: Doctor, John Smith, UNIT. At first glance, some of the items in the list have obvious meanings: "Doctor" is a person's title and "John Smith" is a name. But what is "UNIT"? Also, the first two items may be used in a way that is not obvious. To a computer, these items are just alphanumeric characters with no inherent meaning.

With XML, you can "teach" the browser how to tell the difference between the real name, the alias, and the person's organization. You can also tell the browser how each of these elements should be displayed.

XSL, which stands for Extensible Stylesheet Language, is used with XML or XHTML to describe a styled document. Sounds a lot like CSS, right? However, XSL not only describes styles (like CSS), it goes further to completely describe content organization, layouts, and layout-selection rules (including pagination). In fact, XSL can work with CSS2 to create pages with greater complexity and flexibility than simple CSS can achieve.

XSL (www.w3.org/Style/XSL) converts XML documents into other kinds of documents, such as HTML for display on the Web. This is especially useful for content destined for both screen and print, since it makes it easy to design for both.

Extensible Hypertext Markup Language (XHTML)

XML and XSL (see sidebar "What Are XML and XSL?") hold many promises for Web designers, not the least of which is the ability to separate the display of content from its actual layout. Freeing the content from its layout means that rather than having to sweat the details on each page, you can control the layout for a site from a single location.

But how do you get Web designers to switch from HTML, with which they are comfortable, to the more complex XML?

The answer: XHTML.

XHTML (www.w3.org/TR/xhtml1) is a hybrid of the HTML 4.01 standard (www.w3.org/TR/html401) and XML. Many people hope that XHTML will begin a relatively painless transition from HTML to XML.

XHTML uses the XML Document Type Definitions (DTD)—collections of declarations that tell the browser how to treat the structure, elements, and attributes of the tags that it finds in a document. XHTML uses all the same tags as HTML with the upshot that, although XHTML Web pages can use the strength of XML, the code will still work even if the browser does not understand XML.

continues on next page

What is SVG?

The Scalable Vector Graphics format—SVG, for short—is a method of creating vector graphics on the Web (www.w3.org/Graphics/SVG). Like Flash, rather than plotting each point in the graphic, SVG describes two points and then plots the path between them as a straight line or curve.

Unlike Flash, which uses an editor to create its files and hides much of the code used to create the graphics, SVG uses a variation of XML to create its vector graphics. More important from a DHTML standpoint, SVG graphics can be scripted with the Document Object Model (for more information on the DOM, see Chapter 10), and can include all the DHTML capabilities described in this book.

SVG is currently a W3C recommendation, but although Adobe is offering an SVG browser plug-in, no browser has built-in SVG capabilities. SVG is poised to give Flash some competition.

If the standards are so similar, why change? The W3C offers two good reasons:

◆ The *X* in *XHTML* stands for *extensible*, which means it's much easier to add new capabilities to XHTML than to HTML. The behavior of tags is defined in a DTD rather than by the individual browser, so XHTML is more modular. Therefore, the capabilities of XHTML can be enhanced for future browsers or other Web-enabled devices without sacrificing backward compatibility.

◆ Today, a lot of Web traffic comes from "alternative" platforms, such as TV sets, handheld devices, and telephones. If you think it's hard to code HTML for a few different browsers, imagine coding for dozens of devices. A standard language is needed. In addition, because these devices generally have a smaller band-width, the code needs to be as compact as possible—something for which XHTML is perfect.

If Web designers begin using XHTML now, they can reap the benefits of XML without giving up the HTML skills they worked so long to develop. In fact, if you know HTML, you already know all the XHTML tags. The main thing you will have to learn is how these tags can (and cannot) be used. XHTML is a good deal stricter than HTML in terms of what it allows you to do, but these restrictions lead to cleaner, faster, easier-to-understand HTML code.

✔ Tips

■ It looks as though XHTML and CSS may be the future of Web design. Although browser manufacturers have been slow to adapt these standards, the W3C has made sure that XHTML will always be backward-compatible.

■ Many of the design-related HTML tags (for example, `<font>`), if not already abandoned by the new HTML standard, are slated to be made obsolete in favor of CSS. The W3C calls this situation "depre-cation." Although the tags still work, they are on the way out.

■ You can find further information about HTML at www.w3.org/MarkUp.

CSS AND MARKUP LANGUAGES

Converting HTML to XHTML

So what is the difference between HTML and XHTML? XHTML is far more restrictive than HTML: It will not allow you to bend the rules. However, because XHTML shares the same tags as HTML, it's fairly easy to convert if you keep the following points in mind:

◆ **No overlapping tags.** Most browsers don't care whether HTML tags are properly nested, so the following code works just fine:

```
<p>Bad <b>Nesting</p></b>
```

That is not the case in XHTML. You must use the correct syntax:

```
<p>Good <b>Nesting</b></p>
```

◆ **Tags and attributes have to be lowercase.** XML is case-sensitive, so <li> and <LI> are different tags. Keep all your tags and attributes in lowercase, and you'll be fine.

◆ **Always use an end tag.** Often, Web designers simply slam in a <p> tag to separate paragraphs. With XHTML, however, you have to use this format:

```
<p>Your text</p>
```

◆ **Use a space and slash in empty tags.** The preceding rule doesn't make much sense for <br> or <li> tags, which have no closing tag. Instead, include a space and then a slash in the tag to make it self-closing:

```
<br />
```

◆ **Don't nest links.** In XHTML, the following doesn't work:

```
<a src="this.html">This <a src="that.html">That</a></a>
```

But why would you want to do that in the first place?

◆ **Use** id **and** name **together.** If you're identifying an element on the screen, such as a layer, use both the id and name attributes, except in radio buttons:

```
<div id="object1" name="object"1">object</div>
```

◆ **Place attribute values in quotes.** If a tag contains attributes, the values have to be in quotes. The following example is wrong:

```
<img src=myImage.gif />
```

Use this syntax instead:

```
<img src="myImage.gif" />
```

◆ **Encode the ampersand in URLs or other attribute values.** The ampersand (&) has to be coded as &. The following example is wrong:

```
<img src="bill&ted.gif" />
```

Use this syntax instead:

```
<img src="bill&amp;ted.gif" />
```

◆ **Don't use HTML comments in script or style containers.** One trick I show you in this book is to place HTML comment tags immediately after <style> or <script> tags to hide the code from older browsers. For XHTML, do not do this. The following example is wrong:

```
<style> <!- p { font: times; } //-> </style>
```

Use this syntax instead:

```
<style> p { font: times; } </style>
```

Setting Your DTD

A Document Type Definition, sometimes called a "Doctype" or just "DTD," is a text document that contains the rules for how a particular markup language works. Although anyone can create a DTD, most Web designers will use one of the ones created (and hosted) by the World Wide Web Consortium (**Figure 1.9**).

You can place a tag at the beginning of your code that includes a reference to the DTD for the markup language your Web page uses (**Code 1.1**). However, it's only in the most recent browser versions (Netscape 6 and higher, Mozilla 1, and Internet Explorer 5 for Mac and 6 for Windows) that the Doctype will have any effect on how the content is displayed. If the Doctype is left unspecified, the browser will use *quirks mode*, which will behave like a legacy browser. If a recognizable Doctype is included, the browser will switch to *strict rendering*, which follows the specified standard.

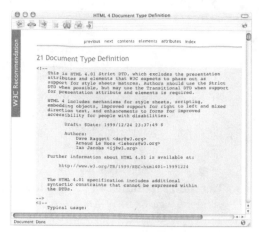

Figure 1.9 A Web browser displaying the HTML 4.01 Strict DTD provided by the World Wide Web Consortium (www.w3.org/TR/REC-html4o/sgml/dtd.html).

Code 1.1 The Doctype tag (which references the DTD file created by the World Wide Web Consortium) is placed at the top of the code.

```
<!DOCTYPE html PUBLIC "-//W3C//DTD HTML
 4.01 Transitional//EN"
    "http://www.w3.org/TR/html4/loose.dtd">
<html>
    <head>
        <title>HTML Transitional
         Doctype</title>
    </head>
    <body>
Content...
</body>
</html>
```

Code 1.2 The HTML Doctypes: Strict, Transitional, and Frameset. Choose one of these to place at the top of your HTML pages.

```
●○○                    Code                    ○
<!DOCTYPE html PUBLIC "-//W3C//DTD HTML
→ 4.01//EN"
       "http://www.w3.org/TR/html4/strict.dtd">


<!DOCTYPE html PUBLIC "-//W3C//DTD HTML
→ 4.01 Transitional//EN"
       "http://www.w3.org/TR/html4/loose.dtd">


<!DOCTYPE html PUBLIC "-//W3C//DTD HTML
→ 4.01 Frameset//EN"
       "http://www.w3.org/TR/html4/frameset.dtd">
```

Code 1.3 The XHTML Doctypes: Strict, Transitional, and Frameset. Because it's XML based, XHTML also requires that you declare the XML version. Choose one of these to place at the top of your HTML pages.

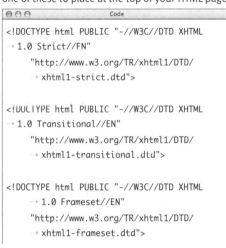

```
●○○                    Code                    ○
<!DOCTYPE html PUBLIC "-//W3C//DTD XHTML
→ 1.0 Strict//FN"
       "http://www.w3.org/TR/xhtml1/DTD/
         → xhtml1-strict.dtd">


<!DOCTYPE html PUBLIC "-//W3C//DTD XHTML
→ 1.0 Transitional//EN"
       "http://www.w3.org/TR/xhtml1/DTD/
         → xhtml1-transitional.dtd">


<!DOCTYPE html PUBLIC "-//W3C//DTD XHTML
       → 1.0 Frameset//EN"
       "http://www.w3.org/TR/xhtml1/DTD/
         → xhtml1-frameset.dtd">
```

For CSS, there are three basic DTDs you need to worry about, which can be specified using the Doctype tags in either HTML (**Code 1.2**) or XHTML (**Code 1.3**):

◆ **Strict:** Assumes that *all* styles will be handled by CSS. Thus no formatting tags are allowed.

◆ **Transitional:** Allows you to use a mixture of CSS and legacy HTML formatting to design your page. Sometimes called "loose."

◆ **Frameset:** Used with HTML documents used to create framesets.

Although the goal is for all Web designers eventually to create strictly coded Web pages (yeah, right), for now, your best bet is to use the transitional form of the Doctype for either HTML or XHTML.

✔ Tips

■ Older browsers that do not recognize DTDs will render the page based on their own definitions.

■ You can also include an XML version definition and encoding value above the XHTML DTD:

```
<?xml version="1.0" encoding=
→ "iso-8859-1"?>
```

However, this can often cause inexplicable errors especially when using ASP, JSP, and PHP. I generally recommend leaving it out.

SETTING YOUR DTD

Kinds of HTML and XHTML Tags

Not all CSS definitions can be applied to all HTML or XHTML tags. Whether a particular CSS property can be applied (or not) depends on the nature of the tag, and for the most part, it's fairly obvious.

For example, you wouldn't expect the text-indent property, which indents the first line of a paragraph, to apply to an inline tag such as <bold>. When you do need some help in this area, Appendix A tells you which properties can be used with a particular kind of HTML or XHTML tag.

Besides the <body> tag, there are three basic types of HTML or XHTML tags:

♦ **Block-level tags** place a line break before and after the element. **Table 1.2** lists the block-level tag selectors that CSS can use.

Table 1.2

Selectors for Block-Level Tags	
SELECTOR	**HTML USE**
blockquote	Quote style
center	Center text
dd	Definition description
dfn	Defined term
dir	Directory list
div	Logical division
dl	Definition list
dt	Definition term
h1–7	Header levels 1–7
li	List item
ol	Ordered list
p	Paragraph
table	Table
td	Table data
th	Table head
tr	Table row
ul	Unordered list

Tags or Selectors: What's the Big Difference?

An HTML selector is the text part of an HTML tag—the part that tells the browser what type of tag it is. So when you define an HTML selector using CSS, you are, in fact, redefining the HTML tag. Although the two elements, tag and selector, seem to be identical, they aren't: If you used the full HTML tag—brackets and all—in a CSS rule, the tag would not work. So it's important to keep these two ideas separate.

Table 1.3

Selectors for Inline Tags	
SELECTOR	HTML USE
a	Anchored link
b	Bold
big	Bigger text
cite	Short citation
code	Code font
em	Emphasis
font	Font appearance
i	Italic
pre	Preformatted text
span	Localized style formatting
strike	Strikethrough
strong	Strong emphasis
sub	Subscript
sup	Superscript
tt	Typewriter font
u	Underlined text

Table 1.4

Selectors for Replaced Tags	
SELECTOR	HTML USE
br	Line break
img	Image embedding
input	Input object
object	Object embedding
select	Select input area
textarea	Text input area

◆ **Inline tags** have no line breaks associated with the element. **Table 1.3** lists the inline-tag selectors that CSS can use.

◆ **Replaced tags** have set or calculated dimensions. **Table 1.4** lists the replaced-tag selectors that CSS can use.

✔ Tips

■ Although the paragraph tag (`<p>`) is often used without its closing `</p>` tag in HTML, the closing tag *must* be included if you want to define something using CSS.

■ Although the break tag (`<br>`) does not have a closing tag, you can add styles to it. However, remember that in XHTML, the break tag becomes `<br />` (with a space between the `br` and the `/`) so that it is self-closing.

KINDS OF HTML AND XHTML TAGS

Who Owns CSS?

On January 12, 1999, Microsoft Corp. (www.microsoft.com) was granted U.S. Patent #5,860,073. This particular patent, titled *Style sheets for publishing system(s)*, covers "the use of style sheets in an electronic publishing system." Sound familiar?

The inventors listed in this patent claim to have developed a system whereby "text, or other media such as graphics, is poured into the display region," at which time style sheets—defined as "a collection of formatting information, such as fonts and tabs"—are applied. This patent seems to overlap concepts laid out in the W3C's specifications for CSS and the Extensible Stylesheet Language (XSL), which have been in development since at least 1994.

What does this mean? It means that Microsoft can now claim as its intellectual property several of the key concepts that make Web-browser technology possible. Theoretically, if you want to use these technologies—or any technology based on them—you now need to sign a licensing agreement with Microsoft. Imagine a world in which every Web site using CSS, dynamic HTML (DHTML), and XSL has to be Microsoft-certified.

The situation may never get that bad, however. Microsoft has reported that it will offer "free and reciprocal" licensing agreements to anyone who wants to use "its" technology, adding that it isn't even clear whether a license will be necessary.

A brief analysis of the patent shows that it has two major flaws, which the W3C and the Web Standards Project (www.webstandards.org) have already been quick to point out:

◆ "The existence of prior art," referring to the fact that style sheets were proposed with the first Web browsers coming out of CERN laboratories in 1994. In fact, style sheets have been around since the 1960s, when they were used for print publications. At best, Microsoft is a Johnny-come-lately to the concept.

◆ The W3C's own licensing ensures that the standards developed under its banner are universally available and royalty-free. Because the W3C first developed the concept of style sheets, its license should hold precedence.

Microsoft had representatives on the committees that created these standards, and its own patent refers to documents produced by the W3C regarding CSS, so it seems highly improbable that this patent would stand up to much scrutiny.

George Olsen of the Web Standards Project questions whether the patent should have been granted in the first place, "because [there] are a number of prior examples of similar technology, including the original proposal for CSS," he says. Also, it is assumed that any organization—Microsoft included—with representatives in the W3C will detail any current or pending patents that might affect the W3C standards under consideration, which this patent certainly did. Yet the W3C first heard of the patent on February 4, 1999, when information about the patent was made publicly available.

So what does this mean to *you?* Probably not much. The W3C has published CSS as an open standard, and the genie is already out of the bottle.

So far, I haven't heard of Microsoft serving anyone a cease-and-desist order for using CSS on a Web site. Still, the point of having an open standard is to allow interested parties to contribute without one entity taking all the credit. Let's hope that this patent won't put a chill on future CSS development.

CSS BASICS

Figure 2.1 An HTML page using CSS to add an image in the background, position the content down and to the right, and format the text.

Figure 2.2 The same content displayed without the benefit of CSS. The page still displays, but without the formatting of Figure 2.1.

CSS lets you control your document's appearance, but the big advantage of using CSS instead of just creating new HTML tags to do the same job is that by changing a definition in a single, centrally located CSS rule, you change the appearance of all the tags controlled by that rule (**Figures 2.1** and **2.2**).

If the rule is in the head of a particular document, the change affects that page. If the rule is in an external file, the change affects every page to which that file is linked—potentially, an entire Web site. On the downside, some browsers don't understand CSS, but those are becoming increasingly rare. Fortunately, they just ignore the CSS code and display the HTML as if it didn't exist. The page may not look as good without CSS, but at least it will still be usable, and if you design it right, the visitor may never think that anything is amiss.

In this chapter, you'll learn how to set up CSS in a variety of places, and methods for different effects.

Adding Styles to an HTML Tag

Although CSS means never having to set the appearance of each tag individually, you still have the freedom to set styles within individual tags, referred to as an *inline* style. This is especially useful for overriding other styles set for the page, if you need to, case by case.

Figure 2.3 shows the general syntax for adding a style directly to an HTML tag.

To set the style properties of individual HTML tags:

1. `<h1 style=`

    Type `style=` in the HTML tag you want to define (**Code 2.1**).

2. `"font:small-caps bold italic 2.5em`
    `→ 'minion web', Georgia, 'Times New`
    `→ 'Roman', Times, serif; color: red;"`

    In quotes, type your style-definition(s) as `property: value`, with a semicolon (;) separating individual definitions. Make sure to close the definition list with quotation marks.

3. `> Alice's Adventures in Wonderland`
    `→ '</h1>`

    After closing the tag, add the content to be styled. Then, if necessary, close the tag pair with the corresponding end tag. **Figure 2.4** shows the code's results.

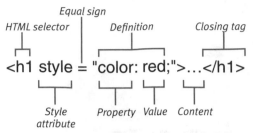

Figure 2.3 The general syntax for defining styles directly in an HTML tag.

Figure 2.4 The styles have been placed directly into the tags.

Code 2.1 Each tag receives instructions on how the content within it should behave, by means of the style attribute.

```
○○○                 Code                    ○
<html>
<head>
</head>
<body style="background: white url(alice23.gif)
→ no-repeat; font-family: arial, helvetica,
→ geneva, sans-serif; word-spacing: 1px;">
     <div style="position: relative; top: 190px;
     → left: 165px; width: 480px;">
<br>
     <h1 style="font: small-caps bold italic
     → 2.5em 'minion web', Georgia, 'Times New
     → Roman', Times, serif; color: red;">
     → Alice's Adventures in Wonderland</h1>
     <h2 style="font: bold 1.5em 'minion web',
     → Georgia, 'Times New Roman', Times,
     → serif;">Lewis Carroll</h2>
     <p style="style: italic; font-family:
     → monospace;">THE MILLENNIUM FULCRUM
     → EDITION 3.0</p>
     <h2>CHAPTER I
     <br>Down the Rabbit-Hole</h2>
     <p><span style="font: 300%/100% serif;
     → color: #999999; margin-right: -3px;
     → ">A</span> lice was beginning to get
     → very tired of sitting by her sister on
     → the bank...</p>
     <p>So she was considering in her own
     → mind...</p>
     <p>There was nothing so <i>very</i>
     → remarkable in that...</p>
     </div>
     </body>
</html>
```

✔ Tips

■ Although you do not gain the benefit of the universal style changes, using CSS in individual HTML tags is nevertheless very useful when you want to override universally defined styles. (See "Determining the Cascade Order" at the end of this chapter.)

■ I've also shown how you can define the <body> tag in this example, but be careful—this can lead to more problems than it's worth (see "Managing Existing or Inherited Property Values" later in this chapter). In addition, both Netscape and Internet Explorer balk at many properties in the <body> tag, especially positioning properties.

■ So as not to confuse the browser, it is best to use double quotes (") around the definition list, and single quotes (') around any values in the definition list, such as font names with spaces.

■ One common mistake I make is to confuse the equal sign (=) with the colon (:). Remember that although the style attribute in the tag uses an equal sign, CSS definition lists always use a colon.

■ You can also apply common styles to an entire Web page (see the following section, "Adding Styles to a Web Page") or to multiple Web pages (see "Adding Styles to a Web Site" later in this chapter).

■ Font names made up of more than two words are placed in single quotes (") when used with a style.

Adding Styles to a Web Page

The main use for CSS is to define style rules for an entire document. To do this, you can include your style rules in the head of the document nestled within a style container (**Figure 2.5**).

While the results of adding style in this manner can look identical to adding the styles directly to an HTML tag (**Figure 2.6**), placing styles in a common location allows you to change the styles in a document from one place. For example, if you use the header level 1 tag in multiple locations in a Web page, you can define the style for h1 tags in the head of your document and it will apply to all <h1> tags in that document.

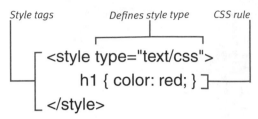

Style tags   Defines style type   CSS rule

Figure 2.5 The general syntax of a CSS style contained placed in the head of an HTML document.

Figure 2.6 Although this figure is a doppelganger of Figure 2.4, the CSS used to create it is located in the head of the document rather than in each individual tag.

Code 2.2 Although the result of this code (Figure 2.6) may look identical to the preceding example (Figure 2.4), the style rules are collected in the head of the document, where they affect all tags within the HTML document.

```
<html>
<head>
    <style type="text/css"><!--
    body {
        background: white url(alice23.gif)
        → no-repeat;
        word-spacing: 1px;
    }

    #content {
        position: relative;
        top: 190px;
        left: 165px;
        width: 480px;
        font-family: arial,helvetica,geneva,
        → sans-serif;
    }

    h1 {
        font: small-caps bold italic 2.5em
        → 'minion web', Georgia, 'Times New
        → Roman', Times, serif;
        color: red;
    }

    h2 {
        font: bold 1.5em 'minion web', Georgia,
        → 'Times New Roman', Times, serif;
    }

    .dropcap {
        font: 300%/100% serif;
        color: #999999;
        margin-right: -3px;
    }
-->
    </style>
</head>
```

(code continues on next page)

To set the style for tags in an HTML document:

1. `<style type="text/css">`

   Type the opening `<style>` tag in the head of your document, defining the `type` as `"text/css"`. This defines the following styles as being not just any style, but CSS (**Code 2.2**).

2. `h1 {`

   Open your rule by typing the selector for the tag to be defined, followed by a curly bracket (`{`). The selector can be any of the following:

   ▲ **An HTML tag selector** (such as `h1`; see "(re)Defining an HTML Tag")

   ▲ **A class selector** (such as `myClass`; see "Defining Classes to Create Your Own Tags")

   ▲ **An ID selector** (such as `#object1`; see "Defining IDs to Identify an Object")

   ▲ **A group of selectors separated by commas** (such as `h1,h2,myclass`; see "Defining Tags with the Same Rules") to receive a common definition list

   ▲ **A group of selectors separated by spaces** (such as `h1 myclass object1`; see "Defining Tags in Context") to receive contextual definitions

3. `font: small-caps bold italic 2.5em` `→ 'minion web', Georgia, 'Times New` `→ 'Roman', Times, serif; color: red;`

   Type the definition(s) to be assigned to this rule as `property: value`, with a semi-colon (`;`) separating individual definitions in the list.

4. Close the rule with a curly bracket (`}`).

5. Repeat steps 2–4 for all the selectors you want to define.

continues on next page

6. </style>

Close the style definition by typing the </style> end tag.

✔ Tips

- You don't have to include type="text/css", because the browser should be able to determine the type of style being used. I always put it there, however, to allow browsers that do not support a particular type of style sheet to avoid the code. It also clarifies to other humans the type being used.

- You can hide your CSS from non-CSScapable browsers by placing the HTML comment tags <!--...--> around all rules within the <style>...</style> tags. Otherwise, these browsers may display the text, which is not very attractive. However, this can cause problems if you are using strict XHTML.

Code 2.2 *continued*

```
<body>

<div id="content">
        <br>


<h1>Alice's Adventures in Wonderland</h1>
        <h2>Lewis Carroll</h2>
        <p style="style: italic; font-family:
→ monospace;">THE MILLNNIUM FULCRUM
→ EDITION 3.0</p>
        <h2>CHAPTER I<br>
           Down the Rabbit-Hole</h2>
        <p><span class="dropcap">A</span>
→ lice was beginning to get very tired
→ of sitting by her sister on the
→ bank...</p>
        <p>So she was considering in her own
→ mind...</p>
        <p>There was nothing so <i>very</i>
→ remarkable in that...</p>
    </div>
</body>
</html>
```

Adding Styles to a Web Site

A major benefit of CSS is that you can create a style sheet for use not just with a single HTML document, but throughout an entire Web site. You can apply this *external* style sheet to a hundred HTML documents—without having to retype the information.

Establishing an external CSS file is a two-step process. First, set up the rules in a text file; then link or import this file into an HTML document, using either the <link> tag or @import (**Figure 2.7**).

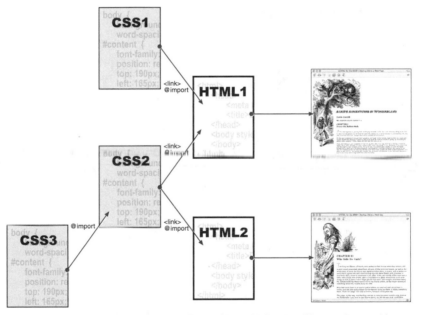

Figure 2.7 External CSS files cannot only be used in multiple HTML files, as shown with CSS2, but an external CSS file can be imported (but not linked) into another external CSS file, as shown with CSS3. Linked or imported CSS files, however, act exactly as if you had typed the code into the file they are linked or imported into.

Creating an External Style Sheet

The first step in using an external style sheet globally in a Web site is to create the text file that holds all of the CSS code. However, unlike adding embedded styles, you do *not* use <style> tags in an external CSS file. This would prevent it from working in most browsers.

To set up an external CSS file:

1. Create a new file, using word processing or other software that allows you to save as a text file; Notepad or SimpleText will do (**Code 2.3**).

2. h1 {

Add CSS rules to the page by typing the selector for the tag to be defined, followed by a curly bracket ({). The selector can be any of the following:

▲ **An HTML tag selector** (such as h1; see "(re)Defining an HTML Tag")

▲ **A class selector** (such as .myClass; see "Defining Classes to Create Your Own Tags")

▲ **An ID selector** (such as #object1; see "Defining IDs to Identify an Object")

▲ **A group of selectors separated by commas** (such as h1,h2,myclass; see "Defining Tags with the Same Rules") to receive a common definition list

▲ **A group of selectors separated by spaces** (such as h1 myclass object1; see "Defining Tags in Context") to receive contextual definitions

Notice that you do not use the <style> tag here. Using that tag in this document will keep it from working in an HTML document.

Code 2.3 default.css: The external CSS "default.css" contains definitions that will be used to create the layout in Code 2.5 and Code 2.6.

```
body {
    background:  white url(alice23.gif)
    → no-repeat;
    word-spacing: 1px;
}
#content {
    font-family: arial, helvetica, geneva,
    → sans-serif;
    position: relative;
    top: 190px;
    left: 165px;
    width: 480px;
}

.dropCap {
    font: 300%/100% serif;
    color: #999999;
    margin-right: -3px;
}
```

Code 2.4 headers.css: The external CSS "headers.css" contains additional definitions for the two header levels that will be used to create the layout in Code 2.5 and Code 2.6. Remember, you can call these files anything you want. I used "headers" as an example.

```
h1 {
    color: red; font: italic small-caps
    → bold 2.5em 'minion web', Georgia,
    → 'Times New Roman', Times, serif;
}

h2 {
    font: bold 1.5em 'minion web', Georgia,
    → 'Times New Roman', Times, serif;
}
```

3. `font: small-caps bold italic 2.5em` `→ 'minion web', Georgia, 'Times New` `→ 'Roman', Times, serif; color: red;`

Type the definition(s) to be assigned to this rule as `property: value`, with a semicolon (`;`) separating individual definitions in the list.

4. Close the rule with a curly bracket (`}`).

5. Repeat steps 2–4 for all the selectors you want to define.

6. Save this document as `default.css`, where "default" is whatever you want to call this file, and ".css" is an extension to identify the file type. You can create and link to as many external CSS files as you want (**Code 2.4**). In this example, I created another external CSS file called "headers.css" to hold the h1 and h2 definitions.

7. Attach this file to an HTML file, using `<link>`, or to an HTML file or another CSS file using `@import`.

✔ Tips

■ Although the external CSS file can have any HTML you want, it's a good idea to use a name that will remind you of what these styles are for. The name "navigation.css," for example, probably is a more helpful name than "ss1.css."

■ A CSS file should not contain any HTML tags (especially not the `<style>` tag) or other content, with the exception of comments and imported styles.

■ You do not have to use the .css extension with CSS files. You could just call this file "default," and it would work just as well. Adding the extension, however, can prevent confusion.

Linking to a Style Sheet

External style sheet files can be used with any HTML file through the `<link>` tag. Linking a CSS file affects the document just as though the styles had been typed directly in the head of the document. **Figure 2.8** shows the general syntax for linking style sheets, while **Figure 2.9** shows the results of linking to a style sheet.

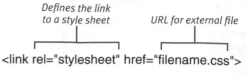

Figure 2.8 The general syntax for linking to an external style sheet.

Figure 2.9 While this page may look exactly the same as Figures 2.4 and 2.6, the CSS used to create it is mostly located in external files that have been linked to.

Code 2.5 Chapter01.html: The majority of the styles applied to this HTML document are being linked to from the external CSS files called default.css and headers.css, shown in Code 2.3 and Code 2.4. The one exception is the *<body>* tag. It is being defined locally to tailor the background image for this page (Figure 2.9).

```
<html>
<head>
    <link rel="stylesheet" href="default.css">
    <link rel="stylesheet" href="headers.css">
    <style type="text/css" media="screen"><!--
        body {
            background: white url(alice23.gif)
            → no-repeat;
        }
    </style>
</head>
<body>
    <div id="content">
        <br>
        <h1>Alice's Adventures in Wonderland
        → </h1>
        <h2>Lewis Carroll</h2>
        <p style="style: italic; font-family:
        → monospace;">THE MILLENNIUM FULCRUM
        → EDITION 3.0</p>
        <h2>CHAPTER I<br>
        Down the Rabbit-Hole</h2>
        <p><span class="dropCap">A</span> lice
        → was beginning to get very tired of
        → sitting by her sister on the
        → bank...</p>
        <p>So she was considering in her own
        → mind...</p>
        <p>There was nothing so <i>very</i>
        → remarkable in that...</p>
    </div>
</body>
</html>
```

To link to an external CSS file:

1. `<link`
Within the `<head>...</head>` of your HTML document, open your `<link>` tag and then type a space (**Code 2.5**).

2. `rel="stylesheet"`
Tell the browser that this will be a link to a style sheet.

3. `href="default.css"`
Specify the location, either global or local, of the CSS file to be used, where *default.css* is the full path and name (including extension) of your CSS document.

4. `>`
Close the `<link>` tag with a chevron (>).

5. `<link rel="stylesheet" → href="headers.css">`
Repeat steps 1–4 to add as many style sheets as you want to link to.

6. `<style type="text/css">...</style>`
Add any additional styles in the head, using the `<style>` tag. You can place a `<style>` tag before the `<link>` tags, if you desire.

Importing a Style Sheet

Another way to bring external style sheets into a document is to use the @import statement. The advantage of importing is that it can not only be used to put an external CSS file in an HTML document file, but also to place one external CSS file in another. **Figure 2.10** shows the general syntax for the @import statement, and **Figure 2.11** shows the result of importing the style sheet.

URL for external file

@import url(filename.css);

Figure 2.10 The general syntax for importing an external style sheet.

Figure 2.11 The same CSS files have been used to create this page as were used for Figure 2.9. This time, however, the files have been imported rather than linked to. In addition, a different background image has been defined for the body.

ADDING STYLES TO A WEB SITE

Code 2.6 Chapter11.html: This example uses @import instead of <link> to add CSS files to this HTML document. As in Code 2.5, the body tag has been defined so that a different background image is used, suitable for this particular chapter.

```
●○○                    Code                    ○

<html>
<head>
    <style type="text/css" media="screen"><!--
        @import url(default.css);
        @import url(headers.css);
        body {
        background: white url(alice40.gif)
        → no-repeat;
        }
    -->
    </style>
</head>
<body>
    <div id="content">
        <br>
        <h2>CHAPTER XI<br>
        Who Stole the Tarts?</h2>
        <p><span class="dropCap">T</span>he
        → King and Queen of Hearts were seated
        → on their throne when they
        → arrived...</p>
        <p>Alice had never been in a court of
        → justice before, but she had read
        → about them in books, and she was
        → quite pleased to find that she knew
        → the name of nearly everything there.
        → 'That's the judge,' she said to
        → herself, 'because of his great
        → wig.'</p>
        <p>The judge, by the way, was the
        → King...</p>
        <p>'And that's the jury-box,' thought
        → Alice, 'and those twelve
        → creatures,'...</p>
    </div>
</body>
</html>
```

To import an external CSS file:

1. `<style type="text/css"`
   Within the head of your HTML document, open a style container (**Code 2.6**).

2. `@import url(default.css);`
   Import the CSS file, replacing "default.css" with the URL of the CSS document to be used. The URL can be global, in which case it would start with `http://`; or it could be local, pointing to a file on the same computer.

3. `@import url(headers.css);`
   Repeat step 2 for as many external CSS documents as you want to link.

4. `body { background:white url`
   `→ (alice40.gif) no-repeat; }`
   You can include additional CSS rules here, if needed (see the previous section, "Adding Styles to a Web Page").

5. `</style>`
   Close the style definition with a style end tag.

✔ Tip

■ Alternatively, you can place @import directly in another external style sheet to import one external style sheet into another. The imported file will be included as part of that external CSS file.

(re)Defining an HTML Tag

Most HTML tags already have built-in definitions. Take the <bold> tag, for example; its built-in property is the equivalent of font-weight: bold.

By adding new definitions to the tag's selector, b, you can change the ... tag pair to have just about any effect you want on the content between them (**Figure 2.12**).

Figure 2.13 shows the general syntax for adding a complete CSS rule using an HTML selector.

HTML selectors can be defined within the <style>...</style> tags in the head of your document (see "Adding Styles to a Web Page" earlier in this chapter) or in an external CSS file that is then imported or linked to the HTML document (see the previous section, "Adding Styles to a Web Site").

Figure 2.12 Several HTML tags have been redefined. Paragraphs <p> now display their text as gray, 12px size, with 1.5 spaces between each line, and using the Verdana font. In addition, images <img> will justify to the right, and italic <i> text will appear bold.

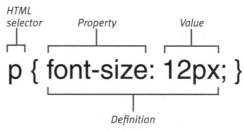

Figure 2.13 The general syntax used to define the styles for an HTML tag.

Code 2.7 Normally, the <p> tag simply puts a space between paragraphs. Add a few styles, however, and the <p> tag changes the color of the text, the font family, the font size, and the line spacing—not bad for one little tag (Figure 2.12).

```
<html>
<head>
    <style type="text/css" media="screen"><!--
        p {
            color: #666666;
            font-size: 12px;
            line-height: 18px;
            font-family: Verdana, Arial,
             → Helvetica, Geneva, sans-serif;
        }
        img {
            float: right
        }
        i {
            font-weight: bold
        }
--></style>
</head>
<body>
    <div align="left">
        <h3>CHAPTER V<br>
        Advice from a Caterpillar</h3>
    </div>
    <p><img src="alice15.gif" height="264"
    → width="200" border="0">The Caterpillar
    → and Alice looked at each other for some
    → time in silence: at last the Caterpillar
    → took the hookah out of its mouth, and
    → addressed her in a languid, sleepy
    → voice.</p>
        <p>'Who are <i>you</i>?' said the
Caterpillar.</p>
</body>
</html>
```

To define an HTML selector:

1. p {

Start with the HTML selector whose properties you want to define, and add a curly bracket ({) to open your rule (**Code 2.7**).

2. color: #666666;

font-size: 12px;

line-height: 18px;

font-family: Verdana, Arial,
→ Helvetica, Geneva, sans-serif;

Type your property definition(s). You can add as many definitions as you want, but the properties have to work with the HTML tag in question. You cannot use text indent, for example, to define the <bold> tag. Check out Appendix A to see which properties can be used to redefine which tags.

3. }

Close your definition list with a curly bracket (}). Forget this, and it will ruin your day!

✔ Tips

■ The syntax is slightly different for redefining an individual HTML tag within a document (see "Adding Styles to an HTML Tag" earlier in this chapter).

■ Redefining a tag does not override that tag's preexisting properties. Thus, <b> still makes text bold no matter what other styles are added to it (see "Managing Existing or Inherited Property Values").

■ Although the <body> tag can also be redefined, it acts like a block-level tag (see "Kinds of HTML and XHTML Tags" in Chapter 1), Internet Explorer for Windows does not accept any positioning controls in the <body> tag.

If you want to position your entire page, you need to place the whole thing in a CSS layer and position it that way (see "Creating a Block-Level Element" in Chapter 5).

Defining Classes to Create Your Own Tags

Using a class selector gives you the ability to set up an independent style that you can then apply to any HTML tag.

Unlike an HTML selector, which automatically defines a particular type of tag, a class is given a unique name that is then specified in the HTML tag or tags you want to use it in with the `style` attribute (**Figure 2.14**).

Figures 2.15 and **2.16** show the general syntax of a CSS class rule.

Class rules can be defined within the `<style>...</style>` tags in the head of your document (see "Adding Styles to a Web Page" earlier in this chapter) or in an external CSS file that is then imported or linked to the HTML document (see "Adding Styles to a Web Site" earlier in this chapter).

Figure 2.14 The class copy has been applied to all of the `<p>` tags, making the font 12px size, 1.5 spaces between lines, and Trebuchet MS font. The `<blockquote>` has its own version of copy as a dependent class to make the text bold, 14px size, a tighter line height, Book Antiqua font, and centered.

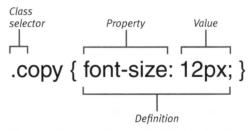

Figure 2.15 The general syntax of a CSS class definition.

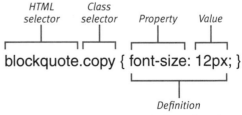

Figure 2.16 The general syntax of a dependent class definition. The definitions for this version of copy will only work if applied to a `<blockquote>` tag.

Code 2.8 A class style can be set up to be applied to any HTML tag, as with copy, or only to specific HTML tags, as with `blockquote.copy`.

```
<html>
<head>
    <style type="text/css" media="screen"><!--
        .copy {
            font-size: 12px;
            line-height: 150%;
            font-family: 'Book Antiqua',
            → 'Times New Roman', Georgia,
            → Times, serif;
        }
        blockquote.copy {
            font-weight: bold;
            font-size: 14px;
            line-height: 16px;
            text-align: center
        }
    --></style>
</head>
<body>
    <p class="copy">Alice glanced rather
    → anxiously at the cook...</p>
    <p class="copy">'Oh, don't bother ME,'
    → said the Duchess...</p>
    <blockquote class="copy">
        <p>'Speak roughly to your little
    → boy,<br>
        And beat him when he sneezes:<br>
        He only does it to annoy,<br>
        Because he knows it teases.'<br>
    </blockquote>
</body>
</html>
```

- You can use `<div>` and `<span>` tags to create your own HTML tags.

- A class name cannot be a JavaScript reserved word. See Appendix B for the list.

To define a class selector:

1. `.copy {`

Type a period (.) and a class name; then open your definition with a curly bracket ({). The class name can be anything you choose, as long as you use letters and numbers.

`copy` is an independent class, so you can use it with any HTML tag you want, with one stipulation: The properties set for the class must work with the type of tag you use it on (**Code 2.8**).

2. `font-size: 12px;`
`line-height: 150%;`
      `font-family: 'Book Antiqua',`
      → `'Times New Roman', Georgia,`
      → `Times, serif;`

Type your definition(s) for this class, making sure to separate definitions with a semicolon (;).

3. `}`

Type a curly bracket (}) to close your rule.

A class will not work until it is specified inside an HTML tag within a document, as in the following exercise.

To apply your class to an HTML tag:

- `<p class="copy">...</p>`

Add `class="className"` to the tag to which you want to apply the class. Notice that although when you defined the class in the `<style>...</style>` tags, it started with a period (.), you do not use the period when referencing the class name in a tag.

✔ Tips

- You can mix a class with ID and/or inline rules within an HTML tag (see "Adding Styles to an HTML Tag," earlier, and the following section, "Defining IDs to Identify an Object").

DEFINING CLASSES TO CREATE YOUR OWN TAGS

39

Defining IDs to Identify an Object

Like the class selector, the ID selector can be used to create unique styles that are independent of any particular HTML tag. Thus, they can be assigned to any applicable HTML tag. **Figure 2.17** shows the general syntax of IDs.

IDs are the cornerstone of dynamic HTML (DHTML), in that they allow JavaScript functions to identify a unique object on the screen. This means that unlike a class, an ID should normally be used only once on a page to define a single element as an object. This object then can be manipulated with JavaScript (**Figure 2.18**).

An ID can be defined within the `<style>...</style>` tags in the head of your document (see "Adding Styles to a Web Page" earlier in this chapter) or in an external CSS file that is then imported or linked to the HTML document (see "Adding Styles to a Web Site" earlier in this chapter).

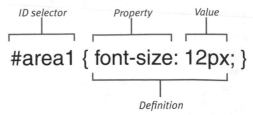

Figure 2.17 The general syntax for an ID definition.

Figure 2.18 By setting the left margin, `area1` has been shifted over to the right, while `image1` has been set to float to the left.

Elements or Objects?

There is often a lot of confusion over the terms *element* and *object* when discussing Web pages. Simply stated, an element is created by open and close markup tags. For example <p>...</p> and all of the content between these two tags (even other tags) form an element. Any tags within the element are referred to as *child* elements, and the surrounding tags are the *parent* element.

An object, on the other hand, is created when an element is given a unique ID that allows the browser to access that element's properties.

See "Understanding the Element's Box" in Chapter 5 for more details on elements and Chapter 10, "The Document Object Model" for more details on objects.

Code 2.9 The ID *area1* is used to define an area of the document to be manipulated (Figure 2.18).

```
<html>
<head>
    <style type="text/css" media="screen"><!--
        #area1 {
            color: red;
            margin-left: 9em;
            position: relative;
        }
        #image1 {
            float: left;
        }
    --></style>
</head>
<body>
    <p>'Well!' thought Alice to herself,
    → 'after such a fall as this, I shall think
    → nothing of tumbling down stairs!...</p>
    <p id="area1"><img id="image1"
    → src="alice06.gif" height="200"
    → width="163" border="0">Down, down, down.
    → Would the fall <i>never</i> come to an
    → end!...</p>
    <p>Presently she began again. 'I wonder
    → if I shall fall right （i）through（i）the
    → earth!...</p>
</body>
</html>
```

- The difference between IDs and classes will become apparent after you've learned more about using CSS positioning and after you've used IDs to create CSS layers. IDs are used to give each element on the screen a unique name and identity. This is why an ID is typically used only once, for one element in a document, to make it an object that can be manipulated with JavaScript.

- An ID name cannot be a JavaScript reserved word. See Appendix B for the list.

To define an ID:

1. #area1 {

   ID rules always start with a number sign (#) and then the name of the ID. The name can be a word or any set of letters or numbers you choose (**Code 2.9**).

2. color: red; margin-left: 9em;
   → position: relative;

   Type your definition(s) for this class, making sure to separate definitions with a semicolon (;).

   You can use an ID with any type of property, but ID selectors are best used to define unique objects on the screen.

3. }

   Type a curly bracket (}) to close your rule.

An ID will not work until it is specified with an individual HTML tag within a document, as in the following exercise.

To apply an ID to an HTML tag:

◆ <p id="area1">...</p>

   Add id="idName" to the HTML tag of your choice, as shown in Code 2.9. The value of the ID attribute will be the name of the ID selector you created, as explained in the previous exercise. Notice, though, that although the number sign (#) is used to define an ID, it is *not* included for referencing the ID in the HTML tag.

✔ Tips

- You can mix an ID with a class and/or inline rules within an HTML tag (see "Adding Styles to an HTML Tag" and "Defining Classes to Create Your Own Tags" earlier in this chapter).

- Although I showed you here how to set up a definition for an ID, you don't *have* to set up a definition to add an ID to a tag and use it as an object with DHTML.

Defining Styles with the Same Rules

If you want two or more selectors to have the same definitions, just put the selectors in a list separated by commas. The general syntax for a definition grouping is shown in **Figure 2.19**.

You can define common attributes in the list and then add rules for each HTML selector individually, if you like, to refine them (**Figure 2.20**).

CSS rules can be defined within the `<style>...</style>` tags in the head of your document (see "Adding Styles to a Web Page" earlier in this chapter) or in an external CSS file that is then imported or linked to the HTML document (see "Adding Styles to a Web Site" earlier in this chapter).

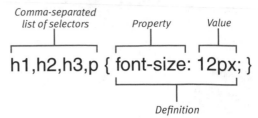

Figure 2.19 The general syntax for a list of selectors all receiving the same definition list.

Figure 2.20 The headers and paragraph all have the same font and margins.

Code 2.10 Save time by combining selectors in a list separated by commas to be given a common set of definitions (Figure 2.22).

```
○ ○ ○                Code                     ○
<html>
<head>
     <style type="text/css" media="screen"><!--
        h1,h2,h3,p {
            font-family: 'Book Antiqua',
            → 'Times New Roman', Georgia,
            → Times, serif;
            margin-left: 10px;
            font-variant: small-caps;
            }
        h1,h2,.dropcap {
            font-size: 1.5em;
            line-height: 100%;
            color: red
                }
        h3 {
            margin-top: 25px;
            border-top: 2px solid black;
        }
        p {
            font-variant: normal;
        }
     --></style>
</head>
<body>
     <h1>Alice's Adventures in Wonderland</h1>
     <h2>Lewis Carroll</h2>
     <h3>CHAPTER I<br>
     Down the Rabbit-Hole</h3>
     <p><span class="dropCap">A</span> lice was
     → beginning to get very tired of sitting
     → by her sister on the bank...</p>
</body>
</html>
```

To group definitions:

1. h1,h2,h3,p {...}

Type the list of selectors (HTML, class, or ID), separated by commas (**Code 2.10**). These selectors all receive the same definitions.

2. h3 {...}

You can then add or change definitions for each selector individually to tailor it to your needs. If you are overriding a definition set in the group rule, make sure these rules come after the group rules in your CSS (see "Determining the Cascade Order").

✔ Tips

■ IDs and/or classes can also be defined in the list:

h1,h2,.dropcap {...}

■ Grouping selectors like this can save a lot of time and repetition. But be careful—by changing the value of any of the properties in the definition, you change that value for every tag in the list.

Defining Styles in Context

When a tag is surrounded by another tag, one inside another, we call the tags *nested*. In a nested set, the outer tag is called the *parent*, and the inner tag is the *child*. You can use CSS to create a rule for a tag if it is the child of another particular tag or tags.

Figure 2.21 shows the general syntax of contextual selectors.

In this example (**Code 2.11**), I've set up the link tags so that they will have a completely different appearance depending on whether the link is in a `<p>` tag or in a `<div>` tag with the menu class (**Figure 2.22**).

To set up a contextual selector:

1. `p a:link {...}`

   `div.menu a:link {...}`

   Type the HTML selector of the parent tag, followed by a space. You can type as many HTML selectors as you want for as many different parents as the nested tag will have, but the last selector in the list is the one that receives all the styles in the rule.

2. `<div class="menu"><a href="#">...`
   `→ </a></div>`

   `<p><a href="#">...</a></p>`

   If, and only if, the `<link>` tag occurs within a paragraph, it appears bright red. And if, and only if, the link is in a `<div>` tag with the menu class, it appears darker crimson, with no underlining.

✔ Tip

- Like grouped selectors, contextual selectors can include class selectors (dependent or independent) and/or ID selectors in the list, as well as HTML selectors.

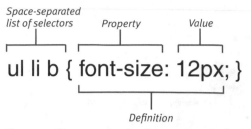

Figure 2.21 The general syntax for a contextual rule.

Figure 2.22 Although all these links use the `<a>` tag, there are two distinct link styles on the page, depending on where the links appear.

Code 2.11 Context-sensitive CSS allows you to set the styles of HTML tags depending on their parents' characteristics. In this example, I've set up two versions of the link style: one to be used if the link is within a paragraph; the other to be used if a link is within a `<div>` tag with the menu class (Figure 2.24).

```
<html>
<head>
    <style type="text/css" media="screen"><!--
    p a:link {
        color: red;
        text-decoration: underline
        }
    div.menu a:link {
        color: #900;
        font-weight: bold;
        text-decoration: none
        }
    div.menu {
```

(code continues on next page)

Code 2.11 *continued*

```
          font: bold 16px 'Trebuchet MS', Arial, Helvetica, Geneva, sans-serif;
          }
     p {
          font: 12px 'Book Antiqua', 'Times New Roman', Georgia, Times, serif;
     }
  --></style>
</head>
<body>
     <div class="menu">
          <a href="#">&lt; Previous Chapter</a> | <a href="#">Next Chapter &gt;</a></div>
     <center>
          <hr>
     </center>
     <h3>CHAPTER VIII<br>
          The Queen's Croquet-Ground</h3>
     <p>A large rose-tree stood near the entrance of the garden: the roses growing on it were white,
  → but there were three gardeners at it, busily painting them red. Alice thought this <a href="#">a
  → very curious thing</a>, and she went nearer to watch them, and just as she came up to them she
  → heard one of them say, 'Look out now, Five! Don't go splashing paint over me like that!'</p>
</body>
</html>
```

Other Selector Groupings

CSS also allows several other selector grouping types, so you can further refine definitions and increase specificity (important for determining the cascade order, as explained later in this chapter). Unfortunately, these different styles are not supported by Internet Explorer for Windows (although they work on Internet Explorer for Mac).

However, if you're coding for Netscape 6, Mozilla 1, Opera 6, or Safari 1 or later, then these groupings can add a lot of power to your style sheets.

Defining parent/child tags

Parent/child selectors work a lot like defining contextual styles, but allows you to set the style only if the tag is a direct child (not a "grandchild") of the tag. The basic structure looks like:

```
<div>em { font-family:times; }
```

In this example, only emphasis <em> tags directly within a div <div> tag will use
→ the times font. If the <em> tag is within a paragraph tag that is within a div
→ tag, then it remains unaffected.

Defining adjacent sibling tag attributes

Known as the *adjacent selector,* this grouping allows you to define a style for the first (and only first) occurrence of a tag after another tag.

```
h1 + p { font-family:times; }
```

In this example, the first paragraph <p> tag after a header level 1 <h1> tag will use the times font.

Defining Link Styles with Pseudo-classes

Most browsers allow you to specify link colors for different states (a link, a visited link, and an active link) in the <body> tag of the document. With CSS, you can define not only color, but also any other CSS properties that you want the links to have.

Although a link is a tag (<a>), its individual attributes are not. To set these properties, you have to use the pseudo-classes associated with each state a link can have: link, visited, hover, and active (**Code 2.12**). See the sidebar "Not Really a Class" and **Table 2.1** for more information on pseudo-classes.

Code 2.12 The four link-style pseudo-classes are link, visited, hover, and active.

```
<html>
<head>
    <style type="text/css" media="screen"><!--
        a:link {
            color:#cc0000;
            font-weight:bold;
        }
        a:visited {
            color:#990000;
            text-decoration:none;
            font-weight:normal;
        }
        a:hover {
            text-decoration:none;
            color:#ff0000;
            cursor:nw-resize;
        }
        a:active {
            color:#990000;
            background-color:#ff0000;
            text-decoration:none;
        }
    --></style>
</head>
<body>
    <h3>CHAPTER XI<br>
    Who Stole the Tarts?</h3>
    <p><a href="index.html">The King</a> and
    → <a href="#">Queen of Hearts</a> were
    → seated on their throne when they arrived,
    → with a great crowd assembled about them--
    → all sorts of little birds and beasts,
    → as well as the whole pack of cards: the
    → <a href="#">Knave</a> was standing
    → before them, in chains, with a soldier
    → on each side to guard him; and near the
    → King was the <a href="#">White Rabbit</
    → a>, with a trumpet in one hand, and a
    → scroll of parchment in the other. In
    → the very middle of the court was a table,
    → with a large dish of tarts upon it:
    → they looked so good, that it made Alice
    → quite hungry to look at them--'I wish
    → they'd get the trial done,' she thought,
    → 'and hand round the refreshments!' But
    → there seemed to be no chance of this, so
    → she began looking at everything about
    → her, to pass away the time.</p>
</body>
</html>
```

Queen of Hearts

Figure 2.23 This is the style for a hypertext link (link pseudo-class).

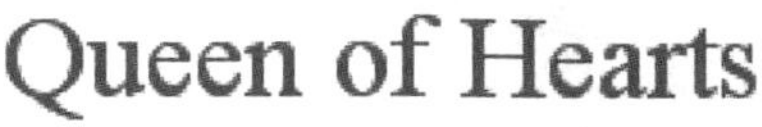

Queen of Hearts

Figure 2.24 The style for a hypertext link that has already been visited (visited pseudo-class).

Queen of Hearts

Figure 2.25 The style for a hypertext link that the mouse pointer is over (hover pseudo-class).

Figure 2.26 The style for a hypertext link that has just been clicked (active pseudo-class).

To set contrasting link appearances:

1. a:link {...}

The link pseudo-class allows you to define the appearance of hypertext links that have not yet been selected (**Figure 2.23**).

2. a:visited {...}

The visited pseudo-class allows you to set the appearance of links that the visitor selected previously (**Figure 2.24**).

3. a:hover{...}

The hover pseudo-class allows you to set the appearance of the link that the mouse pointer is over (**Figure 2.25**).

4. a:active {...}

The active pseudo-class allows you to set the appearance of the link when the visitor clicks it (**Figure 2.26**).

continues on next page

Table 2.1

Pseudo-classes

Pseudo-class	Description	Compatibility
:active	Element being clicked	IE 4, N 6, O 3.5, CSS1, S1
:first-child	Element that is the first child of another element	IE 5*, N 6, O 7, CSS2, S1
:focus	Element that has screen focus	IE 5*, N 6, O 7, CSS2, S1
:hover	Element with mouse-cursor over it	IE 4, N 6, O 3.5, CSS1, S1
:link	Element that has not been visited	IE 4, N 6, O 3.5, CSS1, S1
:visited	Element that has been visited	IE 4, N 6, O 3.5, CSS1, S1

* Mac version only; not available in Windows

✔ Tips

■ The order in which you define your styles makes a difference in certain browsers. In Internet Explorer 5 for Windows, for example, placing the hover pseudo-class before the visited pseudo-class keeps hover from working after a link has been visited. Due to the cascade order (see "Determining the Cascade Order" later in this chapter), active is defined after hover, so in the case of a tie, the active pseudo-class wins. For best results, define your styles in this order: link, visited, hover, and active.

■ The link styles should be inherited by the different states (see "Managing Existing or Inherited Property Values" later in this chapter). (The font you set for the link appearance, for example, should be inherited by the active, visited, and hover states.) But some inconsistencies exist among browsers. To play it safe, I recommend defining all attributes for each link state.

Not Really a Class

CSS-supporting browsers automatically recognize certain special classes, called *pseudo-classes*. Pseudo-classes are tags with unique attributes that can be defined separately. The anchor <a> tag, for example, includes several link states: active, visited, hover, and the default link state. You can define these pseudo-classes individually, as if they were HTML selectors.

Beyond the link pseudo-classes supported in all browsers and the :first-child and :focus pseudo-classes supported in Netscape, CSS also includes several other pseudo-classes not currently supported by Netscape or Internet Explorer (:first, :lang, :left, :right) which are used to address individual pages when printing a Web page.

Text Decoration: To Underline or Not

Underlining has been the standard way of indicating a hypertext link on the Web since its inception. The problem with underlining links is that if you have many links on a page, it becomes an impenetrable mass of lines, and the text is difficult to read. Furthermore, if visitors have underlining turned off, they cannot see links on the page, especially if both link and text colors are the same.

CSS allows you to turn off underlining for links, overriding the visitor's preference. I recommend this practice and prefer to rely on clear color choices to highlight hypertext links. You can use underlining with the hover state, so when visitors place the mouse over a link, they see a clear visual change.

- The Web is a hypertext medium, so it is important that users be able to distinguish among text, links, and visited links. Because you can't count on users having their Underline Links option turned on, it's a good idea to set the link appearance for every document.

- I recommend using caution when changing other attributes for hover. Changing things such as typeface, font size, and weight may cause the text to grow larger than the space reserved for it in the layout forcing the whole page to refresh and the viewer to become annoyed.

- If you use too many colors, your visitors may not be able to tell which words are links and which are not.

- Setting multiple link colors can be useful for showing different kinds of links. For more information on setting multiple link styles on a page, see "Setting Multiple Link Styles" in Chapter 18.

Picking Link Colors

Most browsers default to blue for unvisited links and either red or purple for visited ones. The problem with using two different colors for visited and unvisited links is that visitors may not remember which color is for which type of link. The colors you choose need to distinguish links from other text on the screen and to distinguish among the different states (link, visited, hover, and active), without dominating the screen and becoming distracting.

I recommend using a color for unvisited links that contrasts with both the page's background color and the text color. Then, for visited links, use a darker or lighter version of the same color that contrasts with the background but is dimmer than the unvisited-link color. Brighter unfollowed links will then stand out dramatically from dimmer followed links.

For example, if I were designing a page with a white background and black text, I might use bright red for my links (#ff0000) and pale red (#ff6666) for visited links. The brighter version stands out; the paler version is less distinctive, but still obviously a link.

DEFINING LINK STYLES WITH PSEUDO-CLASSES

Creating Drop Caps with Pseudo-elements

Drop cap–style letters are a time-honored way of starting a new section or chapter of lengthy text by making the first letter of a paragraph larger than subsequent letters and moving the first several lines of text over to accommodate the larger letter. Medieval monks used drop caps with illuminated manuscripts—and now you can use them on the Web (**Figure 2.27**).

You can create a drop cap with CSS by accessing the first letter of the paragraph directly using the `first-letter` pseudo-element.

A *pseudo-element* is a specific, unique part of an element—such as the first letter or first line of a paragraph—the appearance of which can be controlled independent of the rest of the element. For a list of other pseudo-elements, see **Table 2.2**.

CHAPTER VI
Pig and Pepper

or a minute or two she stood looking at the house, livery came running out of the wood- (she conside judging by his face only, she would have called hi was opened by another footman in livery, with a ro noticed, had powdered hair that curled all over the and crept a little way out of the wood to listen.The great letter, nearly as large as himself, and this he Duchess. An invitation from the Queen to play croquet.' The Fr changing the order of the words a little, 'From the Queen. An ir she stood looking at the house, and wondering what to do ne> wood- (she considered him to be a footman because he was i called him a fish)--and rapped loudly at the door with his knuc round face, and large eyes like a frog; and both footmen, Alice She felt very curious to know what it was all about, and crept a by producing from under his arm a great letter, nearly as large solemn tone, 'For the Duchess. An invitation from the Queen to solemn tone, only changing the order of the words a little, 'Fro

Figure 2.27 The drop cap is applied to the first letter of the paragraph, using the `:first-letter` pseudo-element.

Table 2.2

Pseudo-elements

PSEUDO-ELEMENT	DESCRIPTION	COMPATIBILITY
:first-letter	First letter in element	IE 5*, N 6, O 3.5, CSS1, S1
:first-line	First line of text in element	IE 5*, N 6, O 3.5, CSS1, S1
:after	Space immediately before element	N 6, O 5, CSS2, S1
:before	Space immediately after element	N 6, O 5, CSS2, S1

*IE 5.5 for Windows

Code 2.13 The `first-letter` pseudo-element is used to apply a style to just the first letter of a paragraph of text using the class `.dropcap`.

```
<html>
<head>
    <style type="text/css" media="screen"><!--
        p {font: 12px/14px helvetica, arial,
        → sans-serif;}
        p.dropcap: first-letter {
            font: bold 800% times, serif;
            color: red;
            float: left;
            margin-right: 5px;
        }
    --></style>
</head>
<body>
    <h3>CHAPTER VI<br>
    Pig and Pepper</h3>
    <p class="dropcap">For a minute or two she
    → stood looking at the house, and wondering
    → what to do next, when suddenly a footman
    → in livery came running out of the
    → wood...</p>
    <p style="clear:left">'For a minute or two
    → she stood looking at the house, and
    → wondering what to do next, when suddenly
    → a footman in livery came running out of
    → the wood...</p>
</body>
</html>
```

To set a drop cap:

1. `p { font: 12px/14px helvetica,` `→ arial, sans-serif; }`

    Define the paragraph tag to display text in the style you want to use (**Code 2.13**). This example uses 10-point Helvetica with 12-point line spacing. (For help with font sizing, see "Setting the Font Size" in Chapter 3.)

2. `p.dropcap:first-letter {font: bold` `→ 800% times, serif; color: red;` `→ float: left; margin-right: 5px;}`

    Set up a definition for paragraph tags that uses the `first-letter` pseudo-element to make its text bold, eight times larger than the text around it, and with a slight margin to the right so that the drop cap does not bump into the main text. Other text will flow around this text element to the right, because this drop-cap text will float to the left (see "Wrapping Text Around an Element" in Chapter 5).

3. `<p class="dropcap">For a minute or` `→ two... </p>`

    To create a drop cap in your text, simply apply the `dropcap` class to the first paragraph in your text. In this example, the letter appears as 30-point, red, dropped down so its top aligns with the tops of the rest of the characters.

    continues on next page

CREATING DROP CAPS WITH PSEUDO-ELEMENTS

✔ Tips

- To avoid odd positioning, it's a good idea to clear floating in the paragraph immediately after the paragraph with the drop cap in it. To do this, add `clear:left` to the paragraph, either as an inline style or as part of a class or ID.

- Older versions of Internet Explorer render floating letters with their baselines flush with the rest of the text (that is, the bottoms of letters on the same line). Therefore, the letter styled with `dropcap` does not actually drop down.

- Although I set the drop cap up as a class, in theory, you could actually just assign this to the paragraph tag, but then *all* paragraphs in the document would have a drop cap—which is not usually desirable.

- A better alternative than using a class to create the drop cap would be to use the first-child selector (see "Other Selector Groupings" earlier in this chapter) to tell paragraph tags to use the drop-cap style only if immediately preceded by a header level 3 <h3> tag:

  ```
  h3 + p:first-letter {...}
  ```
  Thus, only the first paragraph after a header would receive the drop cap. But, alas, Internet Explorer for Windows does not support first-child selectors.

p { font-size: 12px !important; }

Figure 2.28 The general syntax for making a definition important.

Figure 2.29 Because the <p> tag defines its font size as important, it overrides the later font size set for the copy class, making the text 16px instead of 10px. Because both the <p> tag and copy have !important set for the font family, however, copy takes precedence and the font is Times instead of Arial.

Making a Definition !important

The !important value can be added to a definition to give it the maximum weight in determining the cascade order (see "Determining the Cascade Order" later in this chapter). **Figure 2.28** shows the basic syntax for using !important.

In this example (**Code 2.14**), I have redefined the <p> tag and made the font-size and font-family definitions !important. I have also defined a class called copy that is applied to the paragraph tags with the font family in it defined as !important. As a result, the paragraph text uses the font-size definition from the paragraph-tag rule, but uses the font family and color defined in the copy rule (**Figure 2.29**).

CSS rules can be defined within the <style>...</style> tags in the head of your document (see "Adding Styles to a Web Page" earlier in this chapter) or in an external CSS file that is then imported or linked to the HTML document (see "Adding Styles to a Web Site" earlier in this chapter).

To force a definition to be used always:

1. `p {`

Open a CSS rule with a selector and a curly bracket ({). You can use an HTML selector, class, or ID.

2. `font-size: 16px !important;`

Type a style definition, a space, `!important`, and a semicolon (;) to close the definition.

3. `font-family: arial, helvetica,`
`→ geneva, sans-serif !important;`
`→ color: black; }`

Add any other definitions you desire for this rule, making them `!important` or not as you desire, and then close the rule with a curly bracket (}).

4. `p.copy{...}`

Add any other rules you desire, making their definitions `!important` as needed.

✔ Tips

■ Netscape 4 does not support `!important`.

■ One common mistake is to place the `!important` *after* the semicolon in the definition. This causes the browser to ignore the definition and, possibly, the whole rule.

■ Many browsers allow users to define their own style sheets for use by the browser. Although making a definition `!impor-tant` should override any user-defined styles—even a user's `!important` definitions—I have not found this to be the case in any browser I have tested. In fact, a user-defined style sheet overrides an author-defined style sheet.

Code 2.14 A definition set as `!important` gets top priority when it comes time to determine which definitions are applied to the HTML. In this example, I've set up two rules. The first defines the font size, font family, and color of the <p> tag; the second defines a class called copy for use with the <p> tag, which sets the font size, font family, and text color. Although the copy class should override the font size set in the <p> tag, using `!important` changes this so that the <p> tag's definition takes precedence (Figure 2.26).

```
<html>
<head>
    <style type="text/css" media="screen"><!--
        p {
            font-size: 16px !important;
            font-family: arial, helvetica,
            → geneva, sans-serif !important;
            color: black;
        }
        p.copy {
            font-size: 10px;
            font-family: 'Times New Roman',
            → Georgia, Times, serif !important;
            color: red;
        }
    --></style>
</head>
<body>
    <br>
    <h3>CHAPTER X<br>
    The Lobster Quadrille</h3>
    <p class="copy">The Mock Turtle sighed
    → deeply, and drew the back of one flapper
    → across his eyes. He looked at Alice, and
    → tried to speak, but for a minute or two
    → sobs choked his voice. 'Same as if he
    → had a bone in his throat,' said the
    → Gryphon: and it set to work shaking him
    → and punching him in the back. At last the
    → Mock Turtle recovered his voice, and,
    → with tears running down his cheeks, he
    → went on again:--</p>
</body>
</html>
```

Code 2.15 The <body> tag sets the font style and background color. The font style is inherited by the <p> tag—because the <body> is its parent—but it changes the background color. The <i> tag inherits the <body> and <p> styles but also defines its own background color (Figure 2.28).

```
○ ○ ○                      Code
<html>
<head>

    <style type="text/css">
        body {font: 16pt/20pt times, serif;
→ color: red; background-color: #999999;}
        p {background-color: #cccccc;}

        i {background-color: #ffffff;}

    </style>
</head>
<body>

    <p>She waited for some time without hearing
→ anything more: at last came a rumbling
→ of little cartwheels, and the sound of a
→ good many voices all talking together:
→ she made out the words:<i> 'Where's the
→ other ladder?--Why, I hadn't to bring
→ but one; Bill's got the other--Bill!
→ fetch it here, lad!--Here, put 'em up
→ at this corner--No, tie 'em together
→ first--they don't reach half high enough
→ yet--Oh! they'll do well enough; don't
→ be particular-- Here, Bill! catch
→ hold of this rope--Will the roof bear?
→ --Mind that loose slate--Oh, it's coming
→ down! Heads below!'</i> (a loud crash)--
→ 'Now, who did that?--It was Bill, I
→ fancy--Who's to go down the chimney?--
→ Nay, I shan't! you do it!--That I won't,
→ then!--Bill's to go down--Here,
→ Bill! the master says you're to go down
→ the chimney!'</p>
</body>
</html>
```

Inheriting Properties from a Parent

No, this is not the *Visual QuickStart Guide to Real Estate*. Every HTML tag that can be controlled with CSS, except the <body> tag, has a parent—a container tag that surrounds it.

HTML tags generally assume the styles of any tags that are nested within their parent. This is called inheritance of styles. A color set for the <body> tag, for example, will be used as the color for all tags in the body (**Code 2.15** and **Figures 2.30** and **2.31**).

continues on next page

In some cases, a property is not inherited by its nested tags—obvious properties such as margins, width, and borders. You will probably have no trouble figuring out which properties are inherited and which are not. You wouldn't expect every nested element to have the same amount of padding as its parent, for example.

If you have any doubts, though, check Appendix A, which lists all the properties, as well as whether or not they are inherited.

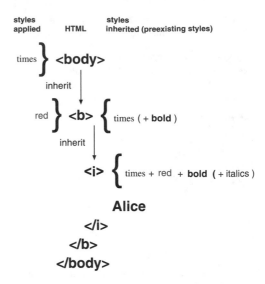

Result

Alice

Figure 2.30 The <body> tag is set to the Times font. This is inherited by the <b> tag, which also has a color style set to red and a pre-existing font-weight style of bold. The <i> tag inherits all of these styles and adds its own pre-existing italic style.

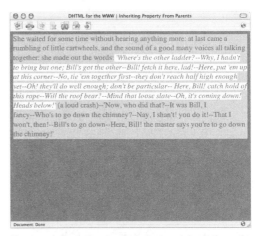

Figure 2.31 Both the <p> and <i> tags inherit the red and Times styles from the <body> tag. The <p> tag overrides the <body> tag's background color with a lighter gray, however, and the <i> tag overrides the <p> tag's background color with white.

Figure 2.32 In a strange turn of events, normal text is bold and bold text is normal.

Managing Existing or Inherited Property Values

By redefining a selector, you do not cause it to lose any of its inherent attributes. A tag redefined with CSS keeps its specified properties. All those properties are displayed, unless the specific existing properties that make up its appearance are changed (**Figure 2.32**).

With CSS, you could make the <b> tag a larger font size and italic, as follows:

```
b {font-size: larger; font-style:
→italic;}
```

Even though it isn't specified in the CSS definition, this text would still be bold. You could, however, set the <b> tag not to be bold by changing the font-weight property, as follows:

```
p b {font-weight: normal;}
```

continues on next page

This overrides the <b> tag's natural state (see **Code 2.16**) whenever bold text is being set within a paragraph.

Properties that are inherited from a parent tag (see the previous section, "Inheriting Properties from a Parent") can likewise be overturned: Simply reset the property in the nested tag's definition list, either in the head style list or directly in a particular tag.

The class .noBold in Code 2.16, for example, can be applied to a <p> tag to override its font-weight definition, which, in this example, has been set to bold.

Code 2.16 In this example, the <p> tag will make text bold unless the text is actually within a <b> tag. In that case, both the inherited bold from the <p> tag and the <b> tag's own inherent boldness are overridden (Figure 2.29).

```
<html>
<head>
    <style type="text/css" media="screen"><!--
        p {font-weight: bold;}
        p b {font-weight: normal;}
        .nobold {font-weight: normal;}
    --></style>
</head>
<body>
    <h3>CHAPTER VII<br>
    A Mad Tea-Party</h3>
    <p>There was a table set out under a tree
    → in front of the house, and the March
    → Hare and the Hatter were having tea at
    → it: a<b> Dormouse was sitting between
    → them, fast asleep, and the other two
    → were using it as a cushion, resting their
    → elbows on it, and talking over its
    → head.</b> 'Very uncomfortable for the
    → Dormouse,' thought Alice; 'only, as it's
    → asleep, I suppose it doesn't mind.'</p>
    <p>The table was a large one, but the three
    → were all crowded together at one corner
    → of it...</p>
    <p class="noBold">'Have some wine,' the
    → March Hare said in an encouraging
    → tone.</p>
</body>
</html>
```

Determining the Cascade Order

Within a single Web page, style sheets may be linked, imported, embedded, or even inlined.

In addition, many browsers allow visitors to have their own style sheets, which they can use to override yours. It's guaranteed, of course, that style sheets from two or more sources being used simultaneously will have conflicting definitions. Who comes out on top? Why do you think they call them *cascading* style sheets?

The following rules determine the cascade order when style sheets conflict:

1. The existence of the `!important` attribute.

Including `!important` with a definition gives it top billing when being displayed (see "Making a Definition `!important`" earlier in this chapter).

Many browsers allow the user to define their own style sheets for use by the browser. In theory, if both the page author and the visitor have included `!important` in their definitions, the author's definition wins. All the browsers I have tested, however, give preferential treatment to styles defined by the user.

2. The source of the rules.

Again, in theory, an author's style sheets override a visitor's style sheets unless the visitor uses the `!important` value. In practice, however, most browsers favor a user's style sheet when determining which definitions are used for a tag.

continues on next page

3. Specificity.

The more specific a rule is, the higher its cascade priority. So the more HTML, class, and ID selectors a particular rule has, the more important it is. In determining this priority, ID selectors count as 100, classes count as 10, and HTML selectors are worth only 1. With this formula, the selectors `ol ol ol.cool` would be weighted at 13 (1+1+1+10=13), whereas p would be 1. This priority setting may seem a bit silly, but it allows context-sensitive and ID rules to carry more weight, ensuring that they will be used.

4. Last one in the pool wins.

CSS gives priority to the last rule listed, in order. This is especially useful if you include an inline definition to override style settings listed in the head.

5. Existing or inherited properties.

Any styles that are inherent to the tag or inherited from parent tags are applied (see the previous section, "Managing Existing or Inherited Property Values").

Following these rules with **Code 2.17** and **2.18**, we get the results shown in **Figure 2.33**.

Code 2.17 global.css: This version provides the default CSS to be used globally in the Web site, and defines a rule for the <h3> tag.

```
h3 { color: blue; }
```

Code 2.18 index.html: The external file global.css is linked to this HTML file. It's defining the color for <h3> tags, but is overridden in the <style> tag. The color set in the <h3> tag itself overrides all other color definitions (Figure 2.30).

```
<html>
<head>
    <style type="text/css" media="screen"><!--
        h3 {
            color: lime
        }
    --></style>
</head>
<body>
    <h3 style="color: red">CHAPTER X<br>
    The Lobster Quadrille</h3>
    <p>The Mock Turtle sighed deeply, and drew
    → the back of one flapper across his
    → eyes...</p>
</body>
</html>
```

Figure 2.33 The <h3> tag is set to have its text appear in blue, and then lime. But the text displays in red, since that's the last color to be defined.

Figure 2.34 What the screen displays is completely different than . . .

Figure 2.35 . . . what the printer prints.

Setting Styles for Print

When most people think of Web pages, they think of them displayed on a screen (**Figure 2.34**). But sooner or later, most people want to print at least some Web pages (**Figure 2.35**). What looks good on the screen, however, does not always look good when printed.

CSS lets us tell the browser to use different style sheets depending on whether the Web page is headed to the computer monitor or to the printer.

To specify a style sheet for a particular medium:

1. Create two external style sheets: one optimized for use on a computer screen and the other tailored for the printed page (see "Adding Styles to a Web Site" earlier in this chapter).

   In this example, the screen version (**Code 2.19**) has white text on a black background—which, although it looks cool on the screen, would not only look messy if printed, but also eat through the toner cartridge. The print version (**Code 2.20**) reverses this with black text on a white (paper) background.

2. `<link href= "print.css"`
   `→ rel="stylesheet" media="print">`

   In the head of your HTML document, type a `<link>` tag that references the print version of the CSS and define `media` as `print` (**Code 2.21**).

Code 2.19 screen.css: This defines how the HTML page in Code 2.21 should be displayed on the screen.

```
body {
    color: white;
    font-family: arial, helvetica, geneva,
    → sans-serif;
    background: black url(alice23.gif)
    → no-repeat;
    word-spacing: 1px;
    position: relative;
    top: 200px;
    left: 165px;
    width: 480px;
}
h1,h2 {
    font: small-caps bold  italic 2.5em
    → 'minion web', Georgia, 'Times New
    → Roman', Times, serif;
}

h2 {
    font-style: normal;
    font-variant: normal;
    font-size: 1.5em;
}
.dropCap {
    font: 300%/100% serif;
    color: #999999;
}
```

Code 2.20 print.css: This defines how the HTML page in Code 2.21 should be displayed when printed.

```
body {
    color: black;
    font-size: 10pt;
    line-height: 12pt;
    font-family: 'Book Antiqua', 'Times New
    → Roman', Georgia, Times, serif;
    background: white no-repeat;
    text-align: justify;
    position: relative;
```

(code continues on next page)

Code 2.20 *continued*

```
        top: 10px;
        left: 40px;
        width: 575px;
}
h1,h2  {
        color: black;
        font: italic small-caps bold 2.5em
        → 'minion web', Georgia, 'Times New
        → Roman', Times, serif;
}
h2 {
        color: black;
        font-style: normal;
        font-variant: normal;
        font-size: 1.5em;
}
.dropCap {
        color: #999999;
        font: 300%/100% serif;
}
```

3. `<link href= "screen.css"` → `rel="stylesheet" media="screen">`
Immediately after the `<link>` tag to the printer version of the CSS, add another `<link>` tag that references the screen version of the CSS, and define `media` as `print`.

✔ Tips

■ The order in which the different CSS files are added to the document is critical, due to the cascade order of styles. If the browser does not understand the media reference, it uses both style sheets.

■ Although several media types are available—including aural (speech), Braille, projection, and handheld—most browsers only support screen and print.

Code 2.21 index.html: The HTML code links to two different CSS files: One is to be used if the file is output to the screen; the other is to be used if the file is output to a printer. Figure 2.34 shows the result for the screen; Figure 2.35 shows the printed result.

```
<html>
<head>
    <link href="print.css" rel="stylesheet" media="print">
    <link href="screen.css" rel="stylesheet" media="screen">
</head>
<body>
    <br>
    <h1>Alice's Adventures in Wonderland</h1>
    <h2>Lewis Carroll</h2>
    <p style="font-family: monospace;">THE MILLENNIUM FULCRUM EDITION 3.0</p>
    <h3>CHAPTER I<br>
    Down the Rabbit-Hole</h3>
    <p><span class="dropCap">A</span>lice was beginning to get very tired of sitting by her sister
    → on the bank, and of having nothing to do: once or twice she had peeped into the book her sister
    → was reading, but it had no pictures or conversations in it, 'and what is the use of a book,'
    → thought Alice 'without pictures or conversation?'</p>
</body>
</html>
```

Adding Comments to CSS

Like any other part of an HTML document, style sheets can have comments. A comment does not affect code; comments only add notes or give guidance to anyone viewing your code. You can include comments in the head of an HTML document or in an external CSS file, as shown in **Code 2.22**.

To include comments in a style sheet:

1. /*

To open a comment area in a style sheet, type a slash (/) and an asterisk (*).

2. selector= HTML tags

Type your comments. You can use any letters or numbers, symbols, and even line breaks (Return or Enter key).

3. */

Close your comment by typing an asterisk (*) and a slash (/).

✔ Tip

■ You cannot nest comments.

Code 2.22 You can use comments to add useful notes to a page without interfering with the code.

```
/* While this sets the apperance of special
→ cases for code
     selector= HTML tags
     rule= the CSS Rule that defines the
     → apperance
     comment= Comments in the CSS */
code.selector { color: #009900; }
code.rule { color: #990099; }
code.comment { color: #cc0000; }
```

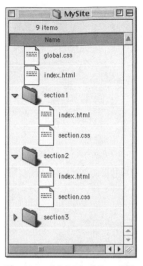

Figure 2.36 A typical tiered file structure that allows different HTML pages to use a global CSS file and then tailors the styles for the particular section with a sectional CSS file. Notice that both sections use a file called "section.css" and not ones called "section1.css" and "section2.css." This allows us to move HTML files between sections without needing to change the URLs used to link or import the documents.

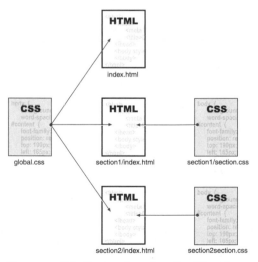

Figure 2.37 This diagram shows how the different HTML files will be linked to the associated CSS files. "global.css" is linked to all three files, while each section's individual "section.css" is linked to refine the page's layout.

Style Sheet Strategies

Here are some useful tips for constructing a site with CSS:

◆ Wherever possible, place your styles in external style sheets (see "Adding Styles to a Web Site" earlier in this chapter).

◆ The power of CSS is that you can place your styles in one common location and change an entire Web site from one place (**Figure 2.36**).

◆ At the top level of your Web site, define a default global.css style sheet that can be applied to your entire Web site.

   Generally speaking, you'll want certain characteristics to be ubiquitous throughout your Web site. You may want all your level 1 headers to be a certain size and font, for example (**Figure 2.37**).

◆ Refine styles at sublevels with a section.css style sheet.

   By doing this, you can change each section or add to the global style sheet. For example, you've already set the size and font for your <h1> tags in the global style sheet, but each section's headers are color-coded. This is your chance to set the color for each section individually.

◆ Use different .css files for distinctive uses.

   Placing all your CSS in one file can lead to larger files and longer download times if you use a lot of CSS. Instead, consider splitting your CSS into several files and importing them as needed for each page.

continues on next page

◆ Place styles in the `<head>` after the JavaScript.

Although you can place the `<style>...</style>` pair anywhere in the head of your document, it's best to place it in one consistent location to make it easier to find. I usually place mine at the bottom, because—well, that's where I put it. Wherever you put your code, be consistent.

◆ Avoid using styles in tags unless you have a compelling reason.

Again, the great thing about CSS is that you can apply styles to multiple tags and change those styles throughout a Web site on a whim. If you define the style directly in the tag, you lose this ability.

FONT CONTROLS

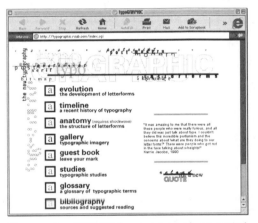

Figure 3.1 typoGRAPHIC (www.rsub.com/typographic) is a great source for learning about the power of typography both on and off the Web.

Figure 3.2 counterSPACE (http://counterspace. motivo.com) also provides insight into typography, all in a beautiful Flash interface.

Typography is one of your most powerful tools for presenting organized, clean-looking documents. For that matter, type is your best tool for presenting chaotic, grungy-looking documents.

The fonts you use go a long way toward getting your message across in just the way you want—whether that message is classical, grunge, or anything in between. Boldface, italic, and other typographic effects help designers guide a visitor's eye around the page (**Figures 3.1** and **3.2**).

CSS gives you the ability to control the appearance of fonts, also known as the *letterforms*, in your Web pages. But with CSS, you can set more than just the font family, boldface and italic attributes, and the limited font sizes available with HTML tags. CSS allows you to go a step further and set generic font families, various levels of boldness, different types of italic, and any font size, using the standard point notation used in the print world.

Understanding Typography on the Web

A *type style* (commonly referred to as a *font family* on the Web) is a category of typefaces (*fonts*) that have similar characteristics. For the Web, there are five basic font families (**Figure 3.3**).

Font Family	Example
serif	Times New Roman
sans-serif	Helvetica and Arial
monospace	Courier New
cursive	*Apple Chancery*
fantasy	Webdings (⌶ 🛍 ✂ ♥ ⓘ ●■ ?)

Figure 3.3 The generic font families and some common examples of each.

◆ **Serif.** A *serif* is the small ornamentation at the end of a letter that gives it a distinguishing quality. Serifs are holdovers from the days of stonecutting and pen strokes. They often improve legibility by making individual letters stand out from their neighbors. Serif fonts generally are best suited for the display of larger text or for smaller printed text. They are not so good for smaller text on a screen, because the serifs often obscure the letter.

◆ **Sans-serif.** As you might guess, *sans-serif* fonts are those fonts without serifs. Although the characters are less distinctive, sans-serif fonts work better for smaller text on a screen.

◆ **Monospace.** Although *monospace* fonts can have serifs or not, their distinguishing feature is that each letter occupies the same amount of space. The lowercase letter *l*, for example, is much thinner than the uppercase letter *M*. In non-monospace fonts, the letter *l* occupies less space than the *M*, but a monospace font adds extra space around the *l* so that it occupies the same amount of space as the *M*. Monospace fonts work best for text that has to be exactly (but not necessarily quickly) read, such as programming code, in which typos can spell disaster.

◆ **Cursive.** *Cursive* fonts attempt to mimic cursive handwriting, usually in a highly stylized manner. Cursive fonts are best reserved for decoration; they are not very good for reading large chunks of text.

◆ **Fantasy.** Decorative fonts that don't fit into any of the preceding categories are referred to as *fantasy* fonts. These fonts usually are extremely ornamental or, in the case of Dingbats, are illustrations or icons. Like cursive fonts, fantasy fonts are best reserved for decoration. You should choose fantasy fonts carefully to reinforce the look and feel of your Web site.

Using type on the Web

Theoretically, you can use any font you want on the Web, but there are three distinctive ways to present text, each with its own strengths and weaknesses:

◆ **HTML text.** The text that you type in your HTML document acts, for the most part, like the text in a word processor. The advantages of HTML text are that it is easy to edit if changes are required, and it can adjust to the width of the screen on which it is being viewed. But HTML text has some severe limitations for design purposes.

By and large, most of the textual control is left up to the visitor's browser, and you can't do things like run text vertically rather than horizontally. Even more stifling is the fact that you are limited to the fonts that are available on the visitor's machine (see "Using Browser-Safe Fonts" later in this chapter). Thus, if you have a specific font on your machine that you want to use, but the person viewing your site doesn't have that font on her machine, you're out of luck.

CSS gives designers greater control of many common typographic features (such as line and word spacing), but even with CSS, HTML text is severely limited, particularly in the special-effects department. This is why many designers turn to text in graphics to get the look they want.

◆ **Graphic text.** Unlike HTML text, graphic text is a graphic (GIF or JPEG) that just happens to have text in it. This means that you can do anything you want in terms of how the text looks and can use any font you want, whether the site visitor has it on his machine or not.

continues on next page

UNDERSTANDING TYPOGRAPHY ON THE WEB

You also have all the limitations that go along with using graphics, such as larger file sizes (larger graphics mean slower download times) and the difficulty of editing text. Graphics also take up a set amount of screen space and may be cut off if the visitor's screen is not large enough.

◆ **Vector text.** Vector text combines the best of both worlds. Like HTML text, it is easy to change and can position itself dynamically, depending on the screen size. But like graphic text, vector text allows you to apply special effects easily (on a slightly more limited scale), and you can use any font that you want.

Vector Text in SVG and Flash

Currently, the only universal way to get vector text into a Web site is to use Macromedia's Flash plug-in. The World Wide Web Consortium (W3C) is working on standards that will allow browsers to display vector text (and graphics) just as they would HTML text.

On the horizon is the Scalable Vector Graphics (SVG) format, which is now a standard from the W3C and is being pushed by its chief developer, Adobe Systems. Although SVG allows the use of vector graphics integrated into HTML documents, like Flash, it relies on a browser plug-in to be displayed. But the Flash plug-in comes standard for most browsers, while the SVG plug-in has to be downloaded and installed, so you can guess which format your users are most likely to use.

Code 3.1 You can specify as many fonts in your definition as you want. Separate names with a comma, and place quotes around font names that contain more than one word.

```
<html>
<head>
    <style type="text/css"><!--
        h1 {
            font-family: Georgia, 'Times New
            → Roman', Times, serif;
        }
        h3 {
            font-family: 'Courier New', Courier,
            → Monaco, monospace;
        }
        .copy {
            font-family: Arial, Helvetica,
            → Geneva, sans-serif;
        }
    --></style>
</head>
<body>
    <hr>
    <h1>ALICE'S ADVENTURES IN WONDERLAND</h1>
    <h3>Lewis Carroll</h3>
    <hr>
    <h3>CHAPTER I<br>
    Down the Rabbit-Hole</h3>
    <p class="copy">Alice was beginning to
    get very tired of sitting by her sister on
    the bank...</p>
</body>
</html>
```

Setting the Font

The font you use to display your text can make a powerful difference in how readers perceive your message. Some fonts are easier to read on the screen; others look better when printed. The font property allows you to determine the visual effect of your message by choosing the font for displaying your text.

In this example (**Code 3.1** and **Figure 3.4**), the level 1 header has been assigned the Times font.

Figure 3.4 The font for the title, subtitle, and text of the page have all been set, thus overriding the default font set in the browser.

To define the font in a rule:

1. `font-family:`

Type the property name font-family, followed by a colon (`:`).

2. `Georgia`

Type the name of the font you want to use.

3. `, 'Times New Roman', palatino`

If you want, you can type a list of fonts separated by commas.

4. `, serif;`

After the last comma, type the name of the generic font family for the particular style of font you're using. **Table 3.1** lists generic values for font families. Although including this value is optional, doing so is a good idea.

✔ Tips

■ When you provide a list of fonts, the browser tries to use the first font listed. If that one isn't available to the browser, it works through the list until it encounters a font that is installed on the visitor's computer. If there are no matches, the browser displays the text in the visitor's default font. The advantage of specifying a generic font is that the browser tries to display the text in the same style of font, even if the specific ones you list are not available.

■ Fonts that contain a space in their names must be enclosed in quotation marks (example: 'New York').

■ Check out "Using Browser-Safe Fonts" on the following page for a list of the fonts that generally are available to browsers.

■ Theoretically, Internet Explorer and Netscape allow you to download a particular font to the visitor's computer and then specify the font by using the `family-name` property. See the sidebar "Downloadable Fonts" for details.

Table 3.1

font-family Values	
VALUE	**COMPATIBILITY**
<family-name>	IE3, N4, S1, O3.5, CSS1
<generic-family>	IE3, N4, S1, O3.5, CSS1
serif	IE3, N4, S1, O3.5, CSS1
sans-serif	IE3*, N4, S1, O3.5, CSS1
cursive	IE4, N4, S1, O3.5, CSS1
fantasy	IE4, N4, S1, O3.5, CSS1
monospace	IE4, N4, S1, O3.5, CSS1
*Internet Explorer 4 for the Mac	

Using CSS vs. the Font Tag

The most common way to set a typeface is by using the `<font>` tag, as follows:

```
<font face="arial,helvetica">Blah,
 'blah, blah</font>
```

But the `<font>` tag is on the way out. The most recent version of the HTML specification from the W3C does not include this tag, noting that fonts should be handled by CSS.

There are two basic problems with the `<font>` tag:

◆ You have to add this tag every time you set a font, which can significantly increase file size.

◆ If you need to change the font attributes, you have to change the attributes in every tag.

CSS solves both of these problems by allowing you to redefine how existing tags treat the text they contain, rather than adding more tags, and by allowing you to control these behaviors from a single line in the document.

Table 3.2

Mac System Fonts	
FONT NAME	STYLES
American Typewriter*	bold
Apple Chancery	
Apple Symbols*	
Arial	bold, italic, bold italic
Arial Black	
Arial Narrow*	bold, italic, bold italic
Arial Rounded MT Bold*	
Baskerville*	bold, italic, bold italic
Big Caslon*	
Brush Script MT*	
Capitals**	
Charcoal**	
Chicago**	
Cochin*	bold, italic, bold italic
Comic Sans MS	bold
Copperplate*	bold
Courier	bold, oblique, bold oblique
Courier New	bold, italic, bold italic
Didot*	bold, italic
Futura*	
Gadget**	
Geneva	
Georgia	bold, italic, bold italic
Gill Sans*	bold, italic, bold italic
Helvetica	bold, oblique, bold oblique
Helvetica Neue*	bold, italic, bold italic
Herculanum*	
Hoefler Text	bold, italic, bold italic
Impact	
Lucida Grande*	bold
Marker Felt*	
Monaco	
New York**	
Optima*	bold, italic, bold italic
Palatino**	bold, italic, bold italic
Papyrus*	
Sand**	
Skia	
Symbol	
Techno**	
Textile**	
Times	bold, italic, bold italic
Times New Roman	bold, italic, bold italic
Trebuchet MS	bold, italic, bold italic
Verdana*	bold, italic, bold italic
VT100*	bold
Webdings	
Zapf Dingbats*	
Zapfino*	

*= as of OS X; ** Only installed in OS X if Classic is installed*

Using browser-safe fonts

Look around the Web, and what do you see? Two fonts: Arial and Times. Virtually every site whose designers made an effort to control the display of text uses either Times or Arial (or its Mac equivalent, Helvetica). This situation came about for one simple reason: Virtually every computer has these two fonts or some variant of them.

I am sick of them.

Don't get me wrong—these are great fonts, easy to read at many sizes. But as I said earlier, typography adds a language to text that goes far beyond the written word.

Web-based typography is mired in using Times for serif fonts and Helvetica/Arial for sans-serif fonts. This arrangement mutes the power of typography, and all Web pages begin to look the same.

What are the alternatives to the "terrible two"? That depends on the computer the person visiting your site is using. Mac and Windows computers have certain standard fonts that should always be installed. In addition, Internet Explorer (which comes installed on most computers these days) installs several additional fonts.

I have compiled lists of browser-safe fonts that should be available on each of the different platforms.

◆ **Apple Macintosh (Table 3.2)**

◆ **Microsoft Windows (Table 3.3)**

◆ **Microsoft Core Fonts (Table 3.4)** are installed with Internet Explorer for both Windows and Mac.

continues on next page

As you can see, there are certainly more than two choices. Appendix D also lists these fonts, with examples of what they should look like and replacement fonts that are similar looking.

✔ Tip

- For more details on Mac fonts, see `developer.apple.com/fonts`. For more details on Windows fonts, see `www.microsoft.com/typography/fonts`. Although listed for Web development, these fonts can be used for any document (presentation, word processed, or whatever) that is being transferred between computers.

Table 3.4

Microsoft Core Fonts	
FONT NAME	**STYLES**
Andale Mono*	
Arial	bold, italic, bold italic
Arial Black	
Comic Sans MS	bold
Courier New	
Georgia	bold, bold italic, italic
Impact	
Times New Roman	bold, italic, bold italic
Trebuchet MS	bold, bold italic, italic
Verdana	bold, bold italic, italic
Webdings	
Adobe Minion Web	

Previously named Monotype.com

NOTE: Internet Explorer installs these fonts, so they may not be available to Netscape users. Still, because most computers come with IE installed, it's a safe bet that these fonts will be on your visitor's machine.

Table 3.3

Windows System Fonts	
FONT NAME	**STYLES**
Arial	bold, italic, bold italic
Arial Black	
Comic Sans MS	bold
Courier New	bold, bold italic, italic
Franklin Gothic Medium*	italic
Georgia	bold, bold italic, italic
Impact	
Lucida Console	
Lucida Sans Unicode	
Marlett	
Microsoft Sans Serif*	
Palatino Linotype	bold, bold italic, italic
Symbol	
Tahoma	bold
Times New Roman	bold, bold italic, italic
Trebuchet MS	bold, bold italic, italic
Verdana	bold, bold italic, italic
Webdings	
Wingdings	

* = as of Windows XP

8pt 12pt 24pt 48pt

Figure 3.5 A few font sizes.

Code 3.2 The font size for the class copy has been set to 12 pixels, blockquotes will appear with a 2-em indent, and level 3 header tags will appear large(r) than the parent's text—which, in this case, is the default size set for the browser.

```
<html>
<head>
    <style type="text/css"><!--
        .copy {
            font-size: 12px;
        }
        blockquote {
            font-size: 2em;
        }
        h3 {
            font-size: large;
        }
    --></style>
</head>
<body>
    <h3>CHAPTER II<br>
    The Pool of Tears</h3>
    <p class="copy">'Curiouser and curiouser!'
    → cried Alice...</p>
    <blockquote>
        ALICE'S RIGHT FOOT, ESQ.<br>
        HEARTHRUG,<br>
        NEAR THE FENDER,<br>
        (WITH ALICE'S LOVE).
    </blockquote>
</body>
</html>
```

Setting the Font Size

HTML gives you seven font sizes, but these are all relative to a default size set by the visitor. With CSS, you can specify the size of the text on the screen using several notations or methods, including the traditional point-size notation, percentage, absolute size, and even a size relative to the surrounding text. **Figure 3.5** shows text in different sizes.

In this example (**Code 3.2** and **Figure 3.6**), I define the class copy to use a font size of 12 pixels and then apply it to paragraphs of text.

Figure 3.6 The size of the font helps determine its legibility and the emphasis it receives on the page. Titles usually are larger than copy, but some text needs a little more attention.

To define the font size in a rule:

1. `font-size:`

Type the property name font-size, followed by a colon (:).

2. `12px;`

Type a value for the font size, which could be any of these options:

- ▲ A length unit (usually, the font size in points)

- ▲ An absolute expression that describes the font size; the expressions are `xx-small`, `x-small`, `small`, `medium`, `large`, `x-large`, and `xx-large`

- ▲ `smaller` or `larger`, to describe the font size in relation to its parent element (see "Inheriting Properties from a Parent" in Chapter 2)

- ▲ A percentage, representing how much larger the text is in proportion to the size of its parent element (75%, for example)

See **Table 3.5** for a list of `font-size` values and their browser compatibility.

✔ Tips

- ■ Although the maximum-size font you can use depends on the visitor's computer, try to stay below 50-point fonts, to be safe.

- ■ Don't limit yourself to the small letters available with HTML. CSS allows you to create dramatic effects for titles by using large letters that download as quickly as any other text.

Table 3.5

font-size Values	
VALUE	COMPATIBILITY
<length>	IE4, N4, S1, O3.5, CSS1
<percentage>	IE4, N4, S1, O3.5, CSS1
smaller	IE4, N4, S1, O3.5, CSS1
larger	IE4, N4, S1, O3.5, CSS1
xx-small	IE4, N4, S1, O3.5, CSS1
x-small	IE4, N4, S1, O3.5, CSS1
small	IE4, N4, S1, O3.5, CSS1
medium	IE4, N4, S1, O3.5, CSS1
large	IE4, N4, S1, O3.5, CSS1
x-large	IE4, N4, S1, O3.5, CSS1
xx-large	IE4, N4, S1, O3.5, CSS1

Pixels and Points

The *point* (abbreviated *pt*) is one way of referring to a font's relative size. A 12-point font is a fairly average size and is comfortable for most readers.

Point sizes are a common way to denote a font's size. The size of a point, however, varies slightly between operating systems, so a font set to 12 points in Windows appears larger than the same font set to 12 points on a Mac.

I occasionally set fonts by using the point size (especially if the page is being printed), but I usually prefer to specify font sizes by using **px**, which defines the size in pixels. Pixels are still a little unreliable, but they usually are more consistent than point size when displaying text on the Web.

Although there is not a one-to-one correlation between pixels and points, **12px** is roughly the same size as **12pt**.

normal *italic oblique*

Figure 3.7 Italic or oblique? To really tell the difference, take a careful look at the letter "i" in both words.

Code 3.3 The `booktitle` class and `<blockquote>` tags will be italicized.

```
<html>
<head>
    <style type="text/css"><!--
        .booktitle {
            font-family: 'times new roman',
            → times, serif;
            font-style: italic;
        }
        blockquote {
            font-family: arial, helvetica, serif;
            font-style: italic;
        }
    --></style>
</head>
<body>
    <h1 class="booktitle">Alice in Wonderland
    → </h1>
    <p><i>How doth the little--</i>&quot;' and
    → she crossed her hands on her lap...</p>
    <blockquote>
        <p>'How doth the little crocodile</p>
        <p>Improve his shining tail,</p>
    </blockquote>
</body>
</html>
```

Making Text Italic

The two kinds of styled text—*italic* and *oblique*—are often confused. An italic font is a special version of a particular font, redesigned with more pronounced serifs and usually a slight slant to the right. An oblique font is simply a font that is slanted to the right by the computer (**Figure 3.7**).

With the `font-style` element, you can define a font as italic, oblique, or normal. When a font is set to italic but does not have an explicit italic version, the font defaults to oblique.

In this example (**Code 3.3** and **Figure 3.8**), the class `booktitle` and any paragraphs within a `<blockquote>` are italicized. The title uses a serif font, so it shows the true italics, while the blockquote is using a sans-serif font, which is actually oblique, even when defined as italics.

Figure 3.8 Book titles and quotes are generally italicized to set them off.

To set font-style in an HTML tag:

1. `font-style:`

   Type the property name font-style, followed by a colon (:).

2. `italic;`

   Type a value for the `font-style`. Your options are (**Table 3.6**)

   ▲ `italic`, which displays the type in an italic version of the font

   ▲ `oblique`, which slants the text to the right

   ▲ `normal`, which overrides any other styles set

✔ Tips

■ Many browsers do not differentiate between italic and oblique, but will simply treat all serif fonts as italic, even when set to oblique.

■ Many Web designers underline words to draw visual attention to them. I recommend using italic or oblique text instead. Underlining often causes the page to look cluttered. More important, underlined text might be confused with hypertext links.

■ Italicized text generally fits into a more compact space than does nonitalic text (called *roman* in traditional typesetting terms) and could be used to save screen space. But be careful—at small point sizes, italic can be difficult to read on the screen.

Table 3.6

font-style Values	
VALUE	COMPATIBILITY
normal	IE4, N4, S1, O3.5, CSS1
italic	IE4, N4, S1, O3.5, CSS1
oblique	IE4, N6, S1, O3.5, CSS1

normal **bold**

Figure 3.9 The difference between normal and bold text is evident here.

Code 3.4 The `bolder` class is used to make boldface text. Italics within a paragraph have been set to non-bold.

```
<html>
<head>
    <style type="text/css"><!--
        body {
            font-size: 24px;
            font-family: 'times new roman',
            → times, serif;
        }
        .bolder {
            font-weight: bolder;
        }
        p i {
            font-weight: normal;
        }
    --></style>
</head>
<body>
    <b>More from <i>Alice in Wonderland</i></b>
    <p><span class="bolder">'I wish I hadn't
    → cried so much!'...</span></p>
    <p><span class="bolder">Just then she heard
    → <i>something</i> splashing about in the
    → pool a little way off...</span></p>
    <p><span class="bolder">'Would it be of any
    → use, now,' thought Alice...</span></p>
    <p><span class="bolder">'Perhaps it doesn't
    → understand English,' thought Alice...
    → </span></p>
    <p><span class="bolder">'Not like
cats!'...</span></p>
</body>
</html>
```

Setting Bold, Bolder, Boldest

In straight HTML, text is either bold or not. CSS provides several more options that allow you to set different levels of boldness for text. Many fonts have various weights associated with them; these weights have the effect of making the text look more or less bold. CSS can take advantage of this feature (**Figure 3.9**).

In this example (**Code 3.4** and **Figure 3.10**), I've created a class called `bolder` to make text bolder than the surrounding text.

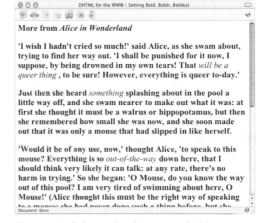

Figure 3.10 All the text has been set to bold except italicized words, which are a normal weight.

To define bold text in a CSS rule:

1. `font-weight:`

Type the property name font-weight, followed by a colon (`:`).

2. `bolder;`

Type the value for the `font-weight` property, using one of these options (**Table 3.7**):

   ▲ `bold`, which sets the font to boldface

   ▲ `bolder` or `lighter`, which sets the font's weight to be bolder or lighter relative to its parent element's weight

   ▲ A value from `100` to `900`, in increments of 100, which increases the weight, based on alternative versions of the font that are available

   ▲ `normal`, which overrides other weight specifications

✔ Tip

■ Use `font-weight` to add emphasis to text, but use it sparingly. If everything is bold, nothing stands out.

Table 3.7

font-weight Values	
VALUE	COMPATIBILITY
normal	IE4, N4, S1, O3.5, CSS1
bold	IE3, N4, S1, O3.5, CSS1
lighter	IE3, N6, S1, O3.5, CSS1
bolder	IE3, N6, S1, O3.5, CSS1
100-900*	IE4, N4, S1, O3.5, CSS1

Depending on available font weights

Font-Weight Numbers

Most fonts do not have nine weights, so if you specify a `font-weight` value that is not available, another weight is used, based on the following system:

   ◆ `100` to `300` use the next-lighter weight, if available, or the next-darker

   ◆ `400` and `500` may be used interchangeably

   ◆ `600` to `900` use the next-darker weight, if available, or the next-lighter

Normal   SMALLCAPS

Figure 3.11 All the letters are capitals, but the first letter is larger than the rest.

Code 3.5 The level 2 header tag is set to be displayed in small caps.

```
<html>
<head>
    <style type="text/css"><!--
        body {
            font-size: 24px;
            font-family: 'times new roman',
            → times, serif;}
        h2 {
            font-variant: small-caps;
        }
    --></style>
</head>
<body>
    <h2>Chapter III<br>
    A Caucus-Race and a Long Tale</h2>
    <p>They were indeed a queer-looking party
    → that assembled on the bank...</p>
</body>
</html>
```

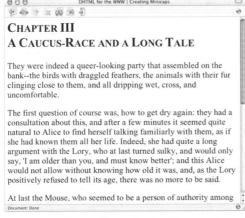

Figure 3.12 Using small caps for the title is an elegant way to set it off from the rest of the text.

Creating Small Caps

Small caps (sometimes referred to as "mini-caps") are useful for emphasizing titles. With small caps, lowercase letters are converted to uppercase, but in a slightly smaller size than regular uppercase letters (**Figure 3.11**).

In this example (**Code 3.5** and **Figure 3.12**), the <h2> tag is used to create a distinctive book title in small caps.

To make a rule for small caps:

1. `font-variant:`

   Type the property name font-variant, followed by a colon (:).

2. `small-caps;`

   Type the value of the font-variant property, using one of these options (**Table 3.8**):

   ▲ `small-caps`, which sets lowercase letters as smaller versions of true uppercase letters

   ▲ `normal`, which overrides other font-variant values that might be inherited

✔ Tip

■ Small caps are best reserved for titles or other special text; they are hard to read at smaller sizes.

Table 3.8

font-variant Values	
VALUE	COMPATIBILITY
normal	IE4, N6, S1, O3.5, CSS1
small-caps	IE4, N6, S1, O3.5, CSS1

Setting Multiple Font Values

Although you can set font properties independently, it is often useful, not to mention more concise, to put all font elements in a single definition. To do this, you use the font property.

This example (**Code 3.6** and **Figure 3.13**) shows a level 1 header tag being defined, along with a class called copy that will be applied to paragraphs of text. In addition, the level 3 header tag is defined with the shorthand font style (see the sidebar "Using the Visitor's Styles" on the next page).

To define several font attributes simultaneously in a rule:

1. font:

   Type the property name font, followed by a colon (:). Then type the values in the following steps (**Table 3.9**):

2. bold

   Type a font-weight value, followed by a space (see "Setting Bold, Bolder, Boldest" earlier in this chapter).

3. italic

   Type a font-style value, followed by a space (see "Making Text Italic" earlier in this chapter).

4. small-caps

   Type a font-variant value, followed by a space (see the previous section, "Creating Small Caps").

5. 2.5em

   Type a font-size value (see "Setting the Font Size" earlier in this chapter).

6. /3em

   Type a forward slash (/), a line-height value, and a space (see "Adjusting Text Spacing" in Chapter 4).

Code 3.6 The <h1> tag and copy class have had the various font styles set at the same time, while the <h3> tag uses a shorthand value to mimic the caption style.

```
<html>
<head>
    <style type="text/css"><!--
        h1 {
            font: bold italic small-caps
            → 2.5em/3em 'minion web', Georgia,
            → 'Times New Roman', Times, serif;
        }
        h3 {
            font: caption;
        }
        .copy {
            font: 10px/20px Arial, Helvetica,
            → Geneva, sans-serif;
        }
    --></style>
</head>
<body>
    <hr>
    <h1>Alice's Adventures In<br>
    Wonderland</h1>
    <h3>Lewis Carroll</h3>
    <hr>
    <h3>CHAPTER I<br>
    Down the Rabbit-Hole</h3>
    <p class="copy">Alice was beginning to
    → get very tired of sitting by her sister
    → on the bank...</p>
</body>
</html>
```

Figure 3.13 You can set all the font properties (and the line height) in a single definition and even instruct the page to use styles defined by the visitor's computer.

7. `'minion web', Georgia,`
   → `'Times New Roman', Times, serif;`

Type a `font-family` value and closing semicolon (refer to "Setting the Font" earlier in this chapter).

✔ Tips

■ If you don't want to set a particular value in the list, don't include it. The browser will use its default value instead.

■ The `font` attribute is a real time-saver, and I try to use it as often as possible. WYSIWYG programs such as GoLive and Dreamweaver, however, tend to default to using the individual attributes.

Table 3.9

font Values	
VALUE	COMPATIBILITY
<font-family>	IE4, N4, S1, O3.5, CSS1
<font-style>	IE4, N4, S1, O3.5, CSS1
<font-variant>	IE4, N4, S1, O3.5, CSS1
<font-weight>	IE4, N4, S1, O3.5, CSS1
<font-size>	IE4, N4, S1, O3.5, CSS1
<font-height>	IE4, N4, S1, O3.5, CSS1
<visitor-style>	IE5, N6, S1, O3.5, CSS2

Using the Visitor's Styles

Wouldn't it be nice if you could match the font styles that the user visiting your page is already using in his browser? You can do this by simply declaring the font style to be one of the following keywords (for example, `font: icon;`):

◆ `caption`: the font style being used by buttons

◆ `icon`: the font style being used to label icons

◆ `menu`: the font style being used in drop-down menus and menu lists

◆ `message-box`: the font style being used in dialog boxes

◆ `small-caption`: the font style being used for labeling small controls

◆ `status-bar`: the font style being used in the window's status bar

Downloadable Fonts

The Holy Grail of Web-based typography is downloadable fonts. Imagine if, rather than having to rely on the limited list of browser-safe fonts or having to create graphics just to get the typeface you want to use, you could send the font to the visitor's computer automatically.

Actually, the CSS Level 2 standard allows for downloadable fonts, so why don't we see downloaded fonts all over the Web? There are several impediments to simple font delivery:

◆ Many fonts are not free. There is some concern among font creators that they will not be compensated if their fonts are distributed over the Web. This assumes that users can download and reuse fonts without having to pay for them.

◆ Windows and Mac fonts are incompatible. You would have to include versions for both platforms.

◆ Font files can be quite large and, thus, take a while to download.

Netscape and Internet Explorer have introduced schemes to overcome these problems and allow font downloading for Web pages. The problem is that you can't simply queue a font like a graphic and have it download. Instead, you have to process the font for the Web. Unfortunately, Netscape and Microsoft came up with incompatible—not to mention difficult—systems for creating downloadable fonts.

For Internet Explorer, you have to convert your fonts to .eot format, using a program called WEFT (www.microsoft.com/typography/web/embedding). This program, however, is Windows-only software.

For Netscape, you have to purchase software from Bitstream to convert your fonts to TrueDoc format (www.truedoc.com). According to Bitstream, this format works in both Netscape and Internet Explorer, but is extremely buggy.

On the distant horizon, CSS3 promises to sort out the font download problems. However, since a new version of Internet Explorer for Windows (the most prevalent browser) is not due until 2005 and there is no guarantee that it will support CSS Level 3, downloading fonts seems to be a moot point for today's Web designers.

TEXT CONTROLS

Text is everywhere around us. Text can be used for everything from listing the ingredients in breakfast cereal to writing an ode to a Grecian urn. It is the best system that humans have yet devised for relating complex thoughts.

Many people think of text as being simply a way of recording spoken words, but typography adds a language to text that goes far beyond the written word.

Typography affects how text appears by controlling not only the shapes and sizes of the letters being used (the font), but also the spaces between letters, words lines, and paragraphs. On the Web, typography has taken up the challenges of displaying text on a computer screen to a wider audience.

Unfortunately, many of the challenges of typography on the Web have come about as a result of a need to circumvent the limitations of the medium.

In this chapter, I'll show you ways to present text using CSS to open up the screen and improve legibility, as well as to draw interest.

Adjusting Text Spacing

One feature of CSS that HTML styles have no parallel for is the ability to easily adjust the space between text, including the space between individual letters (kerning), words, and lines of text in a paragraph (leading). Of course you could resort to nonbreaking spaces and the line break tag to get a similar effect with straight HTML, but these are kludges that are difficult to implement, control, and change. With CSS, you have exact control over all of these elements and you can change them as desired.

Adjusting the space between letters

Kerning refers to the amount of space between letters in a word. More space between letters often improves the readability of the text. On the other hand, too much space can hamper reading by making individual words appear less distinct on the page.

In this example (**Code 4.1** and **Figure 4.1**), extra space is being added between the letters of the word *stretching*.

Code 4.1 Here, I've used letter spacing for a dramatic effect to stretch the word stretching.

```
<html>
<head>
    <style type="text/css"><!--
        .stretch {
            letter-spacing: 2em;
        }
    --></style>
</head>
<body>
    An enormous puppy was looking down at her
    → with large round eyes, and feebly <span
    → class="stretch">stretching</span> out
    → one paw, trying to touch her. 'Poor
    → little thing!' said Alice, in a coaxing
    → tone, and she tried hard to whistle to
    → it; but she was terribly frightened all
    → the time at the thought that it might be
    → hungry, in which case it would be
    → very likely to eat her up in spite of
    → all her coaxing.
</body>
</html>
```

Figure 4.1 This text does what it says.

Table 4.1

letter-spacing Values	
VALUE	COMPATIBILITY
normal	IE4, N6, S1, O3.5, CSS1
<length>	IE4, N6, S1, O3.5, CSS1

To define kerning:

1. letter-spacing:

   Type the letter-spacing property name, followed by a colon (:) in the CSS definition list.

2. 2em;

   Type a value for the letter-spacing property (**Table 4.1**), using either of these:

   ▲ A **length value,** such as 2em, which sets the absolute space between letters

   ▲ normal, which overrides inherited spacing attributes

✔ Tip

■ A positive value for letter-spacing adds more space to the default amount; a negative value closes the space. A value of 0 does not add or subtract space, but prevents justification of the text (see "Aligning Text Horizontally" later in this chapter).

Adjusting space between words

Just like adjusting kerning, adjusting word spacing can both help and hinder legibility. Adding a little space between words on the screen can help make your text easier to read, but too much space interrupts the path of the reader's eye across the screen and, therefore, interferes with reading.

In this example (**Code 4.2** and **Figure 4.2**), some of the words are being pressed illegibly close together, and others are separated to give the text a looser appearance.

Code 4.2 I've set up a class for the title, to space out the words (and the letters). In addition, this code uses a negative value in <p> tags to press the text together and overrides that setting with a positive value in <p> tags with the copy class.

```
<html>
<head>
    <style type="text/css"><!--
        .title {
            word-spacing: 8px;
            letter-spacing: 4px;
        }
        p {
            word-spacing: -8px;
        }
        p.copy {
            word-spacing: 4px;
            letter-spacing: 1px;
        }
    --></style>
</head>
<body>
    Yet more<span class="title"> Alice in
    → Wonderland</span>
    <p>'We indeed!' cried the Mouse, who was
    → trembling down to the end of his tail.
    → 'As if I would talk on such a subject!
    → Our family always <i>hated</i> cats:
    → nasty, low, vulgar things! Don't let me
    → hear the name again!'</p>
    <p class="copy">'I won't indeed!' said
    → Alice, in a great hurry to change the
    → subject of conversation. 'Are you--are
    → you fond--of--of dogs?'...</p>
</body>
</html>
```

Figure 4.2 The space between letters is stretched slightly for a more relaxed appearance and, further down, compressed to be made illegible.

Table 4.2

word-spacing Values	
VALUE	COMPATIBILITY
normal	IE4*, N6, S1, O3.5, CSS1
<length>	IE4*, N6, S1, O3.5, CSS1

IE 6 in Windows

To define word spacing:

1. word-spacing:

   Type the word-spacing property name, followed by a colon (:) in the CSS definition list.

2. 8px;

   Set the value for word-spacing (**Table 4.2**), using either of these:

   ▲ A **length value,** representing the amount of space between words (8px, for example)

   ▲ normal, which overrides inherited values

✔ Tip

■ A positive value for word spacing adds more space to the default, and a negative value closes the space. A value of 0 neither adds nor subtracts space, but prevents justification (see "Aligning Text Horizontally" later in this chapter).

ADJUSTING TEXT SPACING

Adjusting space between lines of text

Anybody who has ever typed a term paper knows that these papers usually have to be double-spaced, to make reading easier and to allow space for comments to be written on the page. Space between lines *(leading)* also can be increased for a dramatic effect by creating areas of negative space between the text. The line-height property adds space between the baselines (the bottoms of most letters) of lines of text.

In this example (**Code 4.3** and **Figure 4.3**), the copy has been double-spaced, and the citation text has its line height set slightly above the font size.

Code 4.3 Text with the class copy will be double-spaced while the <cite> tag will have less than a single space between each line.

```
<html>
<head>
    <style type="text/css"><!--
        .copy {
            font-size: 12px;
            line-height: 2;
        }
        p cite {
            font-size: 12px;
            line-height: 14px;
        }
    --></style>
</head>
<body>
    <p class="copy">After a time she heard a
 → little pattering of feet in the
 → distance...</p>
    <p><cite>Alice took up the fan and gloves,
 → and, as the hall was very hot, she
 → kept fanning herself all the time she
 → went on talking...</cite></p>
</body>
</html>
```

Figure 4.3 The text is double-spaced for regular text. The leading is closer for quotes.

Table 4.3

line-height Values	
VALUE	COMPATIBILITY
normal	IE3, N4, S1, O3.5, CSS1
<number>	IE4, N4, S1, O3.5, CSS1
<length>	IE3, N4, S1, O3.5, CSS1
<percentage>	IE3, N4, S1, O3.5, CSS1

To define leading in a rule:

1. `line-height`:

   Type the `line-height` property name, followed by a colon (`:`), in the CSS definition list.

2. Type the value for `line-height` (**Table 4.3**), using one of these options:

   ▲ A **number** to be multiplied by the font size to get the spacing value (2 for double spacing, for example).

   ▲ A **length value,** such as `24px`. The space for each line of text is set to this size regardless of the designated font size. So if the font size is set to `12px` and the line height is set to `24px`, the text will be double-spaced.

   ▲ A **percentage,** which sets the line height proportionate to the font size being used for the text.

   ▲ `normal`, which overrides inherited spacing values.

✔ Tips

- Adding space between lines of text enhances legibility—especially in large amounts of text. Generally, a line height of 1.5 to 2 times the font size is appropriate for most text.

- To double-space text, set the `line-height` value as either `2` or `200%`. Likewise, `3` or `300%` results in triple-spaced text.

- You can use a negative value to smash text lines together. Although this effect may look neat, it probably won't ingratiate you with your readers.

- Line height can also be defined in the `font` property (see "Setting Multiple Font Values" in Chapter 3).

- You can control the space between individual paragraphs using the `margin` property explained in Chapter 5.

Setting Text Case

When you're dealing with dynamically generated output, you can never be sure whether the text will appear in uppercase, lowercase, or a mixture. With the `text-transform` property, you can control the ultimate case of the text no matter what it begins with.

In this example, the names of the characters have been typed in the HTML (**Code 4.4**) in lowercase characters. When displayed in the browser, however, the text is transformed into its correct format (**Figure 4.4**).

Code 4.4 The class `nameCapitalize`, if invoked, will force words to be displayed with initial capitals.

```
<html>
<head>
    <style type="text/css" media="screen"><!--
        body {
            font-size: 28pt;}
        .nameUppercase {
            text-transform: uppercase;}
        .nameLowercase {
            text-transform: lowercase;}
        .nameCapitalize {
            text-transform: capitalize;}
    --></style>
</head>
<body>
    <p class="nameUppercase">alice uppercase</p>
    <p class="nameLowercase">ALICE LOWERCASE</p>
    <p class="nameCapitalize">alice
    → capitalized</p>
</body>
</html>
```

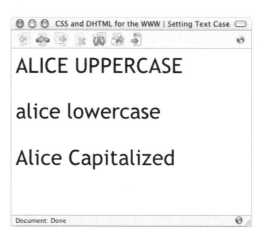

Figure 4.4 Even though the text is lowercase in the HTML, it's displayed in uppercase in the browser.

Table 4.4

text-transform Values	
VALUE	COMPATIBILITY
capitalize	IE4, N4, S1, O3.5, CSS1
uppercase	IE4, N4, S1, O3.5, CSS1
lowercase	IE4, N4, S1, O3.5, CSS1
none	IE4, N4, S1, O3.5, CSS1

To define the text case:

1. text-transform:

   Type the text-transform property name, followed by a colon (:), in the CSS definition list.

2. capitalize

   Type one of the following values for text-transform (**Table 4.4**) to specify how you want the text to be treated:

   ▲ capitalize sets the first letter of each word in uppercase

   ▲ uppercase forces all letters to be uppercase

   ▲ lowercase forces all letters to be lowercase

   ▲ none overrides inherited text-case values and leaves the text as-is

✔ Tips

■ If you want specific text to be uppercase, you should type it as uppercase, so that older browsers won't be left out.

■ The text-transform property probably is best reserved for formatting text that is being created dynamically. If the names in a database are all uppercase, for example, you can use text-transform to make them more legible when displayed.

Aligning Text Horizontally

Traditionally, text is either aligned at its left margin or fully justified (often called *newspaper style*, in which text is aligned at both left and right margins). In addition, for emphasis or special effect, text can be centered on the screen or even right-justified. The text-align property gives you control of the text's alignment and justification (**Figure 4.5**).

Figure 4.5 Aligning text to the left side, the right side, in the center, or equally on both sides.

Code 4.5 I'm setting up classes for all the various justifications.

```
<html>
<head>
    <style type="text/css" media="screen"><!--
        .left {
            text-align: left;}
        .justify {
            text-align: justify;}
        .center {
            text-align: center;}
        .right {
            text-align: right;}
    --></style>
</head>
<body>
    <h2 class="left">Left</h2>
    <p class="left"><i>'You are old, Father
    → William...</i></p>
    <hr>
    <h2 class="right">Right</h2>
    <p class="right"><i>'In my youth,' Father
    → William replied to his son...</i></p>
    <hr>
    <h2 class="center">Center</h2>
    <p class="center"><i>'You are old,' said
    → the youth...</i></p>
    <hr>
    <h2 class="justify">Justified</h2>
    <p class="justify">Hardly knowing what she
    → did, she picked up a little bit of stick,
    → and held it out to the puppy...</p>
</body>
</html>
```

To define text alignment:

1. `text-align:`
   Type the `text-align` property name, followed by a colon (`:`), in the CSS definition list (**Code 4.5**).

2. `left;`
   Set one of the following alignment styles (**Table 4.5**):
   - ▲ `left` to align the text on the left margin
   - ▲ `right` to align the text on the right margin
   - ▲ `center` to center the text within its area
   - ▲ `justify` to align the text on both the left and right sides

✔ Tip

- Fully justifying text may produce some strange results on the screen because spaces between words must be added to make each line the same length. In addition, there is considerable debate about whether full justification helps or hinders readability.

Table 4.5

text-align Values	
VALUE	COMPATIBILITY
left	IE3, N4, S1, O3.5, CSS1
right	IE3, N4, S1, O3.5, CSS1
center	IE3, N4, S1, O3.5, CSS1
justify	IE3, N4, S1, O3.5, CSS1

Aligning Text Vertically

With the vertical-align property, you can specify the vertical position of one element relative to the elements around it, either above or below. This means that vertical-align can be used only with inline element selectors—tags without a break before or after them, such as the anchor (<a>), image (<img>), bold (<b>), and italic (<i>) tags.

Figure 4.6 shows how the different vertical-alignment types should look.

To define vertical alignment:

1. vertical-align:

   Type the vertical-align property name, followed by a colon (:), in the definition list (**Code 4.6**).

2. super;

   Type a value for the vertical alignment of the text (**Table 4.6**). Choose one of these options:

   ▲ super, which superscripts the text above the baseline.

   ▲ sub, which subscripts the text below the baseline.

   ▲ baseline, which places the text on the baseline (its natural state).

   ▲ A **relative value** from **Table 4.7** that sets the element's alignment relative to its parent's alignment. To align the top of your text with the top of the parent element's text, for example, type text-top.

   ▲ A **percentage value,** which raises or lowers the element's baseline proportionate to the parent element's font size (25%, for example).

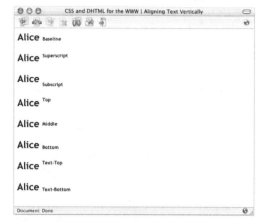

Figure 4.6 There are a variety of ways to align text relative to other text on the screen.

Code 4.6 Here I'm setting up a class for each of the vertical alignments.

```
<html>
<head>
    <style type="text/css" media="screen"><!--
        .superscript {
            vertical-align: super;
            font-size: 12px;}
        .baseline {
            vertical-align: baseline;
            font-size: 12px;}
        .subscript {
            vertical-align: sub;
            font-size: 12px;}
        .top {
            vertical-align: top;
            font-size: 12px;}
        .middle {
            vertical-align: middle;
            font-size: 12px;}
        .bottom {
            vertical-align: bottom;
            font-size: 12px;}
        .texttop {
            vertical-align: text-top;
            font-size: 12px;}
```

(code continues on next page)

Code 4.6 *continued*

```
        .textbottom {
            vertical-align: text-bottom;
            font-size: 12px;}
        .normal {
            font-weight: bold;
            font-size: 24px;}
    --></style>
</head>
<body>
    <p class="normal">Alice <span class=
    → "baseline">Baseline</span></p>
    <p class="normal">Alice <span class=
    → "superscript">Superscript</span></p>
    <p class="normal">Alice <span class=
    → "subscript">Subscript</span></p>
    <p class="normal">Alice <span class=
    → "top">Top</span></p>
    <p class="normal">Alice <span class=
    → "middle">Middle</span></p>
    <p class="normal">Alice <span class=
    → "bottom">Bottom</span></p>
    <p class="normal">Alice <span class=
    → "texttop">Text-Top</span></p>
    <p class="normal">Alice <span class=
    → "textbottom">Text-Bottom</span></p>
</body>
</html>
```

✔ Tips

- Superscript and subscript are used for scientific notation. To express the Pythagorean theorem, for example, you would use superscripts:

  $a^2 + b^2 = c^2$

  A water molecule might be expressed with subscripts as follows:

  $H_2 0$

  However, keep in mind that neither sub- nor superscript will reduce the size of the text, so you may also want to include `font-size` in your definition for true scientific notation style (see "Setting the Font Size" in Chapter 3).

- Superscript is also great for footnotes in the text, which can then be anchor-linked to notes at the bottom of the current page or to another Web page.

Table 4.6

vertical-align Values	
VALUE	COMPATIBILITY
super	IE4, N6, S1, O3.5, CSS1
sub	IE4, N6, S1, O3.5, CSS1
baseline	IE4, N6, S1, O3.5, CSS1
<relative>	IE5*, N6, S1, O3.5, CSS1
<percentage>	IE5**, N6, S1, O3.5, CSS1

* IE5.5 in Windows
** Mac version only; not available in Windows

Table 4.7

Setting an Element's Position Relative to the Parent Element	
TYPE THIS	TO GET THE ELEMENT TO ALIGN LIKE THIS
top	Top to highest element in line
middle	Middle to middle of parent
bottom	Bottom to lowest element in line
text-top	Top to top of parent element's text
text-bottom	Bottom to bottom of parent element's text

ALIGNING TEXT VERTICALLY

Indenting Paragraphs

Indenting the first word of a paragraph several spaces (traditionally, five) is the time-honored method of introducing a new paragraph.

On the Web, however, indented paragraphs haven't worked because most browsers compress multiple spaces into a single space. Instead, paragraphs have been separated by an extra line break.

With the `text-indent` property, you can specify extra spaces at the beginning of the first line of text in a paragraph (**Figure 4.7**).

To define text indentation in a rule:

1. `text-indent:`

Type the `text-indent` property name, followed by a colon (`:`), in the CSS definition list (**Code 4.7**).

2. `10%;`

Type a value for the indent, using either of these options (**Table 4.8**):

▲ A **length value,** such as `2em`. This amount will create a nice, clear indent.

▲ A **percentage value,** which indents the text proportionate to the paragraph's width (`10%`, for example).

✔ Tips

■ You can set the margin of a paragraph to `0` to override the `<p>` tag's natural tendency to add space between paragraphs if you are using indentation to indicate paragraphs.

■ Because indenting is more common in the print world than online, you may want to consider using indents only for the printer-friendly versions of your page.

Figure 4.7 Paragraphs stand out better when they are indented.

Code 4.7 The class copy is set up to indent paragraphs of text 10% of the total screen width. So the wider the screen, the wider the indent.

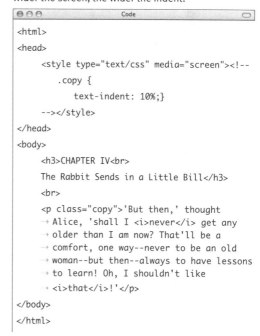

```
<html>
<head>
    <style type="text/css" media="screen"><!--
       .copy {
          text-indent: 10%;}
    --></style>
</head>
<body>
    <h3>CHAPTER IV<br>
    The Rabbit Sends in a Little Bill</h3>
    <br>
    <p class="copy">'But then,' thought
  → Alice, 'shall I <i>never</i> get any
  → older than I am now? That'll be a
  → comfort, one way--never to be an old
  → woman--but then--always to have lessons
  → to learn! Oh, I shouldn't like
  → <i>that</i>!'</p>
</body>
</html>
```

Table 4.8

text-indent Values	
VALUE	COMPATIBILITY
<length>	IE3, N4, S1, O3.5, CSS1
<percentage>	IE3, N4, S1, O3.5, CSS1

Looking Good in Print (on the Web)

I have never seen a paperless office and would be quite surprised if I ever did. But the big promise that came along with the computer was the elimination of paper from our lives—no more filing cabinets, clutter, or dead trees, just an entropy-free utopia in which electrons were constantly recycled and reused, just like in *Star Trek*.

But something tells me that we'll have the technology to fly between the most distant stars before we eliminate paper from our lives.

With the advent of laser and inkjet printers, we seem to be buried under mounds of perfectly printed paper. Even the Web seems to increase the amount of paper we use. If a Web page is longer than a couple of scrolls, most people print it.

But the Web was created to display information on the screen, not on paper. Web graphics look blocky when printed, and straight HTML lacks much in the way of layout controls. That said, you can take steps to improve the appearance of printed Web pages. Looking good in print on the Web may take a little extra effort, but your audience will thank you in the long run.

Here are eight simple things you can do to improve the appearance of your Web page when it gets printed:

◆ **Use CSS.** Cascading style sheets are the future of Web design. CSS allows you to create documents that look as good printed as anything spit out of a word processor.

◆ **Define your media.** CSS allows you to define different style sheets to be used depending on the way the page is displayed—usually on a screen or on paper (see "Setting Styles for Print" in Chapter 2).

◆ **Use page breaks to keep headers with their text.** Although the page-break attribute is not widely supported at this time, it may be a universal standard before long.

◆ **Separate content from navigation.** Try to keep the main content—the part your audience is interested in reading—in a separate area of the design from the site navigation. You can then use CSS to tell the navigation not to display for the print version.

◆ **Avoid using transparent colors in graphics.** This is especially true if the graphic is on a background color or a graphic other than white. The transparent area of a GIF image usually prints as white regardless of the color behind it in the window. This situation is not a problem if the graphic is on a white background to begin with, but the result is messy if the graphic is supposed to be on a dark background.

◆ **Avoid using text in graphics.** The irony of printing stuff off the Web is that text in graphics, which look smooth in the window, look blocky when printed, but regular HTML text, which may look blocky on the screen, prints smoothly on any decent printer. Try to stick with HTML text as much as possible.

◆ **Provide a separate print-ready version of the Web site.** Rather than force visitors to follow every link on your site and print each page along the way, provide a single document for your Web site that visitors can download and print. Adobe Acrobat is a great way to provide this content in a more-or-less universal file format that retains most formatting, fonts, and graphics for delivery over the Web. Find out more about Acrobat at the Adobe Web site (www.adobe.com).

INDENTING PARAGRAPHS

Setting Text and Foreground Color

The color property is used to set the foreground color of an element. Although this property is primarily used to color text, you can also apply it as the foreground color for horizontal rules and form elements (**Figure 4.8**).

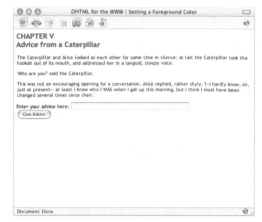

Figure 4.8 The text in the header for this page has been set to red.

Preventing Widows and Orphans

Two unattractive problems can occur when printing Web pages:

◆ *Widows* occur when the last line from the end of a paragraph appears alone at the top of a page.

◆ *Orphans* occur when the first line of the beginning of a paragraph appears alone at the bottom of a page.

Netscape and Internet Explorer for Mac (but *not* Windows) allow you to specify how many lines of text must appear in a paragraph at the top (widow) or bottom (orphan) of a page before a page break is allowed, using the widows and orphans properties:

```
p {

     widows:5;

     orphans:10;

}
```

The above code forces at least five lines of text to appear at the top of a page in a paragraph and at least 10 lines of text to appear at the bottom of a page. Otherwise, the text for the paragraph is forced onto a new page so that it will fit.

It is important to note, however, that these properties do *not* work in Internet Explorer for Windows.

Code 4.8 Color values are added to different classes and tags here to turn them different shades of red.

```
<html>
<head>
    <style type="text/css" media="screen"><!--
        h2 {color: red;}
        form {color: #990000;}
        input {color: rgb(100%, 0%, 0%);}
        .copy {color: rgb(102,102,102)
    --></style>
</head>
<body>
    <h2>CHAPTER V<br />
    Advice from a Caterpillar</h2>
    <p class="copy">The Caterpillar and Alice
    → looked at each other for some time
    → in silence: at last the Caterpillar took
    → the hookah out of its mouth, and
    → addressed her in a languid, sleepy
    → voice.</p>
    <p class="copy">'Who are you?' said the
    → Caterpillar.</p>
    <p class="copy">This was not an encouraging
    → opening for a conversation. Alice
    → replied, rather shyly, 'I--I hardly
    → know, sir, just at present-- at least I
    → know who I WAS when I got up this
    → morning, but I think I must have been
    → changed several times since then.'</p>
    <form action="#" method="get" name=
    → "FormName">
    Enter your advice here: <input type="text"
    → name="textfieldName" size="48"><br>
    <input type="submit" name="advice" value=
    → "Give Advice">
    </form>
</body>
</html>
```

Table 4.9

color Value	
VALUE	COMPATIBILITY
<color>	IE3, N4, S1, O3.5, CSS1

To define the foreground color:

1. `color:`

Type the `color` property name, followed by a colon (:), in the CSS definition list (**Code 4.8**).

2. `red;`

Now type a value for the color you want this element to be (**Table 4.9**). This value can be the name of a color, a hex color value, or an RGB value (see "Values and Units Used in this Book" in the introduction).

✔ Tips

■ Assigning a color to several nested elements can lead to unwanted color changes. The most obvious example is if you set the color in the <body> tag. Internet Explorer 4/5 and Netscape 6 will change the color of all elements in the body. Always consider which tags you redefine and how they might affect other tags on your Web page (see "Inheriting Properties from a Parent" in Chapter 2).

■ A tag's border color can be set by the `color` property but can be overwritten by the `border-color` property (see "Setting an Element's Border" in Chapter 5).

SETTING TEXT AND FOREGROUND COLOR

Decorating Text

Using the `text-decoration` attribute, you can adorn the text in one of four ways: underline, overline, line-through, or blink. Used to add emphasis, these decorations attract the reader's eye to important areas or passages in your Web page (**Figure 4.9**).

To decorate a selector's text:

1. `text-decoration:`

    Type the `text-decoration` property name, followed by a colon (:), in the CSS definition list (**Code 4.9**).

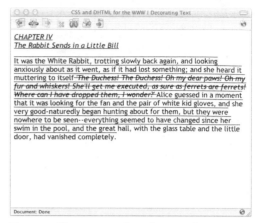

Figure 4.9 There are a variety of ways to decorate your text, but the most useful is underlining. Striking through text is also useful for text that you want to show as being deleted.

Code 4.9 Emphasized text will be underlined unless it is in a paragraph, in which case it will have a line through it and a line over it, which it inherits from the <p> tag.

```
<html>
<head>
    <style type="text/css" media="screen"><!--
        em {
            text-decoration: underline;}
        p em {
            text-decoration: line-through;}
        p {
            text-decoration: overline;}
    --></style>
</head>
<body>
    <em>CHAPTER IV<br>
    The Rabbit Sends in a Little Bill</em>
    <p>It was the White Rabbit, trotting slowly back again, and looking anxiously about as it went, as
    → if it had lost something; and she heard it muttering to itself<em> 'The Duchess! The Duchess!
    → Oh my dear paws! Oh my fur and whiskers! She'll get me executed, as sure as ferrets are ferrets!
    → Where <i>can</i> I have dropped them, I wonder?' </em>Alice guessed in a moment that it was
    → looking for the fan and the pair of white kid gloves, and she very good-naturedly began hunting
    → about for them, but they were nowhere to be seen--everything seemed to have changed since
    ﹅ her swim in the pool, and the great hall, with the glass table and the little door, had vanished
    → completely.</p>
</body>
</html>
```

Table 4.10

text-decoration Values	
VALUE	COMPATIBILITY
none	IE4, N4, S1, O3.5, CSS1
underline	IE3, N4, S1, O3.5, CSS1
overline	IE4, N6, S1, O3.5, CSS1
line-through	IE3, N4, S1, O3.5, CSS1
blink	IE4, N4, S1, O3.5, CSS1

2. underline;

Type a value for the text-decoration property (**Table 4.10**). Choose one of the following:

▲ underline, which places a line below the text

▲ overline, which places a line above the text

▲ line-through, which places a line through the middle of the text (also called "strikethrough")

▲ blink, which causes the text to blink on and off

▲ none, which overrides decorations set elsewhere

✔ Tips

■ If you want to, and as long as the first value is not none, you can have multiple text decorations by adding more values in a list separated by spaces, as follows:

underline overline underline blink

■ Many visitors don't like blinking text, especially on Web pages where they spend a lot of time. In fact many browsers allow the user to disable blinking or simply ignore it. Use this decoration sparingly.

■ I've used strikethrough in online catalogs that include sale prices. I show the original price in strikethrough, with the sale price next to it.

■ Setting text-decoration: none; overrides link underlines in many browsers, even if the visitor's browser is set to underline links. In my experience, many visitors look for underlining to identify links. Although I don't like underlining for links—it clutters the page, and CSS offers many alternatives to identify links—I receive angry e-mails from visitors when I turn off underlining.

DECORATING TEXT

Setting Text Direction

Increasingly, the Web is being used to display text in non-Western languages. The direction of the text (left-to-right or right-to-left) can vary from language to language, so it may be necessary to override the browser's default display direction if you aren't using English (**Figure 4.10**).

To set the direction text is displayed:

1. direction:

Type the direction property name, followed by a colon (:), in the CSS definition list (**Code 4.10**).

2. rtl;

Type a value for the direction (**Table 4.11**). Choose one of the following:

▲ rtl, which displays text right-to-left

▲ ltr, which displays text left-to-right (for Western languages)

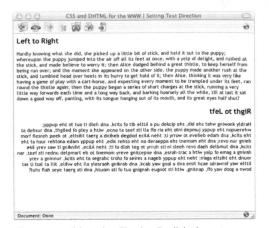

Figure 4.10 Although still using English characters, the second paragraph of text has had its direction reversed.

Table 4.11

direction Values	
VALUE	COMPATIBILITY
rtl	IE5*, N6, S1, CSS2
ltr	IE5*, N6, S1, CSS2

Windows version only. Not available in Mac.

Code 4.10 The class `rightToLeft` is created to force the text to display from right to left even if the browser uses left to right.

```
<html>
<head>
    <meta http-equiv="content-type" content=
    → "text/html;charset=ISO-8859-1">
    <title>CSS and DHTML for the WWW | Setting
    → Text Direction</title>
    <style type="text/css" media="screen"><!--
        .leftToRight {
            direction: ltr;
            unicode-bidi: normal; }
        rightToLeft {
            direction: rtl;
            unicode-bidi: bidi-override; }
    --></style>
</head>
<body>
<h2 class="leftToRight">Left to Right</h2>
    <p class="leftToRight">Hardly knowing what
    → she did, she picked up a little bit of
    → stick, and held it out to the puppy…</p>
    <h2 class="rightToLeft">Right to Left</h2>
    <p class="rightToLeft">Hardly knowing what
    → she did, she picked up a little bit of
    → stick, and held it out to the puppy…</p>
</body>
</html>
```

3. `unicode-bidi:`

Type the `unicode-bidi` property name, followed by a colon (`:`), in the CSS definition list. This property is used to define how the `direction` attribute is used if there are multiple text directions being used in a single Web page.

4. `bidi-override;`

Type a value for the embedded bidirectional code (**Table 4.12**). Choose one of the following:

▲ `bidi-override`, to override the currently set direction for text in the browser. This is needed to truly reverse the text.

▲ `embed`, to embed the bidirectional text within the current direction. This effectively justifies the text to the left (`ltr`) or right (`rtl`), although ending punctuation is shifted.

▲ `normal`, to use the browser's default for embedded bidirectional text.

✔ Tip

■ Keep in mind that this is only effective if the viewer's computer can display the text in the intended language.

Table 4.12

unicode-bidi Values	
VALUE	COMPATIBILITY
bidi-override	IE5*, N6, CSS2
embed	IE5*, N6, CSS2
normal	IE5*, N6, CSS2

Windows version only. Not available in Mac.

SETTING TEXT DIRECTION

105

Setting Page Breaks for Printing

One problem you'll encounter when trying to print a Web site is that pages break wherever they happen to break. A Web page may actually contain several printed pages. So the header for a section might appear at the bottom of a page and its text at the top of the next page.

If you want to force a page break when printing a Web page, use the following code to define an HTML tag (see "Adding Styles to an HTML Tag" in Chapter 2).

In this example, the Web page has a new chapter starting in the middle (**Figure 4.11**). Normally, when this page is printed, this header might appear anywhere on the page. By adding a page break in the <h3> tag (**Code 4.11**), however, you can force the chapter title to appear at the top of a new page when printed (**Figure 4.12**).

Figure 4.11 On the screen, each section immediately follows the preceding one.

Code 4.11 The level 3 header <h3> tag has been set up so that whenever the page is printed, a page break is forced above it.

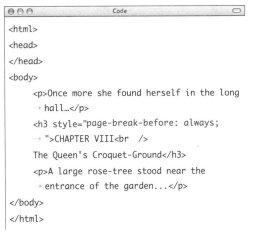

```
<html>
<head>
</head>
<body>
    <p>Once more she found herself in the long
    → hall...</p>
    <h3 style="page-break-before: always;
    → ">CHAPTER VIII<br  />
    The Queen's Croquet-Ground</h3>
    <p>A large rose-tree stood near the
    → entrance of the garden...</p>
</body>
</html>
```

Once more she found herself in the long hall, and close to the little glass table. 'Now, I'll manage better this time,' she said to herself, and began by taking the little golden key, and unlocking the door that led into the garden. Then she went to work nibbling at the mushroom (she had kept a piece of it in her pocket) till she was about a foot high: then she walked down the little passage: and then—she found herself at last in the beautiful garden, among the bright flower-beds and the cool fountains out now, Five! Don't go splashing paint over me like that!'

CHAPTER VIII
The Queen's Croquet-Ground

A large rose-tree stood near the entrance of the garden: the roses growing on it were white, but there were three gardeners at it, busily painting them red. Alice thought this a very curious thing, and she went nearer to watch them, and just as she came up to them she heard one of them say, 'Look out now, Five! Don't go splashing paint over me like that!'

Figure 4.12 When the page is printed, the beginning of the new section forces a page break.

Table 4.13

page-break-before and page-break-after Values	
VALUE	COMPATIBILITY
always	IE4, N7, S1, O5, CSS2
auto	IE4, N7, S1, O5, CSS2

To define a page break for printing:

1. `style type="`
   This CSS property works only if it is included in the `style` attribute of an HTML tag.

2. `page-break-before:`
   Type the `page-break-before` or `page-break-after` property name, followed by a colon (`:`), in the CSS definition list.

3. `always;`
   Type one of the following values (**Table 4.13**) to designate how you want page breaks to be handled:
   ▲ `always`, forces a page break before (or after) the element
   ▲ `auto`, allows the browser to place the page breaks

4. `"`
   Add other styles and then close the `style` attribute with quotation marks (`"`).

✔ Tips

- Remember that this attribute will not work if it is included as part of a CSS rule—only if it is used directly in a tag with the `style` attribute.

- Setting page breaks is a key ingredient in "Looking Good in Print (on the Web)."

SETTING PAGE BREAKS FOR PRINTING

5

ELEMENT CONTROLS

In the physical world, atoms are the building blocks for all larger objects. Every type of atom, or *element*, has its own unique properties, but when bonded with other atoms, they create larger structures with properties different from the parts—molecules.

Likewise, HTML tags are the building blocks of your Web page. Each tag, or element, has its own unique capabilities, and tags can be combined to create a Web page that is greater than the parts.

Whether a tag is by itself or nested deep within other tags, each tag can be treated as a discrete element on the screen and controlled by CSS.

Web designers use the concept of the box as a metaphor to describe the various things that you can do to an HTML element in a window, whether it is a single tag or several nested tags. This box has several properties—including margins, borders, padding, width, and height—that can be influenced by CSS.

In this chapter, I'll show you how to control the box and its properties.

Understanding the Element's Box

The term *element* refers to the various parts of an HTML document that are set off by HTML container tags. The following is an HTML element:

```
<p>Alice</p>
```

This is another HTML element:

```
<div><p><b>Alice<img src="alice11.gif">
→ </b></p></div>
```

The first example is an element made of a single tag. The second example is a collection of nested tags, and each of those nested tags is in turn an individual element. Remember that nested tags are referred to as the children of the tags within which they are nested; those tags in turn are referred to as the parents (see "Inheriting Properties from a Parent" in Chapter 2).

Parts of the box

All HTML elements have four sides: top, bottom, left, and right (**Figure 5.1**). These four sides make up the element's box, to which CSS properties can be applied. Each side of the box has the following properties:

◆ **Width** and **height,** which are the lengths on a side of the element. Top and bottom are the width; left and right are the height. Parallel sides (left/right and top/bottom) have the same length. If you leave width and height undefined, these distances are determined by the browser (see "Setting the Width and Height of an Element" later in this chapter).

◆ **Margin,** which is the space between the border of the element and other elements in the window (see "Setting an Element's Margins" later in this chapter).

◆ **Border,** which is a rule (line) that surrounds the element. The border is invisible unless its color, width, and style—solid, dotted, dashed, and so on—are set (see "Setting an Element's Border" later in this chapter).

◆ **Padding,** which is the space between the border and the content of the element (see "Setting an Element's Padding" later in this chapter).

◆ **Content** and **Background** are at the center of the box. All other CSS properties (font, text, color, background, and lists) apply to this area. (Note: Background properties also apply to the padded area of an element's box.) The content includes all text, lists, forms, and images you care to use.

✔ Tip

■ Element boxes can also wrap around other elements, embedding an element within another (see "Floating Elements in the Window" in Chapter 6).

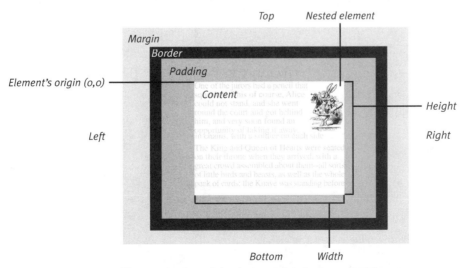

Figure 5.1 An element's box has a margin, a border, and padding on four sides around its central content. The element's width and height can be defined by the author or can be left to the browser's discretion. The origin of an element's box is always its top-left corner.

UNDERSTANDING THE ELEMENT'S BOX

Changing How an Element is Displayed

As explained in the section "Kinds of HTML and XHTML Tags" (Chapter 1), all elements can be classified according to how they're displayed—inline, block, or replaced. By default, every tag has a display style that defines how it will fit with other tags around it.

You can use the `display` property to define whether an element includes line breaks above and below (block), is included inline with other elements (inline), is treated as part of a list, or is displayed at all. **Table 5.1** shows the different values available for the `display` property:

◆ `inline` defines this tag as being an inline tag, suppressing line breaks immediately after the tag.

◆ `block` defines this tag as being a block-level tag, placing a line break above and below the element.

◆ `none` causes this element not to display in CSS browsers. It will be as though the content did not exist on the page.

◆ `list-item` places a list-item marker on the first line of text, as well as a break above and below. This code allows the item to be used as part of a list even if you're not specifically using a list tag.

◆ `table`, or one of the other `table` properties shown in Table 5.1, allows you to turn any tag into part of a data table. Unfortunately, these are not thoroughly implemented in Internet Explorer for Windows, and so may prove of limited use.

◆ `inherit` uses the display value set for the element's parent.

Table 5.1

display Values	
VALUE	COMPATIBILITY
list-item	IE 5, N6, S1, O3.5, CSS1
block	IE4*, N6, S1, O3.5, CSS1
inline	IE4*, N6, S1, O3.5, CSS1
table	IE5**, N6, S1, O3.5, CSS2
table-cell	IE5**, N6, S1, O3.5, CSS2
table-footer-group	IE5**, N6, S1, O3.5, CSS2
table-header-group	IE5, N6, S1, O3.5, CSS2
table-row	IE5**, N6, S1, O3.5, CSS2
table-row-group	IE5**, N6, S1, O3.5, CSS2
none	IE4, N6, S1, O3.5, CSS1

*IE 5.5 Windows
**Mac only, not available for Windows

Code 5.1 You can use the display property to create elements that flow together without line breaks. In this case, we're overriding paragraph tags so that they flow together rather than breaking apart.

```
<html>
<head>
    <style type="text/css" media="screen"><!--
        p.noBreak {
        font-weight: bold;
        display: inline;
        }
    --></style>
</head>
<body>
    <img src="alice29.gif" height="236"
    → width="200" align="right" border="0" />
    <p>First came ten soldiers carrying
    → clubs...</p>
    <p class="noBreak">next the ten
    → courtiers...</p>
    <p class="noBreak">After these came the
    → royal children...</p>
    <p>Next came the guests, mostly Kings and
    → Queens...</p>
    <p>Then followed the Knave of Hearts...</p>
    <p>last of all this grand procession, came
    → THE KING AND QUEEN OF HEARTS.</p>
</body>
</html>
```

Creating an inline element

By definition, an inline element is placed with the content before it and after it on the same line (**Code 5.1** and **Figure 5.2**). You can turn any element (including paragraphs) into inline tags using the inline value in between the two tags.

To set an element to be placed inline:

1. display:

   Start your definition by typing the display property name, followed by a colon (:), in the CSS definition list.

2. inline;

   Type the inline definition for how this element will be displayed.

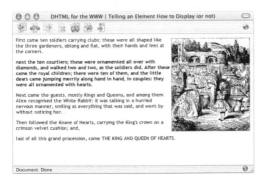

Figure 5.2 Although the <p> tag is a block-level element by default, here it has been set to appear inline, suppressing the break between it and the next <p>.

Creating a block-level element

Block-level elements, which place line breaks immediately above and after the element, are the flip side of inline elements (**Code 5.2** and **Figure 5.3**).

To set an element to be placed as a block:

1. display:

Start your definition by typing the display property name, followed by a colon (:), in the CSS definition list.

2. block;

Type the block definition for how this element will be displayed.

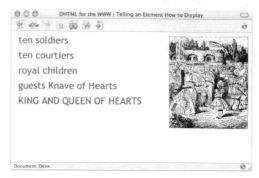

Figure 5.3 Each link is a block-level element, forcing it to appear on a separate line.

Code 5.2 You can use the display property to create elements that are separated from other elements by line breaks. In this example, we will be overriding the link style's natural inline display to create a menu with each option on a new line.

```
<html>
<head>
    <style type="text/css" media="screen"><!--
    a:link.menuLinks {
        font-size: 24px;
        margin: 10px;
        display: block;
    }
    --></style>
</head>
<body>
    <img src="alice29.gif" height="236" width="200" align="right" border="0" /><a class="menuLinks"
    → href="(EmptyReference!)">ten soldiers </a><a class="menuLinks" href="(EmptyReference!)">ten
    → courtiers </a><a class="menuLinks" href="(EmptyReference!)">royal children </a><a
    → class="menuLinks" href="(EmptyReference!)">guests Knave of Hearts </a><a class="menuLinks"
    → href="(EmptyReference!)">KING AND QUEEN OF HEARTS</a>
</body>
</html>
```

CHANGING HOW AN ELEMENT IS DISPLAYED

Code 5.3 You can use the `display` property to create an element that is not (initially) displayed on the Web page. The code will still be there, though. In this case, we are hiding all image tags with the noShow class.

```
<html>
<head>
     <style type="text/css" media="screen"><!--
     img.noShow {
          display: none;
     }
     --></style>
</head>
<body>
     <img class="noShow" src="alice29.gif"
     → height="236" width="200" align="right"
     → border="0" />
     <p>First came ten soldiers carrying
     → clubs...</p>
     <p>next the ten courtiers...</p>
     <p>After these came the royal children...
     → </p>
     <p>Next came the guests, mostly Kings and
     → Queens...</p>
     <p>Then followed the Knave of Hearts...</p>
     <p>last of all this grand procession, came
     → THE KING AND QUEEN OF HEARTS.</p>
</body>
</html>
```

Figure 5.4 The image has been set not to be displayed.

Creating an element that does not display

Although at first glance the none value may seem to be a description of its usefulness, this will actually prove to be one of the most important CSS attributes we'll use with DHTML. By initially setting the display of an element to none, and then resetting the value using JavaScript, we can create several useful interface widgets (**Code 5.3** and **Figure 5.4**).

To set an element to not be displayed:

1. `display:`

   Start your definition by typing the `display` property name, followed by a colon (`:`), in the CSS definition list.

2. `none;`

   Type the none definition for how this element will be displayed.

Turning an element into a list

HTML provides several list tags, but there are times when you need to use a standard HTML tag as a part of a list (**Code 5.4** and **Figure 5.5**).

To set an element to be part of a list:

1. `display:`

   Start your definition by typing the `display` property name, followed by a colon (:), in the CSS definition list.

2. `list-item;`

   Type the `list-item` definition for how this element will be displayed.

✔ Tips

- Any elements given the value `none` will simply be ignored by a CSS browser. Be careful in using `none`, however. Although it is not an inherited attribute, `none` turns off display of the element as well as any children elements within it.

- The `display` property should not be confused with `visibility` (see "Setting the Visibility of an Element" in Chapter 7). Unlike the `visibility` property, which leaves a space for the element, `display: none;` completely removes the element from the page, although it still loads.

- Using JavaScript, you can create a simple collapsible menu by switching `display` between `inline` and `none` to make menu options appear and disappear (see "Creating Collapsible Menus" in Chapter 18).

Code 5.4 You can use the `display` property to turn paragraphs into a numbered list enumerating members of the courtly procession.

```
<html>
<head>
    <style type="text/css" media="screen"><!--
    .list {
        display: list-item;
    }
    --></style>
</head>
<body>
    <img src="alice29.gif" height="236"
    → width="200" align="right" border="0">
    <ol>
    <p class="list">First came ten soldiers
    → carrying clubs...</p>
    <p class="list">next the ten
    → courtiers...</p>
    <p class="list">After these came the
    → royal children...</p>
    <p class="list">Next came the guests,
    → mostly Kings and Queens...</p>
    <p class="list">Then followed the Knave
    → of Hearts...</p>
    <p class="list">last of all this grand
    → procession, came THE KING AND QUEEN
    → OF HEARTS.</p>
    </ol>
</body>
</html>
```

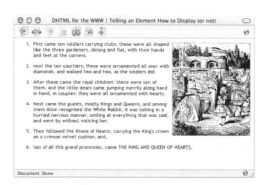

Figure 5.5 The Royal Procession is enumerated to make it easier to follow.

Code 5.5 You can set the width and/or height of an element using a variety of different units. The most common method is to use pixels. But you can also use centimeters, millimeters, inches, and points, among other options.

```
<html>
<head>
    <style type="text/css" media="screen"><!--
    textarea {
        width: 225px;
        height: 100px;
    }
    img {
        float: left;
        width: 5cm;
        height: 8cm;
    }
    .copy {
        float: left;
        width: 225px;
        height: 100px;
    }
    --></style>
</head>
<body>
    <form action="#" method="get">
        <textarea rows="4" cols="40">Alice
        → remained looking thoughtfully at the
        → mushroom for a minute...</textarea>
    </form>
    <img src="alice11.gif" />
    <p class="copy">Alice remained looking
    → thoughtfully at the mushroom for a
    → minute...</p>
</body>
</html>
```

Setting the Width and Height of an Element

The width and height of block-level and replaced elements can be specified with the `width` and `height` properties (see "Kinds of HTML and XHTML Tags" in Chapter 1). Usually, the width and height are determined automatically by the browser and default to being 100% of the available width and whatever height is needed to display all the content. You can use CSS, however, to override both the `width` and `height` properties (**Code 5.5** and **Figure 5.6**).

Figure 5.6 The width and height for the form box, the image (which looks uncomfortably scrunched), and the text block have all been set. Notice that although the form box conforms to both width and height, the text block seems to have only the width set. Height is ignored unless you define the `overflow` property.

To define the width of an element:

1. `width:`

Type the `width` property name, followed by a colon (`:`), in the CSS definition list.

2. `225px;`

Type a value for the element's width, which can be any of the following (**Table 5.2**):

▲ A **length value**

▲ A **percentage,** which sets the width proportional to the parent element's width

▲ `auto`, which uses the width calculated by the browser for the element—usually the maximum distance that the element can stretch to the right before hitting the edge of the window or the edge of a parent element

To define the height of an element:

1. `height:`

Type the `height` property name, followed by a colon (`:`), in the CSS definition list.

2. `100px;`

Type a value for the element's height, which can be any of the following (**Table 5.3**):

▲ A **length value**

▲ A **percentage,** which sets the height proportional to the parent element's height

▲ `auto`, which uses a calculated height determined by the browser—however much space the element needs to display all the content

Table 5.2

width Values	
VALUE	COMPATIBILITY
<length>	IE4, N4, S1, O3.5, CSS1
<percentage>	IE4, N4, S1, O3.5, CSS1
auto	IE4, N4, S1, O3.5, CSS1

Table 5.3

height Values	
VALUE	COMPATIBILITY
<length>	IE4, N4, S1, O3.5, CSS1
<percentage>	IE4, N4, S1, O3.5, CSS1
auto	IE4, N4, S1, O3.5, CSS1

SETTING THE WIDTH AND HEIGHT OF AN ELEMENT

✔ Tips

■ You can resize an image (GIF, PNG, or JPEG) using the width and height properties, thus overriding the width and height set in the image tag. Doing this will more than likely create a severely distorted image, but that can sometimes be a pretty neat effect.

■ Use width and height to keep form fields and buttons a consistent size.

■ Although you can set the height of any element, only elements with replaced tags (see "Kinds of HTML and XHTML Tags" in Chapter 1) will use it. Other tags ignore a height value unless you define what should happen to the overflowing content of the element (see "Setting Where the overflow Content Goes" in Chapter 7).

Setting Maximum and Minimum Width and Height (Mozilla Only)

Although not implemented in Internet Explorer, Mozilla-based browsers (Netscape 6+, Firebird, and Camino) as well as Opera and Safari have all implemented the CSS2 ability to set a minimum and maximum width and height for an element. This can be unbelievably useful for creating flexible designs that will never stretch to unreasonable proportions on larger screens (**Code 5.6**).

To set the maximum and minimum width:

1. max-width: 600px;

   Type the max-width property name, a colon (:), and an appropriate width value (**Table 5.4**). The element will never grow wider than this value regardless of the browser window width (**Figure 5.7**).

Code 5.6 You can set the maximum or minimum width (and height) for an element to allow it to grow and shrink, but not out of bounds. In this code, a minimum and maximum value have been used with a class applied to the <body> tag.

```
<html>
<head>
    <style type="text/css" media="screen"><!--
    .stretchAbility {
        max-width: 600px;
        min-width: 400px;
    }
    --></style>
</head>
<body class="stretchAbility">
    <p>'How queer it seems,' Alice said to
    → herself...</p>
</body>
</html>
```

Table 5.4

max/min-width Values	
VALUE	COMPATIBILITY
<length>	N6, S1, O5, CSS2
<percentage>	N6, S1, O5, CSS2
auto	N6, S1, O5, CSS2

Figure 5.7 Although the browser window stretches farther, the element does not get wider than 600 pixels.

`How queer it seems,' Alice said to herself, `to be going m
rabbit! I suppose Dinah'll be sending me on messages next
began fancying the sort of thing that would happen: `"Miss
here directly, and get ready for your walk!" "Coming in a n
But I've got to see that the mouse doesn't get out." Only I
Alice went on, `that they'd let Dinah stop in the house if
ordering people about like that!'

By this time she had found her way into a tidy little room
in the window, and on it (as she had hoped) a fan and two
pairs of tiny white kid gloves: she took up the fan and a pa
gloves, and was just going to leave the room, when her ey
little bottle that stood near the looking- glass. There was
time with the words `DRINK ME,' but nevertheless she und
put it to her lips. `I know SOMETHING interesting is sure t
she said to herself, `whenever I eat or drink anything; so
what this bottle does. I do hope it'll make me grow large a
really I'm quite tired of being such a tiny little thing!'

It did so indeed, and much sooner than she had expected:
had drunk half the bottle, she found her head pressing ag
ceiling, and had to stoop to save her neck from being brok
hastily put down the bottle, saying to herself `That's quite
hope I shan't grow any more--As it is, I can't get out at the
wish I hadn't drunk quite so much!'

Document: Done

Figure 5.8 Although the browser window is much
smaller, the element does not get smaller than
400 pixels.

Table 5.5

max/min-height Values	
VALUE	COMPATIBILITY
<length>	N6, S1, O5, CSS2
<percentage>	N6, S1, O5, CSS2
auto	N6, S1, O5, CSS2

2. `min-width: 400px;`

Type the `min-width` property name, a
colon (`:`), and an appropriate width value
(Table 5.4). The element will never shrink
to less than this value, regardless of the
browser window width (**Figure 5.8**).

✔ Tips

- The `max-height` and `min-height` properties work very much the same, but are
dependent on the content being displayed, rather than the dimensions of the
browser window (**Table 5.5**).

- Obviously, you don't have to include *both*
the minimum and maximum values.

SETTING THE WIDTH AND HEIGHT OF AN ELEMENT

Setting an Element's Margins

The margin property of an element allows you to set the space between that element and other elements in the window by specifying one to four values (**Code 5.7**) that correspond to all four sides together, the top/bottom and left/right sides as pairs, or all four sides independently (**Figure 5.9**).

Figure 5.9 The margins around the first block of text have been set relative to the live area of the screen.

Code 5.7 You can set all the margins in a single definition or one side at a time, either by defining each side individually, as shown in this code, or by listing each side.

```
<html>
<head>
    <style type="text/css" media="screen"><!--
    p.paragraphtwo {
        margin: 5em;
    }
    h2 {
        margin: 1em;
    }
    p.copy {
        margin: 5em 200px 10% 8em;
    }
    --></style>
</head>
<body>
    <h2>CHAPTER VII<br />
     A Mad Tea-Party</h2>
    <p class="copy">There was a table set out under a tree in front of the house...</p>
    <p class="paragraphtwo">The table was a large one...</p>
</body>
</html>
```

Table 5.6

margin Values	
VALUE	COMPATIBILITY
<length>	IE3, N4, S1, O3.5, CSS1
<percentage>	IE3, N4, S1, O3.5, CSS1
auto	IE3, N4, S1, O3.5, CSS1

To define the margins of an element:

1. `margin:`

   Start your definition by typing the `margin` property name, followed by a colon (:), in the definition list.

2. `5em;`

   Now type a value for the margin, which can be any of the following (**Table 5.6**):

   ▲ A **length value**

   ▲ A **percentage,** which creates a margin proportional to the parent element's width

   ▲ `auto`, which returns control of the margins to the browser's discretion

✔ Tips

■ You can also set each side's margin independently (see "Setting Margins on a Side" on the next page).

■ You can also set margins for the <body> tag, in which case they define the distance at which elements nested in the body should appear from the top and left sides of the browser window. In theory, this would allow you to center the content of a page by setting the margins on both sides to `auto`, however, this tends to be buggy in Internet Explorer for Windows.

■ When setting proportional margins, be aware that you might get very different results depending on the size of the user's window. What looks good at a resolution of 640x480 might be a mess at larger screen sizes.

Setting Negative Margins

Although you can use negative margins (for example, `margin:-5em;`) to create interesting effects for overlapping pieces of text, this method is frowned upon because the various browsers present different results.

Overlapping text is better achieved with CSS positioning (see Chapter 6, "Element Positioning Controls").

Be careful when setting negative margins around a hypertext link. If one element has margins that cause it to cover the link, the link will not work as expected.

Setting margins on a side

If you want to set several margins, you can enter up to four values, separated by spaces, as follows:

```
margin: 5em auto 5em 25%;
```

◆ One value sets the margin for all four sides.

◆ Two values set the top/bottom margins and left/right margins.

◆ Three values set the top margin, the left/right margins (the same), and the bottom margin.

◆ Four values set each individual margin, in this order: top, right, bottom, and left.

You can also set just one side of the box's margins without having to worry about the other three margins. This is especially useful when used with an inline style to override margins set elsewhere. To do this, just specify the margin side you want to define and a legitimate margin value:

```
margin-top: 5em;
```

```
margin-bottom: 10%;
```

```
margin-left: 8em;
```

```
margin-right: 200px;
```

Code 5.8 You can set all the border's attributes in one definition for all four sides, or you can set them individually for each side.

```
⬤⬤⬤                    Code                    ⬭
<html>
<head>
     <style type="text/css" media="screen"><!--
     p {
         border: double 20px #990000;
         padding: 5px;
         width: 230px;
     }
     .frame {
         border-style: dotted inset dashed
         ⇢ solid;
         border-width: 1mm 2pc 3px 3pt;
         border-color: #990000;
         width: 230px;
     }
     --></style>
</head>
<body>
     <div class="frame">
         <img src="alice15.gif" height="264"
         ⇢ width="200" /></div>
     <p>This time Alice waited patiently until
     ⇢ it chose to speak again...</p>
</body>
</html>
```

Table 5.7

border Values	
VALUE	COMPATIBILITY
<border-width>	IE4, N4, S1, O3.5, CSS1
<border-style>	IE4, N4, S1, O3.5, CSS1
<border-color>	IE4, N4, S1, O3.5, CSS1

Setting an Element's Border

To set any of the border attributes for all four sides of the box simultaneously, CSS provides the border property (**Code 5.8** and **Table 5.7**). You can use border to set width, style, and color at the same time (**Figure 5.10**).

Figure 5.10 The border around the image has been set to have a different decoration on each side, while the text below it always has a double rule.

To set the border:

1. border:

Type the border property name, followed by a colon (:), in the CSS definition list.

2. double

Type the name of the style you want to assign to your border. (See **Table 5.9** for a complete list of available border styles.)

Alternatively, you can type none, which prevents the border from appearing.

Table 5.8

border-width Values	
VALUE	COMPATIBILITY
thin	IE4, N4, S1, O3.5, CSS1
medium	IE4, N4, S1, O3.5, CSS1
thick	IE4, N4, S1, O3.5, CSS1
<length>	IE4, N4, S1, O3.5, CSS1
inherit	IE4, N4, S1, O3.5, CSS1

Table 5.9

border-style values	
VALUE COMPATIBILITY	APPEARANCE
dotted	IE4*, N6, S1, O3.5, CSS1
dashed	IE4*, N6, S1, O3.5, CSS1
solid	IE4, N4, S1, O3.5, CSS1
double	IE4, N4, S1, O3.5, CSS1
groove	IE4, N4, S1, O3.5, CSS1
ridge	IE4, N4, S1, O3.5, CSS1
inset	IE4, N4, S1, O3.5, CSS1
outset	IE4, N4, S1, O3.5, CSS1
none	IE4, N4, S1, O3.5, CSS1
inherit	IE4, N4, S1, O3.5, CSS1

IE 5.5 for Windows

Table 5.10

border-color Values	
VALUE	COMPATIBILITY
<color>	IE4, N4, S1, O3.5, CSS1
transparent	IE4, N4, S1, O3.5, CSS1
inherit	IE4, N4, S1, O3.5, CSS1

3. 20px

Type a border-width value, followed by a space. This value can be one of the following (**Table 5.8**):

▲ A **length value;** a value of 0 prevents the border from appearing

▲ A relative-size keyword

4. #990000;

Type a color value, which is the color you want the border to be (**Table 5.10**). This can be the name of the color, a hex color value, or an RGB value.

✔ Tip

■ Most browsers that do not support other border properties usually support the simple border property.

SETTING AN ELEMENT'S BORDER

Decorating an element's border

Although you can use the border attribute to set all the border attributes (style, color, and width) at the same time, you can also set each border attribute individually for the box (**Code 5.9** and **Figure 5.11**), and even on each side (**Figure 5.12**).

Code 5.9 You can set the border-decoration attributes (style, color, and width) for all four sides at the same time, or you can define each side independently.

```
<html>
<head>
    <style type="text/css" media="screen"><!--
    .frame {
        border-style: inset;
        border-color: #ff0000;
        border-width: 10px;
    }
    p.frame {
        padding: 5px;
        border-top: 1px inset red;
        border-right: 8px inset red;
        border-bottom: inset red;
        border-left: 4px inset red;
        border-bottom-width: 2px
    }
    --></style>
</head>
<body>
    <div class="frame">
        <img src="alice06.gif" height="245" width="200" /></div>
    <p class="frame">Alice was not a bit hurt, and she jumped up on to her feet in a moment...</p>
</body>
</html>
```

Figure 5.11
The attributes for the borders have been mixed and matched.

Alice was not a bit hurt, and she jumped up on to her feet in a moment: she looked up, but it was all dark overhead; before her was another long passage, and the White Rabbit was still in sight, hurrying down it. There was not a moment to be lost: away went Alice like the wind, and was just in time to hear it say, as it turned a corner, 'Oh my ears and whiskers, how late it's getting!' She was close behind it when she turned the corner, but the Rabbit was no longer to be seen: she found herself in a long, low hall, which was lit up by a row of lamps hanging from the roof.

Figure 5.12
It's hard to see in a two-color book, but trust me—this border is a beautiful, vibrant, multicolored extravaganza.

To decorate a border:

1. border-style: inset;

   Add the border-style property with one of the following values:

   ▲ A **style name** from Table 5.9

   ▲ none, which prevents the border from appearing

   ▲ inherit to use the parent's border-style value

2. border-color: #ff0000;

   Add the border-color property with one of the following values:

   ▲ A **color value,** which is the color you want the border to be (Table 5.10). This value can be the name of the color, a hex color value, or an RGB value (see "Values and Units Used in This Book" in the introduction).

   ▲ transparent to use no color, allowing colors behind the element to show through.

   ▲ inherit to use the parent's border-color value.

3. border-width: 10px;

   Add the border-width property and one of the following values (Table 5.8):

   ▲ A **keyword;** use thin, medium, or thick

   ▲ A **length value;** a length of 0 prevents the border from appearing

   ▲ inherit to use the parent's border-width value

✔ Tip

■ You do not have to include all the individual border attributes in your definition list, but if you don't, their defaults will be used (see Appendix C).

SETTING AN ELEMENT'S BORDER

Setting and decorating borders on a side

You aren't stuck with having the same border on all four sides. Each border side can also have all its values set independently, as follows:

```
border-top: 1mm dotted #990000;

border-bottom: 3px dashed #990000;

border-left: 3pt solid #990000;

border-right: 2pc inset #990000;
```

This method is especially useful for overriding the border values set by the single border property.

Alternatively, you can also set borders independently for each border style type. CSS gives you the freedom to define the border's appearance one side at a time, as follows:

```
border-style: ridge double dotted dashed;

border-width: 20px 15px 10px 5px;

border-color: red green blue purple;
```

To set each side's border properties separately, you can type from one to four values.

◆ One value sets the border width for all four sides.

◆ Two values set the border width for the top/bottom and left/right sides.

◆ Three values set the top border width, the border width for the left/right sides (the same), and the bottom border width.

◆ Four values set the border width for each side individually, in this order: top, right, bottom, and left.

SETTING AN ELEMENT'S BORDER

Figure 5.13 In Camino (one of the browsers based on Mozilla), the border used to define a link on the page has round rather than square corners.

Your final option for setting a border on a single side (as if you really needed another option) is to combine the two techniques mentioned above allowing you to set a specific style type (style, width, color) for a specific side (top, bottom, left, right):

`border-top-style: ridge;`

`border-top-width: 20px;`

`border-top-color: red;`

Rounding border corners (Mozilla only)

If you're tired of square corners in your designs, but don't want to resort to graphics to create borders, Mozilla-based browsers (Netscape 6+, Firebird, and Camino) have a property that allows you to set the corner radius for borders set using CSS (**Figure 5.13**). Although not part of the official CSS specification and not implemented in Internet Explorer, Safari, or Opera, this Netscape extension can be useful and does not interfere with how borders will appear in those other browsers.

To create rounded corners in Mozilla browsers:

1. `border: solid 1px #f33;`

   Set up the border for the element using any of the methods previously discussed (**Code 5.10**).

2. `-moz-border-radius:`

   After the border definition, type the `-moz-border-radius` property name, followed by a colon (:).

3. `50%;`

   Type a `border-radius` value, followed by a semicolon. This value can be one of the following (**Table 5.11**):

   ▲ A **length value,** which sets the radius of an imaginary circle at the corner, used to round it off. The larger the value the rounder the edge.

   ▲ A **percentage** (`0%` to `50%`), which uses the size of the element to set the corner radius. Higher values produce rounder corners, with `50%` joining corners into a semi-circle.

Code 5.10 Set up the border and then apply the Mozilla border-radius attribute to round off the corners. In this code, the corners of a border used around hypertext links are rounded. This code will be used only by Mozilla-based browsers.

```
<html>
<head>
    <style type="text/css" media="screen"><!--
    a:link.roundedCorners {
        margin: 0;
        padding: 0 2px;
        border: solid 1px #f33;
        -moz-border-radius: 50%;
    }
    a:hover.roundedCorners {
        background-color: #fcc;
        margin: 0;
        padding: 0 2px;
        border: solid 1px #f00;
        -moz-border-radius: 50%;
    }
    --></style>
</head>
<body>
    <p>It was the <a class="roundedCorners"
    → href="http://www.rabbit.com">White
    → Rabbit</a>, trotting slowly back
    → again...</p>
    <p>Very soon the <a class="roundedCorners"
    → href="http://www.rabbit.com">Rabbit</a>
    → noticed Alice...</p>
    <p>`He took me for his housemaid,' she
    → said to herself as she ran. `How
    → surprised he'll be when he finds out
    → who I am! But I'd better take him his fan
    → and gloves--that is, if I can find them.'
    → As she said this, she came upon a
    → neat little house, on the door of
    → which was a bright brass plate with the
    → name `<a class="roundedCorners"
    → href="http://www.rabbit.com">W. RABBIT
    → </a>' engraved upon it...</p>
</body>
</html>
```

Table 5.11

-moz-border-radius Values	
VALUE	COMPATIBILITY
<length>	N6
<percentage>	N6

✔ **Tip**

■ One problem with the way this is implemented is that the browser does not antialias the corners, so rather than smooth curves, we get blocky curves.

Rounding Corners on a Side (Mozilla Only)

In addition to setting the corners for all four sides simultaneously, you can also set each corner's radius independently, using either of two different methods.

The first method involves using the −moz-border-radius property with one to four values, separated by a space:

```
-moz-border-radius: 5px 0px 50% 0%;
```

◆ One value sets all four corner radii.

◆ Two values set the radius for the top-left/bottom-right and bottom-left/top-right corners.

◆ Three values set the corner radius for the top left, bottom left/top right (the same), and the bottom right corners.

◆ Four values set the radius for each corner individually, in this order: top left, top right, bottom right, and bottom left.

Each border radius can also have all its values set independently, as follows:

```
-moz-border-radius-topleft: 5px;
```

```
-moz-border-radius-topright: 0px;
```

```
-moz-border-radius-bottomright: 50%;
```

```
-moz-border-radius-bottomleft: 0%;
```

This method is especially useful for overriding the border values set by the single -moz-border-radius property.

Setting an Element's Padding

At first glance, padding seems to have an effect identical to margins: It adds space around the element's content. The difference is that padding sets the space between the border of the element and its content, rather than between the element and the other elements in the window (**Code 5.11** and **Figure 5.14**).

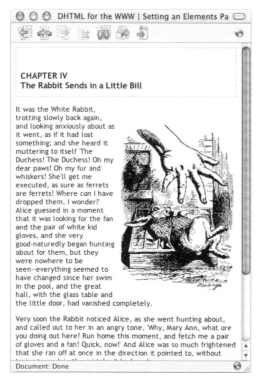

Figure 5.14 The padding moves the chapter title to the bottom-left corner of the box. Note: The element's borders have been turned on (dotted line) so that you can better see the effects of padding.

Code 5.11 You can use one, two, three, or four values with the padding attribute, depending on which sides you want to set.

```
<html>
<head>
    <style type="text/css" media="screen"><!--
    .chpttitle {
        padding: 10% 1cm 10px 0.5em;
        border: dashed 1px silver;
    }
    img {
        padding-top: 25px;
    }
    --></style>
</head>
<body>
    <h3 class="chpttitle">CHAPTER IV<br />
    The Rabbit Sends in a Little Bill</h3>
    <p><img src="alice12.gif" height="287"
    → width="200" align="right" border="0"
    → />It was the White Rabbit, trotting
    → slowly back again...</p>
    <p>Very soon the Rabbit noticed Alice, as
    → she went hunting about, and called out
    → to her in an angry tone...</p>
    <p>'He took me for his housemaid,' she said
    → to herself as she ran...</p>
</body>
</html>
```

Table 5.12

padding Values	
VALUE	COMPATIBILITY
\<length\>	IE4, N4, S1, O3.5, CSS1
\<percentage\>	IE4, N4, S1, O3.5, CSS1

To define padding:

1. `padding:`

   Start your definition by typing the `padding` property name, followed by a colon (:).

2. `10% 1cm 10px .5em;`

   Next, type a value for the element's padding, which can be any of the following (**Table 5.12**):

   ▲ One to four **length values,** which creates padding of the exact size you specify

   ▲ A **percentage,** which creates padding proportional to the parent element's width

   ▲ `inherit` to use the parent's `padding` value

✔ Tips

■ Padding and margins are easily confused because their results often look the same if the border is not visible. Remember: Margins separate one element from other elements, but padding is the space between the border and the content of the element.

■ As with margins, you can type a single value to be set on all sides; type two values for the top/bottom and left/right padding; type three values for the top, bottom, and left/right padding; or type four values to set the top, right, bottom, and left sides (see "Setting margins on a side" earlier in this chapter).

Setting the Background

HTML has allowed us to set background colors and graphics almost since its beginnings. This capability, however, was limited to the background of the entire Web page. Later, you could play around with the background colors of table cells, but that was still very confining.

CSS lets you define the background color and graphic for any individual element on the page, giving you much greater versatility when it comes to designing your Web pages.

You can use the background property to define the background image and color for the entire page or the background image and color immediately behind any individual element on the page (**Code 5.12** and **Figure 5.15**).

Figure 5.15 The background image for the page (the telescoping Alice) appears to the extreme right of the page, and the header has its own distinctive background: a rough texture that repeats only on the left side and is flat gray in the rest.

Code 5.12 This code sets up a background image for the entire page in the <body> tag. The image will be fixed on the right side and will not repeat. In addition, the <h3> tag will have its own background image, which repeats only down the left side of the element.

```
<html>
<head>
    <style type="text/css" media="screen"><!--
    body {
        background: white url(alice05.gif)
        → no-repeat fixed right top;
    }
    h3 {
        background: #999999 url
        → (background_rough.gif) repeat-y
        → left top;
        color: white;
        padding: 20px;
        width: 60%;
    }
    p {
        width: 60%;
    }
    --></style>
</head>
<body>
    <h3>CHAPTER II<br />
    The Pool of Tears</h3>
    <p>'Curiouser and curiouser!' cried
    → Alice...'</p>
</body>
</html>
```

Table 5.13

background Values	
VALUE	COMPATIBILITY
<background-color>	IE4, N4, S1, O3.5, CSS1
<background-image>	IE4, N4, S1, O3.5, CSS1
<background-repeat>	IE4, N4, S1, O3.5, CSS1
<background-attachment>	IE4, N6, S1, O3.5, CSS1
<background-position>	IE4, N6, S1, O3.5, CSS1

Table 5.14

background-color Values	
VALUE	COMPATIBILITY
<color>	IE4, N4, S1, O3.5, CSS1
transparent	IE4, N4, S1, O3.5, CSS1

Table 5.15

background-image Values	
VALUE	COMPATIBILITY
<url>	IE4, N4, S1, O3.5, CSS1
none	IE4, N4, S1, O3.5, CSS1

To define the background:

1. `background:`

Start your definition by typing the `background` property name, followed by a colon (:), then any of the following background values (**Table 5.13**).

2. `white`

Type a value for the color you want the background to be (**Table 5.14**), followed by a space. This value can be the name of the color, a hex color value, or an RGB value.

Alternatively, you could type `transparent`, which tells the browser to use the background-color of elements behind this element.

3. `url(alice05.gif)`

Type a URL for the location of the background image (**Table 5.15**), followed by a space. This location is the image file (GIF, JPEG, or PNG) that you want to use as the background and is either a complete Web address or a local filename.

Alternatively, you can type `none` instead of a URL, which instructs the browser not to use a background image.

continues on next page

SETTING THE BACKGROUND

137

4. `no-repeat`

Type a definition for how you want your background to repeat, followed by a space. Use one of these options (**Table 5.16**):

- ▲ `repeat` instructs the browser to tile the graphic throughout the background of the element both horizontally and vertically.

- ▲ `repeat-x` instructs the browser to tile the background graphic only horizontally. In other words, the graphic repeats in one straight horizontal line along the top of the element.

- ▲ `repeat-y` instructs the browser to tile the background graphic only vertically. In other words, the graphic repeats in one straight vertical line along the left side of the element.

- ▲ `no-repeat` causes the background graphic to appear only once and not tile.

5. `fixed`

Type a keyword for how you want the background "attached"—how it should be treated when the page scrolls—followed by a space. Use one of these options (**Table 5.17**):

- ▲ `fixed` instructs the browser not to scroll the background content with the rest of the element (**Figure 5.16**)

- ▲ `scroll` instructs the background graphic to scroll with the element

Table 5.16

background-repeat Values

VALUE	COMPATIBILITY
repeat	IE4, N4, S1, O3.5, CSS1
repeat-x	IE4, N4, S1, O3.5, CSS1
repeat-y	IE4, N4, S1, O3.5, CSS1
no-repeat	IE4, N4, S1, O3.5, CSS1

Table 5.17

background-attachment Values

VALUE	COMPATIBILITY
scroll	IE4, N6, S1, O3.5, CSS1
fixed	IE4, N6, S1, O3.5, CSS1

Figure 5.16 Although the text has scrolled, the background image for the page (the telescoping Alice) stays in the same place.

Table 5.18

background-position Values	
VALUE	COMPATIBILITY
<percentage>	IE4, N6, S1, O3.5, CSS1
<length>	IE4, N6, S1, O3.5, CSS1
top	IE4, N6, S1, O3.5, CSS1
center	IE4, N6, S1, O3.5, CSS1
bottom	IE4, N6, S1, O3.5, CSS1
left	IE4, N6, S1, O3.5, CSS1
right	IE4, N6, S1, O3.5, CSS1

6. `right top;`

Type two values, separated by a space, to specify where you want the background positioned in relation to the top-left corner of the element. Use one of these values (**Table 5.18**):

▲ A **position keyword,** such as left.

▲ A **length value,** such as –10px. The values can be positive or negative. The first number tells the browser the distance the element should appear from the left edge of its parent; the second value specifies the position from the top edge of the parent.

▲ A **percentage value,** such as 25%. The first percentage indicates the horizontal position proportional to the parent element's size; the second value indicates the vertical position proportional to the parent element's size.

✔ Tips

■ The ability to place graphics behind any element on the screen is a very powerful tool for designing Web pages; it frees you from the constraints of having to create new graphics whenever text changes. You can combine the versatility of HTML text with graphics to create stunning effects (see "Creating Headlines" in Chapter 17).

■ The default state for an element's background is none, so the parent element's background image and/or color will show through unless the background color or background image for that particular child element is set.

■ A fixed background can be particularly effective if you're using a graphic background in your layout to help define the page.

SETTING THE BACKGROUND

Setting a background color

Although you can set all the background properties at once with the background property (see the previous section), you can also set each of the background properties individually.

The ability to set the background color for an HTML page has been around almost since the first Web browsers. With CSS, however, you can define the background color not only for the entire page, but for individual elements as well (**Code 5.13** and **Figure 5.17**).

Figure 5.17 Background colors have been applied to various elements on the screen. Notice that a pink color has been set for the image. This color shows through where the image has been made transparent.

Code 5.13 The background color for the page has been set to gray. Other CSS definitions (<img>, <h3>, <p> with the copy class, and the highlight class) override this background color.

```
<html>
<head>
    <style type="text/css" media="screen"><!--
    body {
        background-color: #cccccc;
    }
    img {
        background-color: #ff9999;
    }
    h3 {
        background-color: #ff9999;
        padding: 10px;
        position: relative;
    }
    p.copy {
```

(code continues on next page)

Code 5.13 *continued*

```
        background-color: rgb(100%,100%,100%);
        padding: 10px;
        position: relative;
    }
    .highlight {
        color: white;
        background-color: black;
    }
    --></style>
</head>
<body>
    <h3>CHAPTER VI<br />
    Pig and Pepper</h3>
    <p class="copy">For a minute or two she
    → stood looking at the house, and
    → wondering what to do next, when suddenly
    → a footman in livery came running out of
    → the wood- (she considered him to
    → be a footman because he was in livery:
    → otherwise, judging by his face only,
    → <span class="highlight">she would have
    → called him a fish</span>)--and rapped
    → loudly at the door with his knuckles. It
    → was opened by another footman in livery,
    → with a round face, and large eyes like
    → a frog; and both footmen, Alice noticed,
    → had powdered hair that curled all over
    → their heads. She felt very curious to
    → know what it was all about, and crept a
    → little way out of the wood to listen.
    → </p>
    <img src="alice21.gif" height="248"
    → width="300" border="0" />
</body>
</html>
```

To define the background color of an element:

1. `background-color:`

   Start your definition by typing the back-ground-color property name, followed by a colon (:).

2. `#cccccc;`

   Type a value for the color you want the background to be (Table 5.14). This value can be the name of the color, a hex color value, or an RGB value.

   Alternatively, you could type transpar-ent, which tells the browser to use the default color set by the browser.

✔ Tip

- The default state for an element's background color is none, so the parent element's background will show through unless the background color or image for that particular child element is set.

Setting a background image

The background attribute (discussed earlier in this chapter) is not the only way to set the background image. CSS offers you the flexibility not only to set the background graphic for a page or an element on the page, but also to dictate how that background graphic should be repeated and positioned (**Code 5.14** and **Figure 5.18**).

Beyond simply setting a background color and image, CSS offers you great flexibility in exactly where the background is placed behind the element, in which direction the background repeats (or even whether it repeats at all), and whether the background will scroll along with its element or stay in a fixed position in the browser window (**Figure 5.19**).

Code 5.14 In this code, a background image is defined for the body of the page. This image is instructed not to repeat, to be fixed, and is positioned up and to the left using negative values. Additionally, the <h3> tag has been defined with a rough background graphic that is repeated only across the top of the element. Finally, so that the text does not overlap the background image, all text has been offset 200 pixels.

```
<html>
<head>
    <style type="text/css" media="screen"><!--
    body {
        background-image: url(alice05.gif);
        background-repeat: no-repeat;
        background-attachment: fixed;
        background-position: -10px -5px;
    }
    h3 {
        background-image:
        → url(background_rough.gif);
        background-repeat: repeat-x;
        background-position: -20px -2px;
        margin-left: 200px;
        padding: 10px;
    }
    .copy {
        margin-left: 200px;
    }
    --></style>
</head>
<body>
    <h3>CHAPTER II<br />

The Pool of Tears</h3>
    <p class="copy">'Curiouser and curiouser!'
    → cried Alice...</p>
    <p class="copy">And she went on planning to
    → herself how she would manage it...</p>
</body>
</html>
```

Figure 5.18 The background image (Alice) appears on the left side of the screen, and the text has been pushed over to the right. The level 3 header also uses a textured background image to add an attractive rule above the chapter title.

Figure 5.19 Although the text has scrolled down, the body's background image stays in place.

To define a background image:

1. `background-image: url(alice05.gif);`

Type the `background-image` property name, followed by a colon (:), and type a URL for the location of the image file (GIF, JPEG, or PNG) that you want to use as the background. It can be either a complete Web address or a local filename.

Alternatively, you can type none instead of a URL to instruct the browser not to use a background image (Table 5.15).

2. `background-repeat: no-repeat;`

Type the `background-repeat` property name, followed by a colon (:), then define how you want your background to repeat by typing one of the following options (Table 5.16):

▲ `repeat` instructs the browser to tile the graphic throughout the background of the element horizontally and vertically

▲ `repeat-x` instructs the browser to tile the background graphic only horizontally, so the graphic repeats in one straight horizontal line along the top of the element

▲ `repeat-y` instructs the browser to tile the background graphic only vertically, so the graphic repeats in one straight vertical line along the left side of the element

▲ `no-repeat` causes the background graphic to appear only once and not tile

continues on next page

SETTING THE BACKGROUND

3. `background-attachment: fixed;`

Type the `background-attachment` property name, followed by a colon (:), then define how you want the background to be treated when the page scrolls by typing one of the following options (Table 5.17):

▲ `fixed` instructs the browser not to scroll the background content with the rest of the element

▲ `scroll` instructs the background graphic to scroll with the element

4. `background-position: -10px -5px;`

Type the `background-position` property name, followed by a colon (:). Then type two values separated by a space, to indicate where you want the background to appear in relation to the top-left corner of the element (usually, the screen). Use one of these values (Table 5.18):

▲ **Length values,** such as `-10px`. The values can be positive or negative. The first number tells the browser the distance the element should appear from the left edge of its parent; the second value specifies the position from the top edge of the parent.

▲ **Percentage values,** such as `25%`. The first percentage indicates the horizontal position proportional to the parent element's size; the second value indicates the vertical position proportional to the parent element's size.

▲ **Definitions** in plain English: `top`, `bottom`, `left`, `right`, or `center`.

✔ Tips

■ Sometimes, a repeating background can be really annoying. It may repeat where it's not wanted, or you may want it to tile in only one direction. CSS gives you supreme control of how background graphics appear through the background-repeat property.

■ You can mix percentage and length values in the same background-position definition, but you cannot mix length or percentages with plain-English keywords.

■ Any background space that does not have a background graphic will be filled with the background color.

Preloading Images

If you are loading many large graphics in your Web site, you can use the display property to preload images on one page for use in another.

For example, if the first page in your site has only a few graphics, but the next page has many, include the <img> tags for the graphics on the second page on page 1 but set their display to none. The graphics will load in the first page but not show up. When the second page loads, the graphics will load from the visitor's cache, which is much faster.

I recommend loading only a few extra graphics on the first page; otherwise, the second page will end up displaying partially loaded images. Use the graphics that will be seen on the page first, and it will look as if your site is loading really fast even with a lot of graphic content.

ELEMENT POSITIONING CONTROLS

One of the obstacles Web designers face is getting a page to look they way they want it to without taking forever to load. Graphics will add text and layout to a design exactly where you want them. Tables can position elements well in the browser window or assemble graphics in jigsaw fashion. However, graphics and tables take more time to render than straight HTML content and can substantially slow down page loading.

Using CSS to create Web layouts provides more accuracy than either graphics or tables, and the results are displayed much faster.

You've already learned how to use CSS to control margins and borders in composition (Chapter 5). CSS further allows you to position elements in the window either exactly (absolutely) or in relation to other elements (relatively). In addition, elements can be made to "float" together, allowing you to create columns and other robust layout formats.

This chapter introduces you to the methods of positioning HTML elements by using CSS, including how to stack elements on top of one another in 3-D and float elements together.

Understanding the Window and Document

A Web page (also referred to as simply the *document*) is displayed within a browser window. Within those rectangular confines, everything that you can present to the viewer is displayed. You can open multiple windows (each displaying its own document), resize and position windows on the screen, and even break the window into smaller windows called *frames*. Everything that you present, however, is displayed within a browser window as part of a document (**Figure 6.1**).

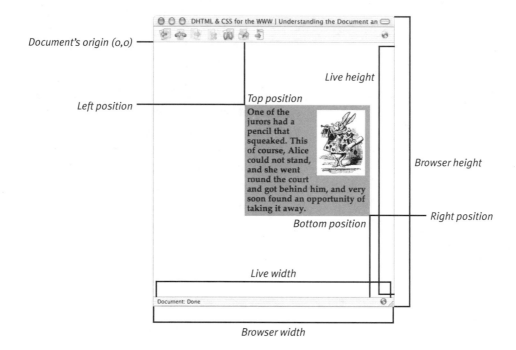

Figure 6.1 The browser window. The element on the gray background has been moved from its normal position to 130 pixels from the top and 190 pixels from the left.

Like the elements contained within it (see "Understanding the Element's Box" in Chapter 5), the window has a width and height, as well as a top, bottom, left, and right. In fact, you can think of the browser window as being the ultimate element in your Web design—the parent of all other elements. Browser windows and documents they contain have three distinct widths and heights and four different sides for setting position.

◆ **Browser width and height** refers to the dimensions of the entire window, including any browser controls and other interface items.

◆ **Live width and height** refers to the *display area* of the browser. The live dimensions, obviously, are always less than the full window dimensions. Generally, when I refer to "the window," I'm referring to the live window area.

◆ **Document width and height,** sometimes called the *rendered* width and height, refers to the overall dimensions of the entire Web page. If the document's width and/or height is larger than the live width and/or height, you'll see scrollbars that let you view the rest of the document.

◆ **Positions (left, top, right, bottom)** are used to set exactly how an element is offset from the sides of the document, its parent element, or from its normal flow position.

✔ Tips

■ In Chapter 11, "Learning About the Environment," we'll learn how to use JavaScript to find all of these different dimensions.

■ *Normal flow* refers to where an element would appear in the Web page if no positioning is applied to it.

Setting the Positioning Type

When you set the attributes of an HTML tag through a selector in a CSS, you effectively single out any content within that tag's container as being a unique element in the window (see "Understanding the Element's Box" in Chapter 5). You can then manipulate this unique element through CSS positioning.

An element can have one of four position values—static, relative, absolute, or fixed—although only the first three are commonly available on most browsers (**Code 6.1**). The position type tells the browser how to treat the element when placing it in the window (**Figure 6.2**).

Using static positioning

By default, elements are positioned as static in the document, unless you define them as being positioned absolutely, relatively, or fixed. Static elements, like the relatively positioned elements explained in the following section, flow into a document one after the next. Static positioning differs, however, in that a static element cannot be explicitly positioned or repositioned.

Using relative positioning

An element that is defined as being relatively positioned will be offset based on its position in the normal flow of the document. This technique is useful for controlling the way elements appear in relation to other elements in the window.

Using absolute positioning

Absolute positioning creates an independent element—a free agent—separate from the rest of the document, into which you can put any type of HTML content you want. Elements that are defined in this way are

Code 6.1 Currently, there are three cross-browser methods for positioning an element in the window: static, relative, and absolute. In addition, some browsers allow you to set a fixed position.

```
<html>
<head>
    <style type="text/css" media="screen"><!--
.stat {
    position: static;
    color: #cccccc;
    font: bold 28pt/normal courier;
}
.abs {
    position: absolute;
    color: #666666;
    font: bold 35pt/normal helvetica;
    top: 25px;
    left: 375px;
    width: 100px;
}
.rel {
    position: relative;
    color: #000000;
    font: bold 12pt/normal times;
    top: 70px;
    left: 25px;
}
    --></style>
</head>
<body>
    <div class="stat">
        'Oh my ears and whiskers, how late it's
        → getting!'</div>

<div class="abs">
        'Oh my ears and whiskers, how late it's
        → getting!'</div>
    <div class="rel">
        'Oh my ears and <span class="rel">
        → whis<span class="rel">kers</span>
        → </span>, how late it's getting!'
        → </div>
</body>
</html>
```

placed at an exact point in the window by means of x and y coordinates. The top-left corner of the document or the element's parent is the origin (that is, coordinates 0,0). Moving an element to a position farther to the right uses a positive x value; moving it farther down uses a positive y value.

Using fixed positioning

Before you get too excited, you should know that fixed positioning currently does not work in all browsers. It does not work in Netscape 6; it does not work in Internet Explorer 5 or 6 for Windows. It *does* work in Netscape 7, Safari 1, Opera 5, and Internet Explorer 5 for the Mac.

Fixing an element's position in the window works almost exactly like absolute positioning: The element is set independently of all other content on the page in a specific position. The big difference is that when the page scrolls in the window, fixed elements stay in their initial positions and do not scroll.

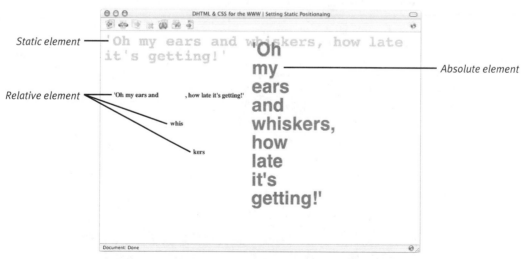

Figure 6.2 Elements being positioned in the window. Notice that the relatively positioned element has relatively positioned elements nested within it, causing the stair-step effect in the text.

To set an element's position type:

1. `position:`

Type the `position` attribute in a rule's definition list or in the `style` attribute of an HTML tag, followed by a colon (`:`).

2. `relative;`

Type the position-type value, which can be one of the following (**Table 6.1**):

▲ `static` flows the content inline, but the position *cannot* be changed by the `top`, `left`, `right`, and `bottom` attributes or by JavaScript.

▲ `relative` places the element inline and allows the position to be set, relative to its normal position, using the `top`, `left`, `right`, and `bottom` attributes or JavaScript.

▲ `absolute` places the element according to the `top`, `left`, `right`, and `bottom` attributes or JavaScript, independently of any other content in its parent (the body of the document or the element within which it's nested).

▲ `fixed` places the element according to the `top`, `left`, `right`, and `bottom` attributes or JavaScript, independently of any other content in its parent, just as with an absolutely positioned element. However, unlike an absolutely positioned element, when the window is scrolled, the element stays where it is as the rest of the content scrolls. (Remember that `fixed` does not currently work in all browsers.)

Table 6.1

position Values	
VALUE	COMPATIBILITY
static	IE4, N4, S1, O5, CSS2
relative	IE4, N4, S1, O5, CSS2
absolute	IE4, N4, S1, O5, CSS2
fixed	IE5*, N7, S1, O5, CSS2

* Not available in Windows

SETTING THE POSITIONING TYPE

3. `top: 70px;`

Now that the position type has been set, you can set the actual position of the element (see "Setting the Position from the Top and Left" and "Setting the Position from the Bottom and Right" later in this chapter).

In addition, setting the position allows you to set the element's *stacking order* (see "Stacking Objects" later in this chapter), *visibility* (see "Setting the Visibility of an Element" in Chapter 7), and *clipping* (see "Setting the Visible Area of an Element" in Chapter 7).

✔ Tips

■ Internet Explorer does not accept position controls in the `<body>` tag. If you need to position the entire body of a Web page, surround all the content with a `<div>` tag and apply positioning to that.

■ After elements have been positioned in the window, you can use JavaScript or other scripting languages to move, hide, or display them (see Part 2 of this book, which discusses DHTML).

■ The `fixed` position in Internet Explorer 5 for the Mac has a severe bug that makes it useless for creating fixed menus in the window (see the sidebar "Is It Fixed?").

■ Browsers that do not understand the `fixed` position type default to `static` for the position type.

Is It Fixed?

The `fixed` position was introduced with CSS Level 2. It shows a lot of promise for user-interface design, especially for allowing a fixed menu in the window that's always available to the visitor. Right now, however, it suffers from several problems:

◆ `fixed` is not supported by the most popular browser being used, Internet Explorer for Windows. Although you cannot set two different position types for the same element, you can create two different style sheets for different browsers (see "Customizing Styles for the OS or Browser" in Chapter 16).

◆ Although Internet Explorer 5 for the Mac supports `fixed`, a strange bug causes the link areas of a fixed element to scroll with the rest of the page. So while the graphic or text for a link stays in a fixed position, the invisible area that gets clicked moves.

Setting an Element's Position

In addition to the margins, which can be specified as part of the box properties (see "Setting an Element's Margins" in Chapter 5), a positioned element can have a top value, a left value, a bottom value, and a right value used to position the element from those four sides.

Setting the position from the top and left

The top and left values are used to set the element's position from the top and left edges of its parent element (the document or the element it's within) or relative to its natural position (**Figure 6.3** and **Figure 6.4**; **Code 6.2**).

To define the left and top positions:

1. position: absolute;

To position an element using the left and top properties, you have to include the position property in the same rule.

2. left:

Type the left property name, followed by a colon (:), in the CSS definition list or in the style attribute of an HTML tag.

3. 12em;

Now type a value for how far to the left the element should appear. You can enter any of the following (**Table 6.2**):

▲ A **length value** to define the distance of the element's left edge from the left edge of its parent or the window

▲ A **percentage value,** such as 55%, to set the left displacement relative to the parent element's width

▲ auto, which allows the browser to calculate the value if the position is set to absolute; otherwise, left will be 0

Code 6.2 After you set the position type, you can set the element's top and left distance from its origin. The origin for the element is the window's top-left corner, its parent's top-left corner, or relative to its own top-left corner.

```
<html>
<head>
     <style type="text/css" media="screen"><!--
#object1 {
     position: absolute;
     left: 12em;
     top: 125px;
     border: solid 2px silver;
}
.changeplace {
     position: relative;
     top: 1cm;
     left: 1cm;
     background-color: #ffcccc;
}
--></style>
</head>
<body>
     <div id="object1">
          <img src="alice27.gif" height="225"
          ➝ width="250" align="left" border="0" />
          <p>'I want a<span class="changeplace">
          ➝ clean cup</span>,' interrupted the
          ➝ Hatter: 'let's all move one place
          ➝ on.'</p>
          <p>He moved on as he spoke, and the
          ➝ Dormouse followed him...</p>
     </div>
</body>
</html>
```

Table 6.2

top and left Values	
VALUE	COMPATIBILITY
<length>	IE4, N4, S1, O5, CSS2
<percentage>	IE4, N4, S1, O5, CSS2
auto	IE4, N4, S1, O5, CSS2

Figure 6.3 The element has been absolutely positioned from the top-left corner of the window and the words *clean cup* have been offset from the top and left of their normal position.

4. `top:`

Type the `top` property name, followed by a colon (`:`), in the CSS definition list or in the `style` attribute of a tag.

5. `125px;`

Type a value for how far from the top the element should appear. You can enter any of the following (Table 6.2):

▲ A **length value** to define the distance of the element's top edge from the top edge of its parent or the window

▲ A **percentage value,** such as 55%, to set the top displacement relative to the window or parent element's height

▲ `auto`, which allows the browser to calculate the value if the position is set to absolute; otherwise, `top` will be `0`

continues on next page

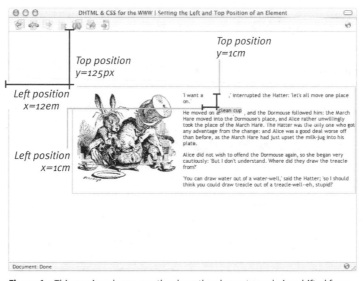

Figure 6.4 This version shows exactly where the elements are being shifted from.

SETTING AN ELEMENT'S POSITION

155

✔ Tips

- You don't have to include both the top and left definitions.

- You can use negative values to move the content up and to the left instead of down and to the right.

- If an element's position is defined as relative, its margins remain unaffected by the top and left properties. This means that setting the top and left margins may cause the content to move outside its naturally defined box and overlap other content.

- Although top and left are not inherited by an element's children, nested elements will be offset along with their parent.

Setting the position from the bottom and right

Although you can accomplish a lot by positioning an element's top and left sides, it can be useful to position the bottom and right sides as well (**Code 6.3**).

CSS Level 2 introduced the ability to set an element's position relative to the right and bottom edges of the element or its surrounding parent (**Figure 6.5** and **Figure 6.6**).

To define the right and bottom positions:

1. position: absolute;

   To position an element by using the right and bottom properties, you have to include the position property in the same rule.

2. right:

   Type the right property name, followed by a colon (:).

Code 6.3 After you set the position type, you can set the element's right and bottom. The positions shift to the right and bottom edges of the element, however, so instead of the top-left corner, the origin will be the bottom-right corner of the window, the parent, or the element itself.

```
<html>
<head>
     <style type="text/css" media="screen"><!--
#object1 {
     position: absolute;
     right: 12em;
     bottom: 125px;
     border: silver solid 2px; }
.changeplace {
     position: relative;
     bottom: 1cm;
     right: 1cm;
     background-color: #ffcccc;}
--></style>
</head>
<body>
     <div id="object1">
        <img src="alice27.gif" height="225"
        → width="250" align="left" border="0" />
        <p>'I want a<span class="changeplace">
        → clean cup</span>,' interrupted the
        → Hatter: 'let's all move one place
        → on.'</p>
        <p>He moved on as he spoke, and the
        → Dormouse followed him...</p>
     </div>
</body>
</html>
```

Table 6.3

bottom and right Values

VALUE	COMPATIBILITY
<length>	IE5, N6, S1, O5, CSS2
<percentage>	IE5, N6, S1, O5, CSS2
auto	IE5, N6, CSS2

Figure 6.5 The element has been absolutely positioned from the bottom-right corner of the window, and the words *clean cup* have been offset from the bottom and right of their normal position.

3. 12em;

Type a value to indicate how far from the right edge of the document the right edge of the element should appear. You can enter any of the following (**Table 6.3**):

▲ A **length value** to define the distance of the element's right edge from the right edge of its parent or the window

▲ A **percentage value,** such as 55%, to set the right displacement relative to the parent element's width

▲ auto, which allows the browser to calculate the value if the position is set to absolute; otherwise, right will be 0

4. bottom:

Type the bottom property name, followed by a colon (:).

continues on next page

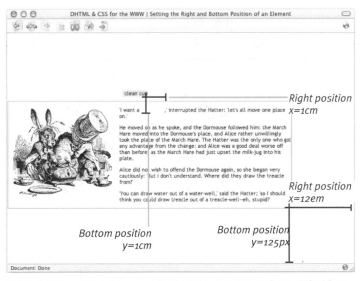

Figure 6.6 This version shows exactly where the elements are being shifted from.

5. 125px;

Type in a value to specify how far from the bottom the bottom edge of the element should appear. You can enter any of the following (Table 6.3):

▲ A **length value** to define the distance of the element's bottom edge from the bottom edge of its parent or the window

▲ A **percentage value,** such as **55%**, to set the bottom displacement relative to the window or parent element's height

▲ auto, which allows the browser to calculate the value if the position is set to absolute; otherwise, bottom will be 0

✔ Tips

■ You can combine left or right positioning with top or bottom.

■ What happens if you set the top/left and bottom/right positions for the same element? The answer depends on the browser, but Internet Explorer always defaults to the top and left positions.

■ What happens if the bottom position has been set, and the element is longer than the height of the page? Normally, the element would go off the bottom of the window, and you could access the rest of the content by using the scroll bar. If the bottom position of the element has been set, though, the element will be pushed up off the top of the window, and you cannot use the scroll bars to access it. So be careful when setting a bottom position for an element.

Code 6.4 Each element is positioned to be offset slightly from the preceding one. The z-index is also set to force element 1 to be on top and then to place elements 2, 3, and 4 underneath.

```
                    Code
<html>
<head>
    <style type="text/css" media="screen"><!--
#element1 {
    position: absolute;
    z-index: 3;
    top: 175px;
    left: 255px;
}
#element2 {
    position: absolute;
    z-index: 2;
    top: 100px;
    left: 170px;
}
#element3 {
    position: absolute;
    z-index: 1;
    top: 65px;
    left: 85px;
}
#element4 {
    position: absolute;
    z-index: 0;
    top: 5px;
    left: 5px;
}
    --></style>
</head>
<body>
    <span id="element1"><img src="alice22.gif"
    → height="147" width="100" /><br
    → clear="all" />
      Element 1 </span><span id=
    → "element2"><img src="alice32.gif"
    → height="201" width="140" /><br
    → clear="all" />
      Element 2 </span><span id=
    → "element3"><img src="alice15.gif"
    → height="198" width="150" /><br
    → clear="all" />
      Element 3 </span><span id=
    → "element4"><img src="alice29.gif"
    → height="236" width="200" /><br
    → clear="all" />
      Element 4 </span>
</body>
</html>
```

Stacking Objects (3-D Positioning)

Although the screen is a two-dimensional area, elements that are positioned can be given a third dimension: a stacking order in relationship to one another.

Positioned elements are assigned stacking numbers automatically, starting with 0 and continuing incrementally with 1, 2, 3, and so on in the order in which the elements appear in the HTML and relative to their parents and siblings. Higher numbers appear above lower numbers. This system is called the *z-index*. An element's z-index number is a value that shows its 3-D relation to other elements in the document or parent element.

If the content of elements overlap each other, the element with a higher number in the stacking order appears over the element that has a lower number.

You can override the natural order of the elements on the page (**Figure 6.7** and **Figure 6.8**) by setting the z-index property directly (**Code 6.4**).

To define an element's z-index:

1. `position: absolute;`

To layer an element in the window, you have to define the `position` property (see "Setting the Positioning Type" earlier in this chapter).

2. `z-index:`

Type the `z-index` property name, followed by a colon (`:`), in the same definition list.

3. `3;`

Now type a positive or negative number (no decimals allowed), or `0`. This step sets the element's z-index in relation to its siblings, where `0` is on the same level (**Table 6.4**).

Alternatively, type `auto` to allow the browser to determine the element's z-index order.

4. `top: 5px;`
`left: 5px; 0;`

Type the element's position.

✔ Tips

- Using a negative number for the z-index causes an element to be stacked that many levels below its parent instead of above.

- You can change the stacking order of elements using JavaScript (see "Moving Objects in 3-D" in Chapter 14).

Table 6.4

z-index Values	
VALUE	COMPATIBILITY
<number>	IE4, N4, S1, O3.5, CSS2
auto	IE4, N4, S1, O3.5, CSS2

Figure 6.7 This version uses the z-indexes set in the code. Notice that although element 1 should be on the bottom of the stack, its z-index has been set to 3, so it appears on top.

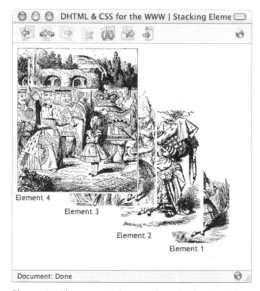

Figure 6.8 The same Web page if you had *not* set the z-index, but kept the natural stacking order. Notice that element 1 is now underneath everything else, because its natural z-index is 0.

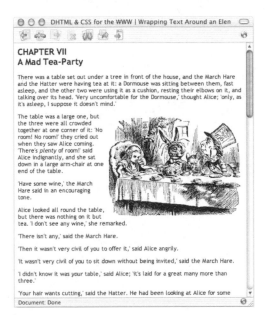

Figure 6.9 The text wraps around the image.

Floating Elements in the Window

In addition to being able to exactly position elements within the document, CSS also allows you to set how an element interacts with other elements by *floating* it.

With HTML you can make text flow around a graphic using the `align` property. CSS takes this technique one step forward by letting you not only flow text around graphics, but also flow text around any element (**Figure 6.9**). You accomplish this feat using the `float` property (**Code 6.5**).

Code 6.5 The `float` property allows you to have either a block of text or a graphic float inside of another block of text. In this example, all images on the page are being defined as floating to the right in the window.

```
<html>
<head>
    <style type="text/css" media="screen"><!--
img {
    float: right;}
    --></style>
</head>
<body>
    <h2>CHAPTER VII<br />
    A Mad Tea-Party</h2>
    <p class="copy">There was a table set out under a tree in front of the house, and the March
    ↪ Hare and the Hatter were having tea at it: a Dormouse was sitting between them, fast asleep, and
    ↪ the other two were using it as a cushion, resting their elbows on it, and talking over its
    ↪ head. 'Very uncomfortable for the Dormouse,' thought Alice; 'only, as it's asleep, I suppose it
    ↪ doesn't mind.'</p>
    <img src="alice25.gif" height="219" width="288" border="0" />
</body>
</html>
```

To define the floating position of a selector:

1. `float:`

   Start your definition by typing the `float` property name, followed by a colon (:).

   In this example, I applied `float` to an image, which has the same effect as setting the `align` property in the `<img>` tag.

2. `right`

   Next, type a keyword to tell the browser to which side of the screen the element should float. Choose one of the following (**Table 6.5**):

   ▲ `right` aligns this element to the right, causing other elements to wrap on the left

   ▲ `left` aligns this element to the left, causing other elements to wrap on the right

   ▲ `none` defaults to the parent element's alignment

✔ Tips

■ You can use `float` with any tag, not just images, to cause text to float around it, so you can have text floating inside other text.

■ In Chapter 17, I'll explain how to use the `float` property to set up separate columns to replace traditional table based layout.

Table 6.5

float Values	
VALUE	COMPATIBILITY
left	IE4, N4, S1, O5, CSS1
right	IE4, N4, S1, O5, CSS1
none	IE4, N4, S1, O5, CSS1

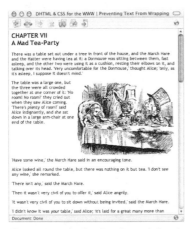

Figure 6.10 Text that has been defined with the nowrap class starts below the image rather than wrapping around it.

Clearing Floating

Sometimes, you may find it necessary to override the float property (**Figure 6.10**). Similar to the clear attribute of the HTML break tag, the CSS clear property allows you to specify whether you want to deny floating around the left, right, or both sides of the element.

To stop text from floating:

1. clear:

   Type the clear property name, followed by a colon (:), in the CSS rule to start your definition (**Code 6.6**).

   continues on next page

Code 6.6 Text given the nofloat class will appear underneath floating elements.

```
<html>
<head>
     <style type="text/css" media="screen"><!--
img {
     float: right;
}
.nowrap {
      clear: right;
}
--></style>
</head>
<body>
     <h2>CHAPTER VII<br />
      A Mad Tea-Party</h2>
     <p class="copy">There was a table set out under a tree in front of the house, and the March
     → Hare and the Hatter were having tea at it: a Dormouse was sitting between them, fast asleep, and
     → the other two were using it as a cushion, resting their elbows on it, and talking over its
     → head. 'Very uncomfortable for the Dormouse,' thought Alice; 'only, as it's asleep, I suppose it
     → doesn't mind.'</p>
     <img src="alice25.gif" alt="Alice at the Tea Party" height="219" width="288" border="0" />
     <p>The table was a large one, but the three were all crowded together at one corner of it: 'No
     → room! No room!' they cried out when they saw Alice coming. 'There's <i>plenty</i> of room!' said
     → Alice indignantly, and she sat down in a large arm-chair at one end of the table.</p>
     <p class="nowrap">'Have some wine,' the March Hare said in an encouraging tone.</p>
</body>
</html>
```

2. `right`

Type the keyword for the side where you want to prevent floating. Choose one of the following (**Table 6.6**):

▲ `left` to prevent floating set for the left side of previous elements

▲ `right` to prevent floating set for the right side of previous elements

▲ `both` to prevent wrapping around elements regardless of the side on which floating was set

▲ `none` to override other `clear` properties

3. `<p class="nofloat">...</p>`

Now whenever you use this class with an HTML tag, the text will not wrap around other tags, regardless of how their `float` property is set.

✔ Tip

■ It's usually a good idea to set headers and titles so that they don't wrap around other objects.

Table 6.6

clear Values	
VALUE	**COMPATIBILITY**
left	IE4, N4, S1, O5, CSS1
right	IE4, N4, S1, O5, CSS1
both	IE4, N4, S1, O5, CSS1
none	IE4, N4, S1, O5, CSS1

CLEARING FLOATING

Figure 6.11 The white-space property allows you to space text and graphics exactly the way you want them. Notice that the picture of Alice has been pushed over with spaces.

Controlling White Space

As mentioned in "Indenting Paragraphs" in Chapter 4, browsers in the past have collapsed multiple spaces into a single space unless the <pre> tag was used. CSS lets you allow or disallow the collapsing of spaces, as well as designate whether text can break at a space (similar to the <nobr> HTML tag).

In this example (**Code 6.7** and **Figure 6.11**), the text has been spaced in odd configurations. If the white-space attribute was not defined for the style, all those spaces would collapse (**Figure 6.12**).

Code 6.7 Adding white-space: pre to the paragraph tag means that all of the spaces will be displayed unless the class .collapse is used, which then allows only one space between characters.

```
<html>
<head>
    <style type="text/css">
        p {
            white-space: pre;
        }
        .collapse {
            white-space: normal;
        }
    </style>
</head>
<body>
    <p>A        L      I      C    E 'S      RIG H
        T F OO T, E S      Q . </p>
    <p class="collapse">H      E      A      R      T      H      R U G       ,</p>
    <p>(W      I      T      H      A      L      I      C    E ' S      L O V E ).
            <img src="alice08.gif" width="200" height="131">
    </p>
</body>
</html>
```

To define white space for a selector:

1. white-space:

Type the white-space property name, followed by a colon (:), in the CSS definition list.

2. pre

Type one of the following values (**Table 6.7**) to designate how you want spaces in text to be handled:

▲ pre, which preserves multiple spaces

▲ nowrap, which prevents line wrapping without a break tag

▲ normal, which allows the browser to determine how spaces are treated; this settings usually forces multiple spaces to collapse into a single space

✔ Tips

■ Do not confuse the <nobr> and <pre> HTML tags with the white-space values of nowrap and pre. Although they do basically the same thing, the HTML tags are being phased out (depreciated) or are not a part of the HTML specification and should not be used.

■ The text content of any tag that receives the nowrap value runs horizontally as far as it needs, regardless of the window's live width. The user may be forced to scroll horizontally to read all the text, so this setting is usually frowned upon.

■ nowrap is great for keeping lines of text in tables together regardless of the width of the table data cell.

Figure 6.12 Without the style, the white spaces collapse.

Table 6.7

white-space Values	
VALUE	COMPATIBILITY
normal	IE5*, N4, S1, O5, CSS1
pre	IE5*, N4, S1, O5, CSS1
nowrap	IE5*, N6, S1, O5, CSS1

IE5.5 for Windows

CONTROLLING WHITE SPACE

ELEMENT VISIBILITY CONTROLS

7

Although the ability to show and hide elements or parts of elements is one of the cornerstones of dynamic HTML (DHTML), the ability to set the visibility of these elements is a feature of CSS.

Keep in mind, however, that until you learn to use JavaScript to change the visibility of an element (see Chapter 11), the visibility controls will not be of much use.

Setting the Visibility of an Element

The visibility property designates whether an element is visible when it is initially viewed in the window. If visibility is set to hidden, the element is invisible but still takes up space in the document, and a big empty rectangle appears where the element should be (**Figure 7.1** and **Figure 7.2**).

To set an element's visibility:

1. position: relative;

   Set the position property to relative or absolute (**Code 7.1**).

2. visibility:

   Type the visibility property name, followed by a colon (:), in the element's CSS definition.

3. hidden

   Now type one of the following keywords to specify how you want this element's visibility to be treated (**Table 7.1**):

   ▲ hidden, which causes the element to be invisible when initially rendered on the screen

   ▲ visible, which causes the element to be visible

   ▲ inherit, which causes the element to inherit the visibility of its parent element

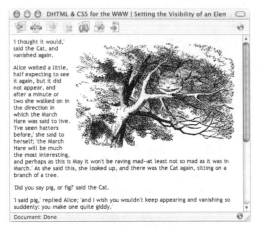

Figure 7.1 In this version, the image's visibility has been left alone, which means that it defaults to visible.

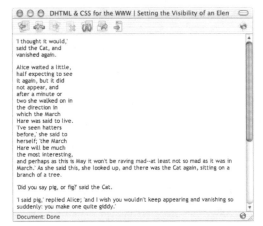

Figure 7.2 This version shows the result of the code. The visibility property has been set to hidden, so there is a blank space where the image should appear.

Code 7.1 The `visibility` property is defined for a class called `hide`, which hides an element in the HTML code.

```
●●●                    Code                    ⬭
<html>
<head>
     <style type="text/css" media="screen"><!--
.hide {
    position: relative;
    visibility: hidden;
}
    --></style>
</head>
<body>
     <span class="hide"><img src="alice24.gif"
→ height="238" width="350" align="right"
→ /></span>'I thought it would,' said the
→ Cat, and vanished again.
     <p>Alice waited a little, half expecting to
→ see it again...</p>
</body>
</html>
```

Table 7.1

Visibility Values	
VALUE	**COMPATIBILITY**
hide	N 4*
hidden	IE4, N4, S1, O3.5, CSS2
show	N4*
visible	IE4, N4, S1, O3.5, CSS2
inherit	IE4, N4, S1, O3.5, CSS2

* Netscape 4 only; not available in Netscape 6

✔ Tips

■ Though the properties seem similar, `visibility` differs radically from `display`. When `display` is set to `none`, the element is wiped out of the document, and no space is reserved for it.

■ Netscape 4 also allowed you to set the visibility using `show` and `hide`, but these values are *not* supported in newer versions of Netscape.

■ I recommend using an ID if you want to define the visibility of a single element on the screen that you might later want to change using JavaScript.

Setting the Visible Area of an Element (Clipping)

Unlike setting the width and the height of an element, which controls its dimensions (see Chapter 5), clipping an element designates how much of that element is visible in the window. The rest of the element's content will still be there, but it will be invisible to the viewer and treated as empty space by the browser (**Figure 7.3**).

To define the clip area of an element:

1. `position: absolute;`

Set the `position` property to `relative` or `absolute` (**Code 7.2**).

2. `clip:`

Type the `clip` property name, followed by a colon (`:`).

3. `rect(15px 350px 195px 50px);`

Type `rect` to define the shape of the clip as a rectangle, then an opening parenthesis (`(`), four values separated by spaces, a closing parenthesis (`)`), and a semicolon (`;`). The numbers define the top, right, bottom, and left lengths of the clip area, respectively. All these values are distances from the element's origin (top-left corner), not necessarily from the indicated side (**Figure 7.4**).

Each value can be either a number with the value type (for example `'px'`) after it , or `auto`, which allows the browser to determine the clip size (usually, 100%). See **Table 7.2** for the browser compatibility of the values.

Figure 7.3 The Cheshire Cat's face is all that appears from this image. The King, Queen, and Jack have all been clipped away.

Code 7.2 The clip region is defined in the `clipInHalf` class, which is then applied to an element in the HTML code.

```
<html>
<head>
    <style type="text/css"><!--
.clipInHalf {
    position: absolute;
    clip: rect(15px 350px 195px 50px);
    top: 0;
    left: 0;
}
    --></style>
</head>
<body>
    <div class="clipInHalf">
        <img src="alice31.gif" height="480"
        → width="379" align="left" /></div>
</body>
</html>
```

Table 7.2

clip Values	
VALUE	COMPATIBILITY
rect (<topLength>, <rightLength>, <bottomLength>, <leftLength>)	IE4*, N4, S1, O7, CSS2
auto	IE4*, N4, S1, O7, CSS2

IE5.5 for Windows

Top clip
y=15px

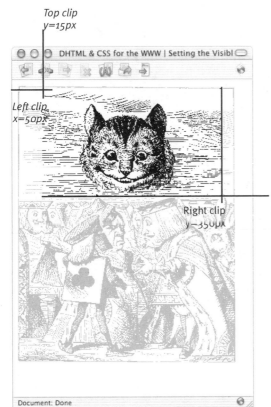

Left clip
x=50px

Right clip
x=350px

Bottom clip
y=195px

Figure 7.4 The clipping region is defined by four values that detail how far from the origin the top, right, bottom, and left edges of the element's visible area should appear.

✔ Tips

- You could simply list the clip values, however, to stay XHTML compliant, you will always need to indicate the units being used with a measurement value.

- The element's borders and padding, but not its margin, will be clipped along with the content of the element.

- Netscape has difficulty trying to apply clipping directly to many tags, including the image tag. Therefore, it is best to use a `<div>` or `<span>` tag when you apply clipping.

- Currently, clips can be only rectangular, but future versions of CSS promise to support other shapes.

- You can change the clipping using DHTML (see "Changing an Object's Visible Area" in Chapter 14).

SETTING THE VISIBLE AREA OF AN ELEMENT

Setting Where the Overflow Content Goes

When an element is clipped, or when the parent element's width and height are less than the area needed to display everything, some content is not displayed. The overflow property allows you to specify how this extra content is treated (**Figure 7.5** and **Code 7.3**).

To define the overflow control:

1. width: 200px;
   height: 200px;

   Type a width and/or height to which the element should be restricted. You could also clip the element (see "Setting the Visible Area of an Element").

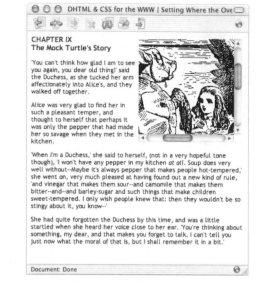

Figure 7.5 Viewers can use the scroll bars to access the overflow content of the element with the image of Alice and the Mock Turtle.

Code 7.3 The class called illustration is set to a height and width of 200 pixels, the overflow (the content that will not fit in this area) is set to auto, and scroll bars will be placed around the element as needed to see the rest of its content. This class is then applied to an element in the HTML code.

```
<html>
<head>
    <style type="text/css" media="screen"><!--
    .illustration {
    width: 200px;
    height: 200px;
    overflow: auto;
    float: right;
    margin: 5px;
}
    --></style>
</head>
<body>
    <div class="illustration">
        <img src="alice35.gif" height="480" width="401" /></div>
    <h3>CHAPTER IX<br />
      The Mock Turtle's Story</h3>
    <p>'You can't think how glad I am to see you again, you dear old thing!' said the Duchess,
      → as she tucked her arm affectionately into Alice's, and they walked off together.</p>
</body>
</html>
```

Table 7.3

overflow Values	
VALUE	COMPATIBILITY
scroll	IE5, N6, S1, O5, CSS2
hidden	IE5, N6, S1, O5, CSS2
visible	IE5, N6, S1, O5, CSS2
auto	IE5, N6, S1, O5, CSS2

2. `overflow:`

Type the `overflow` property name, followed by a colon (`:`).

3. `auto;`

Type in one of the following keywords to tell the browser how to treat overflow from the clip (**Table 7.3**):

- ▲ `scroll`, which sets scroll bars around the visible area to allow the visitor to scroll through the element's content

- ▲ `hidden`, which hides the overflow and prevents the scroll bars from appearing

- ▲ `visible`, to cause even the clipped part of the element to show up, essentially telling the browser to ignore the clipping

- ▲ `auto`, which allows the browser to decide how to treat extra material after clipping

✔ Tips

- ■ If the `overflow` property is not set or set to `auto`, most browsers will ignore the height property set for an element.

- ■ The `overflow` property is also used to define how clipping overflow is treated.

SETTING WHERE THE OVERFLOW CONTENT GOES

Setting an Element's Opacity

Although not a part of the official CSS standard, both Internet Explorer for Windows (not Mac) and Mozilla-based browsers (Netscape 6+, Firebird, Camino) allow you to set the opacity of any element within the Web page (see **Figure 7.6**, **Figure 7.7**, and **Figure 7.8**). However, both browser types implement opacity in completely different ways. Internet Explorer builds on its existing filter functionality (which can be used in a variety of other ways as well), while Mozilla simply adds a new property. However, since one browser will ignore the other browser's code, you can place both definitions in the rule list for the element in question to control its opacity (**Code 7.4**).

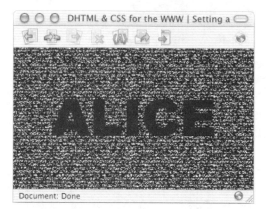

Figure 7.6 The text is at 100% opacity (1.0), so the background does not show through.

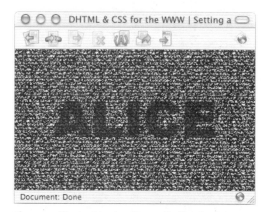

Figure 7.7 The text is at 75% opacity (0.75), so some of the background static shows through.

Figure 7.8 The text is at 50% opacity (0.5), so the words are beginning to fade away.

Code 7.4 Using redundant styles for Internet Explorer (filter) and Mozilla (-moz-opacity) browsers, you can set the opacity of elements and be sure they'll appear the way you want them in most browsers.

```
<html>
<head>
    <style type="text/css" media="screen"><!--
body {
    background-image: url(static.gif)
}
h1 {
    filter:progid:DXImageTransform.Microsoft.
    → BasicImage(opacity=0.75);
    -moz-opacity: 0.75;
    font-size: 72px;
    font-family: 'Arial Black';
    text-align: center;
}
    --></style>
</head>
<body>
    <h1>ALICE</h1>
</body>
</html>
```

To define the opacity of an element:

1. `filter:`

   To control opacity of an element displayed in Internet Explorer for Windows, type the `filter` property name, followed by a colon (`:`), in the definition list.

2. `progid:DXImageTransform.Microsoft.`
   `→ BasicImage(opacity=0.75);`

   Add the `progid` code to define the filter and value being used. You do not want to change this code, except for the value after `opacity`, which can range between `0.0` (completely transparent) and `1.0` (completely opaque).

3. `-moz-opacity:`

   To control the opacity of an element displayed in Mozilla-based browsers, add the `-moz-opacity` property name, followed by a colon (`:`), to the definition list.

4. `0.75;`

   Enter a value for the opacity of the element, which can range between `0.0` (completely transparent) and `1.0` (completely opaque).

✔ Tip

- Opacity changes will *not* work in Internet Explorer for Macintosh, in Safari, or in Opera.

LIST, TABLE, AND INTERFACE CONTROLS

8

One useful feature of HTML is its ability to set up lists that automatically number or bullet themselves. You set up the list, and the browser takes care of the rest. When you add items to the list, the layout adjusts automatically when it's rendered in the window. The available choices, however, are fairly limited with HTML.

CSS gives you many more choices, providing control over the type of marker used to denote the list items, which can be a bullet or an alphanumeric character. You can also create your own bullets and make lists with hanging indents.

In this chapter, I'll show you not only how to whip your lists into shape by using CSS, but how to get the most out of tables and customize parts of the browser interface.

Setting Up a List

You can set all the attributes for a list in one line of code using the list-style property. This gives you access to the list-style-type, list-style-position, and line-style-image properties.

In this example (**Code 8.1**), I've set up a list of cities to which I would like to travel one day and have given them an exciting bullet to add emphasis (**Figure 8.1**).

To define multiple list-style attributes for a selector:

1. list-style:

   Type the list-style property name, followed by a colon (:), and then the list-style values as listed below and in **Table 8.1**.

2. url(bullet1.gif)

   Next, type a list-style-image value. To include your own bullet, you must first create the bullet graphic and then tell the browser where the graphic is located, either the complete Web address or the local file name of the image. (See "Creating Your Own Bullets" later in this chapter for more information.)

3. circle;

   Type a list-style-type value listed in **Table 8.2**, followed by a space, or type none if you want no marker to appear (see the next section, "Setting the Bullet Style," for more information).

Code 8.1 All the list-style properties are set at the same time.

```
<html>
<head>
      <style type="text/css" media="screen"><!--
li {
list-style: url(bullet1.gif) circle inside; }
      --></style>
</head>
<body>
      <h3>Places to go</h3>
      <ul>
          <li>London</li>
          <li>Paris</li>
          <li>Tokyo</li>
          <li>New York</li>
          <li>Slippery Creek</li>
      </ul>
</body>
</html>
```

Figure 8.1 Keep your lists in line using CSS.

Table 8.1

list-style Values

VALUE	COMPATIBILITY
<list-style-type>	IE4, N4, S1, O3.5, CSS1
<list-style-position>	IE4, N6, S1, O3.5, CSS1
<list-style-image>	IE4, N6, S1, O3.5, CSS1

Table 8.2

list-style-type Values

VALUE	COMPATIBILITY
<bullet name>*	IE4, N4, S1, O3.5, CSS1
none	IE4, N4, S1, O3.5, CSS1

See Table 8.4

Table 8.3

list-style-position Values

VALUE	COMPATIBILITY
inside	IE4, N6, S1, O3.5, CSS1
outside	IE4, N6, S1, O3.5, CSS1

4. `inside`

Type a `list-style-position` value (**Table 8.3**), followed by a space. Use either of the following (see "Creating a Hanging Indent" later in this chapter for more information):

▲ `inside`, which aligns subsequent lines of wrapped text with the bullet

▲ `outside`, which aligns subsequent lines of wrapped text with the first letter in the first line of the text

✔ Tips

■ Although I used the list item `<li>` tag in this example, you can turn any element into a list item by adding the CSS list properties along with the definition `display:list-item`.

■ Because each of the multiple values in the preceding exercise is a different type, not all values must be present for this definition to work. Values omitted are set to the default. The following example works just fine:

`list-style: inside;`

■ If the visitor has turned off graphics in the browser, or if a graphical bullet does not load for some reason, the browser uses the `list-style-type` instead.

Setting the Bullet Style

The list-style property gives you control over the type of bullet to be used for list items—not just circles, discs, and squares, but also letters and numerals and dots. Oh, my!

In this example (**Code 8.2**), I have set up my shopping list, using different bullet styles for different types of items (**Figure 8.2**).

To define the bullet style:

1. list-style-type:

Type the list-style-type property name, followed by a colon (:) and one of the values listed below and in Table 8.2.

2. disc;

Type one of the bullet names listed in **Table 8.4**, or type none if you want no marker to appear.

✔ Tip

■ Although we used the list item tag <li> in this example, you can turn any element into a list item by adding the CSS list properties along with the definition display: list-item.

Table 8.4

list-style bullets

NAME	APPEARANCE (VARIES DEPENDING ON SYSTEM)
disc	●
circle	○
square	■
decimal	1, 2, 3
decimal-leading-zero	01, 02, 03
upper-roman	I, II, III
lower-roman	i, ii, iii
upper-alpha	A, B, C
lower-alpha	a, b, c
lower-greek	α, β, χ

Code 8.2 Two classes are created to help with the shopping list. The grocery class uses a disc as its bullet, and computer uses a square.

```
<html>
<head>
        <style type="text/css" media="screen"><!--
li.grocery {
    list-style-type: disc; }
li.computer {
    list-style-type: circle; }
    --></style>
</head>
<body>
        <h3>Shopping list</h3>
        <ul>
            <li class="grocery">Butter</li>
            <li class="grocery">Milk</li>
            <li class="grocery">Cereal</li>
            <li class="computer">5GB Hard drive</li>
            <li class="grocery">Orange juice</li>
            <li class="grocery">Cat Food</li>
            <li class="computer">40MB RAM</li>
            <li class="grocery">Soup</li>
        </ul>
</body>
</html>
```

Figure 8.2 The computer items stand out in the shopping list because they use a different bullet.

Code 8.3 These list items will have an image in front of them rather than a standard bullet.

```
<html>
<head>
    <style type="text/css" media="screen"><!--
li {
    list-style-image: url(bullet1.gif);
    margin-left: 20px;
}
    --></style>
</head>
<body>
    <h2>Things to do</h2>
    <ul>
        <li>write book</li>
        <li>make examples</li>
        <li>edit book</li>
        <li>take holiday in bahammas</li>
        <li>drink pina colladas</li>
    </ul>
</body>
</html>
```

Figure 8.3 Why settle for the same old bullets? Create your own with CSS.

Figure 8.4 An arrow bullet created using a GIF image.

Creating Your Own Bullets

You're not limited to the preset bullet styles built into the browser (see the previous section, "Setting the Bullet Style"). You can also use your own graphics as bullets, in GIF, JPEG, and PNG formats.

In this example (**Code 8.3**), I've set up a list of things to do (**Figure 8.3**) and added emphasis with the arrow bullet (**Figure 8.4**).

To define your own graphic bullet:

1. `list-style-image`:

   Type the `list-style-image` property name, followed by a colon (:).

2. `url(bullet1.gif);`

   To include your own bullet, you have to tell the browser where your bullet graphic is located. Type either the complete Web address or the local file name of the image. In this example, `bullet1.gif` is a local file.

   Alternatively, type `none`, which instructs the browser to override any inherited bullet images (**Table 8.5**).

✔ Tips

- Graphic bullets are a great way to enhance the appearance of your page while minimizing download time.

- Keep in mind that the text being bulleted has to make space for the graphic you use. A taller graphic will force more space between individual bulleted items, and a wider graphic will force bulleted items farther to the right.

Table 8.5

list-style-image Values	
VALUE	COMPATIBILITY
<url>	IE4, N6, S1, O3.5, CSS1
none	IE4, N6, S1, O3.5, CSS1

CREATING YOUR OWN BULLETS

Creating a Hanging Indent

Often, the text of an item in a bulleted list is longer than one line. Using the list-style-position property, you can specify the position of wrapping text in relation to the bullet. Wrapped text that is indented to start below the first letter of the first line of text is called a *hanging indent*.

In this example (**Code 8.4**), I've set up the bullets with two position styles: one to create a hanging indent and the other to align the text with the bullet (**Figure 8.5**).

To define the line position for wrapped text in a list item:

1. list-style-position:

   Type the list-style-position property name, followed by a colon (:).

2. inside;

   Type either of the following to determine how you want the text to be indented (Table 8.3):

   ▲ inside, which aligns subsequent lines of wrapped text with the bullet

   ▲ outside, which aligns subsequent lines of wrapped text with the first letter in the first line of the text

✔ Tip

■ Generally, bulleted lists that have a hanging indent (outside position) stand out much better than those without a hanging indent (inside position).

Code 8.4 Lists are set to display with a hanging indent unless given the class inside, which causes the text to run flush with the bullet.

```
<html>
<head>
     <style type="text/css" media="screen"><!--
li {
     list-style-position: outside;
}
.inside {
     list-style-position: inside;
}
     --></style>
</head>
<body>
     <ul>
          <li>'A knot!' said Alice, always ready
          → to make herself useful, and looking
          → anxiously about her. 'Oh, do let me
          → help to undo it!'</li>
          <li class="inside">'I shall do nothing
          → of the sort,' said the Mouse, getting
          → up and walking away. 'You insult me
          → by talking such nonsense!'</li>
          <li>'I didn't mean it!' pleaded poor
          → Alice. 'But you're so easily
          → offended, you know!'</li>
          <li>The Mouse only growled in reply.</li>
     </ul>
</body>
</html>
```

Figure 8.5 The bullet stands out from the list text.

Code 8.5 The table data cells in the table that receive the class collapsus will share adjacent borders.

```
<html>
<head>
     <style type="text/css" media="screen"><!--
.collapsus {
     border-collapse: collapse;
}
     --></style>
</head>
<body bgcolor="#ffffff">
     <table class="collapsus" width="180"
    → border="5" cellspacing=
    → "5" cellpadding="5">
        <tr>
            <td>a</td>
            <td>b</td>
            <td>c</td>
        </tr>
        <tr>
            <td>d</td>
            <td>e</td>
            <td>f</td>
        </tr>
        <tr>
            <td>g</td>
            <td>h</td>
            <td>i</td>
        </tr>
     </table>
</body>
</html>
```

Collapsing Borders Between Table Cells

Every table data cell defined by the <td> tag has four borders: top, left, bottom, and right. The border-collapse property allows you to set a table so that each table data cell will share its borders with an adjacent table data cell rather than creating a separate border for each (**Code 8.5** and **Figure 8.6**). The actual effects of this, though, will vary slightly from browser to browser (**Figure 8.7**).

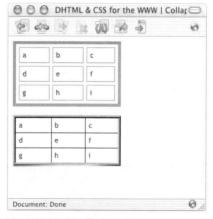

Figure 8.6 In Mozilla-based browsers, the borders become a single line. The top table shows the same code without the border-collapse property.

Figure 8.7 In Internet Explorer for Windows, the borders are collapsed, but the top and left borders disappear because of the 3-D border effect. The top table shows the same code without the border-collapse property.

To collapse the borders in a table:

1. `border-collapse:`

   Type the `border-collapse` property name, followed by a colon (:).

2. `collapse`

   Type either of the following to determine how you want the borders in the table to be treated (**Table 8.6**):

   ▲ `collapse`, which will cause adjacent table data cells to share a common border; you won't be able to set `cell-spacing` if borders are collapsed

   ▲ `separate`, which will cause each table data cell to maintain individual borders

Table 8.6

border-collapse Values	
VALUE	COMPATIBILITY
collapse	IE5.5*, N7, O5, CSS2
separate	IE5.5*, N7, O5, CSS2

* For Windows only

Code 8.6 Text in the `<caption>` tag that uses the `placeCaption` class will be positioned underneath its table.

```
●●●                    Code                    ⬭
<html>
<head>
     <style type="text/css" media="screen"><!--
.placeCaption {
     caption-side: bottom;
}
     --></style>
</head>
<body bgcolor="#ffffff">
     <table width="180" border="5"
   → cellspacing="5" cellpadding="5">
        <caption class="placeCaption">Table
      → 1.1: A Bunch of letters</caption>
        <tr>
            <td>a</td>
            <td>b</td>
            <td>c</td>
        </tr>
        <tr>
            <td>d</td>
            <td>e</td>
            <td>f</td>
        </tr>
        <tr>
            <td>g</td>
            <td>h</td>
            <td>i</td>
        </tr>

</table>
</body>
</html>
```

Table 8.7

caption-side Values	
VALUE	COMPATIBILITY
top	IE5*, N6, S1, O7, CSS2
left	CSS2
bottom	IE5*, N6, S1, O7, CSS2
right	CSS2
*For Mac only	

Setting the Position of a Table Caption

The `<caption>` tag allows you to embed identifying text in a table. You can set the `align` attribute in the table tag to define where the caption should appear in relation to the table, but this is being depreciated in favor of the CSS `caption-side` property, which does the same thing (**Code 8.6** and **Figure 8.8**).

To set the position of a caption in relation to its table:

1. `caption-side:`
   Type the `caption-side` property name, followed by a colon (:).

2. `bottom;`
   Type a keyword indicating on which side of the table you want the caption to appear (**Table 8.7**): top, left, bottom, or right.

✔ Tip

■ Although you should be able to place the caption on any side of the table, currently browsers only support top and bottom.

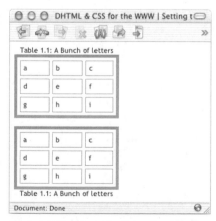

Figure 8.8 The top table shows the default caption position (above the table) while the bottom table uses the `caption-side` property to move the caption to beneath the table.

Changing the Mouse Pointer's Appearance

Normally, the mouse pointer's appearance is determined by the browser. The browser changes the mouse pointer's appearance according to the content over which the pointer currently happens to be resting.

If the pointer is over text, for example, the pointer becomes a text selector. Or if the browser is working and the visitor can't do anything, the pointer becomes a timer, letting visitors know they need to wait.

Sometimes, it's useful to override the browser's wishes and set the appearance of the pointer yourself.

In this example (**Code 8.7**), I've set up different pointer types that depend on the type of object or link over which the pointer is hovering (**Figure 8.9**, **Figure 8.10**, and **Figure 8.11**).

Code 8.7 Because the link leads to a help screen, I've set the help class to change the cursor appearance to the help pointer. In addition, images will have a move pointer, and the entire page will use a pointer that is generally used when resizing the window from the top-left corner.

```
<html>
<head>
    <style type="text/css" media="screen"><!--
body {
    cursor: nw-resize;
}
img {
    cursor: pointer;
}
.help {
    cursor: help;
}
    --></style>
</head>
<body>
    <h3>CHAPTER VIII<br />
    The Queen's Croquet-Ground</h3>
    <p><img src="alice30.gif" height="272"
    → width="200" align="left" border="0"
    → />A large rose-tree stood near the
    → entrance of the garden…</p>
    <p>'I couldn't <a class="help"
    → href="#">help</a> it,' said Five, in a
    → sulky tone; 'Seven jogged my elbow.'</p>
</body>
</html>
```

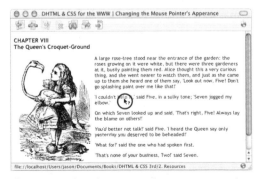

Figure 8.9 The mouse pointer is still an arrow in most places in the window, but it looks different from the standard arrow.

Figure 8.10 When the mouse pointer passes over the help link, it becomes a question mark.

Figure 8.11 When the mouse pointer is over an image, it changes to the move pointer.

Table 8.8

Cursor Types	
NAME	APPEARANCE (VARIES DEPENDING ON OS)
crosshair	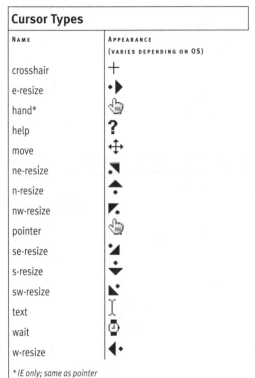
e-resize	
hand*	
help	
move	
ne-resize	
n-resize	
nw-resize	
pointer	
se-resize	
s-resize	
sw-resize	
text	
wait	
w-resize	

* IE only; same as pointer

To set the mouse pointer's appearance:

1. `cursor:`

   Type the `cursor` attribute, followed by a colon (`:`), in the CSS definition list.

2. `help;`

   Type one of the mouse-pointer names listed in **Table 8.8** to specify the pointer's appearance. Alternatively, type one of these other values for `cursor` (**Table 8.9**).

   ▲ `auto` if you want the browser to decide which mouse pointer to use

   ▲ `none` if you want the cursor to disappear altogether

   ▲ `url` and the location of a graphic to use as a custom cursor; this can be either the complete Web address or the local file name of the image

✔ Tips

■ You can use any Web graphic (GIF, PNG, or JPEG), as a custom cursor. Unfortunately, this only works in Internet Explorer 6.

■ Although it's fun to play around with switching the mouse pointers, I've tested this feature on my own Web site and have gotten several e-mails asking me to cut it out. Most Web users have learned to recognize what particular pointers are for and when they should appear. Breaking these conventions tends to confuse people.

Table 8.9

cursor Values	
VALUE	COMPATIBILITY
<cursor type name>	IE5*, N6, S1, O7, CSS2
<URL>	IE6, CSS2
auto	IE5*, N6, S1, O7, CSS2
none	IE5*, N6, S1, O7, CSS2

*IE 5.5/Windows

CHANGING THE MOUSE POINTER'S APPEARANCE

Changing the Scrollbar's Appearance (IE Windows Only)

Internet Explorer (versions 5.5 and above) for Windows allows you to set the color for all or part of the scrollbar (**Code 8.8**). These properties can be applied to the main scrollbar for the page or any scrollbar within the page, such as text-area scrollbars (**Figure 8.12**).

Code 8.8 You can control the color of each part of the scrollbar in Internet Explorer for Windows.

```
<html>
<head>
    <style type="text/css" media="screen"><!--
body {
    scrollbar-base-color: red;
}
textarea {
    scrollbar-3dlight-color: black;
    scrollbar-arrow-color: white;
    scrollbar-darkshadow-color: white;
    scrollbar-face-color: #cccccc;
    scrollbar-highlight-color: black;
    scrollbar-shadow-color: white;
    scrollbar-track-color: gray;
}
    --></style>
</head>
<body bgcolor="#ffffff">
    <textarea style="float: left"
    → name="textareaName" rows="20" cols="45">
'Who cares for you?' said Alice, (she had grown
→ to her full size by this time.) 'You're
→ nothing but a pack of cards!'
    </textarea>
    <img src="alice42a.gif" alt="" height="480"
    → width="360" border="0" />
</body>
</html>
```

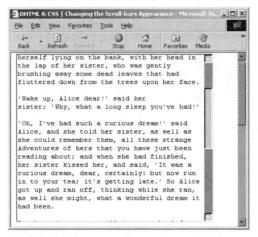

Figure 8.12 The main scrollbar for the page is red and the 3-D appearance for the text-area scrollbar has been reversed.

Table 8.10

scrollbar color properties	
PROPERTY	LOCATION
scrollbar-3dlight-color	Outer top and left sides of scroll face; used to create 3-D effect
scrollbar-arrow-color	Arrows in boxes
scrollbar-base-color	Color used if no other properties set
scrollbar-darkshadow-color	Outer bottom and right sides of scroll face; used to create 3-D effect
scrollbar-face-color	Flat areas in slider, except for track
scrollbar-highlight-color	Inner top and left sides of scroll face; used to create 3-D effect
scrollbar-shadow-color	Inner bottom and right sides of scroll face; used to create 3-D effect
scrollbar-track-color	Flat area that defines the scroller

To set a scrollbar's colors:

1. `scroll-base-color: red;`

   Type the `scroll-base-color` property name, followed by a colon (:), then a color value and a semicolon (;). This will set the overall color scheme for the scrollbar.

2. `scrollbar-3dlight-color: black;`

   Type one of the scrollbar color properties (**Table 8.10**), followed by a colon (:), then a color value and a semicolon (;). These are used to set the color of individual elements in the scrollbar. You do not have to use all of the scroll properties in a definition, but the browser will use default values for those left out.

✔ Tip

■ The "scroll-face" of the scroll bar includes the 3-D beveled edges of the up/down arrows and scroller.

CHANGING THE SCROLLBAR'S APPEARANCE

Part 2
Dynamic HTML

UNDERSTANDING DHTML

Figure 9.1 On the Panic Web site (www.panic.com) you can click an application icon to view details about the product or drag and drop the icon to download the application.

As powerful as cascading style sheets are, they aren't really dynamic per se. They give you control of how a document looks when it's first put on the screen, but what about after that?

Web pages created with CSS can have their properties changed on the fly (that is, dynamically) through a scripting language such as JavaScript.

In addition, dynamic HTML (DHTML) allows users to directly interact with Web pages, and allows you to create far more sophisticated user interfaces than with simple HTML. For example, the Panic software company's Web site uses DHMTL to allow users to quickly download their software (**Figure 9.1**). Clicking the application icon displays more information about the product, but dragging and dropping the same icon downloads the application. This kind of interface would not be possible without DHMTL.

In this chapter, I'll introduce what makes DHTML dynamic and look at how it compares to the other leading dynamic Web technology, Flash.

What Is Dynamic HTML?

I'll let you in on a little secret: There really isn't a DHTML. At least, not in the way that there is an HTML or a JavaScript. HTML and JavaScript are specific, easily identified technologies for the Web. *Dynamic HTML,* on the other hand, is a marketing term coined by both Netscape and Microsoft to describe a set of technologies introduced in their version 4 Web browsers to enhance the interactive capabilities of those browsers (see "The History of DHTML").

These technologies were created or added in an attempt to overcome what were considered to be the chief limitations of Web pages designed with static HTML. Although the Web was great for delivering pages of text and graphics, those who were used to multimedia were left wanting more.

Adding DHTML to your Web site means that your pages can act and react to the user without continually returning to the Web server for more data. In programming terms, placing all of the code in the Web page is called *client-side code.* For you, it means not having to learn programming to create interactive Web sites.

DHTML is a combination of different standards-based Web technologies (CSS, the DOM, JavaScript, and markup languages) that, when used together, allow greater interactivity on your Web page (**Figure 9.2**).

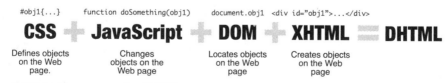

Figure 9.2 The components of DHTML.

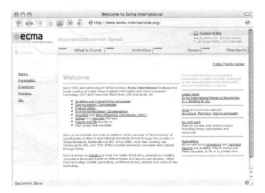

Figure 9.3 The ECMA's (www.ecma-international.org) ECMAScript Web page.

Cascading style sheets (CSS)

CSS allows you to define the properties of any element on the page. Older browsers (such as Netscape 4 and Internet Explorer 4) support CSS Level 1 and CSS-P; most modern browsers support CSS Level 2. CSS is a standard defined by the World Wide Web Consortium (W3C). For more details on CSS, see Chapter 1, "Understanding CSS."

Document Object Model (DOM)

All DHTML-capable browsers have some version of the DOM that you can use to access the properties of any element-turned-object in the browser window. The problem is that the W3C did not standardize the DOM until recently, and older browsers (Netscape 4 and Internet Explorer 4) implemented their own conflicting DOMs. The good news is that the majority of modern browsers now support the W3C DOM and legacy coding is becoming increasingly unnecessary. For more details on the DOM, see Chapter 10, "Events and the DOM."

JavaScript

JavaScript allows you to create simple code to control the behavior of Web page objects. Although Internet Explorer and Netscape do not always agree on the exact implementation of JavaScript, they're close enough that you can work around the inconsistencies.

Unlike CSS and the DOM, JavaScript is *not* a standard set by the W3C. Instead, it has been somewhat standardized by the European Computer Manufacturers Association (ECMA). In fact, it is sometimes referred to as "ECMA script" (**Figure 9.3**).

continues on next page

WHAT IS DYNAMIC HTML?

There were several versions of JavaScript in existence before ECMA started its standards initiative in 1996. Originally, JavaScript was referred to as JScript in Internet Explorer 3.0 and JavaScript in Netscape 2.0. However, today, most browsers support JavaScript 1.2 (its official designation is "Standard ECMA-262") as the JavaScript standard, so that's what we'll be using in this book.

Markup Language

Markup languages are used by Web browsers to define how a Web page should be structured. This can take many forms. HTML (Hypertext Markup Language) is used to define the structure of a Web page, while XML (Extensible Markup Language) can define not only the structure but also the content of a page. In addition, there are several other specialized technologies such as SVG (Scalable Vector Graphics) and SMIL (Synchronized Multimedia Language) used to add graphics and interactivity to the page. All of these languages can work with CSS, JavaScript, and the DOM to create dynamic Web pages.

XHTML (Extensible Hypertext Markup Language) is a hybrid of XML and HTML that is gradually replacing HTML in common use (see **Figure 9.4**). Although DHTML can be applied to a wide variety of markup languages, in this book we'll be coding using the XHTML standard.

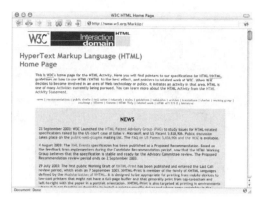

Figure 9.4 The W3C's (www.w3.org) HyperText Markup Language Web page.

The History of DHTML

When dynamic HTML was first being developed in the mid-1990s, Netscape and Microsoft had differing ideas about what technologies should be used to make HTML more dynamic.

Netscape-specific DHTML

Netscape brought several new technologies to the table, hoping to create more dynamic Web pages. Unfortunately, these technologies will never become standards because CSS does most of the same things and is endorsed by the W3C.

JavaScript style sheets (JSS) were introduced in Netscape 4 to offer an alternative to CSS. Like CSS, JSS allows you to define how HTML tags display their content, but JSS uses JavaScript syntax. The only browser that supports JSS, however, is Netscape 4. Not even the latest versions of Netscape support this out-of-date technology. As a result, I do not recommend using JSS.

In addition, Netscape offered layers, which were a prototype for CSS positioning controls. Like them, layers allow you to control the position and visibility of elements on the screen. Again, however, only Netscape 4 supports layers, and Netscape abandoned this technology in favor of CSS positioning. I do not recommend using Netscape layers.

Microsoft-specific DHTML

Much of the Microsoft-specific DHTML is based on proprietary Microsoft software, such as ActiveX technology. Because ActiveX is owned by Microsoft, it is unlikely that it will ever be a cross-browser technology. I do not recommend using ActiveX technologies.

continues on next page

What DHTML *Should* Be

Although there's no official or even standard definition of dynamic HTML, a few things are undeniably part of the DHTML mission:

- DHTML should use HTML or XHTML tags and scripting languages without requiring the use of plug-ins or any software other than the browser.

- DHTML, like HTML, should work (or at least have the potential to work) with all browsers and on all platforms.

- DHTML should enhance the interactivity and visual appeal of Web pages.

Visual filters let you add visual effects to graphics and text in your document. If you've ever worked with Photoshop filters, you'll understand the ways of visual filters. The problem is that these filters are not standard on all browsers, and aren't even supported in all versions of Internet Explorer. I do not recommend using visual filters except in the few cases where a similar effect can be achieved using other code, such as is the case with opacity (see "Setting an Element's Opacity" in Chapter 7).

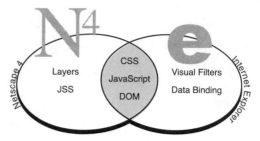

Figure 9.5 Where the two versions of dynamic HTML overlapped is where you find cross-browser DHTML, including CSS, JavaScript, and the Document Object Model (DOM).

Cross-browser DHTML

For years, the inconsistencies in supported technology between the two main browsers had Web developers who wanted to remain cross-browser compatible gnashing their teeth. Fortunately, the Netscape and Microsoft specifications for DHTML did overlap (**Figure 9.5**), and this area of overlap prevented DHTML from becoming just another proprietary technology.

Today, browsers increasingly use the CSS, DOM, and JavaScript standards, and the use of legacy browsers (such as Netscape 4) is diminishing, so DHTML can be used for a wide variety of applications. Although there are still browser inconsistencies, it is becoming easier to code for all browsers with minimal tweaking to accommodate the eccentricities of any particular browser.

Why Should I Use DHTML?

Because you purchased this book, you've already made some commitment to using DHTML. But in case you haven't bought the book and are just flipping through, looking at the cool examples, let me try to make a balanced case for why you should use DHTML in your Web designs—and warn you about some of the troubles you may face.

DHTML advantages

Obviously, DHTML is not without its advantages or no one would use it. It has taken a few years, however, for the power of DHTML to be realized. Here are some advantages to using DHTML:

◆ **Supported by all browsers.** DHTML is completely or partially supported in every major browser since Netscape 4 and Internet Explorer 4, which are used by most of the Web-browsing public. In addition, browsers such as Opera and Safari, and all Mozilla-based browsers support DHTML.

◆ **Open standards.** Because DHTML uses standardized technologies that are open to any browser manufacturer, you can create your pages according to these standards and expect that, for the most part, it will display much the same on any major browser. Although there will be some inconsistencies in how the standards are implemented in each browser, the similarities outweigh the differences.

◆ **Change content on the fly.** One of DHTML's most obvious advantages is that you can make changes to the Web page content after it has loaded, without having to reload it. This is where the *dynamic* in DHTML comes from.

continues on next page

◆ **Small file sizes.** Like HTML, DHTML is created with text files, which are smaller than graphic files and generally render faster than alternatives such as Flash and Java.

◆ **No plug-ins required.** If a browser supports HTML, CSS, JavaScript, and the DOM (which all modern browsers do), it supports DHTML without the need for any additional plug-ins.

◆ **Easy to learn.** If you are already a Web designer, and you know HTML and JavaScript, you are halfway to knowing DHTML.

◆ **Fast development.** Many of the tricks that Web designers produced with graphics and JavaScript can be developed faster with DHTML.

◆ **Faster Web experience.** You can use DHTML to hide, show, and change content without having to load new pages. This capability speeds the performance of your site by requiring fewer calls to the server. In addition, since all DHTML code is text, it allows for fast downloads when compared to other interactive technologies such as Flash.

◆ **No Java programming required.** Although DHTML can do many of the same things and shares some of the same Syntax as Java, you do not have to learn an entire programming language to use it.

DHTML disadvantages

It's not all smooth sailing with DHTML, however. To use DHTML, you need to understand its weaknesses as well as its strengths.

◆ **Browser and operating-system incompatibilities.** The implementation of CSS, JavaScript, and the DOM may vary slightly from browser to browser, and sometimes even between versions of the same browser on different operating systems. Although I've gone to great pains to present workaround solutions in this book, some browsers can do certain things that others simply cannot do (see "Cross-Browser Conundrums" in Chapter 21).

◆ **Picky, picky, picky.** JavaScript and CSS are notoriously finicky when it comes to syntax. Although HTML is very forgiving if you forget a close tag or nest tags that should not be nested, your entire page may go awry if you have one too many brackets in a JavaScript function or forget a semicolon in a CSS definition list. In addition, if you're using XHTML instead of HTML, which is recommended, you won't be able to get away with the mistakes you could in HTML.

◆ **Buggy browsers.** Many browsers have bugs that inexplicably prevent DHTML from working and then suddenly allow it to work. Some bugs have fixes or at least workarounds; others do not.

Flash vs. DHTML

Since their almost simultaneous release in the late 1990's, both Macromedia Flash and DHTML have seemed to be at odds, vying for Web designers' attention as a way to add interactivity to Web sites.

Although DHTML adds interactivity to Web pages by using HTML, CSS, and JavaScript, Flash is a file format that can be integrated into HTML pages but is itself a separate technology that is also delivered through Web browsers (see sidebar "The History of Flash?").

The rest of this book deals with how, where, and why you should use DHTML, but it's also important to understand the strengths and weaknesses of DHTML's chief dynamic competition so that you can better decide which technology to use.

Flash advantages

Flash has scored points with developers for several reasons, not the least of which is its consistency.

◆ **Consistent.** A Flash file will run more or less the same on a Mac using Internet Explorer 5 as it does on a Windows machine running Netscape 4. Unlike HTML, JavaScript, and CSS, which are interpreted variously by the various companies that make Web browsers, a single company (Macromedia) develops Flash. Thus, there are no cross-browser or operating-system incompatibilities.

◆ **Ubiquitous.** According to Macromedia, 95 percent of the Web-browsing public has some version of the Flash plug-in installed. Although this figure may be a tad optimistic, there is a good chance that the audience for your Web site will be able to view Flash content that you include in your Web site.

The History of Flash

Macromedia acquired the vector animation program FutureSplash Animator in 1997. It added interactive and scripting capabilities, renamed the program Flash, and positioned it as a way to create dynamic graphic content for the Web. Up until then, graphics on the Web had been fairly lifeless; animated GIFs were the only substantial way to add motion to the browser window.

Flash changed all that by letting Web designers control the appearance and behavior of Web content.

It's important to remember that Flash is both a program (from Macromedia) and a file format (which has the extension .swf, pronounced *swif*). The file format is now an open standard. Adobe Systems has created its own program for creating Flash movies, called LiveMotion.

◆ **Attractive.** Flash gives designers a wide range of creative tools from which to choose. Also, Flash Web sites win most of the design awards these days.

◆ **Small.** If they're created right, Flash files deliver a lot of dynamic bang for the buck.

Flash disadvantages

Things look good for Flash so far, but there is another side to the story:

◆ **Difficult to learn and create.** HTML, CSS, and JavaScript can be created with a basic text editor. But to create Flash files, you must purchase and learn to use either Macromedia Flash or Adobe LiveMotion. Both of these programs have a difficult learning curve.

◆ **Plug-in phobia.** Although the vast majority of users may have the Flash plug-in, they may not have the most current version; thus, they may not be able to run your cutting-edge Flash movie. To view your site, users have to download the latest version. You could make a similar argument about browsers, but Web surfers traditionally resist downloading plug-ins. In addition, recent legal maneuvers by Eolas (a company that claims to have patented browser plug-ins) has cast doubt on the future of plug-in-based technology in Web browsers. Though this issue is far from settled, it may have a chilling effect on all plug-in technologies, including Flash.

◆ **Bloated downloads.** Although Flash movies can be very small, making them small takes skill and practice. Many enthusiastic designers forget that the people viewing their sites may have slow Internet connections, so downloading these large files can take a long time.

◆ **Usability abuses.** Flash allows greater versatility with the interface design than straight HTML. But with great power comes great responsibility. Designers are more likely to flaunt standard Web interface conventions in Flash designs and this can lead to confusion for the user. See the sidebar "The Great Usability Debate" for more details.

FLASH VS. DHTML

Should I Use DHTML or Flash?

Although I'm biased on this topic, I appreciate the simplicity that DHTML offers Web designers. Which technology you select, however, depends on a variety of factors (**Figure 9.6**). Ask yourself the following questions when determining which technology better satisfies your user-interface needs:

◆ **What technology will my audience have?** Will they have DHTML-capable browsers? Will they have the current Flash plug-in installed? Do they have plug-in phobia? The first rule of design is "Know your audience."

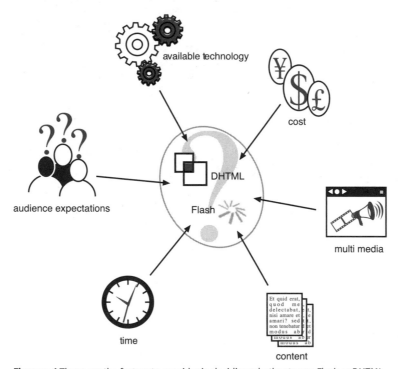

Figure 9.6 These are the factors to consider in deciding whether to use Flash or DHTML.

- **How much money do I have budgeted?** Unlike DHTML, which has no added costs over HTML, Flash requires that you purchase Flash-creation software (either Flash or LiveMotion). These programs can cost several hundred dollars, not to mention the cost of training.

- **Do I need to use sound, animation, or other media on my site?** Flash is much better than DHTML for creating and presenting multimedia content.

- **Am I presenting a lot of text?** HTML and DHTML are more versatile for presenting large amounts of text. Although Flash has made great strides in its print capability, it still can't hold a candle to HTML.

- **How much development and maintenance time do I have?** Generally, DHTML is faster to create, but this depends on which technology you know better.

- **What are my audience's expectations?** If they want fireworks, Flash is the way to go. If they expect a straightforward site or do not like plug-ins, DHTML is the way to go.

The Great Usability Debate

Noted Web usability guru Jakob Nielsen takes a strong position against Flash. In his essay "Flash: 99% Bad" (www.useit.com/alertbox/20001029.html), Nielsen comments that Flash designs have a tendency to break with established Web design conventions, which can lead to confusion for the user.

Since he published this article in October of 2000, Macromedia set up a Web site (www.macromedia.com/devnet/topics/usability.html) to address the issues of usability and Flash. Now even Jakob has softened his views and is publishing articles and giving lectures on how to improve Flash usability in conjunction with Macromedia.

SHOULD I USE DHTML OR FLASH?

THE DOCUMENT OBJECT MODEL AND EVENTS

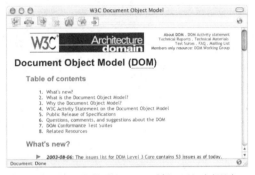

Figure 10.1 The W3C's Document Object Model Web site, keeping the Web safe for your DOM.

The ability to change a Web page dynamically with a scripting language is made possible by the Document Object Model (DOM), which can connect any element on the page to a JavaScript function. This powerful capability allows you not only to change virtually any attribute set for an element, but also any property that can be controlled with CSS.

Although the DOM didn't start out as a standard, the good news is that modern versions of both Netscape and Internet Explorer use the DOM standardized by the World Wide Web Consortium (W3C) (**Figure 10.1**).

In this chapter, you'll learn how to use the W3C's standardized DOM, and how event handlers can be made to trigger actions with the DOM.

Understanding the DOM: Road Map to Your Web Page

When you write a letter to someone, you address the envelope, naming the country, the city, the street, the number, and the person for whom the letter is intended. If you put this process in JavaScript, it might look something like this:

```
usa.newyork.sesameST.123.ernie
```

Using this address, you can send a message to the intended recipient. The postal carrier simply uses the address you list and a road map to find the correct location. As long as there are no other Ernies at 123 Sesame Street in New York, you can feel safe that the addressee will receive your message.

If you need to send a message to someone else who happens to live at the same address as Ernie, however, all you have to do is change the name:

```
usa.newyork.sesameST.123.bert
```

Although the addresses are very similar, each is still unique.

The DOM allows you to find the "address," or *node,* of different elements on your Web page. You can then use JavaScript to send the object at a particular node a message telling the object what to do.

The DOM describes a path starting with the window itself, down through the various objects on the Web page, each element representing a node within the document. For example, **Code 10.1** is broken down into nodes as shown in **Figure 10.2**.

The following example is the path for the image called alice1:

```
window.document.images.alice1
```

This DOM addresses an image in the document in the current window called alice1.

Code 10.1 A simple Web page with its node structure broken down, as shown in Figure 10.2.

```
<!DOCTYPE html PUBLIC "-//W3C//DTD XHTML
→ 1.0 Transitional//EN">
<html>
<head>
    <title>DHTML &amp; CSS for the WWW I
    → Understanding the DOM</title>
</head>
<body>
    <form action="" method="get">
        <input type="text" size="24" />
    </form>
    <div>
        <img src="alice28a.gif" id="alice1" />
        Your Message Here
    </div>
</body>
</html>
```

Should I Use a Name or ID?

To name objects on a page, you can use either the name attribute :

```
<img name="button1"
→ src="button_off.png" />
```

or the id attribute:

```
<img id="button1"
→ src="button_off.png" />
```

However, XHTML is phasing out the use of the name attribute and using id in its place. This is fine for newer browsers, but may cause problems in older browsers. The good news is that in transitional XHTML, you can include both attributes, just in case.

If you needed to access an image called alice2, you would use this DOM:

```
window.document.images.alice2
```

You can use this path to make a JavaScript function send that object a message, such as what image it should be displaying (`src`) or what CSS styles it should use (`style`):

```
window.document.images.alice1.src=
```

```
"alice2.gif"
```

continues on next page

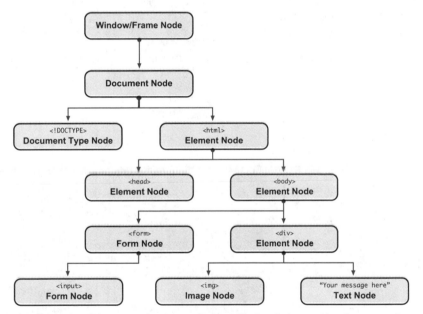

Figure 10.2 The Web page node starts at the top with the window, moving down to each individual element on the page.

UNDERSTANDING THE DOM

Earlier versions of both Netscape and Internet Explorer included their own DOMs, which didn't work the same way. This would be like having two different systems for addressing letters in two different countries. The letters from one country could not be sent to addresses in the other country. The good news is that the W3C published a standardized DOM, to which both Netscape 6+ and Internet Explorer 5+ adhere. In addition, both Safari and Opera also use the W3C standard DOM. Score one for standards! We will be primarily using the W3C standard DOM in this book, but for more details on the older Netscape and Internet Explorer DOMs, see the sidebar "History of the DOM."

Before we learn how to use the DOM to make changes in the Web page, we first need to review a few key ideas: objects and events.

✔ Tips

- Web pages created with CSS can have their properties changed while they are on the screen (that is, dynamically) through a scripting language and the DOM (**Table 10.1**). Because it's available almost universally, most people use JavaScript as their scripting language. CSS, however, can be affected by any scripting language that your browser can handle—VBScript in Internet Explorer, for example.

- When you send a letter within the same country, you don't need to indicate the country in the address. The post office assumes it's going to some place in the same country. The same is true of indicating which window you're referencing with the DOM. It's simply assumed to be the window the code is in. Instead, you begin the DOM with document.

Table 10.1

What the DOM Allows

CAPABILITY	COMPATIBILITY
Change the font and text properties of an element while it's on screen	IE4, N6, S1, O3.5, DOM1
Change the z-index of elements	IE4, N4, S1, O3.5, DOM1
Hide or show elements on the screen	IE4, N4, S1, O3.5, DOM1
Change the position of elements	IE4, N4, S1, O3.5, DOM1
Animate elements on the screen	IE4, N4, S1, O3.5, DOM1
Allow visitors to move objects on the screen	IE4, N4, S1, O3.5, DOM1
Reclip the visible area of an element	IE5, N4, S1, O3.5, DOM1
Change the content of an already-loaded page	IE5, N6, S1, O3.5

CSS Layers?

Often, objects using an ID are referred to as *layers*. These terms can lead to some confusion, however, because the term *layers* was actually coined to describe a similar technology in Netscape. Although any HTML tag can be turned into a CSS layer with the addition of the id attribute, Netscape 4 introduced a <layer> tag to achieve a similar result.

The term *layers* seems to be sticking to CSS objects, however, and Netscape layers have been pretty much forgotten since recent versions of Netscape (6+) do not support them.

To prevent confusion in this book, I will refer specifically to *Netscape layers* and call CSS layers simply *layers*.

History of the DOM

The W3C realized that there would be a need to link scripting languages to objects on a Web page, and it diligently began to work out the best method. Unfortunately, the browser manufacturers couldn't wait, and they introduced their own DOMs before the W3C could set the standard. Better late than never, the W3C released its standardized DOM late in 1998, which has been embraced by the browser-building community.

The Netscape Layer DOM

The Netscape Layer DOM allows you to write scripts to control elements created with the <layer> tag and elements created with CSS positioning. This DOM lets you control the position, visibility, and clipping of the element. Changes made in these properties with either layers or CSS positioning occur on the page immediately.

The Layer DOM does not provide access to CSS properties other than the positioning controls. Thus, you cannot change the font, text, list, mouse, color, background, border, or margin of an object in Netscape 4 after the page has loaded unless you reload the page.

The Layer DOM does not work in Netscape 6 or higher and there was never a version 5 of Netscape. When Netscape started planning Netscape 6 (code-named Mozilla), it decided to start from scratch and attempt to make the browser as standards-compliant as possible. Unfortunately, and to the confusion of many Web designers, this meant abandoning any technologies that were never going to be standards, including the <layer> tag and the Layer DOM.

The Internet Explorer All DOM

The Internet Explorer All DOM allows you to write scripts that can access any element on the screen—at least, any element that Internet Explorer understands. These elements include CSS properties, which let you control the position and visibility of elements on the screen, as well as their appearance. Any changes made in these properties occur on the page immediately, and Internet Explorer rerenders the page to comply.

Thus, any changes made in the font, text, list, mouse, color, background, border, margin, position, or visibility of an object are immediately discernible.

Setting Up an Object

Simply stated, an *object* is an HTML element (see "Understanding the Element's Box" in Chapter 5) that can be uniquely identified in the Web page. The HTML element has a unique address in the browser window that allows it to be accessed by the DOM.

Some objects are accessible by the DOM because of the type of element they are. For example, forms and images can be addressed by using their position in the form or image array for a page. However, this can be difficult to figure out, and it is often much easier to simply give the element a unique identity. Any element in the browser window—at least, any element enclosed within HTML tags—can be identified with an id attribute to give it its own unique address and make it an object, rather than simply an element.

Identifying an HTML element as an object (**Figure 10.3**) allows you to change any of that element's attributes—at least, to the extent that the browser allows.

Figure 10.3 You can act upon the object dynamically using JavaScript and the DOM.

Code 10.2 This code sets up a CSS layer by defining a tag with an ID.

```
○ ○ ○                  Code                        ▭
<!DOCTYPE html PUBLIC "-//W3C//DTD XHTML
→ 1.0 Transitional//EN" "http://www.w3.org/TR/
→ xhtml1/DTD/xhtml1-transitional.dtd">
<html xmlns="http://www.w3.org/1999/xhtml">
<head>
    <meta http-equiv="content-type"
    → content="text/html;charset=utf-8" />
    <title>DHTML &amp; CSS for the WWW |
    → Creating an Object</title>
    <style type="text/css" media="screen"><!--
#object1 {
    position: absolute;
    visibility: visible;
    top: 100px;
    left: 150px;
    width: 210px;
}
    --></style>
</head>
<body>
    <div id="object1">
        <h3>This Is Object 1</h3>
        <img src="alice04.gif" alt="alice"
        → height="298" width="200" border="0" />
    </div>
</body>
</html>
```

To set up an object:

1. #object1 { ... }

   Add an ID rule to your CSS, and define the position as either absolute or relative (see "Defining IDs to Identify an Object" in Chapter 2). You can also add any other definitions you desire, but you must include the position for this object to be a CSS layer (**Code 10.2**).

2. <div id="object1">...</div>

   Apply the ID to an HTML tag—preferably, a <div> tag for absolutely positioned objects or a <span> tag for relatively positioned objects. Notice in this example that not only is the image a part of the object by the text within the <div> tag as well. All elements within the containing tag (the <div> tag, in this example) become a part of the object.

✔ Tip

■ You don't actually have to set the object up as shown in step 1 in order to create an object, all you need to do is add a unique ID to the tag as shown in step 2.

Understanding Events

In the world of JavaScript, *events* occur when something happens in the browser window, usually initiated by the visitor. One example is when the visitor moves the mouse pointer over a link; this action generates a `mouseover` event.

Events can also occur when the browser does something, such as loading a new document (`load`) or leaving a Web page (`unload`).

An *event handler*—which is the event name with the word *on* at the beginning (for example, `onload`)—allows you to define what should happen when a particular event is detected for a particular object (**Figure 10.4**).

Table 10.2 lists some of the more common event handlers that you'll be using. To see all these events on a single page, visit www.webb edenvironments.com/dhtml/eventhandlers, a page I set up to demonstrate how the event handlers work (**Figure 10.5**).

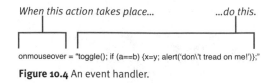

Figure 10.4 An event handler.

Figure 10.5 This Web page contains examples of all the events discussed in this chapter, so you can see them in action.

Table 10.2

Event Handlers

Event Handler	When It Happens	Elements Affected
onload	After an object is loaded	Documents and images
onunload	After the object is no longer loaded	Documents and images
onfocus	When an element is selected	Documents and forms
onblur	When an element is deselected	Documents and forms
onmouseover	When the mouse pointer passes over an area	Links and image map areas
onmouseout	When the mouse pointer passes out of an area	All*
onclick	When an area is clicked in	All*
onmousedown	While mouse button is depressed	All*
onmouseup	When the mouse button is released	All*
onmousemove	As the mouse is moved	Document
onkeydown	While a keyboard key is down	Forms
onkeyup	When a keyboard key is released	Forms
onkeypress	When a keyboard key is down and immediately released	Forms
onresize**	When the browser window or a frame is resized	Document
onmove***	When the browser window is moved	Document

*Images and image maps only in Netscape 4 **Not supported by IE4 ***Not supported by IE4/5 or Netscape 6*

Events and the DOM

If you've used any type of scripting language in an HTML page, you've more than likely seen a DOM in action. The DOM works by describing the path from a JavaScript function to an element on the screen, in response to an event triggered by an action in the browser window (**Figure 10.6**).

✔ Tips

- At first glance, onclick and onmouseup may seem to do the same thing. The click event, however, occurs only after the mouse button has been pressed and released. Both mousedown and mouseup break this action into two separate events, each of which can have a different action associated with it.

- Although the href acts like an onclick event handler, it isn't one, and DHTML code may not run if it's activated from there.

- The event handler can run JavaScript functions, and you can include JavaScript directly in the quotes as well.

- Most changes made in an object's styles with the DOM should be triggered by an event handler. At times, in fact, the JavaScript *must* be triggered by an event to work. I've wasted many, many hours trying to figure out what was wrong with my JavaScript, only to find that I had simply forgotten to trigger the script from an event.

```
          <head>
          <script>
              function toggle() {
                  document.img.button1.src="button_on.gif"
              }
Action    </script>                                               Reaction
          </head>
          <body>
              <a href="nextpage.html" onmouseover="toggle()">
                  <img name="button1" src="button_off.gif">
              </a>
          </body>
```

Action	Event	JavaScript	DOM	Reaction
src="button_off.gif"	onmouseover	toggle()	document.img.button1	src="button_on.gif"
User moves mouse over object	Senses that something has happened to the object	Tells object what to do	locates object on the Web page	Object's image source is changed

Figure 10.6 This process starts with the visitor's action (the mouseover) and ends with the browser's reaction (changing the graphic). In between, the browser senses the action (event), triggers a function, and uses the DOM to change the image's source to a different graphic file.

UNDERSTANDING EVENTS

Using Event Handlers

An event handler connects an action in the browser window to a JavaScript function, which in turn causes some reaction in the browser window.

In this example, when the visitor rolls the mouse over (onmouseover) the diamond graphic (**Figure 10.7**), the original graphic is replaced by a triangle graphic (**Figure 10.8**).

To use an event handler:

1. <a href="#">

   Start the tag to which you want to add an event handler. This typically will either be a link tag (<a>) or one of the form tags (**Code 10.3**) although most browsers will not support events from any object.

2. onmouseover=

   In the tag you started in step 1, type a relevant event handler from Table 10.2, followed by an equals sign (=).

3. "document.getElementById
   → ('object1').src='b_on.gif'"

   Type an opening quote ("), the JavaScript you want executed when the event occurs, and a close quote ("). The JavaScript can be anything you want, including function calls. If you want to run multiple lines of JavaScript off a single event handler, separate the lines with a semicolon (;), but do *not* use a hard return.

Figure 10.7 Before the image is rolled over.

Figure 10.8 After the image is rolled over.

Code 10.3 When the visitor moves the mouse over the area of the link containing the image (b_off.gif), that image changes its source to a different graphic (b_on.gif).

```
<!DOCTYPE html PUBLIC "-//W3C//DTD XHTML
→ 1.0 Transitional//EN" "http://www.w3.org/TR/
→ xhtml1/DTD/xhtml1-transitional.dtd">
<html xmlns="http://www.w3.org/1999/xhtml">
<head>
      <meta http-equiv="content-type"
      → content="text/html;charset=utf-8" />
      <title>DHTML &amp; CSS for the WWW |
      → Detecting Events</title>
</head>
<body>
      <a href="#" onmouseover="document.
      → getElementById('object1').
      → src='b_on.gif'"
         <img id="object1" src="b_off.gif"
         → border="0" />
      </a>
</body>
</html>
```

4. Add as many event handlers as you want to the HTML tag by repeating steps 2 and 3.

5. `>`

   Type a closing chevron (>) to close the tag you started in step 1.

6. `<img src="button_off.gif"`
   `→ id="button1" />`

   Add an image, text, or other HTML content that you want to have trigger the event.

7. `</a>`

   Type the closing tag for the tag you started in step 1.

✔ Tips

■ If you want a single event to perform multiple tasks, add each action inside the quotes, separating actions with a semicolon (;):

   `onclick="action1;action2;action3"`

■ You can not only use event handlers to run JavaScript functions, but also include JavaScript directly inside the quotes.

Where Does the Event Handler Go?

For the sake of backward compatibility with Netscape 4 you will want to place events in the `<body>` tag, `<form>` tags, or link `<a>` tags.

Internet Explorer 4+ and Netscape 6+, however, can generate events from any element in the browser window. Thus, any event handler can be placed with a relevant tag. A `<p>` tag, for example, could support the `onmouseover` event.

Because Netscape 4 accounts for less than 1 percent of the browser market, most designers feel free to use events in an object they desire. If you choose to do this, though, you should consider placing a message on your site for Netscape 4 users letting them know that your site doesn't support their browser.

USING EVENT HANDLERS

Using the DOM

The W3C's ID DOM, or standard DOM, allows you to write scripts that can access any element on the screen (**Figure 10.9**). This allows you to make changes to any CSS property, allowing you to control the position and visibility of objects on the screen, as well as their appearance. Any changes made in these properties occur on the page immediately.

Thus, any changes made in the font, text, list, mouse, color, background, border, margin, position, or visibility of an object are discernible immediately.

To use the DOM to address an object:

1. `var object =`

   Create a variable called `object`, to store the address for the object (see **Code 10.4**).

2. `document.`

   Begin by identifying the object's location. If you're addressing an object on the same page, simply use `document` followed by a period. If you're addressing an object in a different window, start with `window.` and then the window's name with a period after it. If you're addressing an object in a different frame, use `top.` or `parent.` and then the frame's name followed by a period.

3. `getElementById('object1');`

   Add `getElementById` and then, in parentheses, add the ID of the object. The ID can either be the exact object ID in quotes or a string variable that is storing the object ID name.

`document.getElementById('object1').style.top`

Figure 10.9 The Netscape 4 Layer DOM for accessing the CSS top property.

Code 10.4 A JavaScript function using the W3C's ID DOM. The DOM describes a path to a particular layer to find its position and then JavaScript is used to reassign that position.

```
<!DOCTYPE html PUBLIC "-//W3C//DTD XHTML
→ 1.0 Transitional//EN" "http://www.w3.org/TR/
→ xhtml1/DTD/xhtml1-transitional.dtd">
<html xmlns="http://www.w3.org/1999/xhtml">
<head>
    <meta http-equiv="content-type"
    → content="text/html;charset=utf-8" />
    <title>DHTML &amp; CSS for the WWW |
    → Using the DOM</title>
    <script language="Javascript"
    → type="text/javascript">
        function moveObject() {
        var object=document.getElementById
        → ('object1');
        object.style.top=60 + 'px';
        object.style.left=120 + 'px';
    }
    </script>
    <style type="text/css" media="screen"><!--
#object1 {
    visibility:visible;
    position: absolute;
    top: 10px;
    left: 10px
    }
    --></style>
</head>
<body>
    <div id="object1" onclick="moveObject()" >
        This script will run in any browser that
        → uses the W3C's standard<br />
        for DOM, including Internet Explorer 5
        → and Netscape.<br />
            <img src="alice04.gif" height="298"
            → width="200" border="0" />
    </div>
</body></html>
```

Figure 10.10 The object is moving from its original position, across the screen in response to the function that uses the DOM to address the object.

Table 10.3

DHTML-Capable Browsers		
BROWSER	VERSION	DOM
Netscape	4	Layer
	6+	W3C
Internet Explorer	4	All
	5+	All, W3C
	6	All, W3C
Safari	1+	W3C
Opera	3.5+	W3C

4. `object.style.top = 60 + 'px';`

To change an attribute of the object, use the `object` variable with a period after it and then the name of the attribute to be changed. If it's a CSS attribute (for example, `top`), you'll also need to include `style.` before the attribute name (**Figure 10.10**).

✔ Tips

- The code presented here uses the W3C standardized DOM, which will *not* work in Internet Explorer 4 or Netscape 4 (**Table 10.3**). If you need to code for older browsers, see the section "Detecting the DOM Type for Backward Compatibility," later in this chapter.

- Notice that in order to assign a value to `top` or `left` we had to add + `'px'` to the code when assigning the values. In order to be XHTML compliant, all `style` values must be assigned as strings. This is an easy way to turn the number into a string. If your DHTML code doesn't seem to be working, check to make sure that you translated all numeric values into strings.

DHTML in Netscape 4?

One of the many shortcomings of Netscape 4 is that it only allows most events (including `onclick`) to be triggered from the link tag (`<a>`). As if that weren't bad enough, Netscape 4 often uses a very different syntax than Internet Explorer or even Netscape 6+ to do the same things. In this example, we had to code the assignment of our `moveLeft` and `MoveTop` variables because Netscape 4 cannot use strings as values for style properties, which is required for XHTML compatibility. This is just the tip of the iceberg for the kinds of double coding you'll need to do to accommodate Netscape 4. The code in the rest of the book is based on the W3C's standardized DOM, and much of it won't work in Netscape 4. If you need to see examples of code that will work in Netscape 4, you can download it from the support Web site for the second edition of this book: www.webbedenvironments.com/dhtml/2nd/index.html

USING THE DOM

219

Passing Events to a Function

All events in the browser window generate certain information about what occurred, where it occurred, and how it occurred. You can pass this information directly to a JavaScript function so that it can access the object without having to use the `getElementByID` method.

As seems true of all things in Web design, Internet Explorer and Netscape have different methods for implementing event passing. The good news is that the two methods are easy to combine.

To pass an event to a JavaScript function:

1. `function passItOn()`

In the variables being passed to the function, add an **evt** variable to record the event.

2. `var evt = (evt) ? evt :`
`→ ((window.event) ? event : null);`

Internet Explorer uses a slightly different syntax for tracking events. This line of code will bring the Internet Explorer version in line with the W3C standard for the **evt** variable.

3. `alert(evt.clientX);`

You can now use the **evt** variable to access information about the event. In this example, we're accessing the x-position of where the mouse clicked during the event (**Figure 10.11**).

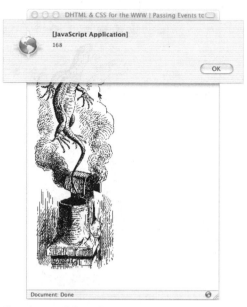

Figure 10.11 Clicking the page displays an alert showing the x-position of where the mouse clicked.

Alert! Results May Vary

If you're using an alert to display the value of the **object** variable (for example, `alert (object)`) you'll see different values depending on which browser you're using. For example, Internet Explorer for Windows will actually show [object]. Rather than showing you the actual value, many browsers will display a variable that is then used to access the object in question. Don't worry, though: This variable contains the same information.

Code 10.5 The event variable passes information about the triggering event to the function, including where the mouse was when it was clicked.

```
<!DOCTYPE html PUBLIC "-//W3C//DTD XHTML
→ 1.0 Transitional//EN" "http://www.w3.org/TR/
→ xhtml1/DTD/xhtml1-transitional.dtd">
<html xmlns="http://www.w3.org/1999/xhtml">
<head>
    <meta http-equiv="content-type"
    → content="text/html;charset=utf-8" />
    <title>DHTML &amp; CSS for the WWW |
    → Passing Events to a Function</title>
    <script><!--
        function passItOn(evt) {
            var evt = (evt) ? evt :
            → ((window.event) ? event : null);
            alert(evt.clientX)
            evt.cancelBubble;
        }
    // -->
</script>
    <style type="text/css" media="screen"><!--
#object1 {
    visibility: visible;
    position: absolute;
    top: 10px;
    left: 10px
    }
    --></style>
</head>
<body>

<div id="object1"  onclick="passItOn(event)">
        <img src="alice13.gif" height="480"
        → width="174" border="0" />
    </div>
</body>
</html>
```

4. `evt.cancelBubble;`

To stop the event from affecting other objects on the page, add `evt.cancelBubble`. This can be left out, but may cause the event to affect other objects on the page unintentionally.

5. `onclick="passItOn(event)"`

Add one or more event handlers to an object to trigger the function (**Code 10.5**). Pass the variable **event** to the function, including information about the triggering event. In this example, the event will fire when the user clicks the image.

✔ Tips

■ The **evt** variable cannot directly access the triggering object. Instead, you'll need to bind the event to an object and then use this ID to access the object. See the following section, "Binding Events to Objects," for more details.

■ Although it may be tempting simply to use event passing in all circumstances to create DHTML, event passing has some shortcomings. For example, Internet Explorer doesn't always respond to events that happen in child elements of the tag containing the event handler. In addition, the object that is being changed is most often not the same object as the one originating the event. I primarily use the `getElementByID` method for the code in this book except where event passing offers a particular advantage.

Binding Events to Objects

Event handlers are most often applied directly to the tag of the object where you want to detect the event. However, another useful technique is to bind an event to one or more objects. You can then use the evt variable to access the object directly and make changes to it without first having to know its ID.

To add a global event handler to a Web page:

1. function initPage() {...}

   Add the function initPage() to your JavaScript. This function prepares the global event handlers to be used, then sets functions to be executed if those events are triggered (**Code 10.6**). Notice that when you call the function:

   document.onclick = errorOn;

   you don't include the parentheses with the function call. You can use any event handler listed in "Understanding Events" earlier in this chapter to set an event for any node in the document.

Code 10.6 The function errorOn() is bound to the document and the function moveTo() is bound to object1.

```
<!DOCTYPE html PUBLIC "-//W3C//DTD XHTML
→ 1.0 Transitional//EN" "http://www.w3.org/TR/
→ xhtml1/DTD/xhtml1-transitional.dtd">
<html xmlns="http://www.w3.org/1999/xhtml">
<head>
    <meta http-equiv="content-type"
    → content="text/html;charset=utf-8" />
    <title>DHTML &amp; CSS for the WWW |
    → Binding Events to an Object</title>
    <script><!--
        function initPage() {
            document.onclick = errorOn;
            document.getElementById('object1').
            → onclick = moveObject;
        }
        function errorOn() {
            alert ('Please do not click here
            → again!')
        }
        function moveObject (evt) {
            var evt = (evt) ? evt : ((window.
            → event) ? event : null);
            var object = document.getElementById
            → (this.id);
            var moveLeft=evt.clientX;
            var moveTop=evt.clientY;
            object.style.left = moveLeft + 'px';
            object.style.top = moveTop + 'px';
        }
// -->
</script>
    <style type="text/css" media="screen"><!--
#object1 {
    visibility: visible;
    position: absolute;
    top: 10px;
    left: 10px;
}
    --></style>
```

(code continues on next page)

Code 10.6 *continued*

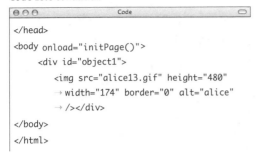

```
</head>
<body onload="initPage()">
    <div id="object1">
        <img src="alice13.gif" height="480"
        → width="174" border="0" alt="alice"
        → /></div>
</body>
</html>
```

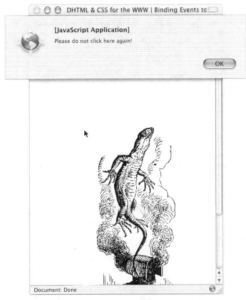

Figure 10.12 Clicking the image causes it to move. Clicking anywhere on the window displays an alert telling you not to click there.

2. `function errorOn(evt) {...}`
`function moveTo() {...}`

Add to your JavaScript the functions that will be run when the events in the function from step 1 are met. In this example, the functions `errorOn()` and `moveObject()` are both triggered when the `onclick` events are triggered in the browser window or on object1. For the `moveObject()` function, we're also passing the `evt` variable to it (see the previous section, "Passing Events to a Function"), allowing us to learn about the triggering event. To address the event we want to change, we can then use

`var object = document.getElementById`
`→ (this.id);`

where `this.id` tells the function to use the ID of the triggering event. This will only work if the event has been bound to the object.

3. `onload="initPage()"`

Add an event handler in the `<body>` tag to trigger the function you created in step 1, which will initialize the bound events for the page (**Figure 10.12**). If this step is left out, nothing will happen.

✔ Tip

- Notice that clicking the image will not only move the image, but also show the alert, because both events are called into play. However, clicking on any empty area of the screen will only trigger the `errorOn()` function.

Using Feature Sensing

The best way to determine whether the browser that is running your script has what it takes to do the job is to ask it. Finding out whether the browser has the feature(s) you need to use is a lot simpler than it sounds and requires only one added line per function.

In most cases, feature sensing is a better alternative than the more common browser sensing (see "Detecting the Browser's Name and Version" in Chapter 11). If the current version of a browser cannot run your script, who's to say that another, more powerful version of the browser won't be released that can run it? Feature sensing will let any able browser that can run the code run it (**Figure 10.13** and **Figure 10.14**).

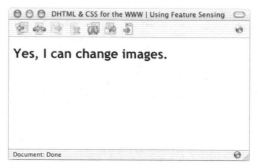

Figure 10.13 This browser can change images.

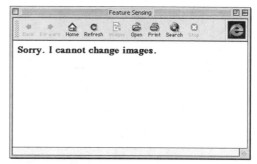

Figure 10.14 Many older browsers, such as Internet Explorer 3, cannot change images. The results now show a different message.

Code 10.7 This code checks to see whether the document.images object is available in this browser, returning "true" if it is.

```
000                    Code
<!DOCTYPE html PUBLIC "-//W3C//DTD XHTML
→ 1.0 Transitional//EN" "http://www.w3.org/TR/
→ xhtml1/DTD/xhtml1-transitional.dtd">
<html xmlns="http://www.w3.org/1999/xhtml">
<head>
    <meta http-equiv="content-type"
    → content="text/html;charset=utf-8" />
    <title>DHTML &amp; CSS for the WWW |
    → Using Feature Sensing</title>
</head>
<body>
    <script language="JavaScript">
        if (document.images) {
            document.writeln('<h1>Yes, I can
            → change images.</h1>');
        }
        else {
            document.writeln('<h1>Sorry.
            → I cannot change images.</h1>');
        }
    </script>
</body>
</html>
```

To sense whether a JavaScript feature is available:

1. if (document.images)

   Within a `<script>` container, set up a conditional statement as shown in **Code 10.7**. Within the parentheses of the if statement, place the JavaScript feature you need to use. In this example, you're checking to see whether the browser can handle the image object.

2. { document.writeln('<h1>Yes,
   → I can change images.</h1>')}

   Within {} brackets, type the JavaScript code you want to execute if this feature is available on this browser.

3. else { document.writeln('<h1>Sorry.
   → I cannot change images.</h1>')}

   You can include an else statement specifying the code to be run in the event that the JavaScript feature for which you're testing is not available.

Detecting the DOM Type for Backward Compatibility

I mentioned earlier that Netscape 4 and Internet Explorer 4 use different DOMs to address objects in the document. This can be a headache if you have to code for both of these browsers. But never fear—there's an easier way to make these two browsers play together, as well as with newer browsers using the W3C standardized DOM.

Like the Rosetta stone, the information returned from detecting the browser's DOM type can translate the DOM for a particular object in the Web page being displayed by the browser. The basic idea is to include methods for all three DOM types in a function called findDOM(), which uses if statements to determine which DOM type to use. A DHTML function then uses findDOM() to build the address for a particular object and access that object's properties (**Figure 10.15**).

To create a backward-compatible DOM wrapper:

1. function findDOM(objectID,
   → withStyle) {...}

   Add the findDOM() function to your JavaScript (**Code 10.8**). This function takes the ID for the desired object and creates an object for the particular browser being used. Then you can use the function to change the object's style properties (if (withSTYLE)) or to change other properties associated with the object.

Figure 10.15 The findDOM() function allows this script to run in any DHTML-capable browser, including Netscape 4 and Internet Explorer 4.

Code 10.8 The Cross Browser DOM script uses feature sensing to determine which DOM type is being used and then uses that information to address the object or the object styles (if the variable with Style is set to 1) using the browser's DOM.

```
<html>
<head>
    <meta http-equiv="content-type"
    → content="text/html;charset=utf-8">
    <title>DHTML &amp; CSS for the WWW |
    → Detecting the DOM Type for Backward-
    → Compatibility</title>
    <script><!--
function findDOM(objectID, withStyle) {
    if (withStyle) {
        if (document.getElementById) return
        → (document.getElementById(objectID).
        → style) ;
        else if (document.all) return
        → (document.all[objectID].style);
        else if ((navigator.appName.indexOf
        → ('Netscape') != -1) && (parseInt
        → (navigator.appVersion) == 4)) return
        → (document.layers[objectID]);
    }
    else {
        if (document.getElementById) return
        → (document.getElementById(objectID)) ;
        else if (document.all) return
        → (document.all[objectID]);
```

(code continues on next page)

Code 10.8 *continued*

```
            else if ((navigator.appName.indexOf
            → ('Netscape') != -1) && (parseInt
            → (navigator.appVersion) == 4)) return
            → (document.layers[objectID]);
        }
    }
function moveObject (objectID) {
    var objectStyle = findDOM(objectID,true);
    if (document.getElementById) {
        moveLeft = 120 + 'px';
        moveTop = 60 + 'px';

}
    else {
        moveLeft = 120;
        moveTop = 60;
    }
    objectStyle.left = moveLeft ;
    objectStyle.top = moveTop;
}
// -->
</script>
    <style type="text/css" media="screen"><!--
#object1 {
    visibility: show;
    position: absolute;
    top: 10px;
    left: 10px
}
    --></style>
</head>
<body>

<div id="object1">
    <a onclick="moveObject('object1')"
    → href="#">
        <img src="alice14.gif" alt="alice"
        → border="0"> </a></div>
</body>
</html>
```

2. `if (document.getElementById) return` `→ (document.getElementById` `→ (objectID).style) ;`

Each DOM type is tested to see whether it's the one used by this browser. If the W3C's ID DOM type is used to locate the object on the Web page the object's address is passed back to the function.

Now that you've translated the various DOMs into one common language, you're ready to use this language to control elements on the screen through a JavaScript function.

3. `var objectStyle = findDOM` `→ (objectID,true);`

In your JavaScript, set up a function that invokes the findDOM() function. In this example, I've set up two variables. This variable records the DOM with the style:

`var objectStyle =` `→ findDOM(objectID,true)`

This variable records the DOM without the style:

`var object = findDOM` `→ (objectID,false);`

4. `onclick="moveObject('object1')"`

Use an event handler to trigger the function you set up in step 3.

✔ Tip

- You can use any name you want for the dom variable, but I prefer to use object-Style if I'm going to use it to access an object's styles, or just plain dom if I'm accessing any other property of the object.

LEARNING ABOUT YOUR ENVIRONMENT

"To change your world, you must first know yourself." I don't know whether this is an ancient proverb or whether I just made it up, but it definitely applies to DHTML. Many of the functions you will be creating to add interactivity to your Web page rely on knowing where something is, how big it is, and what it is doing.

This chapter deals with things that you can learn about the environment in which an object is being displayed—such as the screen size and browser-window size. The two chapters after this will show you how to then find out information about the object itself (Chapter 12) and events triggered by an object (Chapter 13).

Detecting the Operating System

The application-version object (`navigator.appVersion`) will tell you the operating system of the browser used to view the site, although it's embedded in string of other information (**Figures 11.1** and **11.2**). This information can be very useful, especially if you need to overcome font-size inconsistencies or other OS-related incompatibilities.

To detect the operating system being used:

1. `var isMac = 0;`

   Set up three variables (`isMac`, `isWin`, `isOtherOS`) in your JavaScript to record which OS the browser is using. Each of these variables is initially set to 0 (false) and will be reassigned to 1 (true) if the designated operating system is being used (**Code 11.1**).

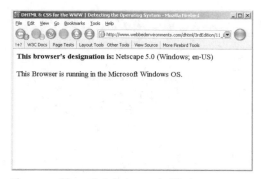

Figure 11.1 The code is being run in Windows.

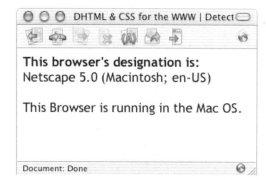

Figure 11.2 The same code is being run on a Mac, although there is no way to tell the difference between the classic Mac OS and OS X.

Code 11.1 This code first writes the complete *appName* and *appVersion* on the page. It then uses that information to determine the operating system so that it can display the correct message.

```
<!DOCTYPE html PUBLIC "-//W3C//DTD XHTML
→ 1.0 Transitional//EN" "http://www.w3.org/TR/
→ xhtml1/DTD/xhtml1-transitional.dtd">
<html xmlns="http://www.w3.org/1999/xhtml">
<head>
    <meta http-equiv="content-type"
    → content="text/html;charset=utf-8" />
    <title>DHTML &amp; CSS for the WWW |
    → Detecting the Operating System</title>
</head>
<script language="JavaScript"
→ type="text/javascript">
var isMac = 0;
var isWin = 0;
var isOtherOS = 0;
</script>
<body>
    <script language="JavaScript"
    → type="text/javascript">
document.write('<b>This browser\'s designation
→ is:</b> ');
document.write(navigator.appName + ' ');
document.write(navigator.appVersion);
    if (navigator.appVersion.indexOf('Mac')
    → != -1) {isMac = 1;}
    else {
        if (navigator.appVersion.indexOf
        → ('Win') != -1) {isWin = 1;}
        else {isOtherOS = 1; }
    }
document.write('<br><br>');
if (isMac) {document.write('This Browser is
→ running in the Mac OS.');}
else {
    if (isWin) {document.write('This Browser
    → is running in the Microsoft Windows
    → OS.');}
    else {
        if (isOtherOS) {document.write
        → ('RESISTANCE IS FUTILE...YOU WILL BE
        → ASSIMILATED');}
    }
}}
</script>
</body>
</html>
```

2. `if (navigator.appVersion.indexOf`
`→ ('Mac') != -1) {isMac = 1;}`

To reassign the variables from step 1, check the name of the OS being used. This code looks for the word *Mac* in the **appVersion**, and changes **isMac** to 1 if it finds it.

3. `else {`

`if (navigator.appVersion.indexOf`
`→ ('Win') != -1) {isWin = 1;}`

To detect whether Windows is being used, you would simply look for *Win* in code version and set **isWin** to 1.

4. `else {isOtherOS = 1; }`

Finally, you need to add a catchall in case another operating system (such as Linux) is being used.

5. `if (isMac) {...}`

Now you can use the variables you set up in steps 1 and 2 for the OS that is being used. In this example I simply have a message written out on the screen to tell the viewer which OS they are using.

✔ Tips

- One of the most common uses of OS detection is to help overcome the font-size and color incompatibilities between the Mac and Windows operating systems (see "Customizing Styles for the OS or Browser" in Chapter 16).

- You could also add detection for a specific operating system besides Macintosh and Windows. All you need to know is how the OS identifies itself in the **appVersion** string and then look for that word using the indexOf method.

DETECTING THE OPERATING SYSTEM

Detecting the Browser's Name and Version

Although feature sensing is better for determining what a browser can and cannot do (see "Using Feature Sensing" in Chapter 10), sometimes you need to be able to tell your code what to do based on the type and version of browser in which the Web page is being viewed (**Figures 11.3** and **11.4**).

Initially, this information comes in two big chunks. The first chunk gives the full name of the browser (`navigator.appName`). The second chunk includes the version of the browser, along with compatibility information and the OS being used (`navigator.appVersion`). Although having the exact name and version of the browser is useful, that information can be a bit bulky when it comes time to code. You can use these chunks to get the data you require and store it in variables for later use (**Code 11.2**).

To determine the browser type and version:

1. `var isNS = 0;`

Set up three variables (`isNS`, `isIE`, `isOtherBrowser`) in your JavaScript to record which browser is displaying the code. These variables are initially set to `0` (false) and will be reassigned to `1` (true) if the designated browser is being used.

2. `if (navigator.appName.indexOf`
`→ ('Netscape') != -1) {isNS = 1;}`

To reassign the variables from step 1, check for the name of the browser. This code looks for the word *Netscape* in the `appName`, and changes `isNS` to `1` if it finds it.

3. `else { if (navigator.appName.indexOf`
`→ ('Microsoft Internet Explorer')`
`→ != -1) {isIE = 1;} }`

Set up an `else` that does the same to `isIE` for *Microsoft Internet Explorer*.

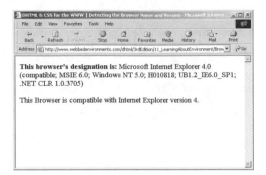

Figure 11.3 The code is being run in Internet Explorer 6 on a Windows machine. Notice that the browser's designation includes (`compatible; MSIE 6.0; Windows NT 5.0`). It will show up, however, as being Internet Explorer 4 so that it can run older JavaScript code.

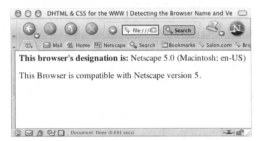

Figure 11.4 The code is being run in Netscape 7 on a Mac. Notice, though, that it claims to be Netscape 5. Although there was never an official release of Netscape 5, it makes a good breaking point between Netscape 4 and Netscape 6, which are completely different browsers.

Feature Sensing or Browser Sensing?

Browser sensing is often used instead of feature sensing to determine whether a DHTML function should be run in a particular browser. Using browser sensing, however, means that you have to know exactly what code will or will not run in the browsers you are including or excluding.

Using browser sensing to determine DHTML compatibility can cause problems, especially when newer browser versions either add new abilities or fix bugs that previously prevented code from working. I recommend using feature sensing if at all possible.

Code 11.2 This code first writes the complete *appName* and *appVersion* on the page. It then uses that information to determine the browser name and version number so it can display the correct message.

```
<!DOCTYPE html PUBLIC "-//W3C//DTD XHTML
→ 1.0 Transitional//EN" "http://www.w3.org/TR/
→ xhtml1/DTD/xhtml1-transitional.dtd">
<html xmlns="http://www.w3.org/1999/xhtml">
<head>
    <meta http-equiv="content-type"
    → content="text/html;charset=utf-8" />
    <title>DHTML &amp; CSS for the WWW |
    → Detecting the Browser Name and Version
    → </title>
</head>
<body>
    <script language="JavaScript"
    → type="text/javascript">
document.write('<b>This browser\'s designation
→ is:</b> ');
document.write(navigator.appName + ' ');
document.write(navigator.appVersion);
var isNS = 0;
var isIE = 0;
var isOtherBrowser = 0;
if (navigator.appName.indexOf('Netscape')
→ != -1) {isNS = 1;}
    else {
    if (navigator.appName.indexOf('Microsoft
    → Internet Explorer') != -1) {isIE = 1;}
        else {isOtherBrowser = 1;}
    }
browserVersion = parseInt(navigator.
→ appVersion);
document.write('<br><br>');
if (isNS) {document.write('This Browser is
→ compatible with Netscape version ');}
    else {
    if (isIE) {document.write('This Browser
    → is compatible with Internet Explorer
    → version ');}
        else {
        if (isOtherBrowser) {document.write
        → ('I do not recognize this browser
        → type. Version = ');}
}}
document.write(browserVersion +'.');
</script>
</body>
</html>
```

4. `else {isOtherBrowser = 1;}`

Finally, add a catch all to detect if the browser is not identifying itself as either Netscape or Internet Explorer.

5. `browserVersion = parseInt(navigator.`
`→ appVersion);`

The number of the browser version is assigned to the variable `browserVersion`.

6. `if (isNS) {...}`

Now you can use the variables you set up in steps 1, 2, and 3 for the particular browser and version.

✔ Tip

■ There are, of course, more than two browsers. But most non–Internet Explorer and non-Netscape browsers show up as one or the other, depending on which browser they are most compatible with. For example, the Opera browser shows up as Microsoft Internet Explorer so it will not be excluded due to browser-sensing Web sites that allow their HTML to be viewed only by particular browsers (**Figure 11.5**).

Figure 11.5 The browser-sensing code is being run in Opera 5. Notice that Opera claims to be Internet Explorer. Most JavaScript code is designed to sense Internet Explorer or Netscape and may exclude other browsers. The Opera browser shows up as Internet Explorer so Opera users will not be left out in the cold.

Finding the Page's Location and Title

The URL (Uniform Resource Locator) of a Web page is its unique address on the Web. The title is the designation you give that page between the `<title>` tags in the head of your document. You can easily display these two useful bits of information on the originating Web page using `self.location` and `document.title` objects (**Code 11.3** and **Figure 11.6**).

To find the page's location and title:

1. `var pageURI = self.location;`

Add the variable `pageURI` to your JavaScript, and assign to it the value `self.location`. This value is the address of your Web page.

2. `var pageTitle = document.title;`

Add the variable `pageTitle` to your JavaScript, and assign to it the value `document.title`. This value is the title of your document—that is, whatever you place between the `<title>` and `</title>` tags on the page.

You can now use these variables for a variety of purposes. The simplest is to write them out on the page, as Code 11.3 does. In addition, I used the page's location to set up the title as a link back to this page.

✔ Tip

- When creating a printer-friendly version of the page, adding the URL for the original link at the bottom is a great way of ensuring that the reader can find the original source.

Code 11.3 The variables `pageTitle` and `pageURI` are defined and then displayed on the page. The URI is also used to create a link back to this page when the user clicks the title.

```
<!DOCTYPE html PUBLIC "-//W3C//DTD XHTML
  1.0 Transitional//EN" "http://www.w3.org/TR/
  xhtml1/DTD/xhtml1-transitional.dtd">
<html xmlns="http://www.w3.org/1999/xhtml">
<head>
     <meta http-equiv="content-type"
        content="text/html;charset=utf-8" />
     <title>DHTML &amp; CSS for the WWW |
        Finding Page Location and Title</title>
</head>
<body>
     <script language="JavaScript"
        type="text/javascript"><!--
var pageURI = self.location;
var pageTitle = document.title;
document.writeln('The location of the page
  titled <i><a href="' + pageURI + '">' +
  pageTitle + '</a></i> is: <br>');
document.writeln(pageURI);
// -->
     </script>
</body>
</html>
```

Figure 11.6 The linked title and page URL are displayed.

Figure 11.7 The live area of the Windows screen includes everything but the bottom menu bar. However, this bar may appear on any side of the screen at the user's discretion.

Determining the Screen Dimensions

The screen—that glowing, slightly rounded panel you stare at all day—is where all the windows that make up your Web site reside. You can try making Web sites with Morse code or punch cards, but trust me on this one: The computer monitor is currently the best medium for displaying Web sites (**Figures 11.7** and **11.8**).

continues on next page

Figure 11.8 The live area of the Mac OS X screen is everywhere but the top menu bar and approximately 6 pixels on the left and right sides. The Mac OS always displays a menu bar at the top of the screen.

What Screen Size Should I Use for My Web Sites?

Although an 800 x 600–pixel screen size has become the design standard for most Web designers, 58 percent of Web users are now using screens as large as 1024 x 768 pixels (according to StatMarket, www.statmarket.com).

Keep in mind, however, that large screen sizes don't necessarily mean that the browser window will be open to that size. Significant content and design elements should be placed "above the fold" so that they're visible without vertical scrolling, and all important user-interface elements must be visible without horizontal scrolling within the 800 x 600 screen.

As with any design issue, it's important to keep your audience in mind. Always try to find out the average size of the monitor being used by the people likely to view your Web site. Although it's useful to know what the average Web browser is using, it could be that 100 percent of your audience falls in that 42 percent of viewers with smaller screen sizes.

One of the frustrations of Web design, however, is never knowing the size of the area in which your design will be placed or how much space is actually available. To find out how much space you're working with, you can use the `screen.width` and `screen.height` objects to find the total dimensions of the screen, and the `screen.availHeight` and `screen.availWidth` objects to find the actual available space on the screen once menus and other interface elements are taken into account (**Code 11.4**).

So why don't you just ask the screen how big it is (**Figure 11.9**)?

To find the screen's dimensions:

1. `var screenHeight = screen.height;`

   Add the variables `screenHeight` and `screenWidth` to your JavaScript, and assign to them the values `screen.height` and `screen.width`, respectively. These variables will now record the *total* height and width of the screen, in pixels.

2. `var liveScreenHeight =`
   → `screen.availHeight;`

   Add the variables `liveScreen-Height` and `liveScreenWidth` to your JavaScript, and assign to them the values `screen.availHeight` and `screen.availWidth`, respectively. These variables will now record the *live* (available) height and width of the screen, in pixels. This differs from the total, in that it does not include any menu bars added by the OS—only the area in which windows can be displayed.

Code 11.4 This code determines both the total and the live dimensions of the entire screen and assigns these values to variables, which it then uses to write the values in the browser window.

```
<!DOCTYPE html PUBLIC "-//W3C//DTD XHTML
→ 1.0 Transitional//EN" "http://www.w3.org/TR/
→ xhtml1/DTD/xhtml1-transitional.dtd">
<html xmlns="http://www.w3.org/1999/xhtml">
<head>
    <meta http-equiv="content-type"
    → content="text/html;charset=utf-8" />
    <title>DHTML &amp; CSS for the WWW |
    → Finding the Screen Dimensions</title>
</head>
<body>
    <script language="JavaScript"
    → type="text/javascript"><!--
var screenHeight = screen.height;
var screenWidth = screen.width;
var liveScreenHeight = screen.availHeight;
var liveScreenWidth = screen.availWidth;
document.writeln('Your total screen height is '
→ + screenHeight + 'px <br><br>');
document.writeln('Your total screen width is '
→ + screenWidth + 'px <br><br>');
document.writeln('Your live screen height is '
→ + liveScreenHeight + 'px <br><br>');
document.writeln('Your live screen width is '
→ + liveScreenWidth + 'px <br><br>');
// -->
    </script>
</body>
</html>
```

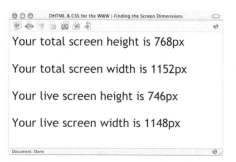

Figure 11.9 The code displays both the total and live dimensions of the screen for my computer.

DETERMINING THE SCREEN DIMENSIONS

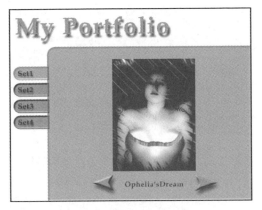

Figure 11.10 An image in all its 32-bit glory.

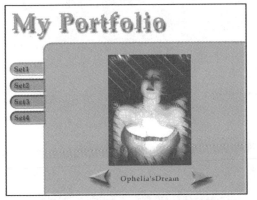

Figure 11.11 The same image in ho-hum 8-bit grayscale. Notice how much rougher the transitions are between areas of color than in the 32-bit version above.

Determining the Number of Colors (Bit Depth)

Once upon a time, color was one of the biggest nightmares a Web designer could face. Not all computers are created equal, especially when it comes to color. On your high-end professional machine, you design a brilliant Web page with bold colors, deep drop shadows, antialiased text, and 3-D buttons (**Figure 11.10**). But on the machine across the hall, it looks like a grainy color photo that's been left out in the sun too long (**Figure 11.11**).

The problem was that some computers displayed millions of colors, while others displayed only a few thousand or *(gasp)* a few hundred or less.

continues on next page

So knowing the number of colors the person viewing your site can actually see might be useful (**Code 11.5**). Older machines are in use, and you may need to be able to design around these machines' limitations (**Figures 11.12** and **11.13**).

To detect the number of colors:

◆ `screen.colorDepth`

The number of colors that the visitor's screen can currently display is in the screen's color-depth object. Using this code will return a color-bit depth value as shown in **Table 11.1**.

✔ Tip

■ Over the past several years, as old machines have been thrown out and new machines brought in, the problem of color has diminished rapidly.

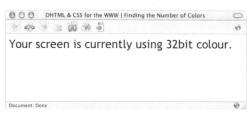

Figure 11.12 The code displays the bit depth of the monitor—in this case, 32-bit.

Table 11.1

Pixel-Depth Values	
COLOR-BIT DEPTH	NO. OF COLORS
4	16
8	256
16	65,536
32	16.7 million

Code 11.5 The function `findColors()` returns one of the values in Table 11.1, depending on the number of colors available on the computer that is being used.

```
<!DOCTYPE html PUBLIC "-//W3C//DTD XHTML
→ 1.0 Transitional//EN" "http://www.w3.org/TR/
→ xhtml1/DTD/xhtml1-transitional.dtd">
<html xmlns="http://www.w3.org/1999/xhtml">
<head>
    <meta http-equiv="content-type"
    → content="text/html;charset=utf-8" />
    <title>DHTML &amp; CSS for the WWW |
    → Finding the Number of Colors</title>
</head>
<body>
    <script language="JavaScript"
    → type="text/javascript"><!--
function findColors() {
    return (screen.colorDepth);
}
document.write('Your screen is currently using '
→ + findColors() + 'bit colour.');
    // -->
    </script>
</body>
</html>
```

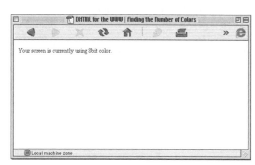

Figure 11.13 The code displays the bit depth of the monitor—in this case, 8-bit.

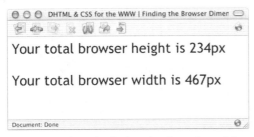

Figure 11.14 The code displays the dimensions of the Netscape browser window.

Determining the Browser Window's Dimensions

In Netscape, the browser window's current width and height can be determined. (Note: Internet Explorer does not support this JavaScript.) This information is the total width and height of the browser window, including all the controls around the display area (**Figure 11.14**), and can be accessed using the outerHeight and outerWidth objects (**Code 11.6**).

Code 11.6 The functions findBrowserHeight() and findBrowserWidth() return the dimensions of the browser window, in pixels. Another feature I added to this code is that when the page is resized, the values are recalculated by reloading the page.

```
<!DOCTYPE html PUBLIC "-//W3C//DTD XHTML 1.0 Transitional//EN" "http://www.w3.org/TR/xhtml1/DTD/
→ xhtml1-transitional.dtd">
<html xmlns="http://www.w3.org/1999/xhtml">
<head>
    <meta http-equiv="content-type" content="text/html;charset=utf-8" />
    <title>DHTML &amp; CSS for the WWW | Finding the Browser Dimensions</title>
    <script language="JavaScript" type="text/javascript"><!--
function findBrowserHeight() {
    if (window.outerHeight != null)
        return window.outerHeight;
    return null;
}
function findBrowserWidth() {
    if (window.outerWidth != null)
        return window.outerWidth;
    return null;
}
    // -->
    </script>
</head>
<body onresize="self.location.reload()">
    <script language="JavaScript" type="text/javascript"><!--
browserHeight = findBrowserHeight();
browserWidth = findBrowserWidth();
if (browserHeight != null) {
```

(code continues on next page)

To find the browser window's dimensions:

1. `window.outerHeight`

   Create a function that returns the value of the outer height of the window. This value is in pixels.

2. `window.outerWidth`

   Create a function that returns the value of the outer width of the browser window. This value is in pixels.

✔ Tip

- The live area of the browser window can be determined in both Internet Explorer and Netscape (see the following section, "Determining the Page's Visible Dimensions").

Code 11.6 *continued*

```
        document.writeln('Your total browser height
        → is ' + browserHeight + 'px <br><br>'); }
        else {document.writeln('The browser
        → window\'s height cannot be determined.
        → <br><br>'); }
if (browserWidth != null) {
        document.writeln('Your total browser width
        → is ' + browserWidth + 'px <br><br>'); }
        else {document.writeln('The browser
        → window\'s width cannot be determined.
        → '); }
        // -->
        </script>
</body>
</html>
```

URI or URL?

Notice that I call the variable that stores the page's location *pageURI* instead of *pageURL*. "URL" stands for Uniform Resource Locator, whereas "URI" stands for Uniform Resource Identifier. What's the difference? Not much, really, but for some reason the World Wide Web Consortium decided that the more commonly used URL was too specific a term and decided to switch to URI instead.

Does this really change your life? No.

Should you start using URI instead of URL when referring to a Web page's address? Only if you want to confuse your friends and impress your enemies.

Determining the Page's Visible Dimensions

Figure 11.15 Loading the page triggers an alert that returns the dimensions of the browser window's live area.

Knowing the size of the browser window is nice (see the previous section, "Determining the Browser Window's Dimensions"), but a much more useful ability is finding the dimensions of the live area in which your content will be displayed (**Figure 11.15**). This is the actual area you have in which to display your Web page, taking into account the current size of the window as well as all of the browser's chrome. These dimensions are available in the clientHeight and clientWidth objects (**Code 11.7**).

Code 11.7 The functions findLivePageHeight() and findLivePageWidth() return the dimensions of the browser window's live area, in pixels.

```
<!DOCTYPE html PUBLIC "-//W3C//DTD XHTML 1.0 Transitional//EN" "http://www.w3.org/TR/xhtml1/DTD/
    xhtml1-transitional.dtd">
<html xmlns="http://www.w3.org/1999/xhtml">
<head>
    <meta http-equiv="content-type" content="text/html;charset=utf-8" />
    <title>DHTML &amp; CSS for the WWW | Finding the Page Dimensions</title>
    <script language="JavaScript" type="text/javascript"><!--
function findLivePageHeight() {
    if (window.innerHeight)
        return window.innerHeight;
    if (document.body.clientHeight)
        return document.body.clientHeight;
    return (null);
}
function findLivePageWidth() {
    if (window.innerWidth)
        return window.innerWidth;
    if (document.body.clientWidth)
        return document.body.clientWidth;
    return (null);
}
function pageDim() {
```

(code continues on next page)

DETERMINING THE PAGE'S VISIBLE DIMENSIONS

To find the dimensions of the live area:

1. `function findLivePageHeight() {...}`

Add the function `findLivePageHeight()` to your JavaScript. This function uses feature sensing to ensure that `document.body.clientHeight` can be used with the browser and then returns the browser's live display height.

2. `function findLivePageWidth() {...}`

Add the function `findLivePageWidth()` to your JavaScript. This function uses feature sensing to ensure that `document.body.clientWidth` can be used with the browser and then returns the browser's live display width.

3. `function pageDim() {...}`

Add a function that calls the `findLivePageHeight()` and `findLivePageWidth()` functions. In this case, we're simply using the functions to display an alert for the current dimensions.

4. `onload="pageDim()"`

Add an event handler to trigger the `pageDim()` function from step 3.

✔ Tips

■ If you're creating a page with content layout dependent on the live page area, you may want to force the page to reload if the user resizes the browser, by placing the following code in the <body> tag:

`onresize="self.location.reload()"`

■ Netscape 6+ can also use the `window.innerHeight` and `window.innerWidth` objects to determine the live page dimensions. However, since Internet Explorer only supports the `clientWidth` and `clientHeight` objects, these are preferred.

Code 11.7 *continued*

```
        livePageHeight = findLivePageHeight();
        livePageWidth = findLivePageWidth();
        alert ('Visible Page Width: ' +
        ⤳ livePageWidth + 'px; Visible Page
        ⤳ Height: ' + livePageHeight + 'px');
}
// -->
</script>
</head>
<body onresize="self.location.reload()"
⤳ onload="pageDim()">
        <div>
            <img src="alice17.gif" height="480"
            ⤳ width="640" border="0" alt="alice" />
        </div>
</body>
</html>
```

Figure 11.16 An alert appears, telling you how far the page has been scrolled, in pixels.

Determining the Page's Scroll Position

CSS positioning works on the basis of offsetting an object from the top and left corners of the page when it loads. If the page scrolls down, however, the origin (top-left corner) scrolls along with it. Fortunately, you can ask the browser how far down (`scrollTop`) or over (`scrollLeft`) it has scrolled (**Code 11.8** and **Figure 11.16**).

Code 11.8 The functions `findScrollLeft()` and `FindScrollTop()` determine the scroll position of the page. You can employ these functions in your Web page in a variety of ways. You can display the result of running the functions directly (as shown in this example) or assign the values to variables that you can use and change.

```
<!DOCTYPE html PUBLIC "-//W3C//DTD XHTML 1.0 Transitional//EN" "http://www.w3.org/TR/xhtml1/DTD/
→ xhtml1-transitional.dtd">
<html xmlns="http://www.w3.org/1999/xhtml">
<head>
    <meta http-equiv="content-type" content="text/html;charset=utf-8" />
    <title>DHTML &amp; CSS for the WWW | Finding the Scroll Position</title>
    <script language="JavaScript" type="text/javascript"><!--
function findScrollLeft() {
    if (document.body.scrollLeft)
        return document.body.scrollLeft;
    return (null);
}
function findScrollTop() {
    if (document.body.scrollTop)
        return document.body.scrollTop;
    return (null);
}
    // -->
    </script>
</head>
<body>
    Scoll the window and then click the image to find your current scroll position.<br />
        <a href="javascript:alert ('Scrolled From Top: ' + findScrollTop() + 'px; Scrolled From Left: ' +
        → findScrollLeft() + 'px');"><img src="alice16.gif" height="477" width="640" border="0" /> </a>
</body>
</html>
```

To find the page's scroll position:

1. `function findScrollLeft() {...}`

Add the function `findScrollLeft()` to your JavaScript. This function uses feature sensing to check that the browser supports `document.body.scrollLeft` and then returns the left scroll position.

2. `function findScrollTop() {...}`

Add the function `findScrollTop()` to your JavaScript. This function uses feature sensing to check that the browser supports `document.body.scrollTop` and then returns the top scroll position.

✔ Tips

■ Netscape 6 (all OSes) does something very silly when a frame's scrolling is set to no. It not only makes the scrollbars disappear, but also prevents the frame from scrolling at all—even when using the JavaScript code presented here. Netscape 7 seems to have corrected this unwanted feature.

■ Netscape can also use the `window.pageXOffset` and `window.pageYOffset` objects to determine the scroll position. However, since Internet Explorer only supports the `scrollLeft` and `scrollTop` methods, these are preferred.

LEARNING
ABOUT AN OBJECT

In Chapter 10, we looked at how to turn an element defined by HTML tags into an object that can then be addressed by the Document Object Model. Using the DOM, you can find out information about the object, such as its size, where it is, and whether it is visible or not.

All the information gained about the environment in the previous chapter was derived from asking the browser questions, such as its type and screen size. In this chapter, we will be looking at what information can be gained by asking objects in the browser window about themselves.

Detecting Which Object Was Clicked

In Chapter 10, I showed you how to use evt to find the object in which an event originated. Using DHTML, though, you can also determine the ID of the object in which the event occurred (**Figure 12.1**). For Internet Explorer, this entails querying the srcElement object; for Netscape, it means using the target object (**Code 12.1**).

Figure 12.1 Pick an Alice, any Alice.

Code 12.1 The findObjectID() function will identify the object that triggered the event by using the evt object that is passed to it.

```
<!DOCTYPE html PUBLIC "-//W3C//DTD XHTML 1.0 Transitional//EN" "http://www.w3.org/TR/xhtml1/DTD/
→ xhtml1-transitional.dtd">
<html xmlns="http://www.w3.org/1999/xhtml">
<head>
    <meta http-equiv="content-type" content="text/html;charset=utf-8" />
    <title>DHTML &amp; CSS for the WWW | Detecting Which Object Was Clicked</title>
    <script language="JavaScript" type="text/javascript"><!--
function findObjectID(evt) {
    var objectID = (evt.target) ? evt.target.id : ((evt.srcElement) ? evt.srcElement.id : null);
    if (objectID)
        alert('You clicked ' + objectID + '.');
    return;
}
    // -->
    </script>
<style type="text/css" media="screen"><!--
#alice1 {
    visibility: visible;
    position: absolute;
    top: 5px;
```

(code continues on next page)

Code 12.1 *continued*

```
                      Code
    left: 5px
}
#alice2 {
    visibility: visible;
    position: absolute;
    top: 150px;
    left: 200px;
}
#alice3 {
    visibility: visible;
    position: absolute;
    top: 5px;
    left: 300px;
}
--></style>
</head>
<body>
    <img id="alice1" onclick="findObjectID
    → (event)" src="alice04.gif" height="448"
    → width="301" border="0" />
    → <img id="alice2" onclick="findObjectID
    → (event)" src="alice22.gif" height="482"
    → width="329" border="0" /> <img id=
    → "alice3" onclick="findObjectID(event)"
    → src="alice30.gif" height="480"
    → width="353" border="0" />
</body>
</html>
```

To determine the element in which the event occurred:

1. `function findObjectID(evt) {...}`

Add the function `findObjectID()` to the JavaScript in the head of your document. This script determines the CSS element on the screen in which the event occurred and then displays an alert telling you which one it was. To do this, we'll need to adapt the event equalizer to find the target (Netscape) or source element (Internet Explorer) of the event, which can then be used to find the object's ID:

```
var objectID = (evt.target) ?
→ evt.target.id : ((evt.srcElement) ?
→ evt.srcElement.id : null);
```

2. `#alice1 {...}`

Set up your CSS elements, using whatever style properties you want. In this example, I set up three images (`alice1`, `alice2`, and `alice3`), each with a unique ID.

3. `onclick="findObjectID(event)"`

Add an event handler to trigger the function you created in step 1, and pass to it the `event` object.

✔ Tip

■ Once the object ID has been found using the `evt` variable, you can then use that to address the object and make changes to its properties.

Determining an Object's Dimensions

All objects have a width and height that determine their dimensions (see "Understanding the Element's Box" in Chapter 5). For images, the width and height are an intrinsic part of the object. For most objects you'll be using the width and height styles to set their dimensions. However, to then find the width and height of an object using JavaScript, you'll use the offsetWidth and offsetHeight objects (**Code 12.2** and **Figure 12.2**).

Figure 12.2 An alert appears, telling you the dimensions of the object—in this case, the object that has the image in it.

Code 12.2 The functions findWidth() and FindHeight() determine the dimensions of an individual object on the page. You can employ these functions in your Web page in a variety of ways. You can display the result of running the functions directly (as shown in this example) or assign the values to variables that you can use and change.

```
<!DOCTYPE html PUBLIC "-//W3C//DTD XHTML 1.0 Transitional//EN" "http://www.w3.org/TR/xhtml1/DTD/
→ xhtml1-transitional.dtd">
<html xmlns="http://www.w3.org/1999/xhtml">
<head>
    <meta http-equiv="content-type" content="text/html;charset=utf-8" />
    <title>DHTML &amp; CSS for the WWW | Finding an Object&rsquo;s Width and Height</title>
    <script type="text/javascript" language="javascript"><!--
function findWidth(objectID) {
    var object = document.getElementById(objectID);
    if (object.offsetWidth)
        return object.offsetWidth;
    return (null);
}
function findHeight(objectID) {
    var object = document.getElementB
yId(objectID);
    if (object.offsetHeight)
        return object.offsetHeight;
    return (null);
}
    // -->
    </script>
```

(code continues on next page)

Code 12.2 *continued*

```
                                        Code
    <style type="text/css" media="screen"><!--
#object1 {
    visibility: visible;
    position: absolute;
    top: 50px;
    left: 100px;
    width: 402px;
    border: solid 2px gray;
}
    --></style>
</head>
<body>
    <script language="JavaScript"
    → type="text/javascript">
        function showDim(objectID) {
            widthObj = findWidth(objectID);
            heightObj = findHeight(objectID);
            alert('Width: ' + widthObj +
            → 'px; Height: ' + heightObj +
            → 'px' );
        }
    </script>
Click me to find my Width and Height!<br />
<br />
    <div id="object1" onclick="showDim
    → ('object1')">
        <img src="alice20.gif" alt="alice"
        → height="480" width="398" border="0"
        → /></div>
</body>
</html>
```

■ Knowing the dimensions of an object helps you move and position the object so that it doesn't go off the screen on the right or bottom, especially when you create scroll bars (see "Creating Scroll Bars for a Layer" in Chapter 18).

To find the width and height of an object:

1. `function findWidth(objectID) {...}`
Add the function `findWidth()` to your JavaScript. This function uses the ID of the object to be addressed—passed to it as the variable `objectID`—to locate the object. It then uses feature sensing to check that `offsetWidth` works in the current browser and returns the object's width if it does.

2. `function findHeight(objectID) {...}`
Add the function `findHeight()` to your JavaScript. This function uses the ID of the object to be addressed—passed to it as the variable `objectID`—to locate the object. It then uses feature sensing to check that `offsetHeight` works in the current browser and returns the object's height if it does.

3. `#object1 {...}`
Set up the IDs for your object(s) with `position`, `left`, and `top` values.

4. `function showDim(objectID) {...}`
Add a JavaScript function that uses the functions you created in steps 1 and 2. In this example, `showDim()` simply assigns the values returned by `findWidth()` and `findHeight()` to variables and then displays the values in an alert.

5. `onclick="showDim('object1')"`
Add an event handler to trigger the function you created in step 4, and pass to it the ID of the object you want to address.

✔ Tips

■ If you test this code on several browsers, you'll notice that the same object comes up with slightly different width and height values. This difference occurs because some browsers (such as Internet Explorer) include the border with the width and height, and others (such as Netscape) do not.

Detecting an Object's Position

You can use CSS to set the top, left, bottom, and/or right positions of elements (see "Setting an Element's Position" in Chapter 6). Then you can use JavaScript to detect those positions and change them to move the objects around.

One major use of DHTML is to make objects move around on the page (see "Moving Objects from Point to Point" in Chapter 14). But to make something move, you need to know where it is.

Finding an object's top and left positions

To *set* the position of an object's top-left corner, you use the CSS `top` and `left` properties. You might, then, assume that you would also use these style properties in JavaScript to find what those values are. However, both Netscape and Internet Explorer use the `offsetLeft` and `offsetTop` object to find this information (**Code 12.3** and **Figure 12.3**).

To find the top and left positions of an object:

1. `function findLeft(objectID) {...}`

Add the function `findLeft()` to your JavaScript. This function uses the ID of the object to be addressed—passed to it as the variable `objectID`—to identify the object. It uses feature sensing to determine whether the browser uses `offsetLeft` and returns the left position of the object as a number if it does.

Figure 12.3 An alert appears, telling you the top and left positions of the object.

Code 12.3 The functions `findLeft()` and `findTop()` detect the position of an individual object on the page. You can employ these functions in your Web page in a variety of ways. You can display the result of running the functions directly (as shown in this example) or assign the values to variables that you can use and change.

```
<!DOCTYPE html PUBLIC "-//W3C//DTD XHTML
→ 1.0 Transitional//EN" "http://www.w3.org/TR/
→ xhtml1/DTD/xhtml1-transitional.dtd">
<html xmlns="http://www.w3.org/1999/xhtml">
<head>
    <meta http-equiv="content-type"
    → content="text/html;charset=utf-8" />
    <title>DHTML &amp; CSS for the WWW |
    → Finding an Object&rsquo;s Left and Top
    → Position</title>
    <script language="JavaScript"
    → type="text/javascript"><!--
function findLeft(objectID) {
    var object = document.getElementById
    → (objectID);
    if (object.offsetLeft)
        return object.offsetLeft;
    return (null);
}
function findTop(objectID) {
    var object = document.getElementById
    → (objectID);
```

(code continues on next page)

Code 12.3 *continued*

```
        if (object.offsetTop)
            return object.offsetTop;
        return (null);
}

    // -->
    </script>
    <style type="text/css" media="screen"><!--
#object1 {
    visibility: visible;
    position: absolute;
    top: 50px;
    left: 100px;
    width: 410px;
    border: solid 2px gray;
}

    --></style>
</head>
<body>
    <script language="JavaScript"
    → type="text/javascript">
        function showPos(objectID) {
            if (objectID) {
                leftPos = findLeft(objectID);
                topPos = findTop(objectID);
                alert('Left: ' + leftPos +
                → 'px; Top: ' + topPos + 'px' );
            }
        }
    </script>
Click me to find my Left and Top Position on the
→ screen!<br />
<br />
    <div id="object1" onclick="showPos
    → ('object1')">
        <img src="alice20.gif" height="480"
        → width="398" border="0" />
    </div>
</body>
</html>
```

2. `function findTop(objectID) {...}`

Add the function `findTop()` to your JavaScript. This function uses the ID of the object to be addressed—passed to it as the variable `objectID`—to identify the object. It uses feature sensing to determine whether the browser uses `offsetTop` and returns the top position of the object as a number if it does.

3. `#object1 {...}`

Set up the IDs for your object(s) with `position`, `left`, and `top` values.

4. `function showPos(objectID) {...}`

Create a JavaScript function that uses the functions you created in steps 1 and 2. In this example, `showPos()` simply assigns the values returned by `findLeft()` and `findTop()` to variables and then displays the values in an alert.

5. `onclick="showPos('object1')"`

Add an event handler to trigger the function you created in step 4, and pass to it the ID of the object you want to address.

✔ Tips

- With Internet Explorer 4+, you can also use the `pixelLeft` and `pixelTop` objects to find the left and top position. However, since `offsetLeft` and `offsetTop` work in both Netscape and Internet Explorer, these are generally preferred.

- You may notice a slight disparity between the position found for the object in Internet Explorer and the one found in Netscape 6. Netscape 6 measures the position from inside the object's border; other browsers measure from outside the border. This generally leads to a disparity of about 4 pixels. You can overcome this by delivering styles tailored to the browser (see Chapter 16, "Customizing Styles for the OS or Browser").

Finding an object's bottom and right positions

Like the top and bottom positions, the bottom and right positions can be determined with JavaScript (**Figure 12.4**). However, you don't do this directly using a particular object. Instead, you find the left or top position of the object and the width or height of the object and add these values (**Code 12.4**).

To find the bottom and right positions of an object:

1. `function findRight(objectID) {...}`

   Add the function `findRight()` to your JavaScript. This function uses the ID of the object to be addressed—passed to it as the variable `objectID`—to find the object. It then uses feature sensing to find the left position (`offsetLeft`) and width (`offsetWidth`) of the object and returns these values added together (see "Determining an Object's Dimensions" and "Finding an Object's Top and Left Positions" earlier in this chapter).

Figure 12.4 An alert pops up to tell you the bottom and right positions of the object.

Code 12.4 The functions `findRight()` and `findBottom()` are used to detect the position of an individual object. You can employ these functions in your Web page in a variety of ways. You can display the result of running the functions directly (as shown in this example) or assign the values to variables that you can use and change.

```
<!DOCTYPE html PUBLIC "-//W3C//DTD XHTML
→ 1.0 Transitional//EN" "http://www.w3.org/TR/
→ xhtml1/DTD/xhtml1-transitional.dtd">
<html xmlns="http://www.w3.org/1999/xhtml">
<head>
    <meta http-equiv="content-type"
    → content="text/html;charset=utf-8" />
    <title>DHTML &amp; CSS for the WWW |
    → Finding an Object&rsquo;s Right and
    → Bottom Position</title>
    <script language="JavaScript"
    → type="text/javascript"><!--
function findRight(objectID) {
    var object = document.getElementById
    → (objectID);
    if (object.offsetLeft) {
        return (object.offsetLeft +
        → object.offsetWidth);
    }
    return (null);
}
function findBottom(objectID) {
```

(code continues on next page)

Code 12.4 *continued*

```
       var object = document.getElementById
       → (objectID);
       if (object.offsetTop) {
           return (object.offsetTop + object.
           → offsetHeight);
       }
       return (null);
}
       // -->
       </script>
       <style type="text/css" media="screen"><!--
#object1 {
       visibility: visible;
       position: absolute;
       top: 50px;
       left: 100px;
       width: 410px;
       border: solid 2px gray;
}
       --></style>
</head>
<body>
       <script language="JavaScript"
       → type="text/javascript">
           function showPos(objectID) {
               rightPos = findRight(objectID);
               bottomPos = findBottom(objectID);
               alert('Right: ' + rightPos +
               → 'px; Bottom: ' + bottomPos +
               → 'px' );
           }
</script>
Click me to find my Right and Bottom positions on
→ the screen!<br />
<br />
       <div id="object1" onclick="showPos
       → ('object1')">
           <img src="alice20.gif" alt="alice"
           → height="480" width="398" border="0"
/></div>
</body>
</html>
```

2. `function findBottom(objectID) {...}`
Add the function `findBottom()` to your JavaScript. This function uses the ID of the object to be addressed—passed to it as the variable `objectID`—to find the object. It then uses feature sensing to find the top position (`offsetTop`) and height (`offsetHeight`) of the object and returns these values added together (see "Determining an Object's Dimensions" and "Finding an Object's Top and Left Positions" earlier in this chapter).

3. `#object1 {...}`
Set up the IDs for your object(s) with `position`, `left`, and `top` values.

4. `function showPos(objectID) {...}`
Create a JavaScript function that uses the functions you created in steps 1 and 2. In this example, `showPos()` simply assigns the values returned by `findRight()` and `findBottom()` to variables and then displays the values in an alert.

5. `onclick="showPos('object1')"`
Add an event handler to trigger the function you created in step 4, and pass to it the ID of the object you want to address.

✔ Tip

- You may notice a slight disparity between the position found for the object in Internet Explorer and the one found in Netscape 6. Netscape 6 measures the position from inside the object's border; other browsers measure from outside the border.

DETECTING AN OBJECT'S POSITION

Finding an Object's 3-D Position

The CSS attribute z-index allows you to stack positioned elements in 3-D (see "Stacking Elements" in Chapter 6). Using JavaScript, you can determine the z-index of individual objects on the screen (**Figure 12.5**) using the style.zIndex object (**Code 12.5**).

But there's a catch: Browsers can't easily see the z-index until it's set dynamically. To get around this little problem, you have to use JavaScript to set the z-index of each object when the page first loads.

Figure 12.5 An alert appears, telling you the layer number of the object clicked.

Code 12.5 The function findLayer() determines the z-index of an individual object on the page after the layers are initialized using initPage().

```
<!DOCTYPE html PUBLIC "-//W3C//DTD XHTML 1.0 Transitional//EN" "http://www.w3.org/TR/xhtml1/DTD/
→ xhtml1-transitional.dtd">
<html xmlns="http://www.w3.org/1999/xhtml">
<head>
    <meta http-equiv="content-type" content="text/html;charset=utf-8" />
    <title>DHTML &amp; CSS for the WWW | Finding the Z Position</title>
    <script language="JavaScript" type="text/javascript"><!--
function initPage() {
    for (i=1; i<=4; i++) {
        var object = document.getElementById('object' + i);
        object.style.zIndex = i;
    }
}
function findLayer(objectID) {
    var object = document.getElementById(objectID);
    if (object.style.zIndex)
        return object.style.zIndex;
    return (null);
}
    // -->
    </script>
    <style type="text/css" media="screen"><!--
#object1 {
    position: absolute;
    z-index: 3;
    top: 175px;
    left: 255px;
}
```

(code continues on next page)

Code 12.5 *continued*

```
#object2 {
    position: absolute;
    z-index: 2;
    top: 100px;
    left: 170px;
}
#object3 {
    position: absolute;
    z-index: 1;
    top: 65px;
    left: 85px;
}
#object4 {
    position: absolute;
    z-index: 0;
    top: 5px;
    left: 5px;
}
    --></style>
</head>
<body onload="initPage();">
    <script language="JavaScript"
    → type="text/javascript">
        function whichLayer(objectID) {
            layerNum = findLayer(objectID);
            alert('Layer: ' + layerNum );
        }
    </script>
        <div id="object1" onclick="whichLayer
        → ('object1')">
            <img src="alice22.gif" height="147"
            → width="100" border="0"
            → alt="alice 1" /><br />
        </div>
        <div id="object2" onclick="whichLayer
        → ('object2')">
            <img src="alice32.gif" height="201"
            → width="140" border="0" alt=
            → "alice 2" /><br />
        </div>
        <div id="object3" onclick="whichLayer
        → ('object3')">
            <img src="alice15.gif" height="198"
            → width="150" border="0"
            → alt="alice 3" /><br />
        </div>
        <div id="object4" onclick="whichLayer
        → ('object4')">
            <img src="alice29.gif" height="236"
            → width="200" border="0"
            → alt="alice 4" /><br />
        </div>
</body>
</html>
```

To find the z-index of an object:

1. `function initPage() {...}`
   Add the `initPage()` function to your JavaScript. This function sets the initial z-index of objects when the page first loads.

2. `function findLayer(objectID) {...}`
   Add the function `findLayer()` to your JavaScript. This function uses the ID of the object to be addressed—passed to it as the variable `objectID`—to find the object. The function then uses this ID to access the `z-index` property and returns that value.

3. `#object1 {...}`
   Set up the IDs for your objects with `position` and `z-index` values.

4. `onload="initPage;"`
   In the <body> tag, use the `initPage()` function to initialize the z-index of all the objects for which you need to know the initial z-index.

5. `function whichLayer(objectID) {...}`
   Create a JavaScript function that uses the functions you created in steps 1 and 2. In this example, `whichLayer()` simply assigns the values returned by `find-Layer()` and then displays those values in an alert.

6. `onclick="whichLayer('object1')"`
   Add an event handler to trigger the function you created in step 5, and pass to it the ID of the object you want to address.

✔ Tip

■ An alternate (though no less complex) method for finding the z-index of any object without first setting the value using JavaScript is presented in "Finding a Style Property's Value" in Chapter 16.

Finding an Object's Visibility State

All objects that have a position set also have a visibility state: hidden or visible (see "Setting the Visibility of an Element" in Chapter 7). This state defaults to visible (**Figure 12.6**).

Unfortunately, browsers cannot access the visibility state that is initially set in the CSS; they're aware of the state only after it has been set dynamically (**Code 12.6**).

To find the visibility of an object:

1. function initPage(objectID, state)
→ {...}

Add the initPage() function to your JavaScript. This function sets the initial visibility of objects when the page first loads.

2. function findVisibility(objectID)
→ {...}

Add the function findVisibility() to your JavaScript. This function uses the ID of the object to be addressed—passed to it as the variable objectID—to find the object on the page. It then uses this ID to access the current visibility property set for the object. Based on that value, the function returns either visible or hidden.

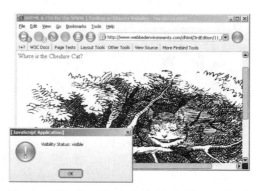

Figure 12.6 The Cheshire Cat is visible, but for how long?

Code 12.6 The function findVisibility() determines the current visibility state of an individual object in the window. This state is either visible or hidden.

```
<!DOCTYPE html PUBLIC "-//W3C//DTD XHTML
→ 1.0 Transitional//EN" "http://www.w3.org/TR/
→ xhtml1/DTD/xhtml1-transitional.dtd">
<html xmlns="http://www.w3.org/1999/xhtml">
<head>
    <meta http-equiv="content-type"
    → content="text/html;charset=utf-8" />
    <title>DHTML &amp; CSS for the WWW |
    → Finding an Object&rsquo;s Visibility</
    → title>
    <script language="JavaScript"
    → type="text/javascript"><!--
function initPage(objectID, state) {
    var object = document.getElementById
    → (objectID);
    object.style.visibility = state;
}
function findVisibility(objectID) {
    var object = document.getElementById
    → (objectID);
    if (object.style.visibility)
        return object.style.visibility;
    return (null);
}
    // -->
    </script>
```

(code continues on next page)

Code 12.6 *continued*

```
 ●●●                    Code                   ○
      <style type="text/css" media="screen"><!--
#object1 {
      visibility: visible;
      position: relative;
      top: 5px;
      left: 5px;
      width: 640px;
}
      --></style>
</head>
<body onload="initPage('object1','visible')">
      <script language="JavaScript"
      → type="text/javascript">
        function showVisibility(objectID) {
           var thisVis = findVisibility
           →(objectID);
           alert('Visibility Status: ' +
           → thisVis );
        }
      </script>

      <a onclick="showVisibility('object1')"
href="#">Where is the Cheshire Cat? </a><br />
        <div id="object1">
           <img src="alice24.gif" alt="alice"
           → height="435" width="640"
           → border="0" />
        </div>
</body>
</html>
```

3. #object1 {...}

Set up the IDs for your objects with position and visibility values.

4. onload="initPage('object1',
   → 'visible')";

In the <body> tag, use the initPage()
function to initialize the visibility of all
the objects for which you need to know
the initial visibility.

5. function showVisibility(objectID)
   → {...}

Create a JavaScript function that uses
the function you created in step 2. In
this example, showVisibility() simply
assigns the values returned by findVis-
ibility() and then displays those values
in an alert.

6. onclick="showVisibility('object1')"

Add an event handler to trigger the function you created in step 5, and pass to it
the ID of the object you want to address.

✔ Tips

- You can also use JavaScript to change
  that state, as explained in "Making
  Objects Appear and Disappear" in
  Chapter 14.

- An alternate (though no less complex)
  method for finding the visibility state of
  any object without first setting the value
  using JavaScript is presented in "Finding
  a Style Property's Value" in Chapter 16.

Finding an Object's Visible Area

The width and height of an object tell you the maximum area of the element (see "Determining an Object's Dimensions" earlier in this chapter). When an object is clipped (see "Setting the Visible Area of an Element" in Chapter 7), the maximum area is cut down, and you can view only part of the object's total visible area. Using JavaScript, you can not only find the width and height of the visible area, but also the top, left, bottom, and right borders of the clipping region (**Code 12.7** and **Figure 12.7**).

Like other CSS visibility properties, however, browsers can't easily read the clipping values until they've been set dynamically. I'll show you a relatively easy workaround for this problem later, changing the clipping area (see "Changing an Object's Visible Area" in Chapter 14.

Figure 12.7 An alert appears, telling us the location of the top border of the clip region

Code 12.7 The functions findClipTop(), findClipRight(), findClipBottom(), findClipLeft(), findClipWidth(), and findClipHeight() find the clip region and borders of an individual object in the window.

```
<!DOCTYPE html PUBLIC "-//W3C//DTD XHTML 1.0 Transitional//EN" "http://www.w3.org/TR/xhtml1/DTD/
→ xhtml1-transitional.dtd">
<html xmlns="http://www.w3.org/1999/xhtml">
<head>
     <meta http-equiv="content-type" content="text/html;charset=utf-8" />
     <title>DHTML &amp; CSS for the WWW | Finding an Object&rsquo;s Clipped Area</title>
     <script language="JavaScript" type="text/javascript">
function setClip(objectID, clipTop, clipRight, clipBottom, clipLeft) {
     var object = document.getElementById(objectID);
     object.style.clip = 'rect(' + clipTop + 'px ' + clipRight + 'px ' + clipBottom + 'px ' +
     → clipLeft +'px)';
}
function findClipTop(objectID) {
     var object = document.getElementById(objectID);
        if (object.style.clip !=null) {
           var clip = findClipArray(object.style.clip);
           return (clip[0]) ;
```

(code continues on next page)

Code 12.7 *continued*

```
        }
        return (null);
}
function findClipRight(objectID) {
    var object = document.getElementById(objectID);
        if (object.style.clip !=null) {
            var clip = findClipArray(object.style.clip);
            return (clip[1]) ;
        }
        return (null);
}
function findClipBottom(objectID) {
    var object = document.getElementById(objectID);
        if (object.style.clip !=null) {
            var clip = findClipArray(object.style.clip);
            return (clip[2]) ;
        }
        return (null);
}
function findClipLeft(objectID) {
    var object = document.getElementById(objectID);
        if (object.style.clip !=null) {
            var clip = findClipArray(object.style.clip);
            return (clip[3]) ;
        }
        return (null);
}
function findClipWidth(objectID) {
    var object = document.getElementById(objectID);
        if (object.style.clip !=null) {
            var clip = findClipArray(object.style.clip);
            return (clip[1] - clip[3]) ;
        }
        return (null);
}
function findClipHeight(objectID) {
    var object = document.getElementById(objectID);
        if (object.style.clip !=null) {
            var clip = findClipArray(object.style.clip);
            return (clip[2] - clip[0]) ;
        }
```

(code continues on next page)

FINDING AN OBJECT'S VISIBLE AREA

Code 12.7 *continued*

```
           return (null);
}
function findClipArray(clipStr) {
     var clip = new Array();
     var i;
        i = clipStr.indexOf('(');
        clip[0] = parseInt(clipStr.substring(i + 1, clipStr.length), 10);
        i = clipStr.indexOf(' ', i + 1);
        clip[1] = parseInt(clipStr.substring(i + 1, clipStr.length), 10);
        i = clipStr.indexOf(' ', i + 1);
        clip[2] = parseInt(clipStr.substring(i + 1, clipStr.length), 10);
        i = clipStr.indexOf(' ', i + 1);
        clip[3] = parseInt(clipStr.substring(i + 1, clipStr.length), 10);
        return clip;
}

     </script>
<style type="text/css" media="screen"><!--
#object1 {
     position: absolute;
     top: 60px;
     left: 0;
     overflow: hidden;
     clip: rect(15px 350px 195px 50px)
}
--></style>
</head>
<body onload="setClip('object1',15,350,195,50)">
<br />
<br />
Clip Dimensions || <a onclick="alert('Clip on Top: ' + findClipTop('object1') + 'px')" href="#">
→ Top </a>| <a onclick="alert('Clip on Left: ' + findClipLeft('object1') + 'px')" href="#">
→ Left </a>| <a onclick="alert('Clip on Bottom: ' + findClipBottom('object1') + 'px')" href="#">
→ Bottom </a>| <a onclick="alert('Clip on Right: ' + findClipRight('object1') + 'px')" href="#">
→ Right </a>|| <a onclick="alert('Clip Width: ' + findClipWidth('object1') + 'px')" href="#">
→ Width </a>| <a onclick="alert('Clip Height: ' + findClipHeight('object1') + 'px')" href="#">
→ Height </a>
     <div id="cobject1">
        <img src="alice31.gif" height="480" width="379" border="0" />
     </div>
</body>
</html>
```

To find the visible area and borders of an object:

1. `function setClip(objectID,state)` `→{...}`

   Add the `setClip()` function to your JavaScript. This function sets the initial clip region of objects when the page first loads, with values the same as those set in the CSS.

2. `function findClipTop(objectID) {...}`

   Add these functions to your JavaScript: `findClipTop()`, `findClipRight()`, `findClipBottom()`, and `findClipLeft()`.

   All these functions do the same thing on different sides of the object. They use the ID of the object to be addressed—passed to the function as the variable `objectID`—to find the object on the Web page. They use the `findClipArray()` function to determine the clip array and then access that array by using 0, 1, 2, 3 for top, left, bottom, and right, respectively.

3. `function findClipWidth(objectID)` `→{...}`

   Add the functions `findClipWidth()` and `findClipHeight()` to your JavaScript. These functions use the ID of the object to be addressed—passed to them as the variable `objectID`—to find the object. The functions then use the object to capture the visible area's height and width by subtracting the top from the bottom value for the height or the left from the right values for the width (see step 3).

   continues on next page

FINDING AN OBJECT'S VISIBLE AREA

4. `function findClipArray(str) {...}`

Add the `findClipArray()` function to your JavaScript. This function translates the string of characters used to store the four clipping sides into an array of numbers, with each number in the array corresponding to a clip dimension.

5. `#object1 {...}`

Set up the IDs for your objects with `position` and `visibility` values.

6. `onload="setClip(...)"`

In the `<body>` tag, use the `setClip()` function to initialize the clip area of all the object(s).

7. `onclick="alert(...)"`

Trigger the functions in steps 3 and 4 from an event handler.

✔ Tips

■ Netscape can also access the clipping values using the `clip.height`, `clip.width`, `clip.top`, `clip.left`, `clip.bottom`, and `clip.right` objects to directly access the values. However, since Internet Explorer does not support this, the array method described here is preferred.

■ An alternate (though no less complex) method for finding the clip area of any object without first setting it using JavaScript is present in "Finding a Style Property's Value" in Chapter 16.

LEARNING ABOUT AN EVENT

In Chapter 10, we looked at how to use event handlers to trigger JavaScript functions. An event handler can be applied to various objects on the page to tell the object how to react when a particular action occurs. However, events also include information about how a particular event was generated such as which event type occurred, what object generated the event, and (for keyboard and mouse events) which button was pressed.

In this chapter, we will learn how to get to the information generated by an event and how to process it.

Detecting Which Event Type Fired

Once an event is fired, the function it triggers doesn't inherently know how it was triggered. The `evt.type` object can tell you what event type was fired, allowing you to write a function that can respond differently depending on how the action was initiated (**Code 13.1** and **Figure 13.1**).

Figure 13.1 The event type that triggered the function (in this case mousedown) is displayed in the alert message.

Code 13.1 The object `evt.type` is used to identify the type of event that triggered the function.

```
<!DOCTYPE html PUBLIC "-//W3C//DTD XHTML 1.0 Transitional//EN" "http://www.w3.org/TR/xhtml1/DTD/
→ xhtml1-transitional.dtd">
<html xmlns="http://www.w3.org/1999/xhtml">
<head>
    <meta http-equiv="content-type" content="text/html;charset=utf-8" />
    <title>DHTML &amp; CSS for the WWW | Detecting Which Event Type Fired</title>
    <script language="JavaScript" type="text/javascript"><!--
function initPage(objectID) {
    var object = document.getElementById(objectID);
    object.onmousedown = findEventType;
    document.onclick = findEventType;
}
function findEventType(evt) {
    var evt = (evt) ? evt : ((window.event) ? event : null);
    if (evt.type)
        alert('This was triggered by a ' + evt.type + ' event.');
}
    // -->
    </script>
    <style type="text/css" media="screen"><!--
#object1 {
    visibility: visible;
    position: absolute;
    top: 50px;
    left: 100px;
    width: 410px;
    border: solid 2px gray;
```

(code continues on next page)

Code 13.1 *continued*

```
  ○○○                Code                ○
}
    --></style>
</head>
<body onload="initPage('object1')">
Click me and I will tell you what type of event
→ this is.<br />
<br />
    <div id="object1">
        <img src="alice06a.gif" height="480"
        → width="392" border="0" alt="alice" />
    </div>
</body>
</html>
```

To find which event type fired:

1. `function initPage(objectID) {...}`

Add the function `initPage()` to your code. You can add bound events to an object, objects, or the entire document (see "Binding Events to Objects" in Chapter 10).

2. `function findEventType(evt) {...}`

Add the function `findEventType()` to your code. This code first uses the event equalizer discussed in Chapter 10 ("Passing Events to a Function") to allow Internet Explorer and Netscape to play together:

`var evt = (evt) ? evt :`
`→ ((window.event) ? event : null)`

It then uses `evt.type` to identify the event that triggered the function. For this example, I simply added an alert to report the event type, but you could use `if` statements to tailor the code for different event types.

3. `onload="initPage('object1')"`

Add an `onload` event handler in the `<body>` tag to trigger the `initPage()` function created in step 1. This sets up the events for the page.

✔ Tip

- Although this example uses event binding, you could also use it with an event handler placed directly in the tag. But remember to pass the event variable in the function call:

`onclick="findEventType(event)"`

Detecting Which Key Was Pressed

Although the onkeydown, onkeyup, and onkeypress events allow you to detect when a key is pressed, they don't tell you which key was actually pressed. To find that out, you'll need to use the evt.charCode object for Netscape or evt.keyCode object for Internet Explorer. Both of these return a numeric value for the key pressed (**Code 13.2** and **Figure 13.2**). You can then use that code to determine the actual key pressed by consulting Appendix E, which lists all of the keyboard characters and their numeric values.

Figure 13.2 The numeric code for the key that the user pressed is displayed in an alert message. In this case, 90 (the character Z).

Code 13.2 The objects evt.charCode (Netscape or any Mozilla-type browser) or evt.keyCode (Internet Explorer) are used to find the code for the key pressed by the user.

```
<!DOCTYPE html PUBLIC "-//W3C//DTD XHTML 1.0 Transitional//EN" "http://www.w3.org/TR/xhtml1/DTD/
 xhtml1-transitional.dtd">
<html xmlns="http://www.w3.org/1999/xhtml">
<head>
    <meta http-equiv="content-type" content="text/html;charset=utf-8" />
    <title>DHTML &amp; CSS for the WWW | Detecting Which Key Was Pressed</title>
    <script language="JavaScript" type="text/javascript"><!--
function initPage() {
    window.document.onkeydown=findKey;
}
function findKey(evt) {
    var evt = (evt) ? evt : ((window.event) ? event : null);
    if (evt.type == 'keydown') {
        var charCode = (evt.charCode) ? evt.charCode : evt.keyCode;
        alert ('Character Code = ' + charCode);
    }
}
    // -->
    </script>
</head>
<body onload="initPage()">
    Press any key to find its character code!<br />
    <br />
</body>
</html>
```

To find which key was pressed:

1. `function initPage() {...}`

   Add the function `initPage()` to your code and bind a `keyDown` event to an object (see "Binding Events to Objects" in Chapter 10). In this example, I wanted to detect whenever a key is pressed with the page loaded, so I used `window.document`. However, you could also bind the event to a form input field to detect key presses only there.

2. `function findKey(evt) {...}`

   Add the function `findKey()` to your code. This code first uses the event equalizer discussed in Chapter 10 ("Passing Events to a Function") to allow Internet Explorer and Netscape to play together:

   ```
   var evt = (evt) ? evt :
   → ((window.event) ? event : null);
   ```

   It then uses either `evt.charCode` if the browser being used is Netscape (or any Mozilla-type browser) or `evt.keyCode` for Internet Explorer to identify the key that was pressed by its numeric value (see Appendix D). For this example, I simply added an alert to report the character value, but you could use `if` statements to tailor the code for different characters.

3. `onload="initPage()"`

   Add an `onload` event handler in the `<body>` tag to trigger the `initPage()` function created in step 1. This sets up the events for the page.

✔ Tip

- This code does not work in Safari 1.

Should I use onkeydown, onkeyup, or onkeypress?

Although the onkeypress and onkeyup event handlers also detect when a key is pressed, onkeydown gives more consistently reliable results between browsers for character detection.

Detecting Which Modifier Key Was Pressed

Unlike other keyboard keys, modifier keys (Shift, Control, Alt/Option, and Command) do not register with a numeric value. Instead, these keys can be detected directly from the event, allowing you to tailor your code depending on which key was pressed (**Code 13.3** and **Figure 13.3**). Each of these keys has its own unique object: `shiftKey`, `ctrlKey`, `altKey`, and `metaKey` (for the Apple Command key).

Figure 13.3 The modifier key that the user pressed is displayed in an alert message.

Code 13.3 The objects `evt.shiftKey`, `evt.ctrlKey`, `evt.altKey`, and `evt.metaKey` are used to test for which modifier key the user pressed.

```
<!DOCTYPE html PUBLIC "-//W3C//DTD XHTML 1.0 Transitional//EN" "http://www.w3.org/TR/xhtml1/DTD/
 → xhtml1-transitional.dtd">
<html xmlns="http://www.w3.org/1999/xhtml">
<head>
     <meta http-equiv="content-type" content="text/html;charset=utf-8" />
     <title>DHTML &amp; CSS for the WWW | Detecting Which Modifier Key Was Pressed</title>
     <script language="JavaScript" type="text/javascript"><!--
function initPage() {
     window.document.onkeydown=findModifierKey;
}
function findModifierKey(evt) {
     var evt = (evt) ? evt : ((window.event) ? event : null);
     if (evt) {
        if (evt.shiftKey) alert ('The Shift key has been pressed');
        if (evt.ctrlKey) alert ('The Control key has been pressed');
        if (evt.altKey) alert ('The Alt/Option key has been pressed');
        if (evt.metaKey) alert ('The Command key has been pressed');
     }
}
     // -->
     </script>
</head>
<body onload="initPage()">
     Press any modifier key (Shift, Control, Option/Alt, or Command)<br />
</body>
</html>
```

To find which modifier key has been pressed:

1. `function initPage() {...}`

Add the function `initPage()` to your JavaScript and bind a `keydown` event to an object (see "Binding Events to Objects" in Chapter 10). In this example, I wanted to detect whenever a key is pressed with the page loaded, so I used `window.document`. However, you could also bind the event to a form input field to detect key presses only there.

2. `function findModifierKey(evt) {...}`

Add the function `findModifierKey()` to your JavaScript. This code first uses the event equalizer discussed in Chapter 10 ("Passing Events to a Function") to allow Internet Explorer and Netscape to play together:

```
var evt = (evt) ? evt :
→ ((window.event) ? event : null);
```

It then evaluates the event for each modifier key object to see if it is true (if that was the key pressed). For this example, I simply added an alert to report which modifier key was pressed, but you could use the `if` statements to tailor the code for different modifiers.

3. `onload="initPage()"`

Add an `onload` event handler in the `<body>` tag to trigger the `initPage()` function created in step 1. This sets up the events for the page.

✔ Tips

- Windows users should know that on the Mac, the Alt key is labeled Option, but they do the same thing.

- On the Mac, the Control key is generally used as a modifier key with the mouse button, in place of the Windows right mouse click.

Detecting Which Mouse Button Was Clicked

DETECTING WHICH MOUSE BUTTON WAS CLICKED

The computer mouse is a key device not only for controlling a computer, but also for navigating Web pages. For the most part, Web pages deal only with one mouse button used to click links, select menus, and choose form fields, radio buttons, and check boxes.

However, using DHTML, you can detect which mouse button is being clicked using the evt.button object, and tailor scripts accordingly (**Code 13.4** and **Figure 13.4**). For example, you may want a link to work as a normal hypertext link when left-clicked but be draggable if right-clicked.

Figure 13.4 The numeric value for the mouse button that the user clicked is displayed in the alert.

Code 13.4 The object evt.button is used to determine which mouse button was clicked to trigger the event.

```
<!DOCTYPE html PUBLIC "-//W3C//DTD XHTML 1.0 Transitional//EN" "http://www.w3.org/TR/xhtml1/DTD/
 xhtml1-transitional.dtd">
<html xmlns="http://www.w3.org/1999/xhtml">
<head>
     <meta http-equiv="content-type" content="text/html;charset=utf-8" />
     <title>DHTML &amp; CSS for the WWW | Detecting Which Mouse Button Was Clicked</title>
     <script language="JavaScript" type="text/javascript"><!--
function initPage(objectID) {
     var object = document.getElementById(objectID);
     object.onmousedown = findMouseButton;
}
function findMouseButton(evt) {
     evt = (evt) ? evt : ((window.event) ? event : null);
     if (typeof evt.button != 'undefined') {
        alert('Mouse Button Value = ' + evt.button);
     }
}
     // -->
     </script>
     <style type="text/css" media="screen"><!--
#object1 {
     visibility: visible;
```

(code continues on next page)

Code 13.4 *continued*

```
      position: absolute;
      top: 50px;
      left: 100px;
      width: 410px;
      border: solid 2px gray
}
      --></style>
</head>
<body onload="initPage('object1')">
      Click me and I will tell you which mouse
    → button you pressed.<br />
      <br />
      <div id="object1">
          <img src="alice06a.gif" height="480"
        → width="392" border="0" alt="alice" />
      </div>
</body>
</html>
```

Table 13.1

Mouse Button Values

Button	Internet Explorer*	Netscape
None	0	null
Left	1	0
Middle	4	1
Right	2	2

*Includes Safari and Opera

To find which mouse button was clicked:

1. `function initPage() {...}`

   Add the function `initPage()` to your JavaScript and bind a `mousedown` event to an object (see "Binding Events to Objects" in Chapter 10). In this example, I wanted to detect whenever a mouse button is pressed anywhere in the Web page, so I used `window.document`. However, you could bind the event to any object on the page.

2. `function findMouseButton(evt) {...}`

   Add the function `findMouseButton()` to your JavaScript. This code first uses the event equalizer discussed in Chapter 10 ("Passing Events to a Function") to allow Internet Explorer and Netscape to play together and then evaluates the `evt.button` object to determine its value. Unfortunately, Netscape and Internet Explorer will report different values (see **Table 13.1**).

   For this example, I simply added an alert to report the value of the mouse button pressed.

3. `onload="initPage('object1')"`

   Add an `onload` event handler in the `<body>` tag to trigger the `initPage()` function created in step 1. This sets up the events for the page.

✔ Tips

- Keep in mind that standard Mac mice only have one button (treated as the left button), and Control-clicking with a Mac mouse is treated as a right-click. Also, many PC mice don't have a middle button.

- Right- or Control-clicking normally brings up a contextual menu. If you use `onmouseup` or `onclick` as the event handler to detect a right-click event, it will be ignored since the contextual menu trumps all other events.

Detecting Where the Mouse Clicked

Remember, no matter where you go, there you are. And if you want to know where you are in the browser window, this is the script for you (**Code 13.5** and **Figure 13.5**).

All mouse-generated events include information in the evt object specifying not only where the event occurred in the browser window (clientX and clientY), but also where within the entire screen (screenX and screenY) the event occurred (**Figure 13.6**).

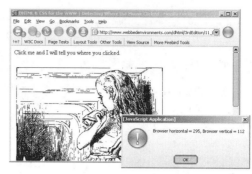

Figure 13.5 An alert tells you where you clicked in the browser window (evt.clientX and evt.clientY).

Code 13.5 The objects evt.clientX and evt.clientY are used to find the mouse's place in the browser window. The objects evt.screenX and evt.screenY are used to measure the mouse's position within the entire screen.

```
<!DOCTYPE html PUBLIC "-//W3C//DTD XHTML 1.0 Transitional//EN" "http://www.w3.org/TR/xhtml1/DTD/
  xhtml1-transitional.dtd">
<html xmlns="http://www.w3.org/1999/xhtml">
<head>
    <meta http-equiv="content-type" content="text/html;charset=utf-8" />
    <title>DHTML &amp; CSS for the WWW | Detecting Where the Mouse Clicked</title>
    <script language="JavaScript" type="text/javascript"><!--
function initPage() {
    document.onclick = findMouseLocation;
}
function findMouseLocation(evt) {
    var evt = (evt) ? evt : ((window.event) ? event : null);
    alert ('Browser horizontal = ' + evt.clientX + ', Browser vertical = ' + evt.clientY);
    alert ('Screen horizontal = ' + evt.screenX + ', Screen vertical = ' + evt.screenY);
}
    // -->
    </script>
    <style type="text/css"
media="screen"><!--
#object1 {
    visibility: visible;
    position: absolute;
    top: 50px;
    left: 100px;
```

(code continues on next page)

Code 13.5 *continued*

```
    width: 410px;
    border: solid 2px gray
}
--></style>
</head>
<body onload="initPage()">
    Click me and I will tell you where you
clicked.<br />
    <br />
        <img src="alice06a.gif" height="480"
        → width="392" border="0" alt="alice" />
</body>
</html>
```

Figure 13.6 An alert tells you where you clicked within the entire window (evt.screenX and evt.screenY).

To find the mouse pointer's position in the browser window:

1. function initPage() {...}

Add the function initPage() to your JavaScript and bind a mouseDown event to an object (see "Binding Events to Objects" in Chapter 10). In this example, I wanted to detect where the mouse is whenever the user clicks anywhere in the window, so I used window.document with the onclick event handler. However, you could bind the event to any object on the page.

2. function findMouseLocation(evt) {...}

Add the function findMouseLocation() to your JavaScript. This code first uses the event equalizer discussed in Chapter 10 ("Passing Events to a Function") to allow Internet Explorer and Netscape to play together. Use the evt.clientX and evt.clientY objects to find the mouse's position in the browser window. Use the evt.screenX and evt.screenY objects to find the mouse's position in the screen. For this example, I simply added an alert to report the mouse's position.

3. onload="initPage()"

Add an onload event handler in the <body> tag to trigger the initPage() function created in step 1. This sets up the events for the page.

continues on next page

✔ Tips

- If you're trying to determine the location of the mouse within the Web page (as opposed to simply the screen) you'll need to add the scroll position values to the mouse position values (see "Determining the Page's Scroll Position" in Chapter 11).

- Netscape can also use the PageX and PageY objects to determine the location within the Web page.

- Although the mouse's y-position in the browser (clientY) is measured from the top of the browser window, its y-position in the screen (screenY) is measured from the bottom of the screen.

BASIC DYNAMIC TECHNIQUES

14

Almost all of DHTML is based on a few basic tricks that allow you to hide and show objects, move them around, and make other changes. For the most part, these techniques are based on the ability to change the CSS properties of an object with JavaScript using the DOM and the `getElementbyId()` method to find it.

In this chapter, we'll look at simple examples of how to create functions that change objects' visibility, position (either to a specific location or by a certain amount), or clipping region. We'll also look at adding content after the page is loaded, and how to control an object between frames and windows. These techniques will be the building blocks from which you can then go on to create a wide variety of dynamic effects.

Making Objects Appear and Disappear

One of the core features of any dynamic Web site is the ability to control the visibility of an element, allowing it to be shown or not shown at any given moment while the visitor is using the Web site. Whether an object is visible or hidden on the page can be changed using JavaScript, but is initially set using CSS, which actually offers two distinct methods for controlling an object's visibility:

◆ Using visibility: hidden will preserve the space needed to show the object even when it's hidden (like the Invisible Man, who still takes up space in his clothes showing his outline, even though you can't see him). When visibility is set back to visible, the object simply fills the space.

◆ Using display: none completely removes the object from display, leaving no space. If the object's display style is then changed to one of the other visible display styles (block, inline, and so on), the object will be placed back into the Web page, even if that means redrawing the page to accommodate the "new" object.

Changing the visibility style

The visibility property allows you to tell an object whether to appear (visible) or not (hidden) on the screen (see "Setting the Visibility of an Element" in Chapter 7). Using JavaScript (**Code 14.1**), you can not only determine the current visibility state (see "Finding an Object's Visibility State" in Chapter 12), but also change the state back and forth (**Figures 14.1** and **14.2**).

Code 14.1 The setVisibility() and toggleVisibility() functions change the visibility state of the designated object in the browser window.

```
<!DOCTYPE html PUBLIC "-//W3C//DTD XHTML
→ 1.0 Transitional//EN" "http://www.w3.org/TR/
→ xhtml1/DTD/xhtml1-transitional.dtd">
<html xmlns="http://www.w3.org/1999/xhtml">
<head>
    <meta http-equiv="content-type"
    → content="text/html;charset=utf-8" />
    <title>DHTML &amp; CSS for the WWW |
    → Making Objects Appear and Disappear |
    → Changing Visibility Style</title>
    <script language="JavaScript"
    → type="text/javascript"><!--
function setVisibility(objectID,state) {
    var object = document.getElementById
    → (objectID);
    object.style.visibility = state;
}
function toggleVisibility(objectID) {
    var object = document.getElementById
    → (objectID);
    state = object.style.visibility;
    if (state == 'hidden')
        object.style.visibility = 'visible';
    else {
        if (state == 'visible')
            object.style.visibility = 'hidden';
    else object.style.visibility = 'visible';
    }
}
    // -->

</script>
    <style type="text/css" media="screen"><!--
#cheshireCat {
    visibility: visible;
    }
    --></style>
</head>
<body onload="setVisibility('cheshireCat',
→ 'visible');">
```

(code continues on next page)

Code 14.1 *continued*

```
        <a onclick="setVisibility('cheshire
        → Cat','hidden');" href="javascript:
        → void('')">Hide the Cat</a> |
        <a onclick="setVisibility('cheshireCat',
        → 'visible');" href="javascript:void('')">
        → Show the Cat</a> |
        <a onclick="toggleVisibility('cheshire
        → Cat');" href="javascript:void('')">
        → Change the Cat's Visibility</a>
            <div id="cheshireCat">
                <img src="alice24.gif" height="283"
                → width="416" border="0" />
            </div>
        <h1>The Cheshire Cat</h1>
</body>
</html>
```

To change the visibility state of an object:

1. `function setVisibility`
`→ (objectID, state) {...}`

Add the function `setVisibility()` to your JavaScript. This function uses the ID of the object to be addressed—passed to it as the variable `objectID`—to find the object to be changed. It can then use this ID to access the object's current `visibility` property and change it to whatever state you specify when you trigger it from an event handler.

continues on next page

Figure 14.1 Before the link is clicked to change the visibility style, the cat is visible with the title underneath the image.

Figure 14.2 After the link is clicked, the Cheshire Cat does its vanishing act, but the title underneath remains in the exact same position because the invisible object still takes up space.

MAKING OBJECTS APPEAR AND DISAPPEAR

277

2. `function toggleVisibility`
`⇢(objectID) {...}`

Add the function `toggleVisibility()` to your JavaScript. This function uses the ID of the object to be addressed—passed to it as the variable `objectID`—to find the object. It then checks the current visibility state of the object and switches it to its opposite.

3. `#cheshireCat {...}`

Set up the IDs for your object(s) with a visibility value.

4. `onload="setVisibility`
`⇢('cheshireCat', 'visible');"`

In the `<body>` tag, use the `setVisibility()` function to initialize the visibility of all the objects for which you need to know the initial visibility. For the `toggleVisibility()` function to work properly, the initial visibility has to be set.

5. `onclick="setVisibility`
`⇢('cheshireCat', 'hidden');"`

Add an event handler to trigger the function you created in step 1, and pass to it the ID for the object you want to address, as well as the visibility state you want it to have.

6. `onclick="toggleVisibility`
`⇢('cheshireCat')"`

Add an event handler to trigger the function you created in step 2, and pass to it the ID for the object you want to address. Repeat this step for each object you defined in step 3.

7. `<div id="cheshireCat">...</div>`

Set up your object(s) that will have visibility changed.

Code 14.2 The setDisplay() and toggleDisplay() functions change the display style of the designated object in the browser window.

```
<!DOCTYPE html PUBLIC "-//W3C//DTD XHTML
→ 1.0 Transitional//EN" "http://www.w3.org/TR/
→ xhtml1/DTD/xhtml1-transitional.dtd">
<html xmlns="http://www.w3.org/1999/xhtml">
<head>
    <meta http-equiv="content-type"
    → content="text/html;charset=utf-8" />
    <title>DHTML &amp; CSS for the WWW |
    → Making Objects Appear and Disappear |
    → Changing Display Style</title>
    <script language="JavaScript"
    → type="text/javascript"><!--
function setDisplay(objectID,state) {
    var object = document.getElementById
    → (objectID);
    object.style.display = state;
}
function toggleDisplay(objectID) {
    var object = document.getElementById
    → (objectID);
```

(code continues on next page)

Changing the display style

The display property allows you to tell an object how it should be treated by the surrounding content, for example, as a block element, an inline element, or as if it weren't there at all (see "Changing How an Element Is Displayed" in Chapter 5). Using JavaScript (**Code 14.2**), you can not only determine the current display state, but also change the state back and forth (**Figures 14.3** and **14.4**).

Figure 14.3 Before the link is clicked to change the display state, the cat is visible with the title underneath the image.

Figure 14.4 After the link is clicked, the Cheshire Cat does its vanishing act, but the title underneath moves up because the object is no longer there. (Unlike in Figure 14.2, where the title stays in the same place.)

To change the display state of an object:

1. ```
   function setDisplay
   → (objectID, state) {...}
   ```
   Add the function setdisplay() to your JavaScript. This function uses the ID of the object to be addressed—passed to it as the variable objectID—to find the object to be changed. It then uses this ID to access the object's current display property and change it to whatever state you specify when you trigger it from an event handler. To hide the object, you'll need to use none for the state.

2. ```
   function toggleDisplay
   → (objectID) {...}
   ```
   Add the function toggleVisibility() to your JavaScript. This function uses the ID of the object to be addressed—passed to it as the variable objectID—to find the object. It then checks the current display state of the object and switches it to either none to hide the object or block (or inline or whatever other display style you choose) to display it.

3. ```
   #cheshireCat {...}
   ```
   Set up the IDs for your object(s) with a display value.

4. ```
   onload="setDisplay
   → ('cheshireCat','block');"
   ```
   In the <body> tag, use the setDisplay() function to initialize the visibility of all the objects for which you need to know the initial display style. For the toggle-Display() function to work properly, the initial display style has to be set.

Code 14.2 *continued*

```
        state = object.style.display;
        if (state == 'none')
            object.style.display = 'block';
        else if (state != 'none')
            object.style.display = 'none';
}

    // -->
    </script>
    <style type="text/css" media="screen"><!--
#cheshireCat {
    display:block;
    }

--></style>
</head>
<body onload="setDisplay('cheshireCat',
→ 'block');">
    <a
onclick="setDisplay('cheshireCat','none');"
→ href="javascript:void('')">Remove the Cat</a> |
    <a onclick="setDisplay('cheshireCat',
    → 'block');" href="javascript:
    → void('')">Display the Cat</a> |
    <a onclick="toggleDisplay('cheshireCat');"
    → href="javascript:void('')">Change the
    → Cat's Display State</a>
        <div id="cheshireCat">
            <img src="alice24.gif" height="283"
            → width="416" border="0" />
        </div>
    <h1>The Cheshire Cat</h1>
</body>
</html>
```

5. `onclick="setDisplay`
   `→('cheshireCat', 'none');"`

Add an event handler to trigger the function you created in step 1, and pass to it the ID for the object you want to address, as well as the visibility state you want it to have. Repeat for each object.

6. `onclick="toggleDisplay`
   `→('cheshireCat')"`

Add an event handler to trigger the function you created in step 2, and pass to it the ID for the object you want to address. Repeat this step for each object.

7. `<div id="cheshireCat">...</div>`

Set up your object(s).

✔ Tips

■ In both examples, we had to use a JavaScript function to initially set the values rather than relying on the CSS. This is needed because JavaScript cannot directly access the value of a style until it has been set using JavaScript. For an alternative method, see "Finding a Style Property's Value" in Chapter 16.

■ In both examples we set up an ID definition in the style container.

MAKING OBJECTS APPEAR AND DISAPPEAR

Moving Objects from Point to Point

Using CSS, you can position an object on the screen (see "Setting an Element's Position" in Chapter 6); then you can use JavaScript to find the object's position (see "Detecting an Object's Position" in Chapter 12). But to make things really dynamic, you need to be able to move things around on the screen by changing the values for the object's position (**Code 14.3** and **Figure 14.5**).

Figure 14.5 The Mad Hatter is dashing for a fresh cup of tea.

Code 14.3 The moveObjectTo() function changes the position of the designated object in the browser window.

```
<!DOCTYPE html PUBLIC "-//W3C//DTD XHTML 1.0 Transitional//EN" "http://www.w3.org/TR/xhtml1/DTD/
→ xhtml1-transitional.dtd">
<html xmlns="http://www.w3.org/1999/xhtml">
<head>
    <meta http-equiv="content-type" content="text/html;charset=utf-8" />
    <title>DHTML &amp; CSS for the WWW | Moving Objects from Point to Point</title>
    <script language="JavaScript" type="text/javascript"><!--
function moveObjectTo(objectID,x,y) {
    var object = document.getElementById(objectID);
        object.style.left = x +'px';
        object.style.top = y + 'px';
}

    // -->
    </script>
    <style type="text/css" media="screen"><!--
#madHatter {
    position: absolute;
    top: 40px;
    left: 30px
}

    --></style>
</head>
<body>
```

(code continues on next page)

```
                      Code                    ◯
     <a onmouseover="moveObjectTo
   → ('madHatter',200,200);" onmouseout=
   → "moveObjectTo('madHatter',30,40);"
   → href="javascript:void('')">I want a
   → fresh cup...</a>
      <div id="madHatter">
         <img src="alice39.gif" height="163"
         → width="200" border="0"
         → alt="alice" />
      </div>
</body>
</html>
```

- If an element's position is defined as relative, its margins remain unaffected by the top and left properties. This means that setting the top and left margins may cause the content to move outside its naturally defined box for that object and overlap other content.

- Although top and left are not inherited by an element's children, nested elements are moved with their parent. Thus, all of the children within an object that is moved left 10 pixels will also be moved 10 pixels, but the individual children will not then move another 10 pixels.

To change the position of an object:

1. `function moveObjectTo`
   `→ (objectID,x,y) {...}`
   Add the function moveObjectTo() to your JavaScript. This function uses the ID of the object to be addressed—passed to it as the variable objectID—to find the object on the Web page. It then uses the x and y values to reset the left and top positions of the object. Remember that to stay XHTML compliant, you cannot simply assign the raw numeric values to the top and left styles, but must assign them as strings. This is why we use +'px'.

2. `#madHatter {...}`
   Set up the IDs for your object(s) with values for position and top and left coordinates.

3. `onmouseover="moveObjectTo`
   `→ ('madHatter',200,200);"`
   Add an event handler to trigger the function you created in step 1, and pass to it the ID for the object you want to address and the new coordinates for the object.

4. `<div id="madHatter">...</div>`
   Set up your object(s).

✔ Tips

- Remember that the position set in Netscape and Internet Explorer may be slightly different due to how they measure the edge of the screen.

- Although I set both top and left positions to move the object, you can use just one of these to have the object move horizontally or vertically.

- You can use negative values to move the content up and to the left instead of down and to the right, but this might move the object off the screen if set relative to the page rather than a parent element.

Moving Objects by a Certain Amount

Moving an object from one precise point to another (as shown in the previous section) is very useful, but to do this you have to know exactly where it is you want to move the object. Often, though, you simply want the object to move by a certain amount from its current location (**Figure 14.6**). To do this, you'll first need to find the location of the object and then add to that the amount by which you want to move it (**Code 14.4**).

Figure 14.6 The Mad Hatter is now staggering for a new cup of tea.

Code 14.4 The moveObjectBy() function changes the position of the designated object in the browser window by a certain amount every time the mouse pointer rolls onto and then off the link.

```
<!DOCTYPE html PUBLIC "-//W3C//DTD XHTML 1.0 Transitional//EN" "http://www.w3.org/TR/xhtml1/DTD/
  xhtml1-transitional.dtd">
<html xmlns="http://www.w3.org/1999/xhtml">
<head>
    <meta http-equiv="content-type" content="text/html;charset=utf-8" />
    <title>DHTML &amp; CSS for the WWW | Moving Things by a Certain Amount</title>
    <script language="JavaScript" type="text/javascript"><!--
function moveObjectBy(objectID,deltaX,deltaY) {
    var object = document.getElementById(objectID);
    if (object.offsetLeft != null) {
       var plusLeft = object.offsetLeft;
       var plusTop = object.offsetTop;
       object.style.left = deltaX + plusLeft +'px';
       object.style.top = deltaY + plusTop + 'px';
    }
}
    // -->
    </script>
    <style type="text/css" media="screen"><!--
#madHatter {
    position: absolute;
    top: 40px;
```

(code continues on next page)

Code 14.4 *continued*

```
                          Code
    left: 30px
    }
    --></style>
</head>
<body>
    <a onmouseover="moveObjectBy
    ('madHatter',75,100);" onmouseout=
    "moveObjectBy('madHatter',-25,-55);"
    href="javascript:void('')">I want a
    fresh cup...</a>
        <div id="madHatter">
            <img src="alice39.gif" height="163"
            width="200" border="0" />
        </div>
</body>
</html>
```

To change the position of an object by a certain amount:

1. function moveObjectBy
    → (objectID, deltaX,deltaY) {...}

    Add the function moveObjectBy() to your JavaScript. This function uses the ID of the object to be addressed—passed to it as the variable objectID—to find the object that's being moved on the Web page. The function then uses offsetLeft and offsetTop to find the current position of the object and adds the deltaX and deltaY values to move the object to its new position.

2. #madHatter {...}

    Set up the IDs for your object(s) with values for position and top and left coordinates.

3. onmouseover="moveObjectBy
    → ('madHatter',75,100);"

    Add an event handler to trigger the function you created in step 1, and to pass it the ID for the object you want to address and the number of pixels you want to move it from its current location. Positive numbers move the object down and to the right; negative move it up and to the left.

4. <div id="madHatter">...</div>

    Set up your object(s).

✔ Tip

■ Netscape doesn't like to have values added directly to the left and top properties. So whereas you can simply use += to add delta values to the current position in Internet Explorer, in Netscape, you have to calculate the current position of the object, add the delta values, and then assign the resulting value to the top. What a pain.

MOVING OBJECTS BY A CERTAIN AMOUNT

285

Moving Objects in 3-D

All positioned objects can be stacked (see "Stacking Elements" in Chapter 6), and you can use JavaScript to find the object's order in the z-index as well as to change that order (**Code 14.5** and **Figures 14.7** and **14.8**).

To set the 3-D position of an object:

1. `var prevObjectID = null;`

`var prevLayer = 0;`

In your JavaScript, initialize two variables:

▲ `prevObjectID`, which stores the ID of the previously selected object

▲ `prevLayer`, which stores the z-index of the previously selected object

2. `function setLayer` `(objectID,layerNum) {...}`

Add the function `setLayer()` to your JavaScript. This function reassigns the z-index of an object to the indicated layer number.

3. `function findLayer(objectID) {...}`

Add the function `findLayer()` to your JavaScript. This function uses the ID of the object to be addressed—passed to it as the variable `objectID`—to find and return the current z-index of the layer.

4. `function swapLayer(objectID) {...}`

Add the function `swapLayer()` to your JavaScript. This function demotes the previously selected layer (if there is one) back to its preceding z-index and then promotes the selected layer (as indicated by the `objectID`) to the top.

5. `#alice1 {...}`

Set up the IDs for your object(s) with position and z-index values.

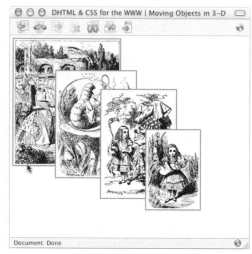

Figure 14.7 This is the stacking order when the page is first loaded.

Figure 14.8 The Queen and Alice now stand in the forefront.

6. `id="alice1"`

Set up your object(s).

7. `onclick="swapLayer('alice1')"`

Add to the layer an event handler that triggers the `swapLayer()` function.

✔ Tip

■ Using a negative number for the z-index causes an element to be stacked that many levels below its parent instead of above.

Code 14.5 The `swapLayer()` function works in conjunction with the `findLayer()` and `setLayer()`functions to pop an object to the top of the stack.

```
<!DOCTYPE html PUBLIC "-//W3C//DTD XHTML 1.0 Transitional//EN" "http://www.w3.org/TR/xhtml1/DTD/
→ xhtml1-transitional.dtd">
<html xmlns="http://www.w3.org/1999/xhtml">
<head>
    <meta http-equiv="content-type" content="text/html;charset=utf-8" />
    <title>DHTML &amp; CSS for the WWW | Moving Objects in 3-D</title>
    <script language="JavaScript" type="text/javascript"><!--
var prevObjectID = null;
var prevLayer = 0;
function setLayer(objectID,layerNum) {
    var object = document.getElementById(objectID);
    object.style.zIndex = layerNum;
}
function findLayer(objectID) {
    var object = document.getElementById(objectID);
    if (object.style.zIndex != null)
        return object.style.zIndex;
    return (null);
}
function swapLayer(objectID) {
    if (prevObjectID != null)
    setLayer(prevObjectID,prevLayer);
    prevLayer = findLayer(objectID);
    prevObjectID = objectID;
    setLayer(objectID,1000);
}
    // -->
    </script>
    <style type="text/css" media="screen"><!--
```

(code continues on next page)

Code 14.5 *continued*

```
#alice1 {
    position: absolute;
    z-index: 3;
    top: 175px;
    left: 255px;
    width: 100;
    border: solid 2px gray;
}
#alice2 {
    position: absolute;
    z-index: 2;
    top: 100px;
    left: 170px;
    width: 140;
    border: solid 2px gray;
}
#alice3 {
    position: absolute;
    z-index: 1;
    top: 65px;
    left: 85px;
    width: 150;
    border: solid 2px gray;
}
#alice4 {
    position: absolute;
    z-index: 0;
    top: 5px;
    left: 5px;
    width: 200;
    border: solid 2px gray;
}
    --></style>
</head>
<body>
    <img src="alice22.gif" height="147" width="100" border="0" id="alice1" onclick="swapLayer
    ➝ ('alice1')" /><br clear="all" />
    <img src="alice32.gif" height="201" width="140" border="0" id="alice2" onclick="swapLayer
    ➝ ('alice2')" /><br clear="all" />
    <img src="alice15.gif" height="198" width="150" border="0" id="alice3" onclick="swapLayer
    ➝ ('alice3')" /><br clear="all" />
    <img src="alice29.gif" height="236" width="200" border="0" id="alice4" onclick="swapLayer
    ➝ ('alice4')" /><br clear="all" />
</body>
</html>
```

Code 14.6 The setClip() function redraws the boundaries of the clipping region set around an object.

```
<!DOCTYPE html PUBLIC "-//W3C//DTD XHTML
→ 1.0 Transitional//EN" "http://www.w3.org/TR/
→ xhtml1/DTD/xhtml1-transitional.dtd">
<html xmlns="http://www.w3.org/1999/xhtml">
<head>
    <meta http-equiv="content-type"
content="text/html;charset=utf-8" />
    <title>DHTML &amp; CSS for the WWW |
    → Finding an Object&rsquo;s Visible
    → Area</title>
    <script language="JavaScript"
    → type="text/javascript">
function setClip(objectID, clipTop, clipRight,
→ clipBottom, clipLeft) {
    var object = document.getElementById
    → (objectID);
    object.style.clip = 'rect(' + clipTop +
    → 'px ' + clipRight + 'px ' + clipBottom
    → + 'px ' + clipLeft +'px)';
}
    </script>
    <style type="text/css" media="screen"><!--
#cheshireCat {
    position: absolute;
    top: 60px;
    left: 0;
    overflow: hidden;
    clip: rect(15px 350px 195px 50px)
}
    --></style>
</head>
<body>
    <a onmouseover="setClip('cheshireCat',35,
    → 320,400,70)" onmouseout="setClip
    → ('cheshireCat',15,350,195,50)"
    → href="javascript:void('')">What is the
    → Cheshire Cat smiling about? </a>
        <div id="cheshireCat">
            <img src="alice31.gif" height="480"
            → width="379" border="0" />
        </div>
</body>
</html>
```

Changing an Object's Visible Area

The clipping region of an object defines how much of that object is visible in the window (see "Setting the Visible Area of an Element" in Chapter 7). If it is left alone, the entire object is visible. But if you clip the object, you can have as much or as little of it visible as you want. You can then use JavaScript to determine the clipping region (see "Finding an Object's Visible Area" in Chapter 12). In addition, DHTML allows you to change the clipping region on the fly allowing you to not just show and hide the entire object, but select parts of it (**Code 14.6** and **Figures 14.9** and **14.10**).

To change the visible area of an object:

1. `function setClip(objectID, clipTop,`
`→ clipRight, clipBottom, clipLeft)`
`→ {...}`

Add the function `setClip()` to your JavaScript. This function uses the ID of the object to be addressed—passed to it as the variable `objectID`—to find the object that will be reclipped. The function then uses the clip style to set a new clipping region for the object.

2. `#cheshireCat {...}`

Set up the ID(s) for your object(s), with values for `clip` (the initial clipping region).

3. `onmouseover="setClip`
`→ ('cheshireCat', 35,320,400,70)"`

Include an event handler to trigger the `setClip()` function. Remember that because this function will be using the DOM, it has to be triggered from an event.

4. `<div id="cheshireCat">...</div>`

Set up your object(s) for which you want to change the clipping region.

✔ Tips

- The element's borders and padding will be clipped along with the content of the element, but its margin will not be.

- Netscape has difficulty applying clipping directly to many tags, including the image tag. Therefore, it's best to use a `<div>` or `<span>` tag when you apply clipping and then place the other content inside of these.

- Currently, clips can be only rectangular, but future versions of CSS promise to support other shapes.

Figure 14.9 What is the Cheshire Cat smiling at? Roll over the link and find out.

Figure 14.10 The Cheshire Cat is smiling because the King can't order his executioner to chop off a head that has no body. This fact makes the Queen of Hearts very, very angry.

Code 14.7 The function writeName() is just one way to use innerHTML to change the content of a layer using input from a form field.

```
● ● ●                    Code
<!DOCTYPE html PUBLIC "-//W3C//DTD XHTML
 ⇢ 1.0 Transitional//EN" "http://www.w3.org/TR/
 ⇢ xhtml1/DTD/xhtml1-transitional.dtd">
<html xmlns="http://www.w3.org/1999/xhtml">
<head>
     <meta http-equiv="content-type"
      ⇢ content="text/html;charset=utf-8" />
     <title>DHTML &amp; CSS for the WWW |
      ⇢ Changing the Content After Loading
      ⇢ </title>
     <script language="JavaScript"
      ⇢ type="text/javascript"><!--
function writeName() {
     var userName = document.getElementById
      ⇢ ('yourName').value;
     var object = document.getElementById
      ⇢ ('response');
     object.innerHTML = '<h1>Hello <i>' +
      ⇢ userName + '</i>!</h1><img
      ⇢ src="alice09a.gif" alt="Alice"
      ⇢ width="278" height="312" border="0"/>'
}
     // -->
     </script>
     <style type="text/css" media="screen"><!--
h1 { color: red; font-size: 48px; font-family:
 ⇢ Georgia, "Times New Roman", Times, serif }
     --></style>
</head>
<body>

<input type="text" id="yourName" size="30" />
     <input type="submit" name="enter"
      ⇢ value="Enter" onclick="writeName()" />
     <div id="response">
Enter your name and press Enter/Return.
     </div>
</body>
</html>
```

Changing an Object's Content

Another important method for making changes to a Web page without having to reload the page is to use the innerHTML object. This allows you to replace or add to the current content within an object, including text and HTML tags. Not only can you change content (for example, changing a layer's visibility), but you can also react to input from the user—for example, from a form field (**Code 14.7** and **Figures 14.11 and 14.12**). This can be an amazingly powerful technique, allowing you to dynamically update content on the fly without having to resort to frames. However, one shortcoming of this technique is that it is not a part of the official ECMA JavaScript standard, but was created by Microsoft for Internet Explorer 4+. The good news is that most browsers including Mozilla browsers (including Netscape 6+), Opera, and Safari are also supporting the method.

To change the content of a layer:

1. `function writeName() {...}`

Add the function `writeName()` to your JavaScript. This function first looks in the form field `yourName` to get its content and assign it to the variable `userName`, and then uses that variable, combined with other text and HTML tags, to change the content of the object named `response` by means of the `innerHTML` object.

2. `<input type="text" id="yourName"`
`→ size="30" />`

Add the input field that is queried by the function from step 1.

3. `onclick="writeName()"`

Add an event handler to trigger the `writeName()` function. In this example, I'm using an input button, but you can use any object type you want.

4. `<div id="response">...</div>`

Set up the object whose content you'll be changing, making sure to give it a unique ID. You can enter the initial content for the object or simply leave it empty to fill in later.

✔ Tips

■ Internet Explorer 4+ can also use a method called innerText to change text bu not add code, but this method is not widely supported.

■ If you simply want to add to the current content in a layer without replacing it, you can use just += rather than = to assign the values. The new content is added after the current content of the layer.

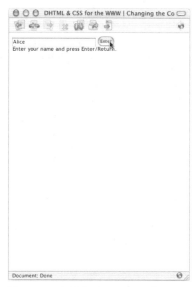

Figure 14.11 Initially the message is to enter your name.

Figure 14.12 After you enter text and click the button, the message is changed without reloading the page or changing the visibility of layers by changing the content of the layer.

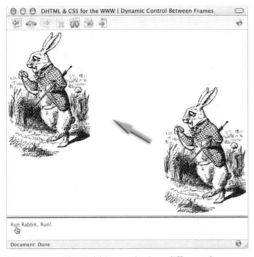

Figure 14.13 The Rabbit may be in a different frame, but the code will hunt him down and make him run.

Code 14.8 In this example, I have set up a frame document (index.html) with frames named "content" and "controls." The frames' sources are content.html and control.html, respectively.

```
<!DOCTYPE html PUBLIC "-//W3C//DTD XHTML
→ 1.0 Frameset//EN" "http://www.w3.org/TR/
→ xhtml1/DTD/xhtml1-frameset.dtd">
<html xmlns="http://www.w3.org/1999/xhtml">
<head>
    <meta http-equiv="content-type"
    → content="text/html;charset=utf-8" />
    <title>DHTML &amp; CSS for the WWW |
    → Dynamic Control Between Frames</title>
</head>
<frameset rows="*,50">
    <frame name="topFrame" src="content.html"
    → noresize="noresize" scrolling="no" />
    <frame name="bottomFrame"
    → src="controls.html" noresize="noresize"
scrolling="no" />
</frameset>
</html>
```

Controlling Objects Between Frames

You can use JavaScript to control objects within one frame without much trouble. Controlling objects in another frame, however, is a little more complicated (**Figure 14.13**). To do this, rather than just passing the function the name of the object you want to change, you also have to pass the function the name of the frame the object is in.

To control elements in other frames:

1. `index.html`

   Set up your frames document (**Code 14.8**), making sure to name the frames that will have dynamic content (**Figure 14.14**). Save this file as index.html.

   continues on next page

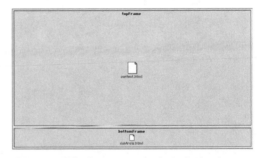

Figure 14.14 The frameset set up by index.html.

2. content.html

Now set up an HTML document with the objects to be controlled from the other frame. Include positioned objects with IDs that can be controlled with JavaScript (**Code 14.9**). In this example, I've set up an object called whiteRabbit. Save this file as content.html.

3. controls.html

Set up the HTML document that will control the element in the other frame. You have to change the function moveObject(), shown in "Moving Objects from Point to Point," to become moveObject-Frame() that uses the function frame-Name—which, along with the objectID variable is used to find the object (**Code 14.10**). Save this file as controls.html.

Now, when you load the file index.html into a Web browser, the files content.html and controls.html are loaded into the frames. The bottom frame (controls) includes a link that controls the object whiteRabbit in the upper frame (content)..

Code 14.9 The object whiteRabbit has been set up and can now be controlled from this frame or any other frame by adding the frame name to the path when finding the object.

```
<!DOCTYPE html PUBLIC "-//W3C//DTD XHTML
→ 1.0 Transitional//EN" "http://www.w3.org/TR/
→ xhtml1/DTD/xhtml1-transitional.dtd">
<html xmlns="http://www.w3.org/1999/xhtml">
<head>
    <meta http-equiv="content-type"
    → content="text/html;charset=utf-8" />
    <title>DHTML &amp; CSS for the WWW |
    → Content Frame</title>
    <style type="text/css" media="screen"><!--
#whiteRabbit {
    position: absolute;
    top: 125px;
    left: 350px
}
    --></style>
</head>
<body>
    <div id="whiteRabbit">
        <img src="alice02.gif" height="300"
        → width="200" border="0" />
    </div>
</body>
</html>
```

✔ Tips

- Notice that the frames use the name attribute rather than id. The name attribute is being phased out for most uses, but frames will still use it.

- This example shows you how to move an object across frames, but you can use any of the other dynamic functions described in this book in your frames.

- For all intents and purposes, a window is like another frame. If you have two windows open, you can use this technique to communicate between two windows, as long as they're named. In addition, this will work with iFrames as well.

Code 14.10 The code in controls.html uses a variation of the moveObject() function presented earlier in this chapter. The main difference is that the function is passed not only the ID of the object to be moved, but also the name of the frame the object is in.

```
Code

<!DOCTYPE html PUBLIC "-//W3C//DTD XHTML 1.0 Transitional//EN" "http://www.w3.org/TR/xhtml1/DTD/
⟶ xhtml1-transitional.dtd">
<html xmlns="http://www.w3.org/1999/xhtml">
<head>
    <meta http-equiv="content-type" content="text/html;charset=utf-8" />
    <title>DHTML &amp; CSS for the WWW | Controls Frame</title>
    <script language="JavaScript" type="text/javascript"><!--
function moveObjectFrame(objectID,frameName,x,y){
    var object = top[frameName].document.getElementById(objectID);
    object.style.left = x + 'px';
    object.style.top = y + 'px';
}
    // -->
    </script>
</head>
<body>
    <a href="javascript:void('')" onmouseover="moveObjectFrame('whiteRabbit','topFrame',10,10)"
    ⟶ onmouseout="moveObjectFrame('whiteRabbit','topFrame',350,125)">Run Rabbit, Run!</a>
</body>
</html>
```

ADVANCED DYNAMIC TECHNIQUES

In Chapter 14, we learned the basic building blocks for creating a dynamic Web site. This includes relatively simple tasks such as changing an object's position and visibility. Now, it is time to combine those techniques to not only change objects spatially, but to add a temporal element so that objects change over time. This will allow us to animate objects and allow greater user interactivity with the objects. In addition, we want to look at ways to make changes to the browser window to place it exactly where it is needed while working.

Making a Function Run Again

To create a dynamic function, you often need to have that function run repeatedly until, well, until you don't want it to run anymore. This recursive running of the function allows you to animate objects or cause objects to wait for a particular event to happen in the browser window before continuing (**Code 15.1** and **Figure 15.1**).

Code 15.1 The setUpAnnoyingFlash() function prepares the initial values of variables that are then run in the annoyingFlash() function. Then annoyingFlash() keeps running, and running, and running…causing the image to appear and disappear at 1-second intervals until the visitor clicks the image while it is showing.

```
○ ○ ○                   Code                   ○
<!DOCTYPE html PUBLIC "-//W3C//DTD XHTML
→ 1.0 Transitional//EN" "http://www.w3.org/TR/
→ xhtml1/DTD/xhtml1-transitional.dtd">
<html xmlns="http://www.w3.org/1999/xhtml">
<head>
     <meta http-equiv="content-type"
     → content="text/html;charset=utf-8" />
     <title>DHTML &amp; CSS for the WWW |
     → Making a Function Run Again</title>
     <script language="JavaScript"
     → type="text/javascript"><!--
var theDelay = 500;
var object = null;
var toStop = 0;
var state = null;
function setUpAnnoyingFlash
→ (objectID,onOffon) {
```

(code continues on next page)

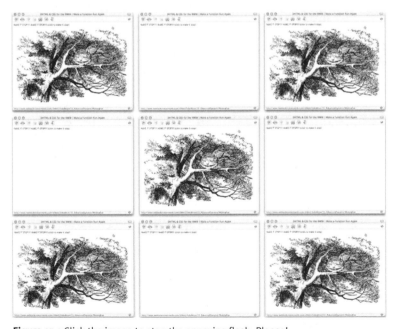

Figure 15.1 Click the image to stop the annoying flash. Please!

Code 15.1 *continued*

```
      if (onOffon == 1) {
          toStop = 1;
          object = document.getElementById
          → (objectID);
          object.style.visibility = 'visible';
          state = 'visible';
          annoyingFlash();
      }
      else toStop = 0;
}
function annoyingFlash() {
    if (toStop == 1) {
        if (state == 'hidden' )
            object.style.visibility = 'visible';
        else {
            if (state == 'visible')
                object.style.visibility =
                → 'hidden';
        else object.style.visibility =
        → 'visible';
        }
        state = object.style.visibility;
        setTimeout ('annoyingFlash()',
        → theDelay);
    }
    else{
            object.style.visibility = 'visible';
            return;
    }
}
    // -->
    </script>
    <style type="text/css" media="screen"><!-
#cheshireCat {
    visibility: visible;
    position: relative
}
    --></style>
</head>
<body onload="setUpAnnoyingFlash
→ ('cheshireCat',1);">
    MAKE IT STOP!!!! MAKE IT STOP!!!
    → (Click to make it stop.)
        <div id="cheshireCat">
            <a onclick="setUpAnnoyingFlash
            → ('cheshireCat',0)" href="#"><img
            → src="alice24.gif" height="435"
            → width="640" border="0" /></a>
        </div>
</body>
</html>
```

To make a function recursive:

1. `theDelay = 500;`

Initialize the global variables:

▲ `theDelay` sets the amount of time in milliseconds between each running of the function. The value 1,000 milliseconds equates to a one-second delay, so 500 is half a second.

▲ `object` is used to record the object that is being changed and is initially set to null.

▲ `toStop` records whether the function should be repeating (1) or not (0).

2. `function setUpAnnoyingFlash`
`→ (objectID, onOffon) {...}`

Add a function that sets initial parameters for the repeating function, then calls the function to start it up. In this example, the function `setUpAnnoyingFlash()` will check to see if the function should be started, finds the object to be used, sets its initial state, and triggers the recursive function. If the variable `onOffon` is 1, the function sets `toStop` to 1 (the function should keep repeating). It uses the ID of the object to be addressed—passed to it as the variable `objectID`—to find the object and then runs the function `annoyingFlash()`. If `onOffon` is 0, this function sets `toStop` to 0, thus stopping the function `annoyingFlash()` from running.

continues on next page

MAKING A FUNCTION RUN AGAIN

3. `function annoyingFlash() {...}`

Add the function you want to repeat. In this example, `annoyingFlash()` is started by the `setUpAnnoyingFlash()` function in step 2. If `toStop` is 1, the visibility is toggled (`visible` if hidden, `hidden` if visible). Then the function runs itself again, using the `setTimeout()` method. The `annoyingFlash()` function keeps running until `toStop` is `0`, in which case the visibility is finally set to `visible` and the function stops running.

4. `#cheshireCat {...}`

Set up the IDs for your object(s) with the relevant styles; in this example, the visibility state.

5. `onload="setUpAnnoyingFlash`
`→ ('cheshireCat',1);"`

Add event handlers to trigger the function you created in step 2, and pass to it the ID for the object. In this example, if you want to have flashing, indicate whether you want the annoying flash to be activated (`1`) or not (`0`).

6. `<div id="cheshireCat">...</div>`

Set up your object(s) as needed, based on the ID from step 4.

✔ Tip

■ When you run this example code, notice that you can click the cat to stop the flashing only while the image is visible. The link is on the page only if the object is visible.

Why setTimeout()?

One common question I get about running a function repeatedly with the `setTimeout()` function is, "Why not just call the function from within itself?" There are two reasons:

◆ Netscape 4 has a bug that causes the entire browser to crash when a function calls itself recursively. Although Netscape 4 does not need to be a going concern, this can be very annoying if a user hits your site using this browser.

◆ `setTimeout()` makes it easy to control a pause between the function's looping back and running again. This can come in handy if you need the function to run more slowly than the computer would run it automatically.

Animating an Object

Document: Done

Figure 15.2 The Mad Hatter dashes across the screen.

Code 15.2 The startAnimate() function finds the initial left and top positions of the object. It also sets up the object's DOM and starts the animation function. The animateObject() function is recursive, so it keeps repositioning the object incrementally until the object reaches its finishing point.

```
Code
<!DOCTYPE html PUBLIC "-//W3C//DTD XHTML
→ 1.0 Transitional//EN" "http://www.w3.org/TR/
→ xhtml1/DTD/xhtml1-transitional.dtd">
<html xmlns="http://www.w3.org/1999/xhtml">
<head>
    <meta http-equiv="content-type"
    → content="text/html;charset=utf-8" />
    <title>DHTML &amp; CSS for the WWW |
    → Animating an Object</title>
    <script language="JavaScript"
    → type="text/javascript"><!--
    var animateSpeed = 5;
    var object = null;
    var fX = null;
    var fY = null;
    var cX = null;
    var cY = null;
    var dX = null;
    var dY = null;
    var stepX = null;
```

(code continues on next page)

When most people think about dynamic techniques, they don't think of simply moving objects from one point to another (see "Moving Objects from Point to Point" in Chapter 14), but of making objects slide across the screen from one point to another or along a curved path. Using a function that runs recursively (see the previous section, "Making a Function Run Again"), you can make any object that has been positioned (see "Setting an Element's Position" in Chapter 6) seem to glide from one point to another (**Figure 15.2**).

Animating an object in a straight line

For a straight line, the process of animation is relatively straightforward: Simply move the object incrementally horizontally and/or vertically step-by-step from its first position to its last position. There is one small snag, though; if the horizontal and vertical distances the object has to move are at all different, you'll need to adjust step movement to get a straight line (**Code 15.2**). This is handled by calculating the slope of the angle between the two points, and using this value to adjust how far the object should be moved in a single step.

ANIMATING AN OBJECT

To animate an object in a straight line:

1. animateSpeed = 5;

Initialize the global variables:

- ▲ animateSpeed sets the amount of delay in the recursive running of the function. The larger the number, the slower the object slides, but the choppier the animation looks.

- ▲ object records the object's address.

- ▲ fX records the final left position of the object.

- ▲ fY records the final top position of the object.

- ▲ cX records the current left position of the object.

- ▲ cY records the current top position of the object.

- ▲ dX keeps track of the amount the object has moved to the left while being animated.

- ▲ dY keeps track of the amount the object has moved from the top while being animated.

- ▲ stepX records how far the object should move horizontally for each step in the animation.

- ▲ stepY records how far the object should move vertically for each step in the animation.

- ▲ slope records the ratio of x to y, for the slant of the object's path from the starting position to its final position. This is used to calculate the x and y step values so that the object goes in a straight line between the two points.

Code 15.2 *continued*

```
        var stepY = null;
        var slope = null;
function initAnimate(objectID,x,y) {
        object = document.getElementById
        → (objectID);
        fX = x;
        fY = y;

cX = object.offsetLeft;
        cY = object.offsetTop;
        dX = Math.abs(fX-cX);
        dY = Math.abs(fY-cY);
        if ((dX == 0) || (dY == 0)) slope = 0;

else slope = dY/dX;
            if (dX>=dY) {
                if (cX<fX) stepX = animateSpeed;
                else if (cX>fX) stepX =
                → - animateSpeed;
                if (cY<fY) stepY =
                → animateSpeed*slope;
                else if (cY>fY) stepY =
                → -animateSpeed*slope;
            }
            else if (dX<dY)  {
                if (cY<fY) stepY= animateSpeed;
                else if (cY>fY) stepY=
                → - animateSpeed;
                if (cX<fX) stepX =
                → animateSpeed/slope;
                else if (cX>fX) stepX =
                → -animateSpeed/slope;
            }
        animateObject()
}
function animateObject()  {
    if ((dX > 0) || (dY > 0)) {
        object.style.left = Math.round(cX)
        → + 'px';
        object.style.top = Math.round(cY)
        → + 'px';
        cX = cX + stepX;
        cY = cY + stepY;
        dX = dX - Math.abs(stepX);
        dY = dY - Math.abs(stepY);
        setTimeout ('animateObject()',0);
    }
    else {
```

(code continues on next page)

Code 15.2 *continued*

```
        object.style.left = fX + 'px';
        object.style.top = fY + 'px';
    }
    return;
}

    //-->
    </script>
    <style type="text/css" media="screen"><!--
#madHatter {
    position: absolute;
    left: 10px;
    top: 10px;
}

    --></style>
</head>
<body onload="initAnimate('madHatter',300,250)">
    <div id="madHatter">
        <img src="alice39.gif" height="163"
width="200" border="0" />
    </div>
</body>
</html>
```

2. `function initAnimate(objectID,x,y)`
   `→ {...}`

   Add the function `initAnimate()` to your JavaScript. This function uses the ID of the object to locate it on the screen, sets the final x,y position of the object (`fX` and `fY`), calculates the current x,y position of the object (`cX` and `cY`), calculates the slope of the animation path, and then uses that to calculate how far the object should move horizontally and vertically for each step in the animation. Finally, this function runs the `animateObject()` function.

3. `function animateObject() {...}`

   Add the function `animateObject()` to your JavaScript. This function checks to see if the object has moved past its final position, then moves the object to its new position, calculates the next position it should be moved to by adding the step variables to the current position, then subtracts how far the object has moved, and then runs the function again. If the object has moved to its final position, it is moved back slightly to compensate and the function ends.

4. `#madHatter {...}`

   Set up the ID for your animated object with values for position and top and left positions.

5. `onload="initAnimate`
   `→ ('madHatter', 200,200)"`

   Add an event handler to trigger the function you created in step 2, passing the function the ID of the object you want to animate and the final position to which you want that object to move.

6. `<div id="madHatter">...</div>`

   Set up the object to be animated.

ANIMATING AN OBJECT

Animating an object in a circle

In many ways, a circular animation is easier to code than a straight line, because you don't need to keep track of the slope. Instead, simply feed the formula the radius of the circle and the script takes it from there (**Code 15.3** and **Figure 15.3**).

To animate an object in a circle:

1. `animateSpeed = 10;`

Initialize the global variables:

▲ `animateSpeed` sets the amount of delay in the recursive running of the function. The larger the number, the slower the object slides, but the choppier the animation looks.

▲ `object` records the object's address.

▲ `cX` records the current left position of the object.

▲ `cY` records the current top position of the object.

▲ `fX` records the final left position of the object.

▲ `fY` records the final top position of the object.

▲ `next` keeps track of the amount the object has moved around the circular path.

▲ `radius` keeps track of the distance from the object to the center of the circle around which the object is being animated.

Figure 15.3 The Mad Hatter dashes around in a circle.

Code 15.3 The circular animation script calculates where the object should be displayed along the radius of a circle, based on a radius you initially feed it.

```
<!DOCTYPE html PUBLIC "-//W3C//DTD XHTML
→ 1.0 Transitional//EN" "http://www.w3.org/TR/
→ xhtml1/DTD/xhtml1-transitional.dtd">
<html xmlns="http://www.w3.org/1999/xhtml">
<head>
    <meta http-equiv="content-type"
    → content="text/html;charset=utf-8" />
    <title>DHTML &amp; CSS for the WWW |
    → Animating an Object</title>
    <script language="JavaScript"
    → type="text/javascript"><!--
var animateSpeed = 10;
var object = null;
var cX = null;
var cY = null;
var fX = null;
var fY = null;
var next = null;
var radius = null;
function initAnimateCircle(objectID,
→ theRadius) {
```

(code continues on next page)

Code 15.3 continued

```
                                              Code

      object = document.getElementById
      ⇥ (objectID);
      radius = theRadius;
      cX = fX = object.offsetLeft;
      cY = fY = object.offsetTop;
      next = 1;
      animateObjectCircle();
}
function animateObjectCircle() {
   if (next < 72) {
      var nX = cX + (Math.cos(next *
      ⇥ (Math.PI/36)) * radius);
      var nY = cY + (Math.sin(next *
      ⇥ (Math.PI/36)) * radius);
      object.style.left = Math.round(nX)
      ⇥ + 'px';
      object.style.top = Math.round(nY)
      ⇥ + 'px';
      cX = nX;
      cY = nY;
      next++;
      setTimeout ('animateObjectCircle()',
      ⇥ animateSpeed);
   }
   else {
      object.style.left = fX + 'px';
      object.style.top = fY + 'px';
   }
   return;
}
   //-->
   </script>
   <style type="text/css" media="screen"><!--
#madHatter {
   position: absolute;
   left: 100px;
   top: 50px;
}
   --></style>
</head>
<body onload="initAnimateCircle
⇥ ('madHatter',10)">
   <div id="madHatter">
      <img src="alice39.gif" height="163"
      ⇥ width="200" border="0" />
   </div>
</body>
</html>
```

2. `function initAnimateCircle`
   `⇥ (objectID,theRadius) {...}`

Add the function `initAnimateCircle()` to your JavaScript. This function uses the ID of the object to locate it on the screen, finds the current x,y position of the object (`cX` and `cY`), and also stores this as the object's final x,y position (`fX` and `fY`). Finally, this function runs the `animateObjectCircle()` function.

3. `function animateObjectCircle() {...}`

Add the function `animateObjectCircle()` to your JavaScript. This function first checks to see if the object has made a full circle (in this example, 72 steps around the circumference). If not, the function calculates the next position of the object along the circumference of the circle, moves the object, increases **next** by 1, and runs the function again. Once the function reaches 72, the object is reset to its initial (final) position. This ensures that the object is exactly positioned in case of any mathematical discrepancies that might offset it by a few pixels and then finishes.

4. `#madHatter {...}`

Set up the ID for your animated object with values for position and top and left positions.

5. `onload="initAnimateCircle`
   `⇥ ('madHatter',10)"`

Add an event handler to trigger the function you created in step 2, passing the function the ID of the object you want to animate and the radius of the circle around which you want to animate it.

6. `<div id="madHatter">...</div>`

Set up the object to be animated.

Making an Object Draggable

Another staple of GUIs is drag-and-drop: the ability to drag windows, files, and whatnot across the screen and drop them into a new element or location.

As an example of this technique, we'll create a poetry kit for a Web page (**Code 15.4** and **Figure 15.4**). You may have one of these games on your own refrigerator right now: Each word is on a magnetic chip, which can be moved around and combined with other chips to make sentences.

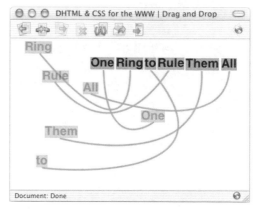

Figure 15.4 Can you figure out the word jumble?

Code 15.4 The three functions `pickIt`, `dragIt`, and `dropIt` allow the visitor to move an object around on the screen.

```
<!DOCTYPE html PUBLIC "-//W3C//DTD XHTML 1.0 Transitional//EN" "http://www.w3.org/TR/xhtml1/DTD/
→ xhtml1-transitional.dtd">
<html xmlns="http://www.w3.org/1999/xhtml">
<head>
     <meta http-equiv="content-type" content="text/html;charset=utf-8" />
     <title>DHTML &amp; CSS for the WWW | Drag and Drop</title>
     <script language="JavaScript">
     <!--
var object = null;
var cX = 0;
var cY = 0;
function initPage () {
     document.onmousedown = pickIt;
     document.onmousemove = dragIt;
     document.onmouseup = dropIt;
}
function pickIt(evt) {
     evt = (evt) ? evt :
((window.event) ? event : null);
     var objectID = (evt.target) ? evt.target.id : ((evt.srcElement) ? evt.srcElement.id : null);
     if (objectID.indexOf('chip')!=-1) object = document.getElementById(objectID);
     if (object) {
        object.style.zIndex = 100;
        cX = evt.clientX - object.offsetLeft;
        cY = evt.clientY - object.offsetTop;
        return;
```

(code continues on next page)

Code 15.4 *continued*

```
        }
        else {
            object = null;
            return;
        }
    }
function dragIt(evt) {
    evt = (evt) ? evt : ((window.event) ?
→ event : null);
    if (object) {
        object.style.left = evt.clientX -
→ cX + 'px';
        object.style.top = evt.clientY -
→ cY + 'px';
        return false;
    }
}
function dropIt() {
    if (object) {
        object.style.zIndex = 0;
        object = null;
        return false;
    }
}
    // -->
    </script>
    <style type="text/css"><!--
.chip {
    color: black;
    font: bold 16pt helvetica, sans-serif;
    background-color: #999999;
    cursor: move;
    position: absolute;
    z-index: 0;
    layer-background-color: #999999;
}
#chip1 {
    top: 123px;
    left: 225px;
}
#chip2 {
```

(code continues on next page)

To set up element dragging:

1. `var object = null;`

    Initialize the following global variables:

    ▲ `object` records the address of the object being moved.

    ▲ `cX` records the current left position of the object.

    ▲ `cY` records the current top position of the object.

2. `function initPage() {...}`

    Add the `initPage()` function to your code. This function sets the event handlers to be automatically triggered for mousedown, mousemove, and mouseup events that occur anywhere on the page (see "Binding Events to Objects" in Chapter 10).

3. `function pickIt(evt) {...}`

    Add `pickIt()` to the JavaScript. This function—which is very much like the `findObject()` function (see "Detecting Which Object Was Clicked" in Chapter 12)—finds the ID of the object that the visitor clicked. If the visitor clicked one of the objects that contains the word chip in its ID, the function sets the z-index of that object to 100, which should place it well above all other objects on the page. Otherwise, if a chip is not clicked, the function does nothing.

4. `function dragIt(evt) {...}`

    Add the `dragIt()` function to your JavaScript. This function will be triggered every time the visitor moves the mouse. The function doesn't do anything unless the visitor clicks one of the chips, in which case the function moves the chip as the visitor moves the mouse.

    continues on next page

5. `function dropIt() {...}`

Add the `dropIt()` function to the JavaScript. This function is triggered when the visitor releases the mouse button. It sets the object's z-index at 0 and then resets the variable `object` to `null`. This releases the object from being dragged dropping it in its new position.

6. `.chip {...}`

Set up a class style to define the appearance of the movable objects on the screen. Make sure to define the chips as being absolutely positioned with a z-index of 0.

7. `#chip1 {...}`

Set up a different ID selector for each object on the screen. Give each object an initial top and left position.

8. `onload="initPage()"`

In the <body> tag, add an `onload` event handler to trigger `initPage()`.

9. `<span id="chip1" class="chip">...`
`↪ </span>`

Set up layers for as many objects as needed, each with its own unique ID.

✔ Tips

- Dragging and dropping has a variety of applications, including allowing you to create movable areas of content and navigation.

- Dragging and dropping code can be very sensitive, so be careful when making changes, and test often to make sure you haven't inadvertently upset the script.

Code 15.4 *continued*

```
          top: 5px;
          left: 25px
}
#chip3 {
          top: 200px;
          left: 45px
}
#chip4 {
          top: 55px;
          left: 55px
}
#chip5 {
          top: 150px;
          left: 60px
}
#chip6 {
          top: 75px;
          left: 125px
}
     --></style>
</head>
<body onload="initPage()" bgcolor="#FFFFFF">
     <span id="chip1" class="chip">One</span>
     ↪ <span id="chip2" class="chip">Ring
     ↪ </span> <span id="chip3" class=
     ↪ "chip">to</span> <span id="chip4"
     ↪ class="chip">Rule</span> <span id=
     ↪ "chip5" class="chip">Them</span>
     ↪ <span id="chip6" class="chip">All</span>
</body>
</html>
```

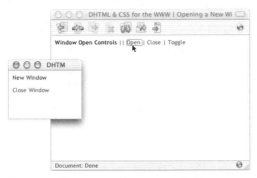

Figure 15.5 The screen with a pop-up window.

Code 15.5 The openWindow(), closeWindow(), and toggleWindow() functions open and close a pop-up window.

```
<!DOCTYPE html PUBLIC "-//W3C//DTD XHTML
1.0 Transitional//EN" "http://www.w3.org/TR/
xhtml1/DTD/xhtml1-transitional.dtd">
<html xmlns="http://www.w3.org/1999/xhtml">
<head>
    <meta http-equiv="content-type"
    content="text/html;charset=utf-8" />
    <title>DHTML &amp; CSS for the WWW |
    Opening a New Window</title>
    <script language="JavaScript"
    type="text/javascript"><!--
var newWindow = null;
function openWindow(contentURL,windowName,
windowWidth,windowHeight) {
    widthHeight = 'height=' + windowHeight +
    'width=' + windowWidth;
    newWindow = window.open(contentURL,
    windowName,widthHeight);
    newWindow.focus()
}
function closeWindow() {
    if (newWindow != null) {
        newWindow.close();
        newWindow = null;
    }
```

(code continues on next page)

Opening a New Browser Window

An often-used interface trick on the Web is opening a new browser window (**Figure 15.5**). These pop-up windows are useful for a variety of purposes, including navigation controls, advertisements, and other content that supplements what's in the main window.

When dealing with pop-up windows, consider three basic functions:

◆ **Open the window.** This function opens a new window and brings it to the front of the screen.

◆ **Close the window.** This function closes the window.

◆ **Toggle the window.** This function can both open and close the window. If the window is not open (closed), the function opens a new window and brings it to the front of the screen. If the window is open, the function closes the window.

To open and close a new browser window:

1. index.html

   Start a new file, and save it as something like index.html. This file will contain the controls that open and close the pop-up window (**Code 15.5**).

2. var newWindow = null;

   Initialize the variable newWindow. This variable will record the current state (open or closed) of the window. null means that the window is closed.

continues on next page

3. ```
function openWindow(contentURL,
→ windowName,windowWidth,
→ windowHeight) {...}
```

   Add the function openWindow() to your JavaScript. This function opens a new window, using these variables:

   ▲ contentURL for the name of the HTML file to be placed in the new window

   ▲ windowName for the name of the new window

   ▲ windowWidth and windowHeight for the width and height of the new window

   The new window is forced to the front of the screen by newWindow.focus().

4. ```
function closeWindow() {...}
```

   Add the function closeWindow() to your JavaScript. This function checks to see whether the pop-up window is, in fact, open. If so, the function tells the window to close and sets the newWindow variable to null (closed).

5. ```
function toggleWindow(contentURL,
→ windowName,windowWidth,
→ windowHeight) {...}
```

   Add the function toggleWindow() to your JavaScript. This function combines the functions added in steps 3 and 4 but allows the window to open only if newWindow is equal to null (closed); otherwise, it closes the window.

6. ```
onunload="closeWindow()"
```

   Optionally, you can add an onunload event handler to force the new window to close when this page (the opening page) is left. This event handler keeps the pop-up window from hanging around when the user moves on.

7. ```
openWindow('newWindow.html',
→ 'myNewWindow',150,50)
```

   Add a function call to your HTML. This function call can be part of an event handler (as shown in step 6) or part of the JavaScript in the href.

**Code 15.5** *continued*

```
}
function toggleWindow(contentURL,windowName,
→ windowWidth,windowHeight) {
    if (newWindow == null) {
        widthHeight = 'height=' + windowHeight
        → + 'width=' + windowWidth;
        newWindow = window.open(contentURL,
        → windowName,widthHeight);
        newWindow.focus()
    }
    else {
        newWindow.close();
        newWindow = null;
    }
}
    // -->
    </script>
</head>
<body onunload="closeWindow()">
    Window Open Controls ||
    → <a href="javascript:openWindow
    → ('newWindow.html','myNewWindow',
    → 150,50)">Open</a> | <a href="javascript:
    → closeWindow()">Close</a> |
    → <a href="javascript:toggleWindow
    → ('newWindow.html','myNewWindow',150,50)
    → ">Toggle</a>
</body>
</html>
```
```

Code 15.6 The file newWindow.html is the Web page that will be used in the pop-up window.

```
<!DOCTYPE html PUBLIC "-//W3C//DTD XHTML
→ 1.0 Transitional//EN" "http://www.w3.org/TR/
→ xhtml1/DTD/xhtml1-transitional.dtd">
<html xmlns="http://www.w3.org/1999/xhtml">
<head>
    <meta http-equiv="content-type"
    → content="text/html;charset=iso-8859-1">
    <title>DHTML &amp; CSS for the WWW |
    → New Window</title>
    <script language="JavaScript"
    → type="text/javascript"><!--
function closeWindow() {
    self.close();
}
    // -->
    </script>
</head>
<body onload="window.moveTo(100,100)"
→ onunload="opener.newWindow = null;">
    New Window
<p>
    <a href="javascript:closeWindow()">
    → Close Window</a>
</p>
</body>
</html>
```

To set up the content for the pop-up window:

1. `newWindow.html`

   Open the file, and save it as something like newWindow.html. This file will be loaded into the pop-up window (**Code 15.6**). You can add anything to this document that you would normally have in a Web page.

2. `function closeWindow() {...}`

   Add the function `closeWindow()` to the JavaScript in this file. When triggered, this function closes the pop-up window.

3. `onload="window.moveTo(100,100)"`

   Add an `onload` event handler to the `<body>` tag to move the window to a particular position on the screen when it first opens (see "Moving the Browser Window" later in this chapter).

4. `onunload="opener.newWindow = null;"`

   In the `<body>` tag, include an `onunload` event handler that sets the variable newWindow in the opening window to `null` if this window is closed. This variable tells the opening window when the pop-up window closes.

5. `<a href="javascript:closeWindow()">` → `CloseWindow</a>`

   Set up a link to trigger `closeWindow()` so that visitors can close this window when they don't need it anymore.

✔ Tips

- Why not always use the toggle version of the open window functions? Generally, toggling the open state of the window is preferable, but sometimes it's useful to have the other two functions, in case you need to make sure the window is either open or closed.

- I especially like using the `closeWindow()` function if I'm using a frame to create my Web site. I place the `onunload` event in the `<frameset>`. When the visitor leaves the site and the frame document unloads, the pop-up window also automatically disappears, preventing any model problems.

- Opening multiple pop-up windows can be a bit problematic because you can't use a variable in place of `newWindow`. Instead, you need to include a separate function for each window (`openWindow1()`, `openWindow2()`, and so on), using a different name for each window (`newWindow1`, `newWindow2`, and so on).

Modal Problems with Pop-Up Windows

Many site developers who use pop-up windows complain about what mode the window is in when it is being used.

Suppose that you use a pop-up window to allow a visitor to enter information in a form that is then used to update information in the main window. What happens if the visitor doesn't enter the information in the pop-up window, doesn't close the window, and returns to the main page? The system is waiting for information that may never come. The visitor might make other changes and return to the pop-up window, enter the information, and really mess up the system.

My advice is simple. If the pop-up window can cause trouble when left open, place the following code in the `<body>` tag of the document in the pop-up window:

```
onblur="self.close();"
```

This code forces the window to close whenever the visitor leaves it. He can always open it again from the main page but cannot return directly to this window.

Figure 15.6 The initial position of the browser window on the screen.

Code 15.7 The JavaScript functions moveTo() and moveBy() move the entire browser window to a certain position on the screen or by a specific amount.

```
<!DOCTYPE html PUBLIC "-//W3C//DTD XHTML
→ 1.0 Transitional//EN" "http://www.w3.org/TR/
→ xhtml1/DTD/xhtml1-transitional.dtd">
<html xmlns="http://www.w3.org/1999/xhtml">
<head>
     <meta http-equiv="content-type"
     → content="text/html;charset=utf-8" />
     <title>DHTML &amp; CSS for the WWW |
     → Moving the Browser Window</title>
</head>
<body>
     <b>Window Controls</b> || <a href=
     → "javascript:moveTo(10,15)">
     → Move to 10, 15</a> | <a href="javascript:
     → moveBy(10,15)">Move By 10, 15</a><br />
     <br />
        <img src="alice42.gif" height="480"
        → width="360" border="0" />
</body>
</html>
```

Moving the Browser Window

When you create a user interface on the Web, it's often helpful to position the browser window on the visitor's computer screen (**Code 15.7** and **Figure 15.6**). This is especially useful if your site will be opening multiple windows and you want to set an initial position so that the windows don't crowd one another (see the previous section, "Opening a New Browser Window").

In addition, you can have a window move from its current position by a certain amount if you want to move windows around in the screen (**Figure 15.7**).

Figure 15.7 After the window has been moved to 10 pixels from the left edge of the screen and 15 pixels from the top.

To set the position of a window on the screen:

1. `functionmoveTo(x,y){...}`

   Add the `moveTo()` JavaScript method to your JavaScript. This built-in JavaScript function tells the browser window to move its top-left corner to the indicated x,y coordinates in relation to the top-left corner of the live screen area (see "Determining the Screen Dimensions" in Chapter 11).

2. `functionmoveBy(dx,dy){...}`

   Add the `moveBy()` code to your JavaScript. This built-in JavaScript function moves the browser window by the x and y amounts (dx,dy) indicated (**Figure 15.8**).

✔ Tip

■ These functions are best used to move a window when it first opens. You do so by placing the `moveTo()` or `moveBy()` code in an `onload` event handler in the `<body>` tag, as shown in the previous section, "Opening a New Browser Window."

Figure 15.8 After the browser window has been moved an additional 10 pixels over and 15 pixels down.

Figure 15.9 The initial size of the browser window.

Changing the Browser Window's Size

When you open a new window, you can set the initial size of that window (see the earlier section, "Opening a New Browser Window"). However, in Mozilla-based browsers (Netscape, Firebird, Camino) you can also resize the window dynamically after the window is open (**Code 15.8** and **Figure 15.9**). Note: This section applies only to Mozilla-based browsers, Safari, and Opera; Internet Explorer does not support this function.

Code 15.8 The changeWindowSize(), magnifyWindow(), and fillScreen() functions control the browser window's size.

```
<?xml version="1.0" encoding="utf-8"?>
<!DOCTYPE html PUBLIC "-//W3C//DTD XHTML 1.0 Transitional//EN" "http://www.w3.org/TR/xhtml1/DTD/
 → xhtml1-transitional.dtd">
<html xmlns="http://www.w3.org/1999/xhtml">
<head>
    <meta http-equiv="content-type" content="text/html;charset=utf-8" />
    <title>DHTML &amp; CSS for the WWW | Changing a Window's Size</title>
    <script language="JavaScript" type="text/javascript"><!--
function changeWindowSize(windowWidth,windowHeight) {
    if (window.outerWidth) {
        resizeTo(windowWidth,windowHeight);
    }
}
function magnifyWindow(dWindowWidth,dWindowHeight) {
    if (window.outerWidth) {
        resizeBy(dWindowWidth,dWindowHeight);
    }
}
function fillScreen() {
    if (window.outerWidth) {
        moveTo(0,0);
        windowWidth = screen.width;
        windowHeight = screen.height;
        resizeTo(windowWidth,windowHeight);

    }
}
```

(code continues on next page)

To change a window's size:

1. function changeWindowSize
→ (windowWidth,windowHeight) {...}

Add the function changeWindowSize()
to your JavaScript. This function first
uses feature sensing to see whether it can
determine the outer width of the browser
window. If so, this browser is a Netscape
browser (see "Determining the Browser
Window's Dimensions" in Chapter 11).
Then the function uses resizeTo() to
change the size of the window to window-
Width and windowHeight (**Figure 15.10**).

Code 15.8 *continued*

```
    // -->
    </script>
</head>
<body>
    Window Size || <a href="javascript:
    → changeWindowSize(300,300)">Resize to
    → 300 by 300</a> | <a href="javascript:
    → magnifyWindow(30,30)">Increase</a> |
    → <a href="javascript:magnifyWindow
    → (-30,-30)">Decrease</a> | <a href=
    → "javascript:fillScreen()">Fill Screen<
    → /a>
    <p><img src="alice04.gif" height="448"
    → width="301" border="0" /></p>
</body>
</html>
```

Figure 15.10 After the window has been resized to
300 x 300 pixels.

Figure 15.11 The window's size has been increased by 30 pixels in both dimensions.

Figure 15.12 The browser window fills the entire screen.

2. `function magnifyWindow(dWindowWidth,`
`→ dWindowHeight) {...}`

Add the function `magnifyWindow()` to your JavaScript. This function first uses feature sensing to see whether it can determine the outer width of the browser window. If so, this browser is a Netscape browser. Then the function uses the JavaScript `resizeBy()` to add or subtract `dWindowWidth` and `dWindowHeight` to or from the window (**Figure 15.11**).

3. `function fillScreen() {...}`

Add the function `fillScreen()` to your JavaScript. This function first uses feature sensing to see whether it can determine the outer width of the browser window. If so, this browser is a Netscape browser. Then the function finds the width and height of the live screen area, moves the top-left corner of the window to the top-left corner of the screen, and resizes the window to the size of the live area of the screen (**Figure 15.12**).

4. `changeWindowSize(300,300)`

Add a function call to whichever function you want to use, passing to it the appropriate parameters. This function call can be associated with an event handler or can be included in the `href` of a link.

CHANGING THE BROWSER WINDOW'S SIZE

Scrolling the Browser Window

Normally, you think of scrolling the Web page as something that the visitor does using the built-in scroll bars on the right side or bottom of the window or frame. You've seen how you can use JavaScript to determine the scroll position of a Web page (see "Determining the Page's Scroll Position" in Chapter 11). Now you'll see how you can force the page to scroll either horizontally or vertically using a simple JavaScript trick (**Code 15.9** and **Figures 15.13** and **15.14**).

Code 15.9 The scrollPage() function takes the coordinates fed to it and scrolls the page to that position.

```
<!DOCTYPE html PUBLIC "-//W3C//DTD XHTML
1.0 Transitional//EN" "http://www.w3.org/TR/
xhtml1/DTD/xhtml1-transitional.dtd">
<html xmlns="http://www.w3.org/1999/xhtml">
<head>
    <meta http-equiv="content-type"
    content="text/html;charset=utf-8" />
    <title>DHTML &amp; CSS for the WWW |
    Changing the Page's Scroll
    Position</title>
    <script language="JavaScript"
    type="text/javascript"><!--
function scrollPageTo(x,y) {
    document.body.scrollLeft = x;
    document.body.scrollTop = y;
    return;
}

    // -->
    </script>
    <style type="text/css" media="screen"><!--
#overHere {
```

(code continues on next page)

Figure 15.13 The links "Down" and "Over" scroll the page horizontally and vertically without using the scrollbars.

Figure 15.14 Clicking "Over" scrolls the Web page to the right, as indicated by the change in the scrollbar position.

Code 15.9 *continued*

```
      visibility: visible;
      position: absolute;
      z-index: 100;
      top: 10px;
      left: 2000px;
      width: 1000px;
      }
#downHere {
      visibility: visible;
      position: absolute;
      z-index: 100;
      top: 2000px;
      left: 10px;
      height: 1000px
}
      --></style>
</head>
<body>
      <a href="javascript:
scrollPageTo(0,1990)">v Down</a> |
→ <a href="javascript:scrollPageTo(1990,0)
→ ">Over &gt;<br style="clear:both" />
            <img src="alice25.gif" height="228"
            → width="300" border="0" /></a>
      <div id="downHere">
            <a href="javascript:scrollPageTo(0,0)
            → ">^ Back to Top</a>
            <p><a href="javascript:scrollPageTo
            → (0,0)"><img src="alice27.gif"
            → height="180" width="200"
            → border="0" /></a></p>
      </div>
      <div id="overHere">
            <a href="javascript:scrollPageTo
            → (0,0)">&lt; Back to Left</a><br
            → style="clear:both" />
            <p><img src="alice26.gif" height="200"
            → width="179" border="0" /></p>
      </div>
      <br clear="all" />
</body>
</html>
```

To scroll a Web page:

1. `function scrollPageTo(x,y) {...}`
   Add the function `scrollPageTo()` to your JavaScript. This function uses the `scrollLeft` and `scrollRight` properties if the browser is determined to be compatible with Internet Explorer, or it uses Netscape's built-in `scrollTo()` function to scroll the page to the specified x and y coordinates.

2. `#overHere {...}`
   Set up the IDs for your object(s) with values for position and top and left positions. In this example, I've set up two objects: one positioned well below the top of the page and one positioned to the far-right side of the page. Now the `scrollPageTo()` function has somewhere to go.

3. `<a href="javascript:scrollPageTo`
   `→ (0,1990)">...</a>`
   Set up a link to trigger the `scrollPageTo()` function, and pass to the function the x and y coordinates to which you want to scroll. Keep in mind that because this function is not addressing a DOM, you don't have to trigger the function call with an event handler.

   continues on next page

✔ Tips

- Although the example in this section still relies on the visitor to click something to cause the page to scroll, you could just as easily have used some other event handler to cause the page to scroll without the direct command of the visitor (by using `onload`, for example). Be careful when doing this, however. If the page suddenly starts jumping around, the effect can be confusing—not to mention unnerving—to the person viewing your Web page.

- Netscape 4 (Windows) and Netscape 6 (all versions) have an unfortunate "feature" that prevents this technique from working in a frame where the scrollbars have been hidden (`scrolling="no"`). Rather than simply making the scrollbars disappear, setting `scrolling` to `no` in these browsers will prevent the frame from scrolling at all—even with JavaScript.

16

Dynamic CSS

In the previous chapters we've looked at ways to change specific CSS attributes for specific effects, such as showing and hiding objects and moving objects across the screen. However, you can make changes to *any* of the CSS properties available (see Appendix A). As a result, you can dynamically control your CSS in the browser window by making changes to styles, with these changes becoming visible immediately—dynamic CSS.

For many years, the full power of dynamic CSS techniques was stymied by the fact that very few of them worked in Netscape 4. However, now that Netscape 4 makes up less than 1 percent of the browser market, a whole new horizon of dynamic techniques is open to Web designers (unless, of course, you know that a significant portion of your likely audience is using Netscape 4).

In this chapter, I'll show you how to add and remove CSS rules and definitions dynamically by learning how to treat style sheets as objects. However, let's first take a look at how to deliver styles tailored for a particular browser or operating system.

Customizing Styles for the OS or Browser

Inconsistencies in how different operating systems and Web browsers display the same HTML code is one of the greatest frustrations Web designers face when using CSS. Although using a Document Type Definition file to force a browser into compatibility (see Chapter 1, "Setting Your DTD") can solve many incompatibility problems, some problems can persist, especially when it comes to matching font sizes, colors, and positioning. Actually, the problem is not with CSS itself, but with the way in which the OSes define font sizes and colors on the screen.

Without getting into the history and technical details, the basic problem is that Windows displays the same-size font larger than a Mac does and displays the same colors a bit darker. This situation can lead to a design that looks great on the Mac but has huge text and dark colors on a PC. In addition, designs that are precisely placed in Internet Explorer can be off by a few unattractive pixels in Netscape.

The answer? Using JavaScript and multiple CSS files tailored to the operating systems and browsers, you can deliver CSS that is targeted for the OS and browser with which your audience is viewing your site (**Figures 16.1, 16.2**, and **16.3**).

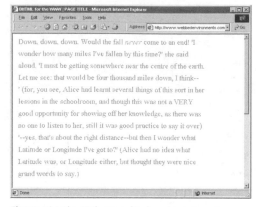

Figure 16.1 The Web page displayed in Internet Explorer for Windows.

Figure 16.2 The same Web page displayed in Firebird (a Mozilla-based browser like Netscape) for the Mac without correction. The text is smaller and much too light.

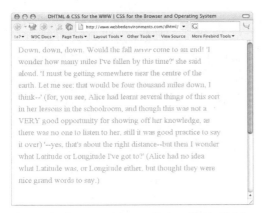

Figure 16.3 The same Web page displayed in Firebird for the Mac with correction. Notice that the text is slightly larger and darker to compensate for the OS and browser.

Code 16.1 The file default.css contains the default styles to be used for the Web pages; it has been optimized for Internet Explorer for Windows.

```
.copy {
    color: #cc3;
    font: 20px/32px "Times New Roman", Georgia,
    → Times, serif;
    width: 500px;
}
body {
    background-color: #fff;
}
```

Code 16.2 The styles in the file mac.css override the ones set in default.css, tweaking the page for the Macintosh by darkening colors, enlarging fonts, and changing the width.

```
.copy {
    color: #bb2;
    font: 23px/35px;
}
```

To set the CSS for the visitor's OS:

1. `default.css`

   Create an external CSS file with the styles to be used in the Web site, and save this file as "default.css" (**Code 16.1**). This file is directly linked to the Web page in step 4. Since Internet Explorer for Windows is the most common browser being used, generally you'll want to optimize the CSS for that.

2. `mac.css`

   Create a second CSS file, and save it as "mac.css" (**Code 16.2**). This version should be used to make the definitions set up in default.css more palatable for Mac users by making the fonts larger and the colors lighter. You don't have to reenter every definition in default.css, because the ones you want from that style sheet cascade down.

3. `netscape.css`

   Create a third CSS file, and save it as "netscape.css" (**Code 16.3**). This version should be used to make the definitions set up in default.css more palatable for Netscape users. Generally, this will involve adjusting the positioning and dimensions of objects.

continues on next page

Code 16.3 The styles in the file netscape.css override the ones set in default.css, tweaking the page for Netscape browsers by increasing the width.

```
.copy { width: 600px; }
```

CUSTOMIZING STYLES FOR THE OS OR BROWSER

4. `<link href="default.css"`
→ `type="text/css" rel="styleSheet" />`

In the head of the HTML document
(**Code 16.4**), link to the default version of
the style sheet.

5. `if (navigator.appVersion.indexOf`
→ `('Mac') != -1) {...}`

`if (navigator.appName.indexOf`
→ `('Netscape') != -1) {...}`

After the `<link>` tag added in step 4,
place JavaScript that checks whether
the browser being used is on a Mac or in
a Netscape-compatible browser (such
as Mozilla or Firebird). If either is, the
`<link>` tag to the Mac or Netscape version of the CSS is "written" into the page
through JavaScript and will be used to
correct the default CSS.

✔ Tips

■ Notice that although the versions of the
class copy in the alternative versions
of the CSS don't include a typeface, the
text still displays in Times. Why doesn't
the definition of the class copy in the
Mac CSS file replace the definition in the
default CSS file? The term *cascading* in
cascading style sheets refers to the ability
to blend definitions, even if they come
from different sources (see "Determining
the Cascade Order" in Chapter 2).

■ You can use the JavaScript trick shown
in this section for many purposes. If you
want to deliver a different style sheet
depending on a preference expressed by
the visitor, for example, you could use
a cookie variable to control which style
sheet is loaded. Such a script gives the
Web designer and the site visitor much
more control over how the page is displayed, and the designer doesn't have to
make a new page for each version.

Code 16.4 This JavaScript detects whether the computer is a Mac and whether the browser identifies
itself as Netscape-compatible. If either condition is
met, additional style sheets are added to the page to
tweak the design.

```
<!DOCTYPE html PUBLIC "-//W3C//DTD XHTML
→ 1.0 Transitional//EN" "http://www.w3.org/TR/
→ xhtml1/DTD/xhtml1-transitional.dtd">
<html xmlns="http://www.w3.org/1999/xhtml">
<head>
    <meta http-equiv="content-type"
    → content="text/html;charset=utf-8" />
    <title>DHTML &amp; CSS for the WWW |
    → CSS for the Browser and Operating
    → System</title>
    <link href="default.css"
    → type="text/css" rel="styleSheet" />
    <script language="JavaScript">
if (navigator.appVersion.indexOf('Mac') != -1)
    document.write('<link href="mac.css"
    → rel="styleSheet" type="text/css">');
if (navigator.appName.indexOf('Netscape')
→ != -1)
    document.write('<link href="netscape.css"
    → rel="styleSheet" type="text/css">');
    </script>
</head>
<body>
    <p class="copy">Down, down, down. Would the
    → fall <i>never</i> come to an end!</p>
    <p class="copy">Presently she began
again.</p>
</body>
</html>
```

Figure 16.4 How the page should look in Netscape 4.

Figure 16.5 Without the CSS-bug fix, after the visitor resizes the screen, the browser's default settings are used to display the page.

Fixing CSS in older versions of Netscape

Netscape 4 has an obvious, and often-complained-about CSS bug. When visitors resize their browsers, all CSS formatting that comes from an external CSS file (one that was imported by the `<link>` tag) mysteriously disappears, as though the linked style sheet never existed. If the visitor reloads the page, however, the CSS reappears (**Figures 16.4** and **16.5**). This bug can be a big turnoff for visitors to your site, especially if they don't know that reloading the page solves the problem.

How do you make sure the page is reloaded after being resized? Just tell the browser to stay on the lookout for size changes and automatically reload itself (**Code 16.5**).

To force the page to reload after resizing:

1. `if (document.layers) {...}`

In the head of your Web page, add code that detects whether the browser uses the layer's Document Object Model. If it does, the code records the current width (`innerWidth`) and height (`innerHeight`) of the visible page area (see "Determining the Page's Visible Dimensions" in Chapter 11).

2. `function reloadPage() {...}`

Add the function `reloadPage()` to your JavaScript. When triggered, this function compares the current width and height of the visible page area with the values recorded in step 1. If the values are different, the page reloads.

3. `onresize = reloadPage;`

Set the `onresize` event to trigger the `reloadPage` function from step 2. If the user resizes the page, changing the visible area of the Web page, the browser reloads the page, restoring the CSS to its rightful place.

Code 16.5 This JavaScript uses feature sensing to identify whether the browser is Netscape 4, and if so, the current page size is then recorded. Then if the browser window is resized, the code forces the page to reload, thus restoring the page's styles.

```
<html>
<head>
     <meta http-equiv="content-type"
     → content="text/html;charset=iso-8859-1">
     <title>DHTML for the WWW |
     → CSS Bug Fix</title>
     <script><!--
if (document.layers) {
     origWidth = innerWidth;
     origHeight = innerHeight;
}
function reloadPage() {
     if (innerWidth != origWidth ||
     → innerHeight != origHeight)
     location.reload();
}
if (document.layers) onresize = reloadPage;
     // -->
     </script>
         <link rel="stylesheet" href=
         → "styles.css">
</head>
<body>
     <h1>Designing with Cascading Style
     → Sheets</h1>
        <p class="copy">Whenever you type in a
section title...</p>
</body>
</html>
```

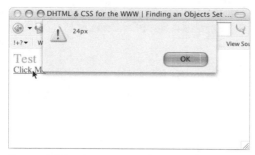

Figure 16.6 An alert appears to let you know what the font-size for object1 has been set to.

Code 16.6 The function findStyleValue() can be used in either Internet Explorer or Netscape to directly query the property values set in a style sheet.

```
<!DOCTYPE html PUBLIC "-//W3C//DTD XHTML
→ 1.0 Transitional//EN" "http://www.w3.org/TR/
→ xhtml1/DTD/xhtml1-transitional.dtd">
<html xmlns="http://www.w3.org/1999/xhtml">
<head>
    <meta http-equiv="content-type"
content="text/html;charset=utf-8" />
    <title>DHTML &amp; CSS for the WWW |
    ⌐ Finding an Object&rsquo;s Set Style
    → Value</title>
    <script language="JavaScript"
    → type="text/javascript"><!--
function findStyleValue(objectID,styleProp,
→ IEStyleProp) {
    var object = document.getElementById
    → (objectID);
    if (object.currentStyle) return object.
    → currentStyle[IEStyleProp]
    else if (window.getComputedStyle) {
        compStyle = window.getComputedStyle
        → (object,'');
        return compStyle.getPropertyValue
        → (styleProp);
    }
}
function displayStyle(objectID) {
    objectFontSize = findStyleValue(objectID,
    → 'font-size','fontSize');
    alert(objectFontSize);
```

(code continues on next page)

Finding a Style Property's Value

Although JavaScript can be used to determine the current value of a CSS property simply enough by using the DOM, it can only do so *after* the style property's value has been set using JavaScript. In other words, JavaScript cannot directly read the styles set in the style sheet. The workaround I've shown in previous examples in this book is simply to initialize the styles in JavaScript (see "Finding an Object's Visibility State" in Chapter 12, for example).

There is a method that allows you to directly query the styles (**Figure 16.6**) however, due to cross-browser differences, the cure may end up being worse than the poison. The biggest problem is that Netscape and Internet Explorer will often deliver the same values, but in completely different formats. For example, while Netscape will always return color in RGB units (regardless of the color units used to define the property in the style sheet), Internet Explorer will always return the color value as set in the style sheet. Another huge disadvantage: This method does not work in Safari or Opera.

Still, in some situations, this solution may be indispensable (**Code 16.6**).

To find the value of a style property as set in a style sheet:

1. `function findStyleValue(objectID, → styleProp,IEStyleProp) {...}`

   Add the function `findStyleValue()` to your Web page. This script uses the `objectID` variable passed to it to address the object and then uses feature sensing to use either the `currentStyle` (for Internet Explorer) or `getPropertyValue` (for Netscape) method to return the style value. Notice that you're actually passing two different versions of the style property being queried. This is because Netscape uses the standard CSS format for the style property, while Internet Explorer uses the style name in JavaScript notation.

2. `function displayStyle (objectID) → {...}`

   Add a function to your Web page that calls the `findStyleValue()` function and pass it the ID for the object you want to query, as well as the style property name in both standard CSS format (for Netscape) and JavaScript format (for Internet Explorer). For example, rather than `font-size`, you would use `fontSize`.

3. `#object1 {...}`

   Set up the object you'll be querying.

4. `displayStyle(...)`

   Add a function call for `displayStyle()`, passing it the object ID for the object you'll be querying.

Code 16.6 *continued*

```
}
    // -->
    </script>
    <style type="text/css" media="screen"><!--
#object1 {
    font-size: 24px;
    color: #ff0000;
    position: relative;
    width: 300px
}
    --></style>
</head>
<body>
    <div id="object1">Test</div>
    <a href="javascript:displayStyle
    → ('object1')">Click Me</a>
</body>
</html>
```

FINDING A STYLE PROPERTY'S VALUE

Code 16.7 The addStyleDef() function changes or adds styles to the definition of a particular object in the browser window. In this code, the visitor can roll over the words *Eat Me* to add a definition to set the font size for object1 to 18px, or *Drink Me* to add a definition to object1 that sets the font size to 4px.

```
<!DOCTYPE html PUBLIC "-//W3C//DTD XHTML
→ 1.0 Transitional//EN" "http://www.w3.org/TR/
→ xhtml1/DTD/xhtml1-transitional.dtd">
<html xmlns="http://www.w3.org/1999/xhtml">
<head>
    <meta http-equiv="content-type"
    → content="text/html;charset=utf-8" />
    <title>DHTML &amp; CSS for the WWW |
    → Adding a Definition</title>
    <script language="JavaScript"
    → type="text/javascript"><!--
function addStyleDef(objectID,styleName,
→ newVal) {
```

(code continues on next page)

Adding or Changing a Style Definition

One powerful feature of dynamic HTML is the ability to change the styles applied to an object. CSS allows you to set up definitions (**Figure 16.7**); JavaScript allows you to change those definitions on the fly by adding new definitions which (because of the cascade order) can replace previous rules (**Figure 16.8**). You can change or add to any CSS property defined for any object on the screen (**Code 16.7**).

Figure 16.7 Before *Eat Me* is moused over, the text is microscopically small.

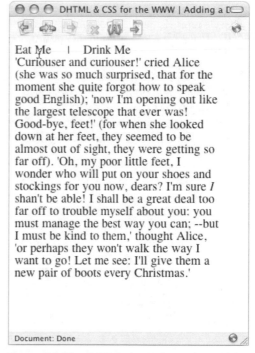

Figure 16.8 After *Eat Me* is moused over, the text has grown from 4 pixels to 18 pixels.

ADDING OR CHANGING A STYLE DEFINITION

To change the definition of an object:

1. `function addStyleDef(objectID,` `→ styleName,newVal) {...}`

   Add the function `addStyleDef()` to your JavaScript. This function addresses the object by its ID, then uses that address to change the style passed to it as `styleName` to the new value (`newVal`).

2. `#object1 {...}`

   Set up the IDs for your object(s) with whatever CSS properties you want to change.

3. `<div id="object1">...</div>`

   Set up your CSS object(s).

4. `onmouseover="addStyleDef` `→ ('object1','fontSize','18px');"`

   Add event handlers to trigger the function `addStyleDef()`. Pass the function the ID for the object you want to address, as well as the style property you want to change and its new value. Notice that the style name is using JavaScript notation.

✔ Tips

- Notice that I've placed the event handler inside the `<div>` tag. Remember, event handlers don't have to appear only in `<link>` tags. For most browsers, events can be triggered from any object in the page.

- Style names that are composed of two or more words are linked with hyphens for CSS (`font-size`). To use them for dynamic CSS, you need to translate style names into the JavaScript naming style (`fontSize`).

Code 16.7 *continued*

```
    var object = document.getElementById
    → (objectID);
    object.style [styleName] = newVal;
}

    // -->
    </script>
    <style type="text/css" media="screen"><!--
#object1 {
    font-size: 4px;
    position: relative;
    width: 300px;
}
#eatMe {
    font-size: 18px;
    margin-right: 20px;
    position: relative;
}
#drinkMe {
    font-size: 18px;
    margin-left: 20px;
    position: relative;
}
    --></style>
</head>
<body>
    <span id="eatMe" onmouseover="addStyleDef
    → ('object1','fontSize','18px');"
    → >Eat Me</span> | <span id="drinkMe"
    → onmouseover="addStyleDef('object1',
    → 'fontSize','4px');">Drink Me</span>
        <div id="object1">
            'Curiouser and curiouser!' cried
            → Alice...</div>
</body>
</html>
```

ADDING OR CHANGING A STYLE DEFINITION

Figure 16.9 Before the link is clicked, the page's default values are used in the window (black text on a white background).

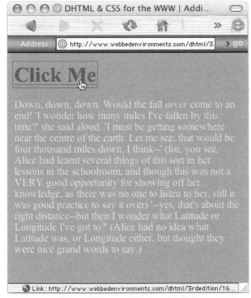

Figure 16.10 After the link is clicked, the new style rule is added to the <body> tag turning the background red and the text white.

Adding or changing styles in Internet Explorer

Although the method for changing styles presented in the previous section works in most modern browsers (Internet Explorer 4+, Netscape 6+, Safari, and Opera), Internet Explorer can also add or change styles by adding new rules to an existing style sheet (**Figures 16.9** and **16.10**).First, you must give the <style> tag an ID that turns it into an object. Then you can use JavaScript to access the style sheet using the DOM to access its properties directly (**Code 16.8**).

JavaScript Naming Convention

JavaScript has a very particular naming convention. Words cannot include periods, hyphens, spaces, or any other separators. Instead, multiple words are expressed in the following manner:

All letters are lowercase except for the first letter of any words after the first word.

The CSS property font-size, for example, would be expressed as fontSize.

I recommend sticking to this naming convention for JavaScript function names and variables, as well as CSS class and ID names, just to make things easier.

To add a new rule to a Web page dynamically in Internet Explorer:

1. `function addStyleDefIE(selector,` → `definition) {...}`

   Add the function *addStyleDefIE()* to your JavaScript. This function adds the new rule to the style sheet that you identify in step 2, using the name of the selector for which you want to add a rule (see "Kinds of Tags" in Chapter 1) and the definition(s) you want to apply to that selector.

2. `id="MyStyles"`

   Add a <style> container in the head of your document—even if you don't set any initial rules—and give it a unique ID that can be used by the function in step 1 to address this style sheet.

3. `onclick="addStyleDefIE('body',` `'background-color:red; color:` → `white;')"`

   Add an event handler to trigger the *addStyleDefIE* function from step 1. Pass to this function the name of the selector for which you want to add a new rule and the definitions you want to assign for this new rule.

✔ Tip

■ One disadvantage of this method is that, according to the XHTML and CSS specifications, style tags are not supposed to have ID attributes. This can cause your Web page to fail HTML and CSS validation.

Code 16.8 The *addStyleDefIE()* function adds a new CSS rule to the style sheet called myStyles.

```
<!DOCTYPE html PUBLIC "-//W3C//DTD XHTML
→ 1.0 Transitional//EN" "http://www.w3.org/TR/
→ xhtml1/DTD/xhtml1-transitional.dtd">
<html xmlns="http://www.w3.org/1999/xhtml">
<head>
    <meta http-equiv="content-type"
    → content="text/html;charset=utf-8" />
    <title>DHTML &amp; CSS for the WWW |
    → Adding a New Rule</title>
    <script language="JavaScript"
    → type="text/javascript"><!--
function addStyleDefIE(selector,definition) {
    document.styleSheets.MyStyles.addRule
    → (selector,definition)
}
    // -->
    </script>
    <style id="MyStyles"><!--
h1 {
    font-size: 24pt
}
body {
    color: gray
}
    --></style>
</head>
<body>
    <h1><a onclick="addStyleDefIE
    → ('body','background-color:red;
    → color: white')" href="#">Click
    → Me</a></h1>
        <p>Down, down, down. Would the fall
        → <i>never</i> come to an end!</p>
</body>
</html>
```

Code 16.9 The setClass() function reassigns the CSS class assigned to a particular object in the browser window.

```
<!DOCTYPE html PUBLIC "-//W3C//DTD XHTML
→ 1.0 Transitional//EN" "http://www.w3.org/TR/
→ xhtml1/DTD/xhtml1-transitional.dtd">
<html xmlns="http://www.w3.org/1999/xhtml">
<head>
    <meta http-equiv="content-type"
    → content="text/html;charset=utf-8" />
    <title>DHTML &amp; CSS for the WWW |
    → Changing a Class</title>
        <script language="JavaScript"
        → type="text/javascript"><!--
function setClass(objectID,newClass) {
    var object = document.getElementById
    → (objectID);
    object.className = newClass;
}
    // -->
    </script>
    <style type="text/css" media="screen"><!--
#object1 {
    position: relative
}
#eatMe {
    margin-right: 20px;
    position: relative
}
```

(code continues on the next page)

Changing an Object's Class

Although being able to add or change an individual definition is great (see the previous section, "Adding or Changing a Style's Definition"), doing this for more than one definition at a time is time-consuming. Instead, you need the ability to change multiple definitions at once (**Figures 16.11** and **16.12**). You can accomplish this task simply by setting up multiple classes and then swapping the entire CSS class assigned to an object (**Code 16.9**).

Figure 16.11 Before the words *Drink Me* are rolled over, the text is very small and black, because its class has been set to copyTiny.

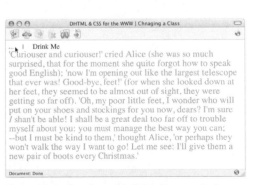

Figure 16.12 After the words *Drink Me* are rolled over, the text is much larger and red because the class has been reassigned to copyHuge.

To change the CSS class of an object:

1. `function setClass(objectID,`
`→ newClass) {...}`

Add the function `setClass()` to your JavaScript. This function uses the ID of the object to find its address, then uses the address to change the CSS class being applied to this object to the new CSS class (`newClass`).

2. `#object1 {...}`

Set up the IDs for your object(s) with whatever styles you desire.

3. `.copyTiny {...}`
`.copyHuge {...}`

Set up the classes that you'll be applying to your objects.

4. `onmouseover="setClass('object1',`
`'copyHuge');`

Add event handlers to trigger the function you created in step 1, and pass it the ID for the object you want to address and the name of the class you want to apply to that object.

5. `<div id="object1">...</div>`

Set up your CSS object(s).

Code 16.9 *continued*

```
#drinkMe {
     margin-left: 20px;
     position: relative
}
.copyTiny {
     color: black;

font-size: 4px;
     position: relative;
     width: 300px;
}
.copyHuge {
     color: red;
     font-size: 24px;
     position: relative;
     width: 600px;
}
.tiny {
     color: red;
     font-size: 4px;
     position: relative;
}
.huge {
     color: black;
     font-size: 18px;
     position: relative;
}
     --></style>
</head>
<body>
     <span id="eatMe" class="huge" onmouseover
     → ="setClass('object1','copyHuge');
     → setClass('drinkMe','huge');this.
     → className = 'tiny';">Eat Me</span> |
     → <span id="drinkMe" class="tiny"
     → onmouseover="setClass('object1',
     → 'copyTiny');setClass('eatMe','huge');
     → this.className = 'tiny';">Drink
     → Me</span>
          <div id="object1" class="copyTiny">
               'Curiouser and curiouser!' cried
                    → Alice...</div>
</body>
</html>
```

Figure 16.13 Before the link is clicked, the text is very large, light-colored, and hard to read.

Figure 16.14 After the link is clicked, the text is displayed in the browser's default style (black text at 12-point font size).

Disabling or Enabling a Style Sheet

Although being able to swap around classes is a quick way to change specific styles, your final alternative for dynamically changing CSS is to swap entire style sheets.

Sometimes, your visitors might want to see just the text without all those fancy styles (**Code 16.10**). Their loss—but everyone has his own taste. Internet Explorer allows you to disable a particular style and then turn it on again to suit your needs (**Figures 6.13** and **6.14**).

To disable a style sheet:

1. `function toggleStyle(objectID) {...}`

Add the function `toggleStyle()` to your code. This function uses the object ID to address a style sheet and then toggle it between being disabled and enabled.

2. `id="strangeStyle"`
`id="dullStyle"`

Set up style sheets in the head of your document. Give each `<style>` tag a unique ID attribute. In this example, I created two styles to toggle between: a style sheet called "strangeStyle" and another called "dullStyle."

3. `onload="toggleStyle('dullStyle');"`

Add an `onload` event handler to the `<body>` tag and disable any style sheets that you don't want to be initially used.

4. `onclick="toggleStyle('strangeStyle')`
`→;toggleStyle('dullStyle');"`

Set up an event handler that calls the `toggleStyle()` function to turn on or off the desired style sheets.

✔ Tip

■ This technique doesn't work in Netscape 6.

Code 16.10 When the word here is clicked, the strangeStyle style sheet is toggled between being disabled (`disabled=true`) and enabled (`disabled=false`).

```
<!DOCTYPE html PUBLIC "-//W3C//DTD XHTML
→ 1.0 Transitional//EN" "http://www.w3.org/TR/
→ xhtml1/DTD/xhtml1-transitional.dtd">
<html xmlns="http://www.w3.org/1999/xhtml">
<head>
    <meta http-equiv="content-type"
    → content="text/html;charset=utf-8" />
    <title>DHTML &amp; CSS for the WWW |
    → Disabling a Style</title>
    <script language="JavaScript"
    → type="text/javascript">
        function toggleStyle(objectID) {
            object = document.getElementById
            → (objectID)
            if (object.disabled==true)
            → object.disabled=false;
            else object.disabled=true;
        }
    </script>
    <style id="strangeStyle"><!--
        .bizzaro {
            color: #eeeeee;
            font: italic 100px fantasy;
        }
    --></style>
    <style id="dullStyle"><!--
        .bizzaro {
            color: #000000;
            font: bold 18px "times new
            → roman", times, serif;
        }
    --></style>
</head>
<body onload="toggleStyle('dullStyle');">
    <span class="bizzaro">'What a curious
    → feeling!'</span><br /> <span id=
    → "styleOff">If you cannot read the above,
    → click --&gt; <span onclick="toggleStyle
    → ('strangeStyle');toggleStyle
    → ('dullStyle');">here</span> &lt;---
    → </span>
</body>
</html>
```

Part 3
Using CSS
and DHTML

LAYOUT AND CONTENT

17

Designers are still discovering the capabilities and limitations of layout with Cascading Style Sheets. Some designers who were initially captivated by the "gee-whiz" abilities of CSS to create dynamic HTML neglected its many layout strengths. In the rush to experiment with the dynamic aspects of CSS, many designers overlooked some of the nuts-and-bolts problems that CSS solves: It facilitates solid, compelling page layout on the Web.

This chapter explores some of the valuable solutions CSS offers for everyday design issues and the best ways to integrate DHTML into the layout.

Importing External Content

Imagine you're designing a large-scale Web site with the same menu on every page. Every time you need to change the menu, you must change every page. Not only is this time-consuming, but the possibility of making mistakes is high. Wouldn't it be nice to have that menu in one file and import it into each page as the visitor uses the Web site? Then you could correct one file and have the changes reflected throughout the site.

To do this, you need a way to import external content into HTML files. There are several methods for dynamically importing content into a Web page, but let's take a look at two that don't require any knowledge of databases or servers.

Importing external JavaScript

As with an external style sheet (see "Adding Styles to a Web Site" in Chapter 2), JavaScript code can be placed in an external file and then imported directly into a Web page as if it had been hard coded into it (**Figure 17.1**). Unlike CSS, though, you use the `<script>` tag to import the external JavaScript file into an HTML document. You can then use the JavaScript file to write HTML code into the page. The advantage of using this method is that you can use the JavaScript to tailor the content as needed (see "To set up a dynamic header and footer" later in this chapter).

To import content using JavaScript:

1. `external.js`

   Create an external JavaScript file, and save it as "external.js" (**Code 17.1**). This file is a text file and can contain any standard JavaScript. To deliver HTML code, use `+=` to add each line of code to the variable `writeExternalCode`, then use `document.write` to place the entire block of code in the Web page.

Figure 17.1 The imported JavaScript writes the title and adds an image to the Web page. Any HTML you wanted can be added this way.

Code 17.1 The external JavaScript (external.js) file can include any JavaScript, but if you want to include HTML content, assign each line to the variable `writeExternalContent` and then use `document.write` to add the code to the Web page.

```
var writeExternalContent = '';

writeExternalContent += '<div style="text-
align:center">';
writeExternalContent += '<h1>Alice In
Wonderland</h1>';
writeExternalContent += '<h3>Chapter 3</h3>';
writeExternalContent += '<img src="alice38.gif"
width="360" height="480" border="0">';

document.writeln(writeExternalContent)
```

Code 17.2 You can place the <script> tag anywhere in your HTML document, but to add visible content, you need to place it in the body of the document.

```
<!DOCTYPE html PUBLIC "-//W3C//DTD XHTML
→ 1.0 Transitional//EN" "http://www.w3.org/TR/
→ xhtml1/DTD/xhtml1-transitional.dtd">
<html xmlns="http://www.w3.org/1999/xhtml">
<head>
     <title>DHTML and CSS for the WWW |
     → Using an External JavaScript File</title>
</head>
<body>
     <script language="JavaScript"
     → src="external.js" name=
     → "externalScript1"></script>
</body>
</html>
```

- Remember, the content to be written using JavaScript has to be inside single quotes ('). If you need to include a single quote in the content you're writing with JavaScript, it has to be proceeded by a backslash (\). So `document.write ('How's it going?');` won't work. Instead, use `document.write` → `('How\'s it going?');`. This technique is referred to as "escaping" the character.

2. ```
<script language="JavaScript"
→ src="external.js" name=
→ "exteralScript1"></script>
```

Importing an external JavaScript file is relatively straightforward. Simply add the `src` attribute to the <script> tag, with the location of the external JavaScript file you created in step 1 (**Code 17.2**). Don't place any code between the opening and closing <script> tags. This method places the external JavaScript in the HTML file at this exact location. If the JavaScript will add HTML tags to the page, those tags will be added to the page in this location, as if they were a part of the original HTML code.

### ✔ Tips

- Although the .js file extension is not required for this to work, it has become the accepted norm and helps differentiate from other file types.

- The drawback of this method is that you have to place every line of HTML code in JavaScript. This can be labor-intensive, and it makes the file harder to debug and fix in most WYSIWYG programs.

- You can import as many different JavaScript files as you want into a single HTML page. In fact, some people build their entire Web sites this way. If you use this technique heavily, though, you may notice that the pages load a bit more slowly than if the code is included directly in the HTML.

- Any JavaScript code placed between <script> tags that include a `src` will be ignored. If you need to put additional JavaScript directly in the page, just add another <script> container (without a source) and place the code there.
```

Using iFrames

The <iframe> tag can be used to place one HTML page within another. This content is treated as though it's in a separate frame; however, it can be positioned as if it were a layer (**Figure 17.2**). The great advantage of using iFrames over JavaScript to import content is that you can then use standard hypertext links to change the content within the frame without having to reload the entire page.

To import content using iFrames:

1. external.html

   Create a new HTML file and save it as external.html (**Code 17.3**). This file doesn't contain the usual <html> open and close tags—which will be supplied by the main document—only the <body> tag and whatever HTML you want to use.

2. <iframe>...</iframe>

   Add the iFrame tags to your HTML at the point where you want the content inserted (**Code 17.4**). You'll also want to set iFrame attributes:

   ▲ id and name are unique identifiers for the frame, which are used to target links (name) or to use JavaScript to locate frame using the DOM (id). Although you may be able to get by with just the id for most browsers, it's generally a good idea to also include the name for some older browsers.

   ▲ src tells the Web page where the initial file to be loaded into the iFrame is located. You can change the content of the frame using targeted links.

   ▲ frameborder sets the thickness of the border around the iFrame. To turn the border completely off (recommended) set this to 0.

Figure 17.2 Most browsers will support iFrames, which allow you to place one HTML file within another. In this case, the image and title are placed into index.html.

Code 17.3 The external content file external.html is being imported into index.html. Notice that you can include the <html>, <head>, and <body> tags.

```
<?xml version="1.0" ?>
<!DOCTYPE html PUBLIC "-//W3C//DTD XHTML
→ 1.0 Transitional//EN" "http://www.w3.org/TR/
→ xhtml1/DTD/xhtml1-transitional.dtd">
<html xmlns="http://www.w3.org/1999/xhtml">
<head>
     <title>DHTML for the WWW | Using iFrames |
     → External File</title>
</head>
<body>
     <div style="text-align:center">
        <h1>Alice In Wonderland</h1>
        <h3>Chapter 2</h3>
        <img src="alice36.gif" height="480"
        → width="360" border="0" />
     </div>
</body>
</html>
```

Code 17.4 The HTML file uses iFrames to import the external content. Remember to set the height of the iFrame carefully so that all of the content is either visible or at least accessible through scrolling.

```
<?xml version="1.0" ?>
<!DOCTYPE html PUBLIC "-//W3C//DTD XHTML
→ 1.0 Transitional//EN" "http://www.w3.org/TR/
→ xhtml1/DTD/xhtml1-transitional.dtd">
<html xmlns="http://www.w3.org/1999/xhtml">
<head>
      <title>DHTML for the WWW |
        → Using iFrames</title>
</head>
<body>
      <iframe
          id="content"
          name="content"
          src="external.html"
          frameborder="0"
          marginwidth="5"
          marginheight="5"
          scrolling="no"
          align="top"
          height="600"
          width="100%">
      <a href="external.html">
        → External Content</a>
      </iframe>
</body>
</html>
```

▲ marginheight and marginwidth set the margin between the frame's edge and the content within it.

▲ scrolling determines whether the frame can be scrolled independent of the rest of the Web page. Setting this to no means that scrolling is not allowed and any content not displayed because the iFrame is too small will be inaccessible. However, the iFrame will still scroll with the rest of the Web page.

▲ align defines how the iFrame is aligned vertically within the page.

▲ width and height are used to define the dimensions of the iFrame.

3. `<a href="external.html">`
`→ External Content</a>`

Inside the `<iframe>` tag, add a link to external.html for browsers that don't support or iFrames.

✔ Tips

■ Many of the iFrame attributes listed here can also be defined using CSS instead of directly in the `<iframe>` tag. The obvious ones are width and height, which directly correspond to CSS properties. However, align corresponds to vertical-align, marginheight and marginwidth correspond to margin-top and margin-left, while frameborder corresponds to border.

■ One problem with using iFrames is in defining the height. Although it would be great if you could just set it to 100 percent and forget about it, it isn't that easy. The main drawback is that when you change the frame's content, it won't automatically resize, so you'll need to either allow scrolling or set the height to handle the tallest content it's likely to display.

Adding Dynamically Generated Content

One problem with designing a large Web site is that it's hard to change the design once you get started.

If you aren't a database guru, but want to be able to tailor the content displayed depending on the page, you can use JavaScript to dynamically "write" content into the page. Using the technique shown in the previous section, you can not only add content to the page, but use JavaScript to generate that content on the fly based on the individual page it's being used in.

In this example, we'll use two different external JavaScript files. The first file (header.js) uses variables on the page into which it's imported to create a header with the page title and other information. The second file (footer.js) dynamically displays the page's title and URL (**Figure 17.3** and **17.4**).

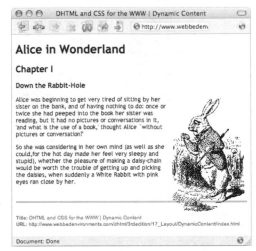

Figure 17.3 The final output with the dynamically generated header and footer in index.html. Because the header and footer code aren't embedded in the page, you can change the layout in the JavaScript files, and those changes will affect every HTML page that uses them.

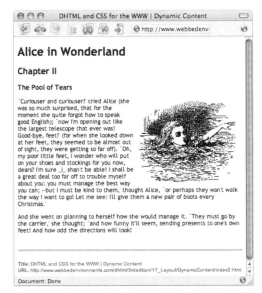

Figure 17.4 However, load the same JavaScript into a different page (index2.html), and you get different results.

Code 17.5 This JavaScript file (header.js) is imported into the top of index.html to create the header for the document.

```
var writeHeader = '';

writeHeader += '<h1>Alice in Wonderland</h1>';
writeHeader += '<h2>';
writeHeader += chpNum;
writeHeader += '</h2>';
writeHeader += '<h3>';
writeHeader += chpTitle;
writeHeader += '</h3>';
writeHeader += '<img src="' + illustration +
'.gif" align="right" />';


document.writeln (writeHeader);
```

Code 17.6 This JavaScript file (footer.js) is imported into the bottom of index.html to create the footer for the document.

```
var writeFooter = '';

writeFooter += '<br /><hr><br clear="all">';
writeFooter += '<span class="pageInfo">';
writeFooter += '<b>Title:</b> ' +
self.document.title;
writeFooter += '<br />';
writeFooter += '<b>URL:</b> <a href="' +
self.location + '">' + self.location + '</a>';
writeFooter += '</span><br />';


document.writeln (writeFooter);
```

To set up a dynamic header and footer:

1. `header.js`

   Create an external JavaScript file, and save it as "header.js." This file will be imported into the top of index.html in step 4. Use the variable `writeHeader` to accumulate the code before using `document.write` to add it as a single block.

   In this example, the header will use variables in index.html to add the title, subtitle, teaser, and date to the Web page (**Code 17.5**).

2. `footer.js`

   Create an external JavaScript file, and save it as "footer.js." This file will be imported at the bottom of index.html in step 4 (**Code 17.6**). Use the variable `writeFooter` to accumulate the code before using `document.write` to add it as a single block.

   In this example, the footer will display the page title—the one between the `<title>` tags, not the JavaScript variable `title`—and the URL for the page, as well as a link to a copyright page and a `mailto` link.

continues on next page

ADDING DYNAMICALLY GENERATED CONTENT

3. `varchpNum = 'Chapter I';`

In a `<script>` tag in the head of the document, include variables to be used by the external content. In this example, we're using three different variables (**Code 17.7**):

▲ `chpNum` records the chapter number for the page.

▲ `chpTitle` records the name of the chapter.

▲ `illustration` records the name of the illustration to be used in the page. This is then used in the header to create an image tag to load the illustration.

4. `<script language="JavaScript"`
→ `src="header.js" name=`
→ `"header"></script>`

In the body of the HTML page, add `<script>` tags, with the sources set to the URLs of the header and footer JavaScript files.

✔ Tips

■ You can place any HTML code in the header and footer. On my Web site, for example, I place all the navigation for the page in external JavaScript files such as these. This allows me to add or delete navigation elements without having to change every page on the site.

■ The variables in step 3 are just examples of the kinds of information you could include on an individual HTML page, for use by a global JavaScript page that is being imported. You can include any type of data about the article, such as volume number, issue number, or its location within the Web site.

Code 17.7 This sample Web page (index.html) imports the header and footer. It also includes several JavaScript variables that add the title, subtitle, teaser, and date to the header of the document.

```
<!DOCTYPE html PUBLIC "-//W3C//DTD XHTML
→ 1.0 Transitional//EN" "http://www.w3.org/TR/
→ xhtml1/DTD/xhtml1-transitional.dtd">
<html xmlns="http://www.w3.org/1999/xhtml">
<head>
    <title>DHTML and CSS for the WWW |
    → Dynamic Content</title>
      <script>
    var chpNum= 'Chapter I';
    var chpTitle= 'Down the Rabbit-Hole';
    var illustration= 'alice02a';
      </script>
      <link href="default.css"
      → rel="stylesheet" />
</head>
<body>
    <script language="JavaScript"
    → src="header.js" name="header"></script>
      <!-- Begin Content -->
      <p>  Alice was beginning to get very
      → tired of sitting by her sister on the
      → bank...</p>
      <!-- End Content -->
    <script language="JavaScript"
    → src="footer.js" name="footer"></script>
</body>
</html>
```

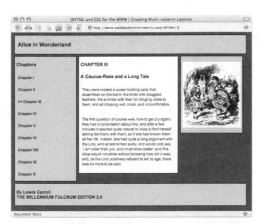

Figure 17.5 The three-column layout with header and footer is a fairly typical design achieved using tables. Here it's created using only CSS. Notice, though, that the columns won't stretch to the height of the longest one as a table would.

Creating Multicolumn Layouts

Although tables have dominated Web site design for years, Web designers increasingly recognize the power of creating layouts using pure CSS. Although CSS positioning—explained in Chapter 6—allows you to precisely control layout on the page, it turns out that these controls are not well suited for dynamic multicolumn layouts. Instead, it's the float property that gives us the most flexible designs (**Code 17.8** and **Figure 17.5**).

Code 17.8 Set up a three-column layout using the float property with three objects to line them up next to each other.

```
<!DOCTYPE html PUBLIC "-//W3C//DTD XHTML 1.0 Transitional//EN" "http://www.w3.org/TR/xhtml1/DTD/
  xhtml1-transitional.dtd">
<html xmlns="http://www.w3.org/1999/xhtml">
<head>
    meta http-equiv="content-type" content="text/html;charset=utf-8" />
    <title>DHTML and CSS for the WWW | Creating Multicolumn Layouts</title>
    <style type="text/css" media="screen"><!--
body {
    font-size: 12px;
    font-family: Arial, Helvetica, Geneva, Swiss, sans-serif;
    line-height: 16px;
    background-color: #333;
}
#page {
    margin: 0 auto;
    width: 760px;
}
#column1, #column2, #column3 {
    margin-right: 5px;
    float: left;
    border:solid 2px black;
}
#column1 {
```

(code continues on next page)

To set up a multicolumn layout using CSS:

1. `#page {...}`

Add an ID to your Web page to define the page. This will contain the header, columns, and footer and should have its width defined. Although this may not seem necessary, it prevents the columns from splitting apart if the browser window isn't wide enough.

2. `#column1, #column2, #column3 {...}`

Set up IDs for each of your columns, defining their common properties. The only mandatory property is `float`, which should be set to `left`. This will cause all three columns to stack next to each other.

3. `#column1 {...}`

You can refine each column to specify its width, background color, and any other properties it doesn't share with the others.

4. `#header, #footer {...}`

Add IDs for the header and the footer that run across the top and bottom of the columns.

5. `<div id="page">...</div>`

In the body of your Web page, set up the `page` object, which will contain all three columns as well as the header and footer.

6. `<div id="header">...</div>`

Add the `header` object within the `page` object.

7. `<div id="column1">...</div>`

Add all three columns within the `page` object. You can place any content you want within these layers—including more columns to split these up further.

Code 17.8 *continued*

```
        background-color: #ccc;
        width: 200px;
}
#column2 {
        background-color: #fff;
        width: 320px;
}

#column3 {
        background-color: #ccc;
        width: 200px;
}
#header, #footer {
        background-color: #ccc;
        display: block;
        margin: 5px 0;
        padding: 5px;
        width: 740px;
        clear: both;
        border: solid 2px black;
}
p {
        padding: 10px;
}
h1 {
        font-size: 1.5em;
        padding: 5px;
}
h2 {
        font-size: 1.25em;
        padding: 5px;
}
.chapter {

margin-top: 0;
        margin-bottom: 3px;
        font-sixe: 10px;
}
        --></style>
</head>
<body>
        <div id="page">
            <div id="header">
                <h1>Alice in Wonderland</h1>
```

(code continues on next page)

Code 17.8 *continued*

```
                                        Code
        </div>
        <div id="column1">
            <h2>Chapters</h2>
            <p class="chapter"><b>Chapter
            ↪ I</b></p>
            <p class="chapter"><b>Chapter
            ↪ II</b></p>
            <p class="chapter"><b>&gt;&gt;
            ↪ Chapter III</b></p>
            <div id="column2">
            <h2>CHAPTER III</h2>
            <h2>A Caucus-Race and a Long
            ↪ Tale</h2>
            <p>They were indeed a queer-looking
            ↪ party that assembled on the
            ↪ bank...</p>
        </div>
        <div id="column3">
            <h2><img src="alice09a.gif"
            ↪ alt="" height="213" width="190"
            ↪ border="0"/></h2>
        </div>
        <br style="clear:both" />
        <div id="footer">
            <h3>By Lewis Carroll<br/>
            THE MILLENNIUM FULCRUM
            ↪ EDITION 3.0</h3>
        </div>
    </div>
</body>
</html>
```

8. `<br style="clear:both" />`

Add a break tag using the `clear:both` style to prevent the content below from floating along with the columns.

9. `<div id="footer">...</div>`

Finally, add the `footer` object at the bottom of the page.

✔ Tips

- Although I used three columns here, you can add as few or as many columns as you want for your design. You can also use this technique to nest columns within columns.

- To see an example of the three-column layout, see the Web site for this book (www.webbedenvironments.com/dhtml). Other "tableless" Web sites include Wired News (www.wired.com) and Macromedia (www.macromedia.com).

- If you design a great layout using CSS without tables, send me the URL (dhtml @webbedenvironments.com). I'd love to check it out.

CREATING MULTICOLUMN LAYOUTS

Styling Tables

Tables have become a staple of Web design. They're still used to control the layout of many of the most popular Web sites you see, although they were never intended to do anything more than display tabular data.

Tables can benefit from CSS: You can set common attributes and change them in a single place without having to go to every `<table>`, `<tr>`, and `<td>` tag and change them individually.

CSS can do many things to make a table layout easier. **Code 17.9** shows how CSS border attributes can be applied to a table (**Figure 17.6**). Although you can use CSS to define tables, all the browser-specific limitations of tables still apply.

Figure 17.6 Tic-tac-toe, anyone? The table's appearance is being controlled with easy-to-change CSS rather than cumbersome tag attributes.

Layout with CSS vs. Tables

Before tables, Web layout consisted of wide pages of text stretching from the left side of the window to the right. Designers had no way to break up this single column of content. Yet most designers came from a print background, and they were used to breaking text into two or more columns.

Tables allow designers to create a layout grid with multiple columns. Although tables were never meant to be the workhorse of Web layout, it was the only game in town until CSS.

Layout with CSS offers two main advantages over table-based layout. The first, although minor, is that CSS layouts will load slightly faster than table-based layouts. More importantly, CSS layouts are extremely modular, allowing you to quickly reshuffle and rearrange layouts without having to rip apart the code (as you have to do with tables).

Initially, Web designers tried to use absolute positioning to exactly place columns across the page. However, this did not deliver satisfactory results, because no content could be placed beneath the columns. So designers went back to the drawing board and found that the unassuming `float` property could be used to simply stack columns next to each other. However, this still has one drawback: the column heights are independent of each other. Unlike with tables, where the shortest column stretches down to the height of the tallest column, CSS columns will abruptly end.

Code 17.9 You can use CSS to set `<table>` tags, which gives you greater flexibility in table layout.

```
 ● ● ●                    Code                     ◯
<!DOCTYPE html PUBLIC "-//W3C//DTD XHTML
→ 1.0 Transitional//EN" "http://www.w3.org/TR/
→ xhtml1/DTD/xhtml1-transitional.dtd">
<html xmlns="http://www.w3.org/1999/xhtml">
<head>
     <title>DHTML and CSS for the WWW |
     → Table Borders</title>
     <style type="text/css" media="screen"><!--
table {
     font: 75px "arial black";
     border: solid 2px red;
}
td {
     text-align: center;
     width: 150px;
     height: 150px;
     border: inset 8px red;
     align: center;
}
td.lightBG { background-color: #cccccc; }
td.darkBG { background-color: #666666; }
     --></style>
</head>
<body>
     <table>
        <tr>
           <td class="darkBG">X</td>
           <td class="lightBG">O</td>
           <td class="darkBG">X</td>
        </tr>
        <tr>
           <td class="lightBG">X</td>
           <td class="darkBG">X</td>
           <td class="lightBG">O</td>
        </tr>
        <tr>
           <td class="darkBG">O</td>
           <td class="lightBG">O</td>
           <td class="darkBG"><br />
           </td>
        </tr>
     </table>
</body>
</html>
```

✔ Tips

■ Without CSS, table borders are fairly boring, and must be set the same on all sides. With CSS, you can set the table borders on each side individually, greatly enhancing the layout possibilities. For example, you could set up borders only underneath each row for a subtle effect.

■ CSS also allows you to collapse the borders between table data cells as explained in Chapter 8.

STYLING TABLES

A (Brief) History of Web Layout with Tables

Without tables, the Web might never have taken off as the multimedia medium of choice for millions of users around the world. So it might be surprising to hear that there was a lot of grumbling when Netscape introduced tables with Navigator 1, because they weren't part of the World Wide Web Consortium's HTML standards.

Since that time, tables have become the standard for anyone who wants more than a lump of text and graphics on a Web page.

Styling Forms

There are no special styles or values specific to forms, but they are elements of Web design that can benefit from style changes—although this can lead to some controversy. The appearance of all form elements (fields, text areas, buttons, pop-up menus, check boxes, and so on) are defined by the operating system of the viewer. By changing the appearance of these buttons from the standard look, you run the risk of confusing visitors. Therefore it's very important to make sure that your form elements will look like form elements (**Figure 17.7**).

Although you can apply styles directly to a form element tag, this can often lead to problems. For example, if you apply a border to an <input> tag, the border will not only appear around form fields, but also around radio buttons and check boxes which may not look that great. Instead, it's best to create classes directly associated with a form element type (**Code 17.10**):

◆ `fieldset` applies a title and border around a content area. Although most often used with forms, there's no reason not to use this with other content as well, including paragraphs and links.

◆ `legend` is used as the title in the `fieldset` and must appear immediately after the opening `fieldset` tag.

◆ `label` is used with text that appears next to form elements to tell the viewer what the form field is for.

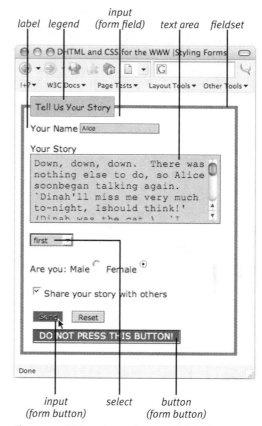

Figure 17.7 CSS can be used to completely change the appearance of form elements from their standard look. But beware: Some users may get confused if you stray too far from the norm.

Code 17.10 There are several different form elements that you can apply styles to. This code shows you how to use classes with form elements. Of course, you don't have to define all form elements in your code.

```
<!DOCTYPE html PUBLIC "-//W3C//DTD XHTML
→ 1.0 Transitional//EN" "http://www.w3.org/TR/
→ xhtml1/DTD/xhtml1-transitional.dtd">
<html xmlns="http://www.w3.org/1999/xhtml">
<head>
    <title>DHTML and CSS for the WWW |
    → Styling Forms</title>
    <style type="text/css" media="screen"><!--
fieldset.formFieldSet {
    padding: 10px;
    width: 325px;
    border: solid 5px #f00;
}
legend.formLegend {
    font-size: 14px;
    font-family: "Zapf Chancery",
    →"Comic Sans MS", cursive;
    background-color: #fcc;
    padding: 5px;
    border: solid 2px #f00;
}
label {
    font-size: 14px;
    font-family: Verdana, Arial, Helvetica,
    → sans-serif;
    vertical-align: middle;
}
textarea.formTextArea {
    font-family: "Courier New", Courier,
    → Monaco, monospace;
    background-color: #ccc;
    padding: 5px;
    width: 300px;
    height: 100px;
    border: solid 1px #f00;
}
select.formPopup {
    font-size: 12px;
    font-family: Verdana, Arial, Helvetica,
    → sans-serif;
    background-color: #ccc;
    border: solid 1px #f00;
}
```

(code continues on next page)

- ◆ **textarea** defines a box with multiple rows where text can be entered. Generally these are used where more than a couple of words need to be recorded.

- ◆ **select** presents multiple options presented as a drop-down or multiple-select menu.

- ◆ **input** (form field) defines a single row used to enter a few words of text.

- ◆ **input** (form button) creates a simple button used to submit or reset forms.

- ◆ **button** (form button) offers another way to create buttons to submit or reset forms.

✔ Tips

- ■ The Mac OS X browsers Safari and Camino will only apply font style changes made to **input**, **textarea**, or **select** form elements. All other styles, including background and border changes, are ignored.

- ■ Notice that in the example code I also included a version of the input form button using hover. This will actually change the appearance of the form button when the user rolls over it. Unfortunately the rollover trick won't work in Internet Explorer for Windows, which only supports hover with hypertext links.

Code 17.10 *continued*

```
                                        Code
input.formField {
    font-size: 10px;
    font-family: Helvetica, Geneva, Arial, SunSans-Regular, sans-serif;
    background-color: #ccc;
    padding: 2px;
    border: solid 1px #f00;
}
input.formButton {
    font-size:12px;
    font-family: Verdana, Arial, Helvetica, sans-serif;
    background-color: #ccc;
    margin: 5px;
    border: solid 1px #f00;
}
input.formButton:hover {
    font-size: 12px;
    font-family: Verdana, Arial, Helvetica, sans-serif;
    background-color: #f00;
    margin: 5px;
    border: solid 1px #ccc;
}
button.formButton {
    color: #fff;
    font-size: 14px;
    font-family: Verdana, Arial, Helvetica, sans-serif;
    background-color: #f00;
    margin: 5px;
    border: solid 2px #333;
}
    --></style>
</head>
<body bgcolor="#ffffff">
    <fieldset class="formFieldSet">
        <legend class="formLegend">Tell Us Your Story</legend>
        <form id="FormName" action="" method="get">
            <p><label>Your Name</label> <input class="formField" type="text" name="textfieldName"
            ⇢ size="24" /></p>
            <p></p>
            <p><label>Your Story<br/>
                </label><textarea class="formTextArea" name="textareaName" rows="4"
                ⇢ cols="40">Down, down, down. There was nothing else to do, so Alice soon began
                ⇢ talking again...
                </textarea></p>
            <p><select class="formPopup" name="selectName" size="1">
                <option value="one">first</option>
```

(code continues on next page)

STYLING FORMS

Code 17.10 *continued*

```
                <option value="two">second</option>
                <option value="three">third</option>
            </select></p>
            <p><label>Are you: Male</label><input class="formButton" type="radio" name="radiogroup"
            → value="radioValue" /> <label>Female</label><input class="formButton" type="radio"
            → name="radiogroup" value="radioValue" /> <br /><br />
            <input class="formButton" type="checkbox" name="checkboxName" value="checkboxValue"
            → /><label>Share your story with others</label></p>
            <p><input class="formButton" type="submit" name="submit" value="Send"/> <input
            → class="formButton" type="reset" /><button class="formButton" name="buttonName"
            → type="button">DO NOT PRESS THIS BUTTON!</button></p>
        </form>
    </fieldset>
</body>
</html>
```

Styling Frames

One of the most frustrating aspects of using frames is the clunky-looking borders that standard HTML puts between them (**Figure 17.8**). When you use the `background` property, however, you can use any border design you dream up (**Figure 17.9**).

Although these borders can be placed only along the left side or top of an individual frame, they're still very useful for showing boundaries between frames.

To create a frame border:

1. `border.gif`

   Create the frame-border graphic. For this example, I'm using an ornate design that I saved as "border.gif" (**Figure 17.10**). You can use anything you want for this graphic.

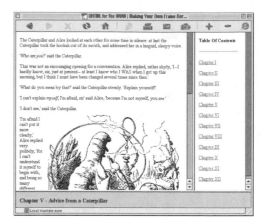

Figure 17.8 A frameset with the default frame borders.

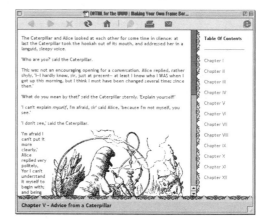

Figure 17.9 A frameset created with CSS, showing an ornate red border separating the frames.

Figure 17.10 The two graphics used to create the borders for the right and bottom frames. Remember, you can use anything you want for these. Go wild.

Code 17.11 The frameset document.

```
<!DOCTYPE html PUBLIC "-//W3C//DTD XHTML
→ 1.0 Frameset//EN" "http://www.w3.org/TR/
→ xhtml1/DTD/xhtml1-frameset.dtd">
<html xmlns="http://www.w3.org/1999/xhtml">
<head>
     <title>DHTML and CSS for the WWW |
     → Styling Frames</title>
</head>
<frameset rows="*,40" border="0"
→ frameborder="no" framespacing="0">
     <frameset cols="*,150" border="0"
     → frameborder="no" framespacing="0">
        <frame name="centerFrame"
        → src="center_frame.html"
        → noresize="noresize" />
        <frame name="rightFrame"
        → src="right_frame.html"
        → noresize="noresize" />
     </frameset>
     <frame name="bottomFrame"
     → src="bottom_frame.html"
     → noresize="noresize" scrolling="no" />
</frameset>
</html>
```

2. `index.html`

Create a frame document, and save it as "index.html" making sure that you turn off the default border (**Code 17.11**):

```
border="0" framespacing="0"
→ frameborder="no"
```

continues on next page

3. `right_frame.html`

Use the `background` property in the `<body>` tag of an HTML document (**Code 17.12** and **17.13**) to place the border graphic from step 1 in the background of the desired frame(s). Repeat this graphic either horizontally (`repeat-x`) or vertically (`repeat-y`) for a full border (see "Setting the Background" in Chapter 5).

✔ Tips

■ Remember that in addition to the border, you can give separate styles to each frame. Each frame is a different Web page and can, thus, include completely different styles, including backgrounds, colors, and fonts. However, it is a good idea to keep the frames visually similar so that they mesh well together.

■ The design of the border can be anything you want, and it can be as thick or thin as you want. Just remember that the image repeats along whichever axis you specify.

■ These borders have one big drawback compared with the default frame-border style: Neither you nor the visitor can use these borders to resize the frame.

Code 17.12 A frame with a custom vertical border set.

```
<!DOCTYPE html PUBLIC "-//W3C//DTD XHTML
→ 1.0 Transitional//EN" "http://www.w3.org/TR/
→ xhtml1/DTD/xhtml1-transitional.dtd">
<html xmlns="http://www.w3.org/1999/xhtml">
<head>
    <title>DHTML and CSS for the WWW |
    → Right Frame</title>
    <style type="text/css" media="screen"><!--
body {
    background: white url(border2.gif)
    → repeat-y;
    margin-left: 20px;
}
    --></style>
</head>
<body>
    <h4>Table Of Contents</h4>
    <hr align="left" width="90%" />
    <p><a href="#">Chapter I</a></p>
</body>
</html>
```

Code 17.13 A frame with a custom horizontal border set.

```
<!DOCTYPE html PUBLIC "-//W3C//DTD XHTML
→ 1.0 Transitional//EN" "http://www.w3.org/TR/
→ xhtml1/DTD/xhtml1-transitional.dtd">
<html xmlns="http://www.w3.org/1999/xhtml">
<head>
    <title>DHTML and CSS for the WWW |
    → Bottom Frame</title>
    <style type="text/css" media="screen"><!--
body {
    background: silver url(border1.gif)
    → repeat-x;
}
    --></style>
</head>
<body>
    <h3>Chapter V - Advice from a
    → Caterpillar</h3>
</body>
</html>
```

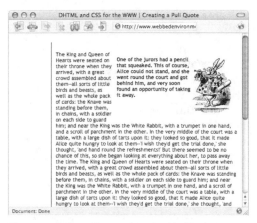

Figure 17.11 The pull quote is embedded in the text. Although I only placed text and graphics in here, you could really use it for anything, including navigation menus.

Creating a Pull Quote

A common layout technique is to take a quote out of the main copy of an article or story and highlight it in what is called a pull quote. To do this, we will float a small, relatively positioned element inside a larger, absolutely positioned element.

The power of CSS layout comes from its ability to position content precisely in the window. When a relatively positioned element is nested in an absolutely positioned element, the former uses its parent's top-left corner as its origin. When this relatively placed element is placed inside an absolutely placed element (**Code 17.14**), it moves with the absolute element (**Figure 17.11**).

Code 17.14 Two classes are created, one defined as absolutely positioned (mainCopy) and the other defined as relatively positioned (pullQuote). The relative class is then used with a <p> tag and is nested within a <div> tag defined with the absolute class. This allows all the content for this page to be moved over to the right. Notice the string of <br /> tags at the end of the code outside the absolute element: They overcome a bug in Internet Explorer that would prevent the scroll bars from appearing.

```
<!DOCTYPE html PUBLIC "-//W3C//DTD XHTML 1.0 Transitional//EN" "http://www.w3.org/TR/xhtml1/DTD/
 xhtml1-transitional.dtd">
<html xmlns="http://www.w3.org/1999/xhtml">
<head>
    <title>DHTML and CSS for the WWW | Creating a Pull Quote</title>
    <style type="text/css" media="screen"><!--
.mainCopy {
    padding: 10px;
    position: absolute;
    left: 100px;
    border-style: none none none solid;
    border-width: 0 0 0 1px;
    border-color: #000000;
}
.pullQuote {
    font-weight: bold;
    padding: 1em;
    position: relative;
    width: 275px;
    float: right;
```

(code continues on next page)

To nest a relative element within an absolute element:

1. `.mainCopy{...}`

   Create an absolutely positioned class. In this example, I've set up a class that off-sets itself 100 pixels to the left and places a thin solid border down the left side of the element.

2. `.pullQuote {...}`

   Create a relatively positioned class. In this example, the class will float to the right, text will be bold, padding is set to one em space, and the element will be 275 pixels wide.

3. `<div class="mainCopy">`

   `<p class="pullQuote">...</p>`

   `</div>`

   In the body of your document, set up a `<div>` tag defined with the `mainCopy` class; then place a tag with the relatively positioned class inside that.

✔ Tip

■ One problem with having the majority of your content placed in an absolute element is that Internet Explorer will not register the height of the element when the page first loads. The result is that even if the content goes off the bottom of the page, no scroll bar appears. However, the user can still use the arrow keys to move the page up or down, and if the user resizes the page, the scroll bar will appear. The only way you can ensure that the scroll bar appears is to place a series of `<br />` tags to force the page down below the fold.

Code 17.14 *continued*

```
}
    --></style>
</head>
<body>
    <div class="mainCopy">
        <p class="pullQuote"><img
        → src="alice37.gif" height="136"
        → width="100" align="right" />One of
        → the jurors had a pencil that
        → squeaked. This of course, Alice could
        → not stand, and she went round the
        → court and got behind him, and very
        → soon found an opportunity of taking
        → it away.</p>
            <p>The King and Queen of Hearts were
            → seated on their throne when they
            → arrived, with a great crowd
            → assembled about them...</p>
    </div>
    <br /><br /><br /><br /><br /><br /><br
    → /><br /><br /><br /><br /><br /><br
    → /><br /><br /><br /><br /><br /><br
    → /><br /><br /><br /><br /><br /><br
    → /><br /><br /><br /><br /><br /><br
    → /><br /><br /><br /><br /><br /><br
    → /><br /><br /><br /><br /><br /><br
    → /><br />
</body>
</html>
```

Code 17.15 Applying a background graphic to a header is fairly straightforward, but the possibilities are infinite.

```
<!DOCTYPE html PUBLIC "-//W3C//DTD XHTML
→ 1.0 Transitional//EN" "http://www.w3.org/TR/
→ xhtml1/DTD/xhtml1-transitional.dtd">
<html xmlns="http://www.w3.org/1999/xhtml">
<head>
     <title>DHTML for the WWW |
     → Creating Headlines</title>
     <style type="text/css" media="screen"><!--
h3.offset {
     color:#000000;
     font-size: 14px;
     font-family: Verdana, Arial, Helvetica,
     → sans-serif;
     font-weight: bold;
     background-color: #ccc;
     padding: 3px;
     position: relative;
     width: 440px;
     border: solid 1pt;
}
h3.graphic {
     color: white;
     font: bold 16px helvetica, sans-serif;
     background: black url(background_
     → headline.gif) no-repeat;
     padding: 10px;
     width: 400px;
}
p {
     font: 10pt / 14pt Times, serif;
     width: 400;
     left-margin: 25px;
}
     --></style>
</head>
<body>
     <h3 class="offset">CHAPTER VII<br />
          A Mad Tea-Party</h3>
     <p>The table was a large one...</p>
     <h3 class="graphic">CHAPTER VII<br />
          A Mad Tea-Party</h3>
     <p>There was a table set out under a tree
     → in front of the house...</p>
</body>
</html>
```

Creating Headlines

One hassle in Web design is headlines created from a graphic, which usually means creating a new graphic for every headline. Using the CSS background property, however, you can create as many different title graphics as you want—without having to create new graphics and without incurring the additional download time involved with using text in graphics (**Code 17.15**).

To create a headline with a graphic background:

1. `background_headline.gif`

Create and save your background in a graphics program. Call the graphic something like "background_headline.gif" (**Figure 17.12**).

2. `h3.graphic {...}`

Add a CSS rule for the `<h3>` tag, with an associated class of `graphic` (see "Defining Classes to Create Your Own Tags" in Chapter 2). Include the `background` attribute, and point to the graphic you created in step 1 (see "Setting the Background" in Chapter 5).

Note: You don't have to call the class created here `graphic`; you may call it anything you want.

3. `<h3 class="graphic">CHAPTER VII<br>` `→ A Mad Tea-Party </h3>`

Your background graphic will appear behind all level-three headings in your document, as long as you include the `class` attribute and set it to the class you added in step 2 (**Figure 17.13**).

✔ Tips

- You can set the other heading levels the same way. You can use different graphics or use the same graphic by grouping the selectors (see "Combining Styles with the Same Rules" in Chapter 2).

- Play around with different graphics in the background. One background that I set up for a Web site used a gradient that started with a color on the left side and faded into the background on the right (**Figure 17.14**).

Figure 17.12 The background graphic that will be tiled behind headlines.

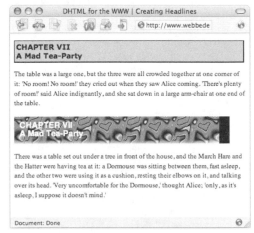

Figure 17.13 Two header examples. Play around with other graphics, different borders, and even different padding in the titles for other effects.

Figure 17.14 The headers About the Site and Reading the Code are both HTML text on a background graphic.

Code 17.16 The fixed header style is set as an ID that is then applied to a `<div>` tag.

```
<?xml version="1.0" ?>
<!DOCTYPE html PUBLIC "-//W3C//DTD XHTML
→ 1.0 Transitional//EN" "http://www.w3.org/TR/
→ xhtml1/DTD/
→ xhtml1-transitional.dtd">
<html xmlns="http://www.w3.org/1999/xhtml">
<head>
     <title>DHTML and CSS for the WWW |
     → Creating a Fixed Header</title>
     <style type="text/css" media="screen"><!--
#header {
     color: red;
     font-size: 16px;
     font-family: "Times New Roman", Georgia,
     → Times, serif;
     font-weight: bold;
     background-color: #aaa;
     visibility: visible;
     padding: 5px;
     position: fixed;
     z-index: 1000;
     top: 0;
     left: 0;
     width: 110%;
}
     --></style>
</head>
<body>
     <div id="header">
         <i>Alice In Wonderland</i> By Lewis
         → Carrol</div>
     <br />
     <p>'I'm sure those are not the right
words,' said poor Alice...</p>
</body>
</html>
```

Creating a Fixed Header

One principle of good Web design is to let people know where they are at all times. Unfortunately, Web pages scroll and important information about the page being viewed, such as its header, can scroll off the top.

Using CSS, you can fix the header at the top of the Web page (**Code 17.16**) so that no matter how far visitors scroll, they always know where they are in the Web site (**Figure 17.15**).

You should know up front, however, that Internet Explorer 5/6 (Windows) and Netscape 6 (Mac and Windows) do not support fixed positioning. However fixed positioning is supported in Netscape 7, Firebird, Opera 3.5+, and Safari.

Figure 17.15 Even though the text has scrolled up, the header stays at the top of the browser window.

To set a fixed header:

1. `#header {`

Open a definition list with either a class or an ID. In this example, I created an ID called `header`.

2. `position: fixed;`

Type the `position` attribute, and give it the `fixed` value.

3. `color: red;`

Add any other definitions to the list that you want to use to create the header. This example displays the header in red on a gray background.

4. `}`

Close the definition list with a curly bracket (}).

5. `<div id="header"> <i>Alice In`
`→ Wonderland </i> By Lewis`
`→ Carroll</div>`

Add the ID to the desired element. In this example, I use a `<div>` tag to set off the title of the page.

✔ Tips

■ Remember that this technique won't work in all browsers. Browsers that don't recognize the fixed position treat the header as a static element, and it scrolls with the rest of the page. The rest of the CSS formatting will work, however. This might also be a good place to customize the CSS for the OS and browser, to allow the fixed element to be absolutely placed in Internet Explorer for Windows.

■ Although it would be great if you could also place links in this fixed header, a bug in Internet Explorer 5 for the Mac makes links in a fixed element almost useless (see the sidebar "Is It Fixed?" in Chapter 6).

```
<!DOCTYPE html PUBLIC "-//W3C//DTD XHTML
→ 1.0 Transitional//EN" "http://www.w3.org/TR/
→ xhtml1/DTD/xhtml1-transitional.dtd">
<html xmlns="http://www.w3.org/1999/xhtml">
<head>
    <title>DHTML and CSS for the WWW |
    → Creating a Simple Drop Shadow</title>
    <style type="text/css" media="screen"><!--
#title {
    font: bold 75px "Hoefler Text", serif,
    → "Times New Roman", Georgia, Times;
    position: relative;
    top: 5px;
    left: 5px;
}
#text {
    color: #000000;
    position: relative;
    z-index: 2;
    top: 0;
    left: 0;
}
#shadow {
    color: #999999;
    position: absolute;
    z-index: 1;
    top: 4px;
    left: 4px;
}
    --></style>
</head>
<body>
    <div id="title">
        <span id="text">Alice in Wonderland
        → </span>
        <span id="shadow">Alice in Wonderland
        → </span>
</div>
    <p>Down, down, down. Would the fall
    → <i>never</i> come to an end! 'I wonder
    → how many miles I've fallen by this
    → time?'</p>
</body>
</html>
```

Creating a Drop Shadow

Another popular special effect on the Web is the drop shadow. Drop shadows make text (especially large headlines and titles) stand out from the rest of the page, adding emphasis and impact. Before CSS, however, the only way to create drop shadows for the Web was to create a graphic of the text and its shadow. Now, a little CSS trickery lets you do the same thing without resorting to graphics (**Figure 17.16**).

To create a CSS drop shadow:

1. #title {...}

In your CSS rules list (**Code 17.17**), create three ID selectors called title, text, and shadow. Both title and text should be positioned relatively; shadow should be positioned absolutely and slightly offset from its top-left corner.

continues on next page

Figure 17.16 For a drop-shadow effect, simply place two identical layers one on top the other, with one layer lighter than the other.

2. `<div id="title">...</div>`

Create a `title` object. This will contain both the foreground (`text`) and background (`shadow`) layers, and allow you to position these elements on the page as one unit.

3. `<span id="text">...</span>`

In the `title` layer, add the `text` layer for the foreground text.

4. `<span id="shadow">...</span>`

Immediately after the `text` layer, add the `shadow` layer, containing the same text as the `text` layer. This layer will be the text's shadow.

✔ Tips

- Note: A non-CSS-capable browser reading a page that uses this drop-shadow technique will display the text one line after the next, which may not look very appealing (**Figure 17.17**).

- You can play with different colors for the drop shadow or even use different fonts for the foreground text and the drop shadow if you're feeling like a complete nut.

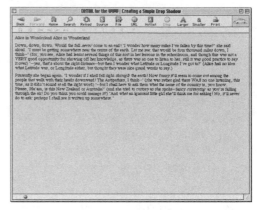

Figure 17.17 What a non-CSS-capable browser sees.

NAVIGATION AND CONTROLS

Navigation is what makes the Web run. Navigation can come in many flavors: main menus, submenus, auxiliary menus, image maps, hypertext links, and other schemes that allow visitors to move from page to page. A well-planned navigation scheme lets visitors get to the information they want with minimal fuss. Poorly planned navigation leads to blindness, low sex appeal, and sometimes death. Even worse, poor navigation may upset site visitors enough that they will never return.

Beyond navigating between Web pages, a truly dynamic Web site allows visitors to interact with the pages by changing the content after it has loaded. You must provide controls that permit that interaction.

In this chapter, I'll look at some effective ways to create dynamic navigation that gives visitors maximum flexibility and allows you to maximize the impact of your content.

In addition to navigation, I'll show you how to add interactive functions that give visitors greater control over the way the Web page is presented to them.

Setting Multiple Link Styles

Although links may be used for different purposes on a Web page (some may be in menus while others are in paragraphs) and in different locations (some may be on a dark background and others on a light background) HTML only allows you to define a single color for *all* links on the page.

However, you often need to define completely different styles for links depending on their use and location on the page. In Chapter 2, I showed you how to set styles for four different link state pseudo-classes (link, visited, hover, and active). You can also associate any class with the appearance of a link pseudo-class or define the pseudo-class contextually within other HTML tags, allowing you to define styles based on the use of the link (**Code 18.1**).

This gives you great design power. If you want the links in your navigation menus to be a different color from the links in a paragraph, for example, you can set up two independent link styles. Although they're both hypertext links, menu links can appear in red, while text links appear in green (**Figure 18.1**).

Figure 18.1 The two link styles in context on the Web page.

Code 18.1 Two link styles have been added. The first style sets up a class called menu that can be applied to links. The second style defines how links should look when they're nested within a <p> tag.

```
<!DOCTYPE html PUBLIC "-//W3C//DTD XHTML
→ 1.0 Transitional//EN" "http://www.w3.org/TR/
→ xhtml1/DTD/xhtml1-transitional.dtd">
<html xmlns="http://www.w3.org/1999/xhtml">
<head>
    <title>DHTML and CSS for the WWW |
    → Setting Multiple Hypertext Link
    → Apperances</title>
    <style type="text/css" media="screen"><!--
a.menu:link {
    color: #cc0000;
    font-weight: bold;
    text-decoration: none;
}
a.menu:active {
    color: #666666;
    font-weight: bold;
    text-decoration: none;
}
a.menu:visited {
    color: #cc0000;
    font-weight: bold;
    text-decoration: none;
}
a.menu:hover {
    color: #ff0000;
    text-decoration: none;
    cursor: move;
}
p a:link {
    color: #00cc00;
    font-weight: bold;
}
p a:active {
    color: #666666;
    text-decoration: none;
}
p a:visited {
    color: #00cc00;
    font-weight: normal;
    texl-decoration: none;
}
p a:hover {
```

(code continues on next page)

Code 18.1 *continued*

```
       color: #00ff00;
       text-decoration: none;
       cursor: nw-resize;
}

       --></style>
</head>
<body>
       <h3><a class="menu" href="#">&lt;Previous
→ Chapter</a> | <a class="menu"
→ href="#">Next Chapter &gt;</a></h3>
       <h3>CHAPTER XI<br />
       Who Stole the Tarts?</h3>
          <p><a href="index.html">The King</a>
          → and <a href="#">Queen of Hearts</a>
          → were seated on their throne when they
          → arrived...</p>
</body>
</html>
```

<Previous Chapter

Figure 18.2 The style for menu links as defined by the menu class.

Queen of Hearts

Figure 18.3 The style for links in a paragraph (in reality, these links should be green).

To set up multiple link styles:

◆ a.menu:link{...}

You can set up link styles as part of a true class if you place a period (.) and the name of the class before the colon (:). In this example, link styles have been set up for the class menu that is applied as a class to the link tag (<a>) (**Figure 18.2**).

or

◆ p a:link{...}

You can also set link styles contextually so they have a certain appearance if their parent is a particular tag. In this example, the link tag (<a>) has the defined appearance if it's within a paragraph tag (<p>) (**Figure 18.3**).

✔ Tips

■ Setting multiple link colors can be useful for showing many different kinds of links. For example, you might also want links that go outside your site to be a different color.

■ If you use too many colors, your visitors may not be able to tell which words are links and which are not.

SETTING MULTIPLE LINK STYLES

Creating Image Rollovers with CSS

When most developers consider using rollovers for navigation, they immediately assume that JavaScript will be required for the effect. However, CSS offers a much simpler, elegant, and robust solution using the background and padding properties with the link pseudo-classes (**Figure 18.4**).

The obvious advantage of this system is that the images used for rollovers no longer require any JavaScript to set up (**Code 18.2**). So if you move the link, the rollover effect goes along with it, and you can easily make changes to the rollover just by changing the style sheet.

To add CSS image rollovers to a Web page:

1. bg_link.png

   Create individual images for each of the states you'll be using, and save them with whatever filenames work best for you; I used "bg_link," "bg_visited," "bg_hover," and "bg_active" (**Figure 18.5**). The images shouldn't use a height much larger then the font size you're using for your text. You can use any graphic format supported by browsers (generally GIF, PNG, or JPEG).

Code 18.2 Set the default link style to offset the text with padding and place the image to the left of the text. Then set up definitions for each link pseudo-class defining the background to be used for that state.

```
<!DOCTYPE html PUBLIC "-//W3C//DTD XHTML
→ 1.0 Transitional//EN" "http://www.w3.org/TR/
→ xhtml1/DTD/xhtml1-transitional.dtd">
<html xmlns="http://www.w3.org/1999/xhtml">
<head>
    <title>DHTML &amp; CSS for the WWW |
    → Creating Image Rollovers with CSS</title>
    <style type="text/css" media="screen"><!--
a {
    text-decoration: none;
    background-repeat: no-repeat;
    background-position: left top;
    padding-left: 17px;
}
a:link {
    color: #c00;
    background-image: url(bg_link.png);
}
a:visited {
    color: #900;
    background-image: url(bg_visited.png);
}
a:hover {
    color: #f00;
    background-image: url(bg_hover.png);
}
a:active {
    color: #090;
    background-image: url(bg_active.png);
}
    --></style>
</head>
<body>
    <p><a href="ch1" onfocus="if(this.blur)
    → this.blur();">Chapter 1</a></p>
    <p><a href="ch2" onfocus="if(this.blur)
    → this.blur();">Chapter 2</a></p>
    <p><a href="ch3" onfocus="if(this.blur)
    → this.blur();">Chapter 3</a></p>
    <p>'Oh, I've had such a <a href="#"
    → onFocus="if(this.blur)this.blur();
    → ">curious dream!</a>' said Alice...</p>
</body>
</html>
```

Figure 18.4 The images next to links are actually part of the background behind the text.

Figure 18.5 The four different link background graphics: bg_link, bg_visited, bg_hover, and bg_active.

Getting Rid of Those Annoying Active Link Borders

Internet Explorer 5 introduced (and many other browsers have adapted) what might be one of the most aggravating features possible to Web designers: the active link border. Those are the boxes that appear around a link after it has been clicked. They can interfere with your design, especially if you're using CSS image rollovers or if the links are in a frame, so the border persists even after the linked page has loaded. There is a way to get rid of these, however. Simply place the following code in the links for which you want to turn active link borders off:

```
onfocus="if(this.blur)this.blur();"
```

This tells the link to blur itself if it's focused, thus getting rid of the border.

2. `a{...}`

In your HTML document, set up a general definition for the <a> tag, or for a class associated with the <a> tag (`a.myClass{...}`). The rules set here will then be applied to all of the link pseudo-classes without having to repeat them.

Set the background not to repeat, position it at the top left of the link area and then add enough padding to the left side so that the text isn't on top of the image (generally, the width of the image plus a few pixels).

3. `a:link{...}`

Now add the definitions for all of the link pseudo-classes, defining the background image for each rollover state. You can, of course, include whatever other style changes you want to make. In this example, I'm also changing the text color.

✔ Tips

■ If you use GIF images for your rollover images, you can use GIF animation for a little extra spice.

■ This is a great technique to combine with setting up classes for different link styles (see "Setting Multiple Link Styles" earlier in this chapter).

■ I say in the steps to add enough padding so that the text doesn't overlap the image. However, this can sometime be a nice effect if designed well. For example, you might use a slight gradient behind the link that goes under the text and have the color change with the different states.

■ In this example, the image is placed to the left of the link, but you could just as easily place the image on the right by changing the background position and adding padding to the right instead of the left.

Adding Pop-Up Hypertext

Hypertext gives site visitors extra information as needed. But to access that information, they have to click a link, which opens a new document and replaces what they were reading with the new material. This setup can be highly distracting, not to mention confusing, when trying to return to the originating link.

Wouldn't it be better if that information—written or visual—simply appeared below the link when the mouse passes over it (**Code 18.3**)? That arrangement would truly be hypertext (**Figure 18.6** and **Figure 18.7**).

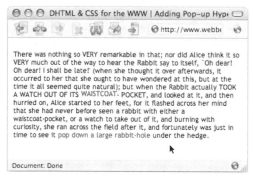

Figure 18.6 When the visitor moves the mouse pointer over the link…

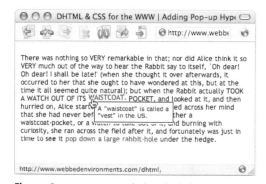

Figure 18.7 …text appears below the link.

Code 18.3 This pop-up code uses information from the event to place an object below the link that triggered it.

```
<!DOCTYPE html PUBLIC "-//W3C//DTD XHTML
→ 1.0 Transitional//EN" "http://www.w3.org/TR/
→ xhtml1/DTD/xhtml1-transitional.dtd">
<html xmlns="http://www.w3.org/1999/xhtml">
<head>
    <title>DHTML &amp; CSS for the WWW |
    → Adding Pop-up Hypertext</title>
    <script type="text/JavaScript"
language="javascript"><!--
        var objPopUp = null;
        function popUp(event,objectID) {
            objPopTrig = document.
            → getElementById(event);
            objPopUp = document.
            → getElementById(objectID);
            xPos = objPopTrig.offsetLeft;
            yPos = objPopTrig.offsetTop +
            → objPopTrig.offsetHeight;
            if (xPos + objPopUp.offsetWidth >
            → document.body.clientWidth) xPos =
            → xPos - objPopUp.offsetWidth;
            if (yPos + objPopUp.offsetHeight >
            → document.body.clientHeight) yPos =
            → yPos - objPopUp.offsetHeight -
            → objPopTrig.offsetHeight;
            objPopUp.style.left = xPos + 'px';
            objPopUp.style.top = yPos + 'px';
            objPopUp.style.visibility =
            → 'visible';
        }
        function popHide() {
            objPopUp.style.visibility =
            → 'hidden';
            objPopUp = null;
        }
//--> </script>
    <style type="text/css" media="screen"><!--
body {
    margin: 0px;
    padding: 0px;
}
p {
    padding: 10px;
```

(code continues on next page)

Code 18.3 *continued*

```
}
a:link {
    white-space: nowrap;
}
.popUp {
    font-size: 10px;
    font-family: Verdana, Arial, Helvetica,
    → sans-serif;
    background-color: #ffffcc;
    visibility: hidden;
    margin: 0 10px;
    padding: 5px;
    position: absolute;
    width: 125px;
    border: solid 1px black;
}
    --></style>
</head>
<body>
    <p> TOOK A WATCH OUT OF ITS <a
    → id="pop1" onmouseover="popUp
    → (this.id,'popUp1')" onmouseout=
    → "popHide()" href="#">WAISTCOAT</a>-
    → POCKET, </p>
        <div id="popUp1" class="popUp">
            A "waistcoat" is called a "vest"
            → in the US.</div>
        <div id="popUp2" class="popUp">
            Take the blue pill!</div>
</body>
</html>
```

To add pop-up hypertext:

1. `var objPopUp = null;`

Initialize the variable `objPopUp`, which will keep track of which pop-up message is being displayed.

2. `function popUp(evt,objectID) {...}`

Add the function `popUp()` to the JavaScript. This function identifies which object triggered the function (`objPopTrig`) and the pop-up object to be displayed (`objPopUp`), then determines where the pop-up should be displayed taking into account the width and height of the display area so that it's always visible. Finally, the function positions the object and shows it.

3. `function popHide() {...}`

Add the function `popHide()` to the JavaScript. This function hides the pop-up object and sets the variable `objPopUp` back to null.

4. `.popUp {...}`

Add the `popUp` class to the CSS. This class will be applied to all pop-up objects and sets their basic appearance.

5. `id="pop1"`

In a container tag, add an ID to define the object. Remember, each object needs a unique ID. The container tag can be anything you want that can use the `onmouseover` and `onmouseout` event handlers, but the link tag (`<a>`) is most commonly used.

6. `onmouseover="popUp(this.id,'popUp1')"`

In the same container tag, add an `onmouseover` event handler that triggers the `popUp()` function, passing it the ID for "this" object and the ID for the pop-up object you want displayed.

continues on next page

ADDING POP-UP HYPERTEXT

7. `onmouseout="popHide()"`

   After the `onmouseover` event handler, add an `onmouseout` event handler to trigger the `popHide()` function, which hides the pop-up object.

8. `<div id="popUp1" class="popUp">...`
   `→ </div>`

   For each hypertext pop-up object, create an object with the class set to `popUp` and a unique ID, which will then be passed to the `popUp()` function you created in step 6.

✔ Tips

- Notice that the links associated with the pop-up text go nowhere (actually, they link to the top of the page using #). You could, however, link to documents that elaborate on the concepts presented in the pop-up text or to anything else you want to use. Or you could use a simple function that returns no value, to have the links do nothing when clicked. You decide.

- You can use pop-up text as tool tips that explain the purpose of a particular link in the navigation.

- You can include pop-up text in an image map. This technique is nice if you have a large graphic with areas that need explanation.

Code 18.4 The code first initializes several variables to control the menus and their appearance. The most important of these is numDropMenu which you will need to change depending on how many menus you are using. The initDropMenu() function sets up the global event handlers for the menus. The function showDropMen() is then responsible for positioning and displaying the menu, while hideDropMenu() will make it vanish when no longer needed.

```
<!DOCTYPE html PUBLIC "-//W3C//DTD XHTML
→ 1.0 Transitional//EN" "http://www.w3.org/TR/
→ xhtml1/DTD/xhtml1-transitional.dtd">
<html xmlns="http://www.w3.org/1999/xhtml">
<head>
    <title>DHTML and CSS for the WWW |
    → Drop-down Menu</title>
        <script language="JavaScript"
        → type="text/javascript">
            var objNavMenu = null;
            var prevObjNavMenu = null;
            var prevObjDropMenu = null;
            var numDropMenu = 3;
            ////// link styles
            var bgLinkColor = '#cccccc';
            var bgLinkHover = '#ffffff';
            var bgLinkActive = '#000000';
            var linkColor = '#000000';
            var linkHover = '#000000';
            var linkActive = '#ffffff';
```

(code continues on next page)

Creating Drop-Down Menus

Drop-down menus have been a favorite GUI device for years. The menu header appears as a single word at the top of the window or screen and when clicked, it displays a list of further options. In a File menu, for example, you might find Save, Close, and Print.

Now you can achieve the same effect on the Web with DHTML (**Code 18.4**). As with most drop-down menu systems, this Web-based version allows you to mouse over a menu header (**Figures 18.8** and **18.9**) and then click to show the menu immediately underneath it (**Figure 18.10**). You can place anything you want in these menus: not just links, but also forms, images, or any other content.

Figure 18.8 The menu headers.

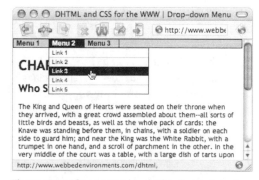

Figure 18.10 After a menu header has been clicked.

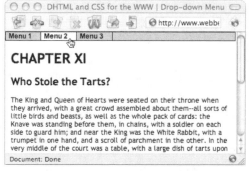

Figure 18.9 When a menu header is rolled over, the rollover effect turns the background gray. What you don't see is that the page has switched off the global event that would hide menus when the page is clicked.

To add drop-down menus:

1. `var objNavMenu = null;`

Initialize the global variables you'll be using. One variable you'll need to pay special attention to is the number of drop menus (numDropMenu), which records the total number of menus on the page. You can also set the colors used for the rollovers.

Because of some slight positioning differences between Internet Explorer and other browsers, we're also going to have to determine whether the code is being run in Internet Explorer.

2. `function initDropMenu ()`

Add the function `initDropMenu()` to your JavaScript. This function sets a global event handler to hide any visible menus whenever the visitor clicks the screen.

The function then uses the variable numDropMenu set in step 1 to cycle through each menu header (`objNavMenu`) and menu (`objDropMenu`) to hide the menus and set how menu headers and menus should behave when moused over, moused out, and clicked.

3. `function menuHover(e) {...}`

Add the function `menuHover()` to your JavaScript. This function is used to disable the global menu hiding set in step 2 whenever the mouse is over a menu header. It also sets the background and foreground color of the menu header to create a rollover effect (white background with black text). We could control the rollover using the `a.hover` pseudo-class, *but* Internet Explorer only supports `hover` in link tags, and we'll be setting up the menu headers using `div` tags.

Code 18.4 *continued*

```
var isIE = null;
if (navigator.appName.indexOf
➝('Microsoft Internet Explorer')
➝!= -1) isIE=1;
function initDropMenu () {
    document.onclick = hideDropMenu;
    for (i=1; i<=numDropMenu; i++) {
        menuName = 'dropMenu' + i;
        navName = 'navMenu' + i;
        objDropMenu = document.
        ➝getElementById(menuName);
        objNavMenu = document.
        ➝getElementById(navName);
        objDropMenu.style.
        ➝visibility = 'hidden';
        objNavMenu.onmouseover =
        ➝menuHover;
        objNavMenu.onmouseout =
        ➝menuOut;
        objNavMenu.onclick =
        ➝showDropMenu;
    }
    objNavMenu = null;
    return;
}
function menuHover(e) {
    document.onclick = null;
    hoverObjNavMenu = document.
    ➝getElementById(this.id);
    if (hoverObjNavMenu !=
    ➝objNavMenu) {
        hoverObjNavMenu.style.color =
        ➝linkHover;
        hoverObjNavMenu.style.
        ➝backgroundColor =
        ➝bgLinkHover;
    }
}
function menuOut (e) {
    document.onclick = hideDropMenu;
    outObjNavMenu = document.
    ➝getElementById(this.id);
    if (outObjNavMenu !=
    ➝objNavMenu) {
        outObjNavMenu.style.color =
        ➝linkColor;
        outObjNavMenu.style.
        ➝backgroundColor =
        ➝bgLinkColor;
    }
}
```

(code continues on next page)

CREATING DROP-DOWN MENUS

Code 18.4 *continued*

```
 ●  ●  ●              Code                ⊂⊃
      function showDropMenu(e) {
        menuName = 'drop' + this.id.
         → substring(3,this.id.length);
        objDropMenu = document.
         → getElementById(menuName);
        if (prevObjDropMenu ==
         → objDropMenu) {
             hideDropMenu();
           return;
        }
        if (prevObjDropMenu != null)
         → hideDropMenu();
        objNavMenu = document.
         → getElementById(this.id);
        if ((prevObjNavMenu !=
         → objNavMenu ) ||
         → (prevObjDropMenu == null)) {
            objNavMenu.style.color =
             → linkActive;
            objNavMenu.style.
             → backgroundColor =
             → bgLinkActive;
        }
        if (objDropMenu) {
            xPos = objNavMenu.
             → offsetParent.offsetLeft +
             → objNavMenu.offsetLeft;
            yPos = objNavMenu.
             → offsetParent.offsetTop +
             → objNavMenu.offsetParent.
             → offsetHeight;
            if (isIE) {
               yPos -= 1;
               xPos -= 6;
            }
            objDropMenu.style.left =
             → xPos + 'px';
            objDropMenu.style.top =
             → yPos + 'px';
            objDropMenu.style.
             → visibility = 'visible';
            prevObjDropMenu =
             → objDropMenu;
            prevObjNavMenu = objNavMenu;
        }
      }
      function hideDropMenu() {
        document.onclick = null;
        if (prevObjDropMenu) {
            prevObjDropMenu.style.
             → visibility = 'hidden';
```

(code continues on next page)

4. `function menuOut(e) {...}`

Add the function `menuOut()` to your JavaScript. This function reinstates the global menu-hiding event handler when the visitor moves their mouse out of a menu header. It also sets the menu header back to its normal style (gray background with black text).

5. `function showDropMenu(e) {...}`

Add the function `showDropMenu()` to your JavaScript. This function is triggered when the visitor clicks a menu header. It first hides the menu currently showing (`prevObjDropMenu`) using the `hideDropMenu()` function you'll add in step 6. It then sets the style for the menu header option so that it looks selected (white text on a black background), and positions and shows the appropriate menu.

Notice that we use the `isIE` function from step 1 to tweak the positioning slightly for Internet Explorer.

6. `function hideDropMenu() {...}`

Add the function `hideDropMenu()` to your JavaScript. This function disables the global `onclick` event and then hides any menus that are showing and sets the menu header style to its normal state (gray background with black text).

7. `body {...}`

One thing that will greatly equalize the positioning of elements between the different browsers is to set the padding and margins for the body to 0. There will still be some discrepancy, but not nearly as much.

8. `#menuBar {...}`

Set up an ID for the menu bar, which will hold the menu headers. Beyond using relative positioning, the exact style is up to you.

continues on next page

9. `.menuHeader {...}`

Set up a class to define the appearance of the menu headers. Remember, rather than links (`<a>`) we'll be setting these up using `<div>` tags. This class will set the initial appearance of the menu headers, which are then changed by the JavaScript depending on the current hover state. Make sure to use relative positioning, but the rest of the styles are up to you.

10. `a.menuLink {...}`

Set up the style for the drop-down menu links, setting each of the link pseudo-classes.

11. `.menuDrop {...}`

Set up a class to define the drop-down menu's appearance. Make sure to use absolute positioning, set the z-index above all other layers, and set the visibility to `hidden`.

12. `onload="initDropMenu()"`

In the `<body>` tag, add an `onload` event handler to trigger the `initDropMenu()` function when the page loads.

13. `<div id="menuBar">...</div>`

Set up the menu bar layer using `<div>` tags and the `menuBar` ID.

14. `<div id="navMenu1"`
`→ class="menuHeader">...</div>`

Inside the menu bar layer, use `<div>` tags and the `menuHeader` class to add a menu header for each menu. You can add as many menu headers as you want, but make sure that each one has a unique navMenu ID (navMenu1, navMenu2, navMenu3, and so on). Remember to set the variable `numMenus` in step 1 to the number of menus you create here.

Code 18.4 *continued*

```
          prevObjDropMenu = null;
          prevObjNavMenu.style.color =
          → linkColor;
          prevObjNavMenu.style.
          → backgroundColor =
          → bgLinkColor;
        }
        objNavMenu = null;
      }
    </script>
    <style type="text/css" media=
    → "screen"><!--
body {
    margin: 0px;
    padding: 0px;
}
#page {
    margin: 10px;
}
#menuBar {
    color: #999999;
    font-size: 12px;
    font-family: arial, Helvetica, sans-serif;
    font-weight: bold;
    text-align: left;
    text-transform: capitalize;
    display: block;
    margin-bottom: 5px;
    position: relative;
    top: 0px;
    left: 0px;
    right: 0px;
    width: 99%;
    overflow: hidden;
    vertical-align: middle;
    border: solid 1px #000000;
    background-color: #cccccc;
}
.menuHeader {
    color: #000000;
    text-decoration: none;
    white-space: nowrap;
    cursor: pointer;
    padding: 5px;
    margin: 0px;
    padding-right: 15px;
    display: inline;
    position: relative;
    border-right: 1px solid #000000;
```

(code continues on next page)

Code 18.4 *continued*

```
}
a.menuLink {
    display: block;
    padding: 2px 5px;
    border-top: 1px solid #cccccc;
}
a.menuLink:link {
    color: #000000;
    text-decoration: none;
}
a.menuLink:visited {
    color: #000000;
    text-decoration: none
}
a.menuLink:hover {
    color: #ffffff;
    background-color: #000000;
    text-decoration: none;
}
a.menuLink:active {
    color: #ffffff;
    text-decoration: none;
    background-color: #cc0000;
}
.menuDrop {
    color: #999999;
    font-size: 10px;
    font-family: arial, Helvetica, sans-serif;
    background-color: #ffffff;
    background-repeat: repeat;
    visibility: hidden;
    margin: 0;
    padding: 0;
    position: absolute;
    z-index: 1000;
    top: 60px;
    left: 0;
    width: 175px;
    height: auto;
    border-style: solid;
    border-width: 0 1px 1px;
    border-color: #003365
}
        --></style>
</head>
<body bgcolor="#ffffff"
onload="initDropMenu()">
    <div id="menuBar">
```

(code continues on next page)

15. `<div id="dropMenu1"`
`class="menuDrop">...</div>`

For each menu header you created in step 14, you should now create the menu to go under it, using `<div>` tags and the `menuDrop` class. These menus are absolutely positioned, so the code can come anywhere in the HTML, but make sure that each has a unique dropMenu ID (`dropMenu1`, `dropMenu2`, `dropMenu3`, and so on).

CREATING DROP-DOWN MENUS

Code 18.4 *continued*

```
                <div id="navMenu1" class="menuHeader">Menu 1</div><div id="navMenu2" class="menuHeader">
                → Menu 2</div><div id="navMenu3" class="menuHeader">Menu 3</div>
        </div>
        <div id="dropMenu1" class="menuDrop">
            <a class="menuLink" href="#" onfocus="if(this.blur)this.blur();">Link 1</a>
            <a class="menuLink" href="#" onfocus="if(this.blur)this.blur();">Link 2</a>
            <a class="menuLink" href="#" onfocus="if(this.blur)this.blur();">Link 3</a>
            <a class="menuLink" href="#" onfocus="if(this.blur)this.blur();">Link 4</a>
            <a class="menuLink" href="#" onfocus="if(this.blur)this.blur();">Link 5</a>
        </div>
        <div id="dropMenu2" class="menuDrop">
            <a class="menuLink" href="#" onfocus="if(this.blur)this.blur();">Link 1</a>
            <a class="menuLink" href="#" onfocus="if(this.blur)this.blur();">Link 2</a>
            <a class="menuLink" href="#" onfocus="if(this.blur)this.blur();">Link 3</a>
            <a class="menuLink" href="#" onfocus="if(this.blur)this.blur();">Link 4</a>
            <a class="menuLink" href="#" onfocus="if(this.blur)this.blur();">Link 5</a>
        </div>
        <div id="dropMenu3" class="menuDrop">
            <a class="menuLink" href="#" onfocus="if(this.blur)this.blur();">Link 1</a>
            <a class="menuLink" href="#" onfocus="if(this.blur)this.blur();">Link 2</a>
            <a class="menuLink" href="#" onfocus="if(this.blur)this.blur();">Link 3</a>
            <a class="menuLink" href="#" onfocus="if(this.blur)this.blur();">Link 4</a>
            <a class="menuLink" href="#" onfocus="if(this.blur)this.blur();">Link 5</a>
        </div>
        <div id="page">
        <h1>CHAPTER XI</h1>
        <h2>Who Stole the Tarts?</h2>
        <p>The King and Queen of Hearts were seated on their throne when they arrived...</p>
        </div>
</body>
</html>
```

Figure 18.11 The list of menu options is in the left frame, and the content is in the right.

Figure 18.12 The submenus of Menu 1 and Menu 3 contain links that target the right frame.

Creating Collapsible Menus

Anyone who has used a GUI—whether Mac-, Windows-, or UNIX-based—has watched menus in a window collapse and expand. Click a folder, and its contents are displayed below the folder; the other files and directories move down to accommodate the expanded content. In Windows, you click plus and minus signs. On the Mac, you click triangles. You can achieve a similar effect on the Web using the `display` property (**Figures 18.11** and **18.12**).

To create a collapsing/expanding menu:

1. `function toggleClamShellMenu`
`→(objectID) {...}`

Add `toggleClamShellMenu()` to your JavaScript (**Code 18.5**). This function uses the `objectID` variable to locate the menu object. It then sets the `display` of that object to `none` if it's already `block` or `block` if it is already `none`. The effect is that the menu seems to appear and pushes everything after it down.

continues on next page

Code 18.5 The `toggleClamShellMenu()` function (located in the file menu.html, which is displayed in a frameset) shows or hides submenus.

```
<!DOCTYPE html PUBLIC "-//W3C//DTD XHTML 1.0 Transitional//EN" "http://www.w3.org/TR/xhtml1/DTD/
→ xhtml1-transitional.dtd">
<html xmlns="http://www.w3.org/1999/xhtml">
<head>
    <title>DHTML and CSS for the WWW | Creating Collapsible Menus</title>
        <script language="javascript" type="text/javascript"><!--
function toggleClamShellMenu(objectID) {
    var object = document.getElementById(objectID);
    if (object.style.display =='block') object.style.display='none';
    else object.style.display='block';
    return;
}

    // -->
```

(code continues on next page)

2. `#menu1 {...}`

Create an ID rule for each of your collapsible menus, setting the display property to none (see "Setting How an Element Is Displayed" in Chapter 5). This way, the menus don't appear when the document first loads.

3. `toggleClamShellMenu('menu1')`

Set up links for each menu that will be used to trigger the function you created in step 1. The function should be passed the ID for the menu that is to be shown.

4. `<span id="menu1">...</span>`

Set up a `<span>` tag surrounding the element (graphic or text) that will make up the menu, and assign it an ID.

Code 18.5 *continued*

```
        </script>
        <style type="text/css"><!--
body {
    font-family: "Trebuchet MS", Arial,
    → Helvetica, Geneva, sans-serif;
    background-color: silver;
}
.menuHead {
    color: #c00;
    font-size: 14px;
    font-family: "Trebuchet MS", Arial,
    → Helvetica, Geneva, sans-serif;
    font-weight: bold;
    text-decoration: none;
    border-top: 1px solid #300;
}
.menuOption {
    color: #f00;
    font-size: 12px;
    font-family: "Trebuchet MS", Arial,
    → Helvetica, Geneva, sans-serif;
    margin-left: 10px;
}
#menu1 { display: none; }
#menu2 { display: none; }
#menu3 { display: none; }
        --></style>
</head>
<body>
    <a href="home.html" target="content">
    → <b>Home</b></a><br /><br />
    <a class="menuHead" href="javascript:
    → toggleClamShellMenu('menu1')">&gt;
    → Menu 1</a><br />
        <span id="menu1">
            <a class="menuOption" href=
            → "option1.html" target="content"
            → >Option 1</a><br />
            <a class="menuOption" href=
            → "option2.html" target="content"
            → >Option 2</a><br />
            <a class="menuOption" href=
            → "option3.html" target="content"
            → >Option 3</a><br />
```

(code continues on next page)

Code 18.5 *continued*

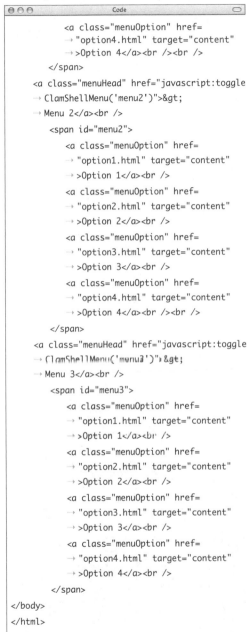

```
            <a class="menuOption" href=
            → "option4.html" target="content"
            → >Option 4</a><br /><br />
        </span>
    <a class="menuHead" href="javascript:toggle
    → ClamShellMenu('menu2')">&gt;
    → Menu 2</a><br />
        <span id="menu2">
            <a class="menuOption" href=
            → "option1.html" target="content"
            → >Option 1</a><br />
            <a class="menuOption" href=
            → "option2.html" target="content"
            → >Option 2</a><br />
            <a class="menuOption" href=
            → "option3.html" target="content"
            → >Option 3</a><br />
            <a class="menuOption" href=
            → "option4.html" target="content"
            → >Option 4</a><br /><br />
        </span>
    <a class="menuHead" href="javascript:toggle
    → ClamShellMenu('menu3')">&gt;
    → Menu 3</a><br />
        <span id="menu3">
            <a class="menuOption" href=
            → "option1.html" target="content"
            → >Option 1</a><br />
            <a class="menuOption" href=
            → "option2.html" target="content"
            → >Option 2</a><br />
            <a class="menuOption" href=
            → "option3.html" target="content"
            → >Option 3</a><br />
            <a class="menuOption" href=
            → "option4.html" target="content"
            → >Option 4</a><br />
        </span>
</body>
</html>
```

✔ Tips

■ You can use any elements in these menus, including graphics, forms, and lists. The design is up to you.

■ This expanding/collapsing menu technique doesn't work in Netscape 4. Moreover, because the `display` property of the menus is set to `none`, the menus do not appear. If you're also coding for Netscape 4, you can use the Browser CSS customization script to change the `display` definition of the menu class to `block` (see "Customizing Styles for the OS or Browser" in chapter 16).

Preventing Navigation Noise

One of my chief gripes about most Web sites is the overabundance of unorganized links. You've probably seen sites with long lists of links that stretch off the window. These links add visual noise to the design and waste precious screen space without assisting navigation.

Web surfers rarely take the time to read an entire Web page. Instead, they scan for relevant information. But human beings can process only so much information at a time. If a Web page is cluttered, visitors must wade through dozens or hundreds of links to find the one path to the information they desire. Anything designers can do to aid visitors' ability to scan a page, such as organizing links in lists and hiding sublinks until they're needed, will improve the Web site's usability. Drop-down, sliding, and collapsible menus area a great way to organize your page to prevent navigation noise.

Creating Sliding Menus

Are you tired of sites that have the same old sidebar navigation? Are your menus taking more and more valuable screen real estate from the content? Are your pages cluttered with links that visitors need only when they're navigating, not when they're focusing on the content?

If you answered "yes" to any of these questions, I have a simple solution: Allow visitors to pull out menus or put them away as needed (**Code 18.6** and **Figures 18.13**, **18.14**, and **18.15**).

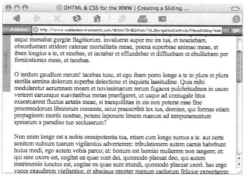

Figure 18.13 The menu tab is visible.

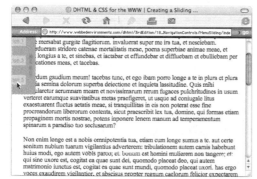

Figure 18.14 After the tab is clicked, the menu begins to slide out.

Code 18.6 The `setMenu()` function prepares the menu for the `slideMenu()` function, which slides out the menu by animating it.

```
<!DOCTYPE html PUBLIC "-//W3C//DTD XHTML
 1.0 Transitional//EN" "http://www.w3.org/TR/
 xhtml1/DTD/xhtml1-transitional.dtd">
<html xmlns="http://www.w3.org/1999/xhtml">
<head>
    <title>DHTML &amp; CSS for the WWW |
     Creating a Sliding Menu</title>
        <script language="JavaScript"><!--
            var open = 0;
            var slideSpeed = 10;
            var object = null;
            function setMenu (objectID) {
                object = document.getElementById
                 (objectID);
                if (open) { fX = -80; cX = 0;
                 open = 0; }
                    else { fX = 0; cX = -80;
                     open = 1; }
                slideMenu(cX,fX);
            }
            function slideMenu (cX,fX) {
                if (cX != fX) {
                    if (cX > fX) { cX -=
                     slideSpeed; }
```

(code continues on next page)

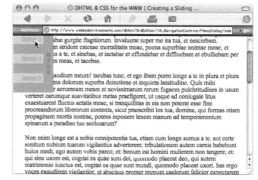

Figure 18.15 The menu is fully extended and can be used to navigate the site.

Code 18.6 *continued*

```
             else { cX += slideSpeed; }
             object.style.left = cX + 'px';
             setTimeout('slideMenu(' + cX +
          → ',' + fX + ')', 0);
             }
        return;
        }
    // -->



</script>


<style type="text/css"><!--
body { margin-left: 30px; }
#mainMenu {
     top: 0;
     left: -80px;
}
.menu { position: fixed; }
a:link {
     color: red;
     font: bold 12px "Trebuchet MS", Arial,
      → Helvetica, Geneva, sans-serif;
}
     --></style>
</head>
<body>
     <span id="mainMenu" class="menu">
        <table width="100" border="0"
frame="frame" cellspacing="0"
→ cellpadding="5" bgcolor="#999999">
           <tr>
              <td align="right"
bgcolor="#cccccc" width="80"><a href=
→ "#">Option 1</a></td>
              <td rowspan="6" width="10">
                 <div align="left">

         (code continues on next page)
```

To set up a sliding menu:

1. `var open = 0;`

Initialize the variables:

▲ `open` records whether the menu is open or closed.

▲ `slideSpeed` records how many pixels the menu should move in an animation cycle. The larger the number, the faster the menu appears to move.

▲ `object` records the object's address on the screen. This is initially set to `null`.

2. `function setMenu (objectID) {...}`

Add `setMenu()` to your JavaScript. This function sets the starting (`cX`) and final (`fX`) points for the sliding menu, based on whether the menu is open or not. `cX` defines the current location of the left edge of the menu and ranges between –80 and 0. The low value depends on the width of your menu minus the width of the tab.

When `cX` is –80, for example, the first 80 pixels of the menu are off the screen to the left. Only the menu tab, which is about another 20 pixels, is visible on the screen, and the menu is closed.

When `cX` is 0, the left edge of the menu is against the left edge of the window, and the menu is open. This function also resets the `open` variable to 0 (closed) if it was open or 1 (open) if it was closed. The last thing it does is start the `slideMenu()` function.

continues on next page

CREATING SLIDING MENUS

3. `function slideMenu (cX,fX) {...}`

Add `slideMenu()` to your JavaScript. This function first checks to see whether the current position (`cX`) is equal to the final position (`fX`). If so, the function stops running. If the positions are not the same, the function subtracts or adds a number of pixels (based on the `slideSpeed` variable set in step 1) to `cX`, depending on whether the menu is opening or closing.

It also sets the left edge of the menu to this new position. The function then starts over with the new `cX` value. `slideMenu()` continues to loop this way until `cX` increases or decreases to equal `fX`, creating the illusion that the menu is sliding across the screen.

4. `.menu {...} #mainMenu {...}`

In the head of the document, set up a style sheet with one general class that collects all the common properties of the menus (`.menu`) and an ID for each menu you'll be setting up. In this example, I set up a single menu called mainMenu. Notice that the left margin in `.menu`, which will change when the `slideMenu()` function is run, has an initial position of `-80`. This setting does not hide the menu; it leaves a small tab visible.

5. `<span id="mainMenu"`
`→ class="menu"> '...</span>`

In the body of the page, create the menu. In this example, the menu is made from a table that is used to control the layout.

6. `setMenu('mainMenu')`

Somewhere in the exposed part of the menu (the area sticking out from the edge) add a call to the `setMenu()` function. When clicked, this link will cause the menu to slide back and forth.

Code 18.6 *continued*

```
            <a href="javascript:
          → setMenu('mainMenu')"
          → onFocus="if(this.blur)
          → this.blur();"><img src=
          → "menuTab.gif"
          → height="100" width="15"
          → border="0" /></a></div>
        </td>
      </tr>
      <tr>
        <td align="right" width="80"><a
        → href="#">Option 2</a></td>
      </tr>
      <tr>
        <td align="right"
        → bgcolor="#cccccc" width="80"><a
        → href="#">Option 3</a></td>
      </tr>
      <tr>
        <td align="right" width="80"><a
        → href="#">Option 4</a></td>
      </tr>
      <tr>
        <td align="right"
        → bgcolor="#cccccc" width="80"><a
        → href="#">Option 5</a></td>
      </tr>
      <tr>
        <td align="right" width="80"><a
        → href="#">Option 6</a></td>
      </tr>
    </table>
  </span>
  <p>Et quid erat, quod me delectabat,
  → nisi amare et amari? ...</p>
</body>
</html>
```

✔ Tips

■ You can set up as many menus as you want, each between its own <span> tags and each with a different ID. Make sure to move the top margin down for each menu so that it doesn't overlap the menu above it. You can use any type of content between the <span> tags—graphics, hypertext links, forms, and so on—to create your menus.

■ What happens in older browsers that do not support DHTML depends on how you construct the menu. In this example, the menu would simply appear on the left side of the page. If you nested the menu in a table with content on the right, it would look like a normal (nondynamic) sidebar.

Using Access Keys to Improve Accessibility

Although most people coming to your Web site will be using their mouse to control what's going on, there are many potential visitors who, for a variety of reasons, may not be able to use a mouse as effectively or at all. To accommodate visitors who are using a keyboard or speech-recognition system to navigate the Web, you can include the accesskey attribute for important links:

```
<a href="index.html"
→ accesskey="h">Home</a>
```

Whenever the user presses the H key, this link will receive focus and they can then press (or speak) Return to access the page.

CREATING SLIDING MENUS

Creating a Remote Control

Whether you are channel-surfing or Web-surfing, a remote control can make the experience more convenient and comfortable. On the Web, a remote control is a small browser window with links that change the content in the main browser window (**Figure 18.16**).

To set up remote control, open a new browser window (see "Opening a New Browser Window" in Chapter 15) and place in it an HTML file with links that target the main browser window.

To create a remote control:

1. `var remote = null;`

In the Web page from which viewers will open the remote control, initialize the variable `remote` to `null`, indicating that the remote is not open (**Code 18.7**).

2. `window.name = "content";`

To target content back to this window, the window has to have a name. In this example, the main window is called `content`.

Figure 18.16 The links in the remote-control window target the main window.

Code 18.7 Placed in the index.html file, the openRemote() function can open an external window with a variety of sizes and uses.

```
● ● ●                    Code                    ◯
<!DOCTYPE html PUBLIC "-//W3C//DTD XHTML
→ 1.0 Transitional//EN" "http://www.w3.org/TR/
→ xhtml1/DTD/xhtml1-transitional.dtd">
<html xmlns="http://www.w3.org/1999/xhtml">
<head>
     <title>DHTML and CSS for the WWW |
     → Creating a Remote Control</title>
        <script><!--
var remote = null;
window.name = "content";
function openRemote(contentURL,windowName,
→ x,y) {
     widthHeight = 'height=' + y +
     → ',width=' + x;
     if (remote) remote.focus();
     else var remote = window.open(contentURL,
     → windowName,widthHeight);
}
        // -->
        </script>
        <style type="text/css" media=
        → "screen"><!--
h1 {
     color: silver;
     font-size: 36px;
     font-family: palatino, "Times New Roman",
     → Georgia, Times, serif;
}
        --></style>
</head>
<body onload="openRemote('remote.html',
→ 'remote',150,300)">
     <b><a href="javascript:openRemote('remote.
     → html','remote',150,300)">Open Remote
     → Control </a>
        <h1>Home</h1>
     </b>
</body>
</html>
```

3. `function openRemote(contentURL,`
   `→ windowName,x,y) {...}`

   Add openRemote() to the JavaScript. This function first checks to see whether the remote is open. If it is, the window is given focus so that it pops to the top of the screen. If it isn't already open, this function opens a new browser window that is x wide by y tall. This window is called windowName. The source is contentURL.

4. `openRemote('remote.html','remote',`
   `→ 150,300)`

   The function in step 3 that opens the remote has to be triggered, either by an event handler or through a link. The source file, window name, and dimensions of the new window need to be passed to the function.

5. `controls.html`

   All links in the control page should target the main frame (content, in this example), as follows (**Code 18.8**):

   `target = "content"`

   In this example, I use onload in the <body> tag to move the new remote window to a set position on the screen. When the page closes (unloads), the JavaScript tells the main window that the frame has closed by resetting the remote variable to null.

   This file contains a simple function, closeWindow(), which closes the window when a link is clicked.

   continues on next page

✔ Tips

■ A remote control can contain anything you can put in an HTML document, but keep in mind that it has to fit into the dimensions you defined in the openRemote() function.

■ Unlike a standard window, a remote window does not display menus, browser navigation (back and forward arrows), the current URL, or anything other than the basic border around the window. This border (called the *chrome*) does include the standard Close button in the top-right corner, allowing the visitor to close the remote at any time.

■ To open the remote, you have to run the openRemote() function. You can do this in several ways, such as having it open automatically when the main browser window opens (onload) although many browsers and Internet service providers will block these "pop-ups." It is a good idea, therefore, to include a link that allows visitors to reopen the remote if they close it or to bring the remote to the front if it disappears behind another window.

■ Notice that the openRemote() function gives the remote focus—that is, places it on top of any other windows on the screen. Without this, if the remote window were already open but covered by another window, the window would simply reload without coming to the front. Visitors to your site could be confused if they clicked the link to reopen the remote and nothing appeared.

Code 18.8 The controls.html file is where the action is. The controls change the content of the main window and also provide a link to close the remote window. This code also uses the opener JavaScript method that allows you to directly access the window from which this window was opened.

```
<!DOCTYPE html PUBLIC "-//W3C//DTD XHTML
→ 1.0 Transitional//EN" "http://www.w3.org/TR/
→ xhtml1/DTD/xhtml1-transitional.dtd">
<html xmlns="http://www.w3.org/1999/xhtml">
<head>
     <title>DHTML &amp; CSS for the WWW |
     → Controls</title>
        <base target="content" />
              <script><!--
function closeWindow() {
    top.self.close();
}
    // -->
    </script>
</head>
<body onload="window.moveTo(100,100)"
→ onunload="if (opener) opener.remote =
→ null;">
        <div onclick=" closeWindow()">&lt;
        → Close&gt</div>
        <h2>Menu</h2>
        <p><a href="index.html">Home</a></p>
        <p><a href="page1.html">Page 1</a></p>
        <p><a href="page2.html">Page 2</a></p>
        <p><a href="page3.html">Page 3</a></p>
</body>
</html>
```

CREATING A REMOTE CONTROL

Ideas for the Remote Control

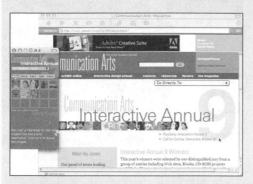

Figure 18.17 Communication Arts uses the remote as a tour guide to the best the Web has to offer.

Figure 18.18 Netscape uses the remote to spotlight ads.

Figure 18.19 Kairos uses the remote not only for navigation, but also for links to other resources inside and outside the Web site.

But wait! That universal remote is good for much, much more. Try these exciting ideas on your site:

◆ **Web tour.** If you have a page of your favorite Web sites, consider placing it in a remote control. Without a remote, visitors have to keep going back to your page; with a remote, they can keep the links in one window while surfing in another. Check out the winners in the interactive section of the Communication Arts Web tour (http://www.commarts.com/CA/interactive/cai03/) for an example of how this feature works (**Figure 18.17**).

◆ **Spotlight.** Many sites use a remote-control window to draw attention to particular areas. News, special offers, and other information can be placed in the remote control. Unfortunately, some sites (such as Netscape, www.netscape.com) use this technique to "pop-up" annoying advertisements every time you visit a new page (**Figure 18.18**).

◆ **Control pad.** You can add functionality to a site by making the remote a control pad. Kairos (english.ttu.edu/kairos/3.2; **Figure 18.19**), an academic-journal site, uses a remote control with two frames. The left frame contains the links; the right frame displays information about the journal, links to search engines, and links to other reference materials.

Creating Scroll Bars for a Layer

Without scroll bars, a GUI would be about as useful as a car without a steering wheel. Scroll bars allow you to place an infinite amount of information in a finite space and move that information around as needed. Because the computer's operating system defines the look and feel of the scroll bars, however, they often limit the design of Web interfaces.

Still, if you can animate a layer (see "Animating an Object" in Chapter 15) then you can scroll the layer up and down (**Figures 18.20** and **18.21**).

Figure 18.20 I used this technique in a Web site I designed for the independent film *The Sandman* (www.sandmanfilm.org).

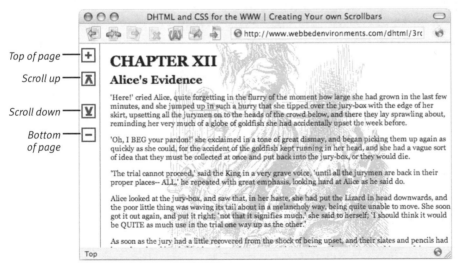

Top of page ⎯⎯ ⊞
Scroll up ⎯⎯ ⊼
Scroll down ⎯⎯ ⊻
Bottom of page ⎯⎯ ⊟

Figure 18.21 The controls allow the visitor to scroll up or down the page, jump to the bottom, and jump back to the top.

Code 18.9 In index.html, set up two frame columns: a narrow column on the left for the scroll bar, and the rest of the space to hold the content.

```
<!DOCTYPE html PUBLIC "-//W3C//DTD XHTML
→ 1.0 Frameset//EN" "http://www.w3.org/TR/
→ xhtml1/DTD/xhtml1-frameset.dtd">
<html xmlns="http://www.w3.org/1999/xhtml">
<head>
    <title>DHTML and CSS for the WWW |
    → Creating Scroll Bars for a Layer</title>
</head>
    <frameset cols="90,*" border="0"
    → frameborder="no" framespacing="0">
        <frame name="scrollBar"
        → src="scrollBar.html" marginwidth="0"
        → marginheight="0" noresize="noresize"
        → scrolling="no" />
        <frame name="content"
        → src="content.html" noresize="noresize"
        → scrolling="no" />
    </frameset>
</html>
```

To set up scroll bars:

1. `index.html`

   Create a frameset file, and save it as "index.html" (**Code 18.9**). Set up two frame columns (**Figure 18.22**). The first column (named scrollBar) is a narrow frame containing the source scrollBar.html; the second (named content) contains the file content.html.

   continues on next page

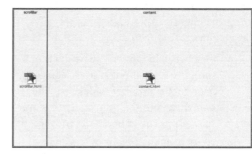

Figure 18.22 The frameset used to hold scrollBar.html on the left and the pages it will be scrolling on the right.

Navigation for Nondynamic Browsers

Almost everyone surfing the Web today uses a browser that supports JavaScript. But a few browsers don't support JavaScript, and some people turn JavaScript off in their browsers.

You still need to provide these Web surfers some basic navigation and possibly some content that you otherwise would include dynamically.

Simply use the <noscript> tag to hold content that is only to be seen if JavaScript is not available:

```
<noscript>

Content for non-dynamic browser goes here

</noscript>
```

The result is that browsers that do not support scripting languages ignore the <noscript> tags and display whatever is between them.

2. scrollBar.html

Create an HTML file, and save it as "scrollBar.html" (**Code 18.10**). This file will contain the scroll-bar controls. Steps 3 through 13 apply to this file.

3. var scrolling = 0;

In the <script> tags of scrollBar.html, initialize the following variables:

▲ scrolling sets whether the layer is currently scrolling.

▲ yT records the current top position of the scrolling layer.

▲ lT sets the initial position of the top of the layer.

▲ yI sets the increment by which the scrolling layer should move. You can change this number as desired. The higher the number, the faster the layer scrolls, but the choppier its movement.

▲ yH records the height of the layer.

▲ object records the address for the scrolling layer to access its properties.

4. function startScroll(objectID,
→ frameName,direction) {...}

Add startScroll() to the JavaScript. This function sets scrolling to 1 (on), identifies the current location of the top of the layer (yT), the height of the layer (–25, to leave a margin at the bottom), and then triggers the scroll() function.

Code 18.10 The file scrollBar.html, with JavaScript for scrolling layers, goes in the scrollBar frame. The scroll() function animates the scrollArea in the content frame, and URT() and URB() take it to the top or bottom.

```
<!DOCTYPE html PUBLIC "-//W3C//DTD XHTML
→ 1.0 Transitional//EN" "http://www.w3.org/TR/
→ xhtml1/DTD/xhtml1-transitional.dtd">
<html xmlns="http://www.w3.org/1999/xhtml">

<head>
    <title>Sliding Menu</title>
        <script language="JavaScript"><!--
            var scrolling = 0;
            var yT = 5;
            var lT = 5;
            var yI = 15;
            var yH = 0;
            var object = null;
        function startScroll(objectID,
        → frameName,direction) {
            object = top[frameName].document.
            → getElementById(objectID);
            scrolling = 1;
            yT = object.style.top;
            pxLoc = yT.indexOf('px');
            if (pxLoc >= 1) yT = yT.
            → substring(0,pxLoc);
            yH = document.body.clientHeight -
            → object.offsetHeight - 25;
            scroll(direction);
        }
        function scroll(direction) {
            if (scrolling == 1) {
                if ((direction == 1) &&
                → (yT <= lT)) {
                    yT = (yT/1) + yI;
                    if (yT > lT) yT = lT;
                    object.style.top = yT +
                    → 'px'; }
                else {
                    if ((direction == 0) &&
                    → (yT >= yH)) {
                        yT -= yI;
                        if (yT < yH) yT = yH;
                        object.style.top = yT +
                        → 'px'; }
                }
```

(code continues on next page)

Code 18.10 *continued*

```
                yT = object.style.top;
                pxLoc = yT.indexOf('px');
                if (pxLoc >= 1) yT = yT.
                → substring(0,pxLoc);
                code2run = 'scroll('+ direction
                → + ')';
                setTimeout(code2run,0);
        }
        return false;
    }
    function stopScroll() {
        scrolling = 0;
        return false;
    }
    function URB(objectID,frameName) {
        var object = top[frameName].
        → document.getElementById
        → (objectID);
        yH = document.body.clientHeight -
        → object.offsetHeight - 25;
        object.style.top = yH +'px';
    }
    function URT(objectID,frameName) {
        var object = top[frameName].
        → document.getElementById
        → (objectID);
        object.style.top = lT + 'px';
    }
    // -->
    </script>
    <style type="text/css"
    → media="screen"><!--
body {
    background: white url(bg_scroll.gif)
    → repeat-y 33px 30px;
    margin-left: 3px; }
a { text-decoration: none; }
        --></style>
</head>
<body>
    <a onmousedown="startScroll('scrollArea',
    → 'content',1); return false;" onmouseup=
    → "stopScroll();" onmouseover="window.
    → status='Up'; return true;" href="#"
    → onfocus="if(this.blur)this.blur();">
```

(code continues on next page)

5. `function scroll(direction) {...}`

   Add `scroll()` to the JavaScript. This function moves the layer up or down incrementally based on the variable `yI` from step 3; the direction depends on the `direction` variable: 1 for up, 0 for down. The function will continue to run while `scrolling` is equal to 1.

6. `function stopScroll() {...}`

   Add `stopScroll()` to the JavaScript. The function sets the variable `scrolling` to 0 (off), stopping the layer from scrolling.

7. `function URB(objectID,frameName)`
   → `{...}`

   Add `URB()` to the JavaScript. This function scrolls instantly to the bottom of the page (moves the bottom of the layer to the bottom of the window).

8. `function URT(objectID,frameName)`
   → `{...}`

   Add `URT()` to the JavaScript. This function scrolls instantly to the top of the window (moves the top of the layer to the top of the window).

9. `startScroll('scrollArea',`
   → `''content',1); return false;`

   The controls have to be set up as links with event handlers. To add a scroll-up event, trigger `startScroll()` with the `onmousedown` event handler in the <body> tag. Pass the function the ID of the object to be scrolled, the name of the frame that contains the object, and a 1 (up).

continues on next page

10. `startScroll('scrollArea',`
    `→ 'content',0);`

    Trigger `startScroll()` with the event handler `onmousedown`. Pass the function the ID of the object to be scrolled, the name of the frame that contains the object, and a `0` for down.

11. `stopScroll()`

    To stop the layer from scrolling, use the `stopScroll()` function with the event handler `onmouseup`.

12. `URT('scrollArea','content')`

    To get to the top of the layer, trigger the `URT()` function, and pass it the ID of the object and the name of the frame that contains the object.

13. `URB('scrollArea','content')`

    To get to the bottom of the layer, use the `URB()` function, and pass it the ID of the object and the name of the frame that contains the object.

Code 18.10 *continued*

```
            <img id="up" src="up_off.gif"
          → height="25" width="25" border="0"
          → vspace="5" />
        </a><br />
        <a onmousedown="URT('scrollArea',
        → 'content'); return false;" onmouseover=
        → "window.status='Top'; return true;"
        → href="#" onfocus="if(this.blur)this.
        → blur();">
            <img id="top" src="top_off.gif"
          → height="25" width="25" border="0"
          → vspace="5" />
        </a><br /><br />
        <a onmousedown="URB('scrollArea',
        → 'content'); return false;" onmouseover=
        → "window.status='Bottom'; return true;"
        → href="#" onfocus="if(this.blur)this.
        → blur();">
            <img id="bottom" src="bottom_off.gif"
          → height="25" width="25" border="0"
          → vspace="5" />
        </a><br />
        <a onmousedown="startScroll('scrollArea',
        → 'content',0); return false;" onmouseup=
        → "stopScroll();" onmouseover="window.
        → status='Down'; return true;" href="#"
        → onfocus="if(this.blur)this.blur();">
            <img id="down" src="down_off.gif"
          → height="25" width="25" border="0"
          → vspace="5" />
        </a>
</body>
</html>
```

Code 18.11 The file content.html in the content frame contains the layer scrollArea which is scrolled from the scrollBar frame.

```
000                    Code                    ◯
<!DOCTYPE html PUBLIC "-//W3C//DTD XHTML
→ 1.0 Transitional//EN" "http://www.w3.org/TR/
→ xhtml1/DTD/xhtml1-transitional.dtd">
<html xmlns="http://www.w3.org/1999/xhtml">
<head>
    <title>DHTML &amp; CSS for the WWW |
→ Content Page</title>
        <meta name="Author"
        → content="Jason Cranford Teague" />
        <meta name="keywords"
        → content="Jason Cranford Teague" />
        <style type="text/css"><!--
body {
    color: black;
    font-size: 12px;
    font-family: Georgia, "Times New Roman",
    → Times, serif;
    line-height: 14px;
    background: white url(bg_alice40a.gif)
    → no-repeat fixed center;
    margin right: 10px;
}
#scrollArea {
    position: absolute;
    top: 5px;
    left: 15px; }
        --></style>
</head>
<body>

<div id="scrollArea">
        <h1>CHAPTER XII</h1>


<h2>Alice's Evidence</h2>
        <p>'Here!' cried Alice, quite
        → forgetting in the flurry of the
        → moment how large she had grown in the
        → last few minutes... </p>
        <h2>THE END</h2>
    </div>
</body>
</html>
```

14. content.html

Create an HTML file, and save it as "content.html" (**Code 18.11**). This file will contain the layer that is being scrolled. Steps 15 and 16 apply to this file.

15. #scrollArea {...}

Set up an ID called scrollArea in content.html. This layer should be positioned absolutely.

16. <span id="scrollArea">...</span>

Set up the scrollArea layer in either a <div> or <span> tag (see "Setting up an Object" in Chapter 10).

✔ Tips

■ I added a simple graphic-toggling function to this example so the controls will appear to light up when clicked.

■ Use return false; in the event handlers for the scroll controls to prevent the pop-up menu from appearing on the Mac.

■ You can also place the controls in the same HTML file as the layer (content.html) and then take out the frame reference when you're using getElementById.

■ *URT* stands for *ubiquitous return to top*, and *URB* stands for—you guessed it—*ubiquitous return to bottom*. Unlike most return-to-top buttons on most Web pages, these controls are always available.

397

Using Input from a Form Field

The most common way users interact with a Web page is with the mouse. You can also use forms to receive input from visitors and then perform a specific action. In Chapter 14, I showed you how to move objects from point to point, but you defined those points. Now it's the visitors' turn to define the movement, by allowing them to enter coordinates into form fields (**Code 18.12** and **Figures 18.23** and **18.24**).

To receive visitor input through a form:

1. function moveObjectTo(objectID, → formNum) {...}

Add moveObjectTo() to the JavaScript at the head of your document. This function moves the element from its current position to a new position (see "Moving Objects from Point to Point" in Chapter 14), based on the values in the xVal and yVal fields of the specified form (form-Num) which is based on the placement of the form in the Web page. The first form is form 0, while subsequent forms are 1, 2, 3, etc...

Code 18.12 For this example, we are adapting the moveObjectTo() function to read values from form input fields.

```
<!DOCTYPE html PUBLIC "-//W3C//DTD XHTML
→ 1.0 Transitional//EN" "http://www.w3.org/TR/
→ xhtml1/DTD/xhtml1-transitional.dtd">
<html xmlns="http://www.w3.org/1999/xhtml">
<head>
    <title>DHTML &amp; CSS for the WWW I
    → Using Input from a Form Field</title>
        <script language="JavaScript">
function moveObjectTo(objectID,formNum) {
    x = document.forms[formNum].xVal.value;
    y = document.forms[formNum].yVal.value;
    var object = document.getElementById
    → (objectID);
    object.style.left = x + 'px';
    object.style.top= y + 'px';
}
    </script>
</head>
<body>
    <div id="object1" style=" visibility:
    → visible; position: absolute; top: 36px;
    → left: 137px;">
        <img src="coco.jpg" height="168"
        → width="138" border="0" />
        <h2>meep</h2>
    </div>
    <form id="form1" action="#" method="get">x:
    → <input type="text" name="xVal"
    → size="3" /><br />
        y:<input type="text" name="yVal"
        → size="3" /><br />
        <input onclick="moveObjectTo
        → ('object1',0)" type="button"
        → value="Move" />

</form>
</body>
</html>
```

Figure 18.23 Enter the coordinates to move Coco the Cat around on the screen.

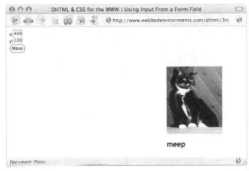

Figure 18.24 The cat has moved to the indicated coordinates. Good kitty!

2. `<div id="object1" style="position:`
`→ absolute; top: 36px; left: 137px;`
`→ visibility: visible;">...</div>`

Set up a CSS layer positioned with the `top` and `left` properties.

3. `<form action="#" name="form1"`
`→ method="get">...</form>`

Set up a simple form, and give it a name.

4. `<input type="text" name="xVal"`
`→ size="3">`

Add form fields that allow visitors to enter the x and y coordinates of the object's new position.

5. `<input type="button" value="Move"`
`→ 'onclick="moveObjectTo`
`→ '('object1',0)">`

Add a form button that triggers moveO-bjectTo(). Pass the function the ID of the object you want to move and the number of the form you created in step 3. Remember, each form is automatically numbered by the Web page, with the first form on the page being 0. Clicking this button causes the element to move to the specified coordinates.

Follow the Mouse Pointer

Like scroll bars (see "Creating Your Own Scroll Bars" in earlier in this chapter), the mouse pointer is part of the user interface over which designers have limited control. Although some browsers also let you control the pointer's appearance to a limited degree (see "Changing the Mouse Pointer's Appearance" in Chapter 8), you're stuck with the pointers provided by the browser.

By using a bit of DHTML, however, you can create a layer that follows the mouse on the screen (**Code 18.13**). In browsers that allow you to set the pointer's appearance to none, you can thus replace the pointer with a graphic of your own devising (**Figure 18.25**).

Code 18.13 A global event handler allows you to track the path of the mouse and move an object along with it.

```
<?xml version="1.0" encoding="utf-8"?>
<!DOCTYPE html PUBLIC "-//W3C//DTD XHTML
→ 1.0 Transitional//EN" "http://www.w3.org/TR/
→ xhtml1/DTD/xhtml1-transitional.dtd">
<html xmlns="http://www.w3.org/1999/xhtml">
<head>
    <title>DHTML for the WWW |
    → Follow the Mouse</title>
        <script language="javascript">
        <!--
    var evt = null;
function initPage() {
    document.onmousemove = followMe;
}
function followMe(evt) {
    var evt = (evt) ? evt : ((window.event) ?
    → event : null);
    var object = document.getElementById
    → ('spotLight');
        object.style.left = evt.clientX -
        → (object.offsetWidth/2) + 'px';
        object.style.top = evt.clientY -
        → (object.offsetHeight/2) + 'px';
        return;
}
```

(code continues on next page)

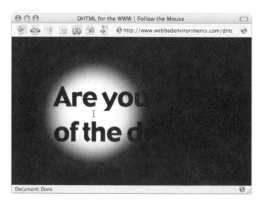

Figure 18.25 This technique creates a flashlight effect. The text is black on a black background. The white graphic moves below the text but above the background, causing the text to show up only when the mouse is over it.

Code 18.13 *continued*

```
      // -->
         </script>
         <style type="text/css"
media="screen"><!--
#spotLight {
      position: absolute;

z-index: 0;
      top: 20px;

left: 20px;
}
#content {
      font: bold 50px fantasy;
      position: absolute;
      z-index: 100;
      top: 100px;
      left: 100px;
}
body {
      color: black;
      background-color: black;
      cursor: none;
}
         --> </style>
</head>
<body onload="initPage()">
      <span id="spotLight"><img
   → src="spotLight.gif" height="300"
   → width="300" /></span>
         <div id="content">
             Are you afraid of the dark?</div>
</body>
</html>
```

To create an object that follows the mouse pointer:

1. `var evt = null;`

   In the JavaScript, initialize the `evt` variable to `null`.

2. `function initPage() {...}`

   Add `initPage()` to the JavaScript. This function sets up a global event handler (see "Binding Events to Objects" in Chapter 10); whenever the mouse moves, the `followMe()` function executes.

3. `function followMe(evt) {...}`

   Add `followMe()` to the JavaScript. This function moves a specific object (in this example, `spotLight`), so the center of the object follows the mouse as it moves.

4. `#spotLight {...}`

   Set up the ID for the object you'll be controlling with the mouse's movement, making it absolutely positioned. The initial top and left positions don't matter, because they'll change as soon as the visitor moves the mouse pointer.

5. `onload="initPage()"`

   When the page loads, the default events need to be initialized, so place an `onload` event handler in the `<body>` tag to run the `defaultEvents()` function.

6. `<span id="spotLight">...</span>`

   Set up the layer that will be moved by the mouse movement. Although this example places a graphic in this layer, you can use HTML text, GIF animations, or anything else that can go in a CSS layer.

continues on next page

✔ Tips

- Although you can place anything you want in the layer to be moved, larger objects take longer for the computer to draw and redraw, so their movement will appear slower and choppier than that of smaller items.

- You can combine this technique with a variety of other techniques for some stunning effects. You could use layers in different z-indexes (see "Stacking Elements [3-D Positioning]" in Chapter 6) to create a puzzle Web page (**Figure 18.26**). Or you can use a PNG graphic to create a crosshair target (**Figure 18.27**).

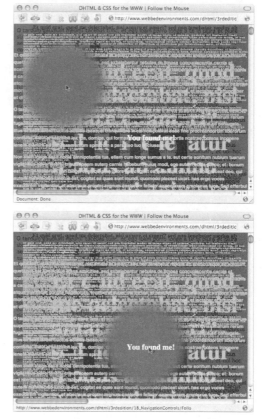

Figure 18.26 The screen is a mess of overlapping text, with a hole that moves around below the mouse pointer until the visitor finds the magic link.

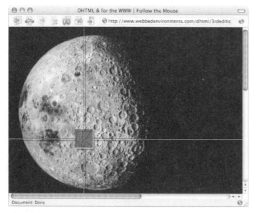 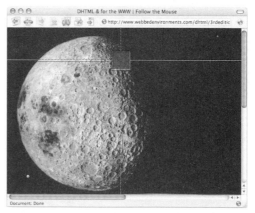

Figure 18.27 The crosshair moves over the intended target. I used a PNG graphic in this example to get the transparent middle and drop shadow, so this graphic will not work in every browser.

Figure 18.28 The slide-show controls allow you to move forward or backward in the show.

Code 18.14 The slide-show code allows you to move forward or backward through a stack of images.

```
<!DOCTYPE html PUBLIC "-//W3C//DTD XHTML
→ 1.0 Transitional//EN" "http://www.w3.org/TR/
→ xhtml1/DTD/xhtml1-transitional.dtd">
<html xmlns="http://www.w3.org/1999/xhtml">
<head>
    <title>DHTML and CSS for the WWW |
    → Creating a Slide Show</title>
        <script><!--
slideT = new Array();
slideC = new Array();
slideT[0] = 5;
slideC[0] = 1;
slideT[1] = 3;
slideC[1] = 1;
function nextSlide(setNum) {
    var objectID = 'slide' + setNum +
    → slideC[setNum];
    var object = document.getElementById
    → (objectID);
    object.style.display = 'none';
    if (slideT[setNum] == slideC[setNum])
    → slideC[setNum] = 1;
    else slideC[setNum]++;
    var objectID = 'slide' + setNum +
    → slideC[setNum];
```

(code continues on next page)

Creating a Slide Show

If you want to show a series of photos (or other content) in order, presenting them in slide-show format may be useful. You may even want to run two or more slide shows simultaneously to display different aspects of your work (**Figure 18.28**).

A slide show hides and shows objects (see "Making Objects Appear and Disappear" in Chapter 14) using the display property (**Code 18.14**). This allows you to preload a number of images (or other content) and then page through them without having to reload the Web page, thus creating a faster Web experience.

To set up a slide show:

1. slideT = new Array();

   Initialize two new arrays. The first array, slideT[n], records the number of slides in a slide show; the second array, slideC[n], records the current slide being displayed.

2. slideT[0] = 5;

   For each slide show, initialize the slideT array with the total number of slides.

3. slideC[0] = 1;

   For each slide show, initialize the slideC array to 1 (the first slide in the show).

4. function nextSlide(setNum) {...}

   Add nextSlide() to the JavaScript. This function hides the currently displayed slide and shows the following slide in order. If the current slide is the last slide in the show, the function loops to the first slide.

continues on next page

5. `function previousSlide(setNum) {...}`

Add `previousSlide()` to the JavaScript. This function hides the currently displayed slide and shows the preceding slide in order. If this slide is the first slide in the show, the function loops to the last slide.

6. `#slideSet0, #slideSet1 {...}`

Set up an ID for each slide set, and call it `slideSetn` where *n* is the slide set's number. This layer is relatively positioned.

7. `.slides {...}`

Set up a class that will be applied to all the slides; this class is called (oddly enough) "slides." This should be positioned relatively.

8. `#slide01, ... #slide11 {...}`

Set up IDs for all the slides, giving each one a number. The first digit of the slide's number corresponds to its set and the second digit indicates its order in the set. So `slide01` is the first slide in slide set 0.

9. `<div id="slideSet0">...</div>`

Set up a CSS layer, and define it with the `slideSetn` class.

10. `<div class="slides" id="slide01">`
`→ '...</div>`

For each slide in the show, set up a nested layer inside the layer you created in step 9, using the slide's numbered ID. Place the content of the slide in that layer.

11. `onclick="previousSlide(0)"`

Add a link to trigger the `previousSlide()` function for this slide set.

12. `onclick="nextSlide(0)"`

Add a link to trigger the `nextSlide()` function for this slide set.

✔ Tip

■ DHTML slide shows can contain any HTML code you want, not just images.

Code 18.14 *continued*

```
        var object = document.getElementById
        → (objectID);
        object.style.display = 'block';
}
function previousSlide(setNum) {
        var objectID = 'slide' + setNum +
        → slideC[setNum];
        var object = document.getElementById
        → (objectID);
        object.style.display = 'none';
        if (slideC[setNum] == 1) slideC[setNum] =
        → slideT[setNum];
        else slideC[setNum]--;
        var objectID = 'slide' + setNum +
        → slideC[setNum];
        var object = document.getElementById
        → (objectID);
        object.style.display = 'block';
}

        // -->
        </script>
        <style type="text/css"><!--
#slideSet0, #slideSet1 {
        background-color: silver;
        text-align: center;
        margin-bottom: 10px;
        padding: 5px;
        position: relative;
        width: 140px;
        height: 140px;
        layer-background-color: silver; }
.slides {
        position: relative;
        z-index: 1;
}
.setTitle, .slideTitle {
        font-family: "Trebuchet MS", sans-serif;
}
.setTitle {
        color: #900;
        font-size: 14px;
        font-weight: bold;
}
.slideTitle {
        color: #666;
```

(code continues on next page)

Code 18.14 *continued*

```
     font-size: 12px;
}
.controls {
    position: relative;
    z-index: 10;
}
#slide01, #slide11 { display: block; }
#slide02, #slide03, #slide04, #slide05, #slide12, #slide13 { display: none; }
        --></style>
</head>
<body>
    <div id="slideSet0">
        <div class="setTitle">Pictures of Jocelyn</div>
        <div id="slide01" class="slides">
          <div class="slideTitle">Slide 1</div>
            <img src="0010s.gif" height="67" width="100" border="0" /></div>
        <div id="slide02" class="slides">
            <div class="slideTitle">Slide 2</div>
            <img src="0016s.gif" height="67" width="100" border="0" /></div>
        <div id="slide03" class="slides">
            <div class="slideTitle">Slide 3</div>
            <img src="0021s.gif" height="67" width="100" border="0" /></div>
        >
        <div class="controls">
            <a href="javascript:previousSlide(0)" style="margin: 10px;"><img src="back.gif"
            → height="11" width="11" border="0" /></a><a href="javascript:nextSlide(0)"
            → style="margin: 10px;"><img src="next.gif" height="11" width="11" border="0" /></a></div>
    </div>
    <div id="slideSet1">
        <div class="setTitle">Jocelyn's Family</div>
        <div id="slide11" class="slides">
            <div class="slideTitle">Slide 1</div>
            <img src="0007s.gif" height="100" width="67" border="0" /></div>
        <div id="slide12" class="slides">
            <div class="slideTitle">Slide 2</div>
            <img src="0012s.gif" height="100" width="67" border="0" /></div>
        <div id="slide13" class="slides">
            <div class="slideTitle">Slide 3</div>
            <img src="0014s.gif" height="100" width="67" border="0" /></div>
        <div class="controls">
            <a href="javascript:previousSlide(1)" style="margin: 10px;"><img src="back.gif" height="11"
            → width="11" border="0" /></a><a href="javascript:nextSlide(1)" style="margin: 10px;"><img
            → src="next.gif" height="11" width="11" border="0" /></a></div>
    </div>
</body>
</html>
```

GoLive CS Primer

GoLive CS is a complete Web site–creation package that bundles together *WYSIWYG* (What You See Is What You Get) and HTML editors. It started life as CyberStudio and was created by a company called GoLive. Both the software and the company were eventually purchased by Adobe Systems Inc., which has made the program a shining star in its Web-development-software lineup.

GoLive has evolved over the years to encompass JavaScript editing, CSS, and dynamic HTML tools. It includes these tools in an easy-to-use environment. The tags are located conveniently and can be altered from various palettes, allowing you to see your changes as you make them.

Especially exciting in this version of GoLive is the introduction of a complete CSS editor, with real-time editing features, which you'll learn more about as you work through this chapter. You'll also learn to create DHTML and CSS in GoLive, including how to add external style sheets and animate multiple objects through complex paths.

The GoLive Interface

Although GoLive was not originally created by Adobe, recent versions of the program have benefited from the influence of Adobe's interface standards. Adobe included additional functionality while keeping the interface well organized and simple to use.

GoLive's WYSIWYG interface allows even novice Web designers to create Web pages, yet this program also includes some of the best code-editing tools (for HTML, JavaScript, and CSS) available to professionals.

The GoLive interface can be broken into several areas: the document window, toolbar, and the Inspector, Objects, and other individual palettes (**Figure 19.1**).

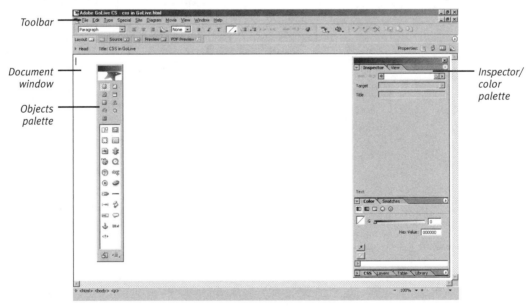

Figure 19.1 The GoLive interface which includes the document window, toolbar, site controls, and various palettes.

Figure 19.2 The document window in the Layout mode. You can add, change, and move elements without having to know a single HTML tag.

Figure 19.3 The document window in Source mode. All the code for the Web page (including JavaScript and CSS) can be edited directly in this window.

Figure 19.4 Outline mode also allows you to edit the code in a Web page, but it shows the code hierarchically. This feature is especially valuable for validating your code.

Document window

The document window is where the code for an individual Web page can be viewed and changed in a variety of modes, each supporting a different way of interacting with the page's content. To switch among these various modes, simply click the tabs at the top of the window.

◆ **Layout Editor** is the most like working in a word processor. Rather than deal with HTML tags, you design the page using visual tools rather than code-oriented ones (**Figure 19.2**).

◆ **Frames Editor** allows you to view and edit the frame layout of a page.

◆ **Source Editor** allows you to edit the raw HTML, CSS, and JavaScript source code (**Figure 19.3**).

◆ **Outline Editor** is useful for viewing the structure of a Web page (**Figure 19.4**).

◆ **Preview mode** allows you to view the page as it should appear in a browser. It also lets you play around with different variables, such as CSS support, to see how the page might appear in a variety of environments. If the page includes framesets, Frames Preview mode is also available.

◆ **PDF Preview** allows you to view the file as a PDF. You can generate PDF files from all of your HTML documents in Adobe GoLive CS, a nice feature that allows you to provide an alternative format for those who require it.

THE GoLIVE INTERFACE

409

Toolbar

The toolbar provides shortcuts to the most common styles and tasks in a thin ribbon across the top of the screen (although you can move it anywhere you want).

The toolbar is contextual, meaning that its tools change depending on what is displayed and selected in the document window. If you're editing text in Layout mode, for example, you'll see text tools that control header level, alignment, and font size (**Figure 19.5**). If you select a layer, the toolbar changes to allow you to control the layer's size, position, and alignment (**Figure 19.6**).

Figure 19.5 The toolbar changes many of its options depending on which element is selected in the document window. This figure shows what the bar looks like when text is selected.

Figure 19.6 This figure shows what the toolbar looks like when a layer is selected. Notice that certain elements (document selection, browser preview, and online help) stay consistent.

Objects palette

The Objects palette (which you can see in Figure 19.1) allows you to drag and drop various HTML features onto a page. The Objects palette is organized into the following categories:

- **Basic** includes basic elements such as those for comments, images, line breaks, and Flash and other objects.

- **Form elements** include a variety of form elements and controls.

- **Frame and framesets** allow you to add elements required by frame and frameset documents.

- **Diagram** is a powerful feature that allows you to create rich diagrams showing the hierarchy of your site and where various assets fall within that site.

- **SMIL elements** (which stands for "Synchronized Multimedia Integration Language," an XML-based multimedia language) help you add SMIL to your pages.

- **Smart objects** allow you to add any other kind of Adobe format file (such as a PDF) and this interesting GoLive feature will process it as an optimized Web graphic and place it in your page.

- **Head elements** give you immediate access to elements used within HTML <head> tags.

- **Site items** let you modify a variety of site-related features, including font sets and color schemes.

- **QuickTime elements** give you instant access to certain aspects of QuickTime, allowing you to create rich multimedia pages.

Inspector and palettes

GoLive offers a number of special palettes that give you access to a multitude of features and functions. You can show or hide palettes by choosing them from the Window menu. These (in addition to the Objects palette) are the most important palettes for CSS and DHTML:

◆ **Color.** This palette allows you to select foreground and background colors.

◆ **Inspector.** This palette allows you to set attributes for the selected object in the document window. The inspector is a contextual palette, so its options depend on what objects are selected in the document window.

◆ **Source code.** This palette allows you to view and change the source code while you're in the document window's Layout mode. Alternatively, you can use Source mode or split the view between Layout and Source by choosing View > Show Split Source.

Other tools

GoLive includes an excellent FTP client and site-management tools. Various options allow you to manage your site and even selectively upload only those files that have changed since the last upload.

GoLive includes a robust spelling checker, as well as tools that predict download times, alert you to potential problems in various browsers, and check all your links to ensure that they're valid.

In addition, GoLive provides several editors for new Web technologies, including CSS and JavaScript.

CSS button

Figure 19.7 The CSS button opens the CSS editor.

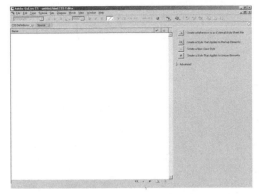

Figure 19.8 The CSS editor as it looks when you first open it.

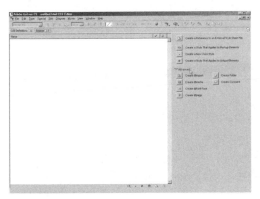

Figure 19.9 The CSS editor, with the Advanced options open.

Adding CSS

Part I of this book deals with style sheets. GoLive includes an assortment of tools that help you add and control the CSS in a Web page or an entire Web site (see "Adding Styles to a Web Page" and "Adding Styles to a Web Site" in Chapter 2).

To add CSS to a Web page:

1. Open a new or existing HTML file by choosing File > New Page, File > Open, or File > New Special and then choosing a specific markup language (this is helpful if you want to work in XHTML, for example). Be sure your page is saved.

2. With the document window in Layout mode (see the previous section, "The GoLive Interface"), click the CSS button in the top-right corner of the window (**Figure 19.7**).

3. With the CSS editor open (**Figure 19.8**), click the Advanced arrow, to see the full features within the editor interface (**Figure 19.9**).

4. Click the button for the CSS selector type you want to use: markup elements, class, or ID (see "The Parts of a CSS Rule" in Chapter 1). For this example, go ahead and click Create a Style That Applies to Markup Elements, and name the selector "h1."

   A new style element for h1 appears in the CSS definitions window, and the CSS editor changes to allow you to input the features for this class.

   continues on next page

ADDING CSS

5. Set the CSS definitions you want to use. Notice the live-updating feature in the editor, which gives you a preview of how the style will look (**Figure 19.10**).

6. After you add all the CSS definitions and rules you want to use, you can click the Source tab to see the CSS source.

7. Return to your HTML document and add an h1 element with some text to view the styles (**Figure 19.11**).

This technique will create embedded CSS. You can also set up external CSS files and then use GoLive to create a link to your Web page.

Setting up and linking to an external CSS file:

1. With the HTML document you worked on in the previous exercise open, click the CSS button.

The CSS Editor opens.

2. In the right pane, click the Create a Reference to an External Style Sheet File button. The editor will change to allow you to input your external style sheet information.

Figure 19.10 Applying styles using the CSS editor. Notice the live-update editing in the bottom pane, showing the way the styles you create will look.

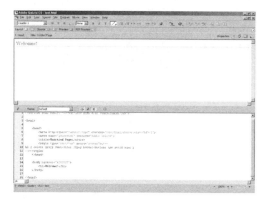

Figure 19.11 Viewing the resulting styles and source code with embedded style.

ADDING CSS

Figure 19.12
Creating an external
style sheet.

3. In the Reference text field, type the name of the CSS file, in this example, test.css. You can also change the media type and add other features here, but if you're not too familiar with what these things are yet, just leave everything else as is (**Figure 19.12**).

4. Click Create and save your style sheet.

5. In the CSS editor, choose a CSS selector type: markup elements, class, or ID.
A new style element appears in the CSS definitions window. Name the element.

6. Use the CSS editor to set your style definitions.

7. Save the file. Now the HTML file can access the styles in the external file.

8. Repeat steps 1 through 5 for as many external style sheets as you want to add.

✔ Tip

■ Avoid uppercase letters when you write style classes. This will help you avoid browser conflicts, especially in the case (if you'll pardon the pun) of XHTML, which requires that all elements and attribute names be lowercase. If you have an uppercase selector, such as H1, in a style sheet that's being used with an XHTML document, your styles will not be interpreted.

How to modify properties with the CSS editor

The CSS editor provides instant access to a variety of style properties. Once you create a selector, you can apply styles to it using the following tabs within the CSS editor:

◆ **Selector and properties.** This tab shows the complete CSS rule being edited. You can make changes directly to both the selector and the properties in this tab (**Figure 19.13**).

◆ **Font properties.** Modify the font properties (as described in Chapter 3) of a given selector (**Figure 19.14**).

◆ **Text properties.** Style your element with text variants, alignment, letter and word spacing and other properties, as described in Chapter 4 (**Figure 19.15**).

◆ **Block properties.** Use these properties (as described in Chapters 5, 6, and 7) to define the dimensions and positioning of a given element (**Figure 19.16**).

◆ **Margin and Padding properties.** Add margins and padding to your element, as described in Chapter 5 (**Figure 19.17**).

◆ **Border and Outline properties.** Add attractive borders to elements, using the properties described in Chapter 5 (**Figure 19.18**).

◆ **List Item and other properties.** Modify your lists and various display styles in this tab, using the properties described in Chapter 8 (**Figure 19.19**).

◆ **Background properties.** Add a background image, position, and effects, and choose your element's background image here, as described in Chapter 5 (**Figure 19.20**).

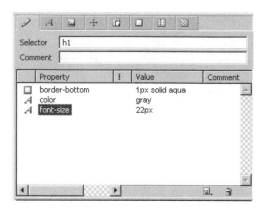

Figure 19.13 The CSS Editor, Selector and Properties view.

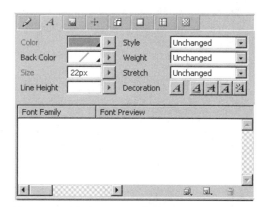

Figure 19.14 The Font properties tab.

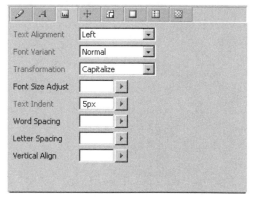

Figure 19.15 The Text properties tab.

ADDING CSS

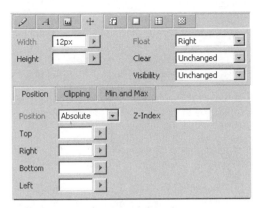

Figure 19.16 The Block properties tab.

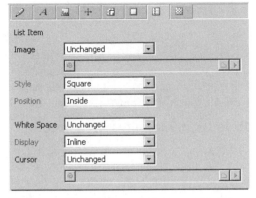

Figure 19.19 The List Item and other properties tab.

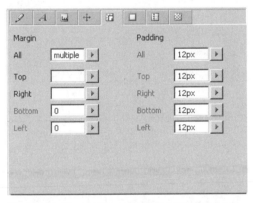

Figure 19.17 The Margin and Padding properties tab.

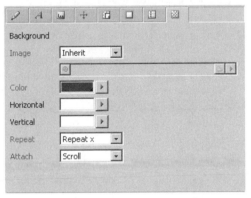

Figure 19.20 The Background properties tab.

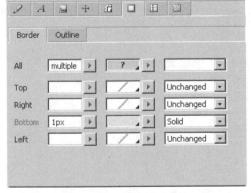

Figure 19.18 The Border and Outline properties tab.

ADDING CSS

Adding a Floating Box

Earlier in this book, I showed you how to set up a CSS box (layer) by turning an element into an object (see "Setting up an Object" in Chapter 10). GoLive refers to a CSS element box as a *floating box,* or a *layer.*

To add a CSS layer to a Web page:

1. With the document window open in Layout mode, double-click the Layer button in the basic-view Objects palette (**Figure 19.21**).

The layer (floating box) now appears in the document window as a numbered rectangle. The numbers correspond to the order in which the layers were created.

2. Move the mouse pointer to any edge of the layer so that the I-beam pointer changes to a hand (**Figure 19.22**). Click to select the object or drag the layer anywhere you want in the window.

3. To change the size of the box after you've selected it, drag one of the handles on any side or corner of the layer (**Figure 19.23**).

Figure 19.21 Adding a layer from the Objects palette.

Figure 19.22 When a layer has been added to the page, you can select the entire layer by clicking one of its borders.

Figure 19.23 When a layer is selected, you can change its width or height by dragging one of the handles.

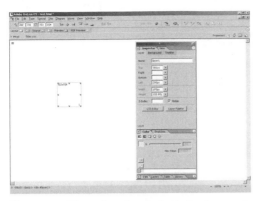

Figure 19.24 When a layer is selected in the document window in Layout mode, the inspector palette allows you to change that layer's properties.

Figure 19.25
You can use the Background tab of the inspector to change the selected layer's background color and image.

To change the CSS layer's properties:

1. With the layer selected in the document window, use the inspector palette to adjust the layer's properties (**Figure 19.24**).

   The inspector palette also includes animation controls, which are discussed in the next section, "Adding DHTML Animation."

2. Type a name for this layer.

   This name will be used as the layer's unique ID in the CSS.

3. Type top and left positions for the layer (see "Setting an Element's Position" in Chapter 6).

4. Type a width and height for the layer (see "Setting the Width and Height of an Element" in Chapter 5).

5. Type the depth of the layer, which will be used for the object's z-index (see "Stacking Elements" in Chapter 6).

6. Specify whether you want the layer to be visible (see "Setting the Visibility of an Element" in Chapter 7).

7. To set the background color or image, click the Background tab within the inspector (**Figure 19.25**).

✔ Tips

- Remember that a CSS layer is an element that has a unique ID, has a position type, and usually is in a <div> tag.

- GoLive assumes that the CSS layer will be positioned absolutely (see "Setting an Element's Position" in Chapter 6). You can use the inspector palette to set up relatively positioned layers.

ADDING A FLOATING BOX

Adding DHTML Animation

Earlier in this book, I showed you how to create simple point-to-point animations (see "Animating an Object" in Chapter 15). Although this technique is highly effective for moving a single object along a simple path, more complex animations are better created with a program such as GoLive, because the calculation and timing involved are difficult to hand-code.

In the following example, I've set up five layers, each with a different letter of Alice's name (**Figure 19.26**). As the animation runs, the letters will move around the page to spell *ALICE*.

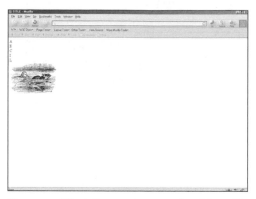

Figure 19.26 The letters start out unordered, but will eventually move to create the name "Alice".

To create an animation with GoLive:

1. Set up a CSS layer (see the previous section, "Adding a Floating Box"), and add any content you want. Make sure the inspector palette is open to the Timeline tab (**Figure 19.27**).

2. With the layer selected, click the Open Timeline Editor button in the inspector, or in the top-right corner of the document window, immediately to the left of the CSS button.

The timeline editor window opens (**Figure 19.28**).

Figure 19.27
The Timeline tab of the inspector palette.

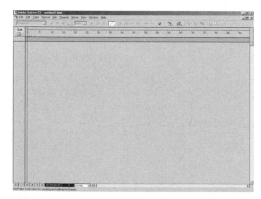

Figure 19.28 The DHTML timeline editor window, as it looks when first opened.

Figure 19.29 Select a curved path and record your animation.

3. With the layer still selected in the document window, in the inspector, choose Curve from the Animation drop-down menu, then click the Record button (**Figure 19.29**).

4. Move the object along the path you want it to follow.

   In the timeline editor window, you see a rectangle with a dot for each point in the animation (**Figure 19.30**). These points are called *keyframes*.

5. Repeat steps 1 through 4 for each layer you want to animate.

When this page is loaded into a Web browser, the layers should move around as programmed (**Figure 19.31**).

Keyframe

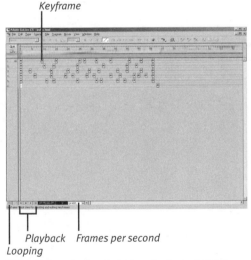

Playback   Frames per second
Looping

Figure 19.30 Viewing the animation in the DHTML timeline editor.

Figure 19.31 The final animation results.

DREAMWEAVER MX 2004 PRIMER

Dreamweaver started its life as a visual editor for Web development, and has integrated more and more tools for both client- and server-side languages, including HTML, XHTML, scripting, and, of course, CSS. It was usually thought of as a WYSIWYG layout program that relied on third-party software to provide rigorous HTML-editing capabilities. But this situation has changed. With the most recent release, Dreamweaver MX 2004, the software has become one of the premier Web design and development tools offering visual editing, server-side languages and live server editing, and includes significant support for Web standards.

Dreamweaver MX 2004 incorporates a bevy of other tools and utilities as well, such as FTP and site management, and it allows you to create templates that make updates to your site a breeze. In addition, because Macromedia is also the developer of Flash MX, Dreamweaver includes several tools that allow you to add Flash text and buttons even if you don't own Macromedia Flash (see "Flash vs. DHTML" in Chapter 9).

In this chapter, I'll show you how to set up CSS using Dreamweaver's tools, work with new Dreamweaver features such as CSS template designs, and use the Tag Inspector to work more efficiently with CSS.

The Dreamweaver Interface

Macromedia worked hard between each release to develop Dreamweaver from a simple DHTML generator into a full-featured Web-design program, and the results are impressive. Although early releases of this software suffered from a lack of integration between the code and WYSIWYG editors, the most recent release has real-time integration between the two editing modes so that changes made in one mode are reflected in the other instantly.

Dreamweaver MX 2004 provides an easy-to-use layout mode that allows you to add, move, and delete page elements directly on the page while it generates the HTML or XHTML code in the background. You can edit the source code directly, however, if you feel more comfortable doing things that way.

Document window

You create individual Web pages in the document window, interacting with the pages' code in a variety of ways, depending on your needs and preferences. You can switch among the following views by clicking the buttons at the top of the document window.

◆ **Design view** shows how the page should look when it's displayed in a browser window. You can move and change elements around on the screen as desired (**Figure 20.1**).

◆ **Code view** allows you to interact directly with the tags used to generate your Web pages (**Figure 20.2**).

◆ **Split view** splits the document window into two panes, allowing you to work in both code and design modes simultaneously. Changes you make in one area affect the other when you switch from one pane to the other (**Figure 20.3**).

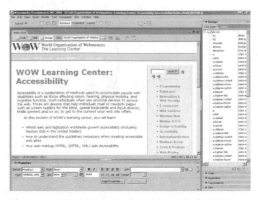

Figure 20.1 Working in Design view, with the CSS Styles tab open in the Design panel. Here, you can add and move page elements around just as you would in a print publishing program.

Figure 20.2 The Dreamweaver document window in Code view. You can edit all of the code for the page (HTML, JavaScript, and CSS) directly in this mode.

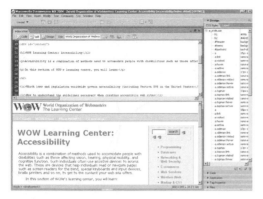

Figure 20.3 The Dreamweaver document window in Split view. Here, you can work with the design or code and see the results in the other window as you make changes.

Property inspector

The property inspector allows you to control all the attributes of the selected page element in the document window. This includes shortcuts to common tags and styles that might be used with the selected element, as well as to input fields that allow you to define the element's properties.

Because these options vary depending on the element that is selected, the Properties toolbar displays options contextually. If you're editing text, for example, you see options for setting the header level, alignment, font size, and other text attributes (**Figure 20.4**). If you select a layer in the document window, the Properties toolbar changes to allow you to control the size, position, and visibility of the layer (**Figure 20.5**).

Figure 20.4 The Properties toolbar options change depending on the element selected in the document window. These are the options when text is selected.

Figure 20.5 Here, the Properties toolbar has changed to reflect the attributes of a selected layer.

Panel groups

You can access Dreamweaver MX 2004's many panels from the Window menu. These panels add features and functionality to the program, but can be closed when they aren't needed (which, for many of them, is most of the time). These are the most important palettes for CSS and DHTML:

◆ **Design.** This panel allows instant access to your CSS information, including CSS and Layer editing options.

◆ **Code.** Snippets of HTML and JavaScript code are available in this panel, along with the contents of several Web reference books.

◆ **Tag Inspector.** This helpful panel, enhanced for Dreamweaver MX 2004, includes three important areas: *Attributes* shows a selected tag's attributes; *Behaviors* shows any behavior associated with a selected tag; and *Relevant CSS* shows all the CSS styles being applied to a selected element.

◆ **Files.** With the Files panel open, you'll always be able to see the location of various files within your site. You can also keep your assets easily identified and modified through this panel.

CSS tools in Dreamweaver

Dreamweaver provides all the tools you would expect in a robust Web-editing package, including a spelling checker, code-validation checkers, and a link checker. In addition, Dreamweaver can create a wide range of documents using multiple languages on either the client or the server side.

Dreamweaver MX 2004 has made major advancements in the area of CSS support. These are some of the new features:

- **Better CSS rendering within Design view.** In the past, Dreamweaver had limited CSS support within this view. Now, it can handle far more explicit CSS rendering. It's not quite perfect, as it doesn't display hover techniques and other effects, but it's definitely a step in the right direction.

- **Default formatting with CSS.** In the past, Dreamweaver used `<font>` tags and other presentational HTML tags (those tags concerned with visual display) to format text. While you can still change preferences in Dreamweaver to allow you to work in this way, Dreamweaver now uses CSS for visual presentation, which is the current recommended best practice. That Dreamweaver MX writes CSS for visual presentation by default rather than using tags that clutter your documents helps make your documents more standards-compliant, which in turn makes life a lot easier on you!

- **CSS templates.** Along with templates for a range of document types, Dreamweaver MX 2004 offers a number of CSS designs that you can modify for your needs. For more about this, see "Working with Dreamweaver CSS Templates" later in this chapter.

- **Tag Inspector/Relevant CSS.** The Relevant CSS tab within the Tag Inspector panel immediately shows you which styles are being applied to a given element. You can also make modifications to those styles directly within the tab.

THE DREAMWEAVER INTERFACE

Adding CSS

In Part I of this book, I showed you how to add style sheets to your Web pages. Dreamweaver includes an assortment of tools that take some of the drudgery out of creating and maintaining well-formed style sheets. You can use Dreamweaver to add CSS to a single Web page or to an entire Web site (see "Adding Styles to a Web Page" and "Adding Styles to a Web Site" in Chapter 2).

To add CSS to a Web page:

1. Open a new or existing HTML file by choosing File > New or File > Open.

2. In the CSS Styles tab of the Design panel (choose Window > CSS Styles to open the panel, if necessary), click the New CSS Style button (**Figure 20.6**).

   The New CSS Style dialog box appears (**Figure 20.7**).

3. Choose the CSS selector types you want to use (see "The Parts of a CSS Rule" in Chapter 1). Class, if you want to add a class; Tag, or Advanced if you'd like to use an ID or advanced selector types.

4. Click the This document only radio button to include your new style in the <style> tag of this page, then click OK.

5. In the CSS Style Definition window, specify the CSS definitions you want to use (**Figure 20.8**).

   You can click Apply at any time to view the changes you're making in the document window.

6. After you define all the CSS rules you want to use, click OK to return to the document window.

   All of your style information will now be added to the document. But remember, these styles will relate only to this document.

Figure 20.6 The CSS Styles tab shows all the classes that are available in this document (in this figure, none).

Figure 20.7 The New CSS Style dialog box allows you to select the type of style you're adding and whether to put it in an external style sheet or embed it in the document.

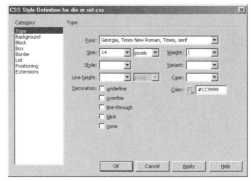

Figure 20.8 The CSS Style Definition dialog box can be considered Dreamweaver's primary CSS-editing interface.

Setting up and linking to an external CSS file:

1. Open a new or existing HTML file.

2. In the CSS Styles tab of the Design panel, click the New CSS Style button.
   The New CSS Style dialog box opens.

3. Choose the CSS selector types you want to use: Class, Tag, or Advanced (to use an ID or advanced selector types).

4. Make sure that the New Style Sheet File radio button is selected, then click OK.

5. The Save Style Sheet File As dialog box opens. Name your CSS file, being careful to include the .css suffix in your file name.
   This will create a new external CSS file, which Dreamweaver MX 2004 automatically links to the current Web page. Alternatively, you can edit a style sheet that is already linked to this page by selecting it from the drop-down menu.

6. Set the CSS styles you want to use.
   You can click Apply at any time to view the changes you're making in the document window.

7. After you define all the CSS rules you want to use, click OK to return to the document window.

8. If you set up any classes, use the CSS Styles tab of the Design panel to set that class for the selected object in the document window.

✔ Tip

■ Dreamweaver doesn't allow you to add styles, so you're stuck with using the styles it knows. You can add style rules directly in Code view, however.

ADDING CSS

The CSS Style Definition window

When you're adding or editing a CSS rule, you'll use the CSS Style Definition window to enter your values for each rule. The CSS Style Definition window comprises the following categories:

◆ **Type.** Set type features including font, size, weight, line height, and decoration, as described in Chapters 3 and 4 (**Figure 20.9**).

◆ **Background.** Set background styles including color and background image and positioning, as described in Chapter 5 (**Figure 20.10**).

◆ **Block.** Set alignment and display styles, as described in Chapters 4 and 5 (**Figure 20.11**).

◆ **Box.** Set styles relating to the positioning, padding, and margins of a given element, as described in Chapters 5 and 6 (**Figure 20.12**).

◆ **Border.** Set borders for an element including style, width, and color, as described in Chapter 5 (**Figure 20.13**).

◆ **List.** Control the way your lists are displayed, as described in Chapter 8 (**Figure 20.14**).

◆ **Positioning.** Set your element's CSS positioning features, as described in Chapter 6 (**Figure 20.15**).

◆ **Extensions.** These styles include new or browser-specific CSS such as cursor and page break (**Figure 20.16**).

Figure 20.9 Setting type styles using the CSS Style Definition window.

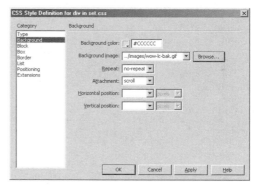

Figure 20.10 You can set a range of background features such as color, image, and image behavior in the Background category.

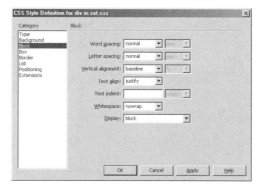

Figure 20.11 The Block category allows you to set word and letter spacing, alignment, indent, whitespace, and display styles.

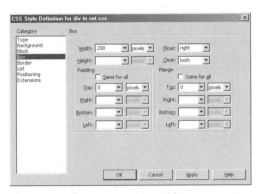

Figure 20.12 The Box category provides a way to manage the width, height, float, padding, and margin styles of an element.

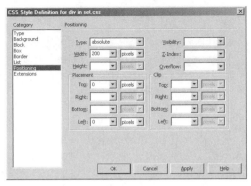

Figure 20.15 Positioning offers a variety of styles that enable you to position your element on the page and manage positioning features.

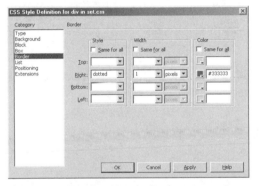

Figure 20.13 Here I'm using the Border category to create a dotted right border with a width of 1 pixel for my selected element.

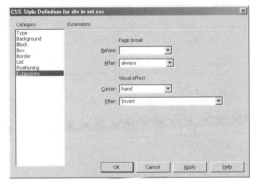

Figure 20.16 Extensions are advanced or proprietary (non-standard) features found within some Web browsers.

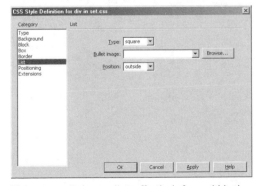

Figure 20.14 Style your lists effectively from within the List category of the CSS Style Definition window.

Adding a Layer

You create what Dreamweaver MX 2004 refers to as a "layer" when you define an element with a unique ID and give it a position type (absolute or relative). Dreamweaver layers are associated with a `<div>` tag (see "Setting up an Object" in Chapter 10), and allow you to position elements on a page in more flexible ways than using HTML tables. Dreamweaver gives you easy access to the attributes available for layers.

To add a CSS layer to a Web page:

1. With the document window open in Design view or Split view, drag the Draw Layer icon from the Layout toolbar above the document window and drop it in the document window's layout pane (**Figure 20.17**).

   The layer now appears as a rectangle in the document window.

2. Move the mouse pointer to any edge of the layer (**Figure 20.18**), then click to select the layer, or drag and position the layer anywhere you want in the window.

3. To change the size of the box after you've selected it, drag one of the handles on any side or corner of the layer (**Figure 20.19**).

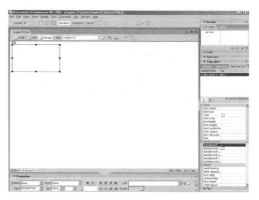

Figure 20.17 Add a new layer to your Web page by dragging the Draw Layer icon from the toolbar above the document window.

Figure 20.18 To select the entire layer, click any edge.

Figure 20.19 You can change the size and position of a layer directly by dragging one of the handles on its side.

Figure 20.20 The Properties toolbar gives you access to all the layer's properties that are controlled by CSS.

To change the CSS layer's attributes:

1. With the layer selected in the document window, use the Properties toolbar to adjust the layer's attributes (**Figure 20.20**).

2. Type a name for this layer.
This name will be used as the object's unique ID in the CSS.

3. Type top and left positions (see "Setting an Element's Position" in Chapter 6) for the layer.

4. Type a width and height for the layer (see "Setting the Width and Height of an Element" in Chapter 5).

5. Type the layer's z-index (see "Stacking Elements" in Chapter 6).

6. Specify whether you want the layer to be visible (see "Setting the Visibility of an Element" in Chapter 7).

7. Set the background color and/or image (see "Setting the Background" in Chapter 5).

8. If you'd like to assign a class style to the layer, select the class from the Class drop-down.

9. Set the left, top, right, and bottom edges of the clipping region, if applicable; then specify how the overflow should be treated (see "Setting the Visible Area of an Element" and "Setting Where the Extra Content Goes" in Chapter 7).

✔ Tip

■ Dreamweaver places all the layer's CSS inline in the `<div>` tag rather than setting up an ID in the `<style>` tag. I like to create IDs in the `<style>` tag or in an external CSS file, but Dreamweaver's method works, too. You can always remove the inline CSS and add it manually to an embedded or external style sheet.

ADDING A LAYER

Working with Dreamweaver CSS Templates

One of the exciting new additions to Dreamweaver MX 2004 is CSS templates. You can use these templates to immediately style documents, or use them as a guide and modify them with the techniques described earlier in this chapter to create a different look.

The templates are grouped into these categories:

◆ **Basic.** Basic CSS templates style your page with a specific font.

◆ **Colors.** Add color schemes to your page with these helpful templates.

◆ **Forms.** CSS can be used to style forms in ways unavailable to designers in HTML, and Dreamweaver MX 2004 even includes one template specifically addressing accessibility.

◆ **Full Design.** These templates include styles for everything from paragraphs to tables and forms.

◆ **Link Effects.** This template defines several link effects that you can use to modify your documents for more compelling visual design.

◆ **Text.** Similar to Basic CSS templates, these templates style pages with fonts, in a variety of specific ways, such as for accessibility.

◆ **Page Designs (CSS).** These templates incorporate CSS for layout, so you can create a complete design by simply attaching one of these style sheets to your content document and applying the styles. While the actual designs may leave a bit to be desired visually, the templates are an excellent way to get more familiar with using CSS for layouts and to learn how modifications will dramatically change the look and feel of a page.

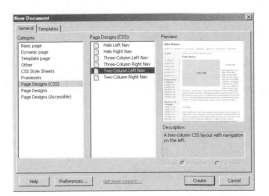

Figure 20.21 Selecting a pure-CSS Page Design template, in this case a two-column layout with left navigation.

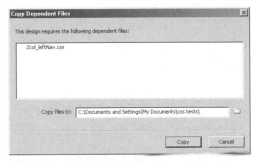

Figure 20.22 Copy the template file to the location where you're saving your work.

Figure 20.23 This is the newly templated page in Design view.

Since you already know how to link a style sheet to your pages, I recommend going ahead and trying out a few of these templates. In the following exercise, you'll work with a full CSS page design and make some simple modifications, giving you a feel for how you can combine Dreamweaver CSS tools and the new templates into a variety of options.

To create a layout using a Dreamweaver CSS template:

1. In order to work with full page design templates, you first need to define your site. For this example, I simply called mine "CSS Tests" and set everything up to run locally.

2. Select File > New. In the New Document window, select Page Designs (CSS) within the Category pane (**Figure 20.21**).

3. The available templates appear in the center pane. Choose Two-Column Left Nav, and click Create.

4. Dreamweaver will first ask you to save the HTML document. Name it "css-test.html" and click Save.

5. The Copy Dependent Files dialog box appears (**Figure 20.22**). This will link the style sheet to your document. Click Copy.

6. The page design will now load in Design view (**Figure 20.23**).

As you can see, the page is ready for you to add your own text and images and already contains numerous features that most Web sites use. But what if you don't like the colors, borders, and design of the page elements? Not to worry—you can modify the design using the Relevant CSS tab of the Tag Inspector panel.

To modify a template design:

1. With your css-test.html document open, open the Tag Inspector, then click the Relevant CSS tab (**Figure 20.24**).

2. The Relevant CSS tab has two views: Category view shows the CSS styles by category and List view shows a list of styles. Click the Show Category View button.

3. Click anywhere in the document once, and the Relevant CSS panel updates to show the styles influencing the element you clicked. Click Site Name to see the styles for that header.

4. Make sure the Font category is open in the Relevant CSS tab. To change the font color properties, simply click the color box to open the color picker (**Figure 20.25**).

5. Click a color, and the element is updated with the color you chose. For this example, I chose a dark red, #660000.

6. To get rid of the navigation bar borders, click in the navigation bar once. It has a number of selectors, so you may have to find the parent selector to change a feature.

7. Under the Border category, find the border-right property. Click the style once, then delete the style completely. This removes the right border of the navigation bar.

8. Do the same for the border-bottom property, ridding the navigation bar of all its borders.

Continue modifying properties as you see fit, changing the color scheme—even adding background graphics to elements. You'll begin to see how using the CSS page design template as a guide can combine with your own design savvy to create great-looking CSS-based pages.

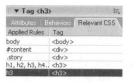

Figure 20.24 Use the Relevant CSS tab of the Tag Inspector panel.

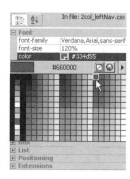

Figure 20.25 Make direct changes to the style sheet using the Relevant CSS tab.

DEBUGGING
YOUR CODE

If you are using CSS or DHTML to create your Web pages, eventually you will have bugs. Like death and taxes, problems with your code are inescapable.

I've tested and retested the code in this book on the most popular browsers and operating systems available and hope that it's as bug-free as humanly possible. You will inevitably have to adapt the code for your own use, however. You'll have to change variables, values, URLs, and styles. You may have to combine code from different examples. You may even have to write your own functions from scratch.

This means bugs.

In this chapter, I'll guide you through some of the most common problems, help you identify and fix them, and (I hope) keep you from smashing your monitor with a heavy mallet when things go wrong. Also, remember that you can download all the code in this book from www.webbedenvironments.com/dhtml.

Troubleshooting CSS

All too often, you carefully set up your style sheet rules, go to your browser, and see... nothing. Don't worry, this happens to everyone.

Check the following

There are many things that might be preventing your style sheet rules from working properly; most of them are easily spotted. **Figure 21.1** points out some common problems you may encounter.

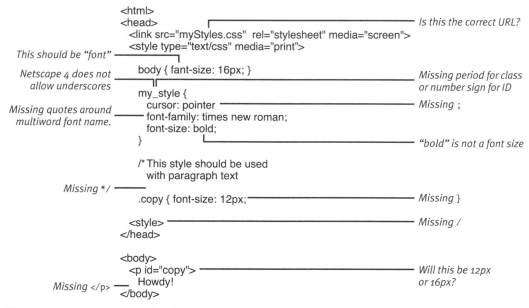

Figure 21.1 Errors are inevitable, but don't let them ruin your day. This figure shows examples of some of the most common CSS problems.

◆ **Are the properties you're using available for your platform and browser?** Many properties are not supported by Internet Explorer and/or Netscape—it depends on the operating system being used. Check Appendix A to see whether the property works with the intended browser and OS.

◆ **Does your selector contain typos?** If you forget the opening period or number sign (#) for classes and IDs, they won't work.

◆ **Do the properties contain typos?** Typos in one property can cause the entire rule to fail.

◆ **Are the values you're using permitted for that property?** Using improper values may cause a definition to fail or behave unpredictably.

◆ **Are you missing any semicolons?** A missing semicolon at the end of a definition will cause the entire rule to fail.

◆ **Did you open and close the definition list with curly brackets?** If not, there's no telling what will happen.

◆ **Did you remember to close all your multiline comment tags?** If not, the rest of the CSS is treated as a comment (see "Adding Comments to CSS" in Chapter 2).

◆ **Are the HTML tags set correctly in the document?** Remember that you have to use an end </p> to make the paragraph tag work properly with CSS (see "Kinds of Tags" in Chapter 1).

continues on next page

TROUBLESHOOTING CSS

◆ **If your rules are in the head, did you use the <style> tag correctly?** Typos in the <style> tag mean that none of the definitions are used. In addition, if you set the media type the styles will only affect output to that medium. So, setting the media type to print will prevent those styles from affecting content displayed on the screen (see "Adding Styles to a Web Page" in Chapter 2).

◆ **If you are linking or importing style sheets, are you retrieving the correct file?** Check the exact path for the file. Also, remember that you should not include the <style> tag in an external CSS file (see "Adding Styles to a Web Site" in Chapter 2).

◆ **Do you have multiple, perhaps conflicting, rules for the same tag?** Check your cascade order (see "Determining the Cascade Order" in Chapter 2).

If all else fails, try these ideas

If you've looked for the above errors and still can't get your code to work, here are a few more things to try.

◆ **Delete the rules and retype them.** When you can't see what's wrong, retyping code from scratch sometimes fixes it.

◆ **Test the same code on another browser and/or OS.** It's possible that a property is buggy and doesn't work correctly in your browser. It's even possible that the browser doesn't allow that property to work with that tag.

◆ **Give up and walk away from the project.** Just joking—though you might want to take a 15-minute break before looking at the problem again.

◆ **If nothing else works, try a different solution to the design problem.**

Figure 21.2 The W3C's CSS Validator.

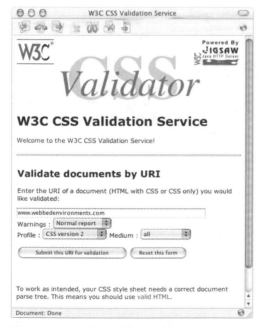

Figure 21.3 I want the Validator to check my webbedENVIRONMENTS site, so I entered the URL for my site's external CSS file.

Validating Your CSS

Although both Dreamweaver and GoLive will make sure your CSS code is accurate, the World Wide Web Consortium (W3C) provides a Web site called the CSS Validator that lets you check your CSS to confirm that it meets the requirements set in the W3C standards.

To use the W3C's CSS Validator:

1. Point your Web browser to jigsaw.w3.org/css-validator/.

2. Click the method by which you want to validate your CSS (**Figure 21.2**).

   You can enter a URL (by URI), enter the CSS code directly in a form (with a text area), or upload your files (by upload). In this example, you'll submit a URL.

3. Enter the URL of the Web site or style sheet (**Figure 21.3**).

   I recommend entering the *exact* URL of the style sheet.

continues on next page

4. Specify how you want warnings to be presented and the type of validation you want to use (usually, CSS2), then click Submit this URI for validation.

The validation takes only a few seconds. You're given a report of errors and other possible problems in your CSS (**Figure 21.4**).

✔ Tips

■ Anyone who creates a Web page can display the Made with Cascading Style Sheets icon (**Figure 21.5**); however, only pages that pass muster with the CSS Validator should display the W3C CSS validation icon (**Figure 21.6**).

■ Although you don't have to have valid CSS for the browser to display your code, the validation process often helps locate code errors.

Figure 21.4 Everything is looking good. Any problems will be reported specifying what is wrong and where, and suggesting fixes.

Figure 21.5 Say it loud, say it proud: Made with CSS.

Figure 21.6 If your CSS passes muster, you too can display the Valid CSS icon.

Figure 21.7 Type `javascript:` in the location bar.

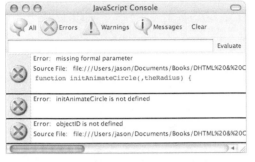

Figure 21.8 The error screen in Firebird, which is a Mozilla-based browser.

Figure 21.9 An error message in Internet Explorer.

Troubleshooting JavaScript

Although JavaScript is not a true programming language like Java, you must still use logic to construct the actions that should take place. Things inevitably go wrong.

Unlike CSS, though, JavaScript doesn't require you to eyeball the code to figure out what's wrong. Most browsers display an error message that details what went wrong and where.

To view JavaScript errors:

◆ In Netscape 6+, Mozilla, or FireBird, type `javascript:` in the browser's location bar (**Figure 21.7**) or choose Tools > JavaScript Console. A window like the one shown in **Figure 21.8** appears. It displays any JavaScript errors that occur in open windows.

◆ In Internet Explorer, JavaScript errors appear as soon as they occur, unless you set your preferences not to show errors (**Figure 21.9**).

After the error has been detected and located, you can check the code and even use JavaScript to track down the problem (**Figure 21.10**).

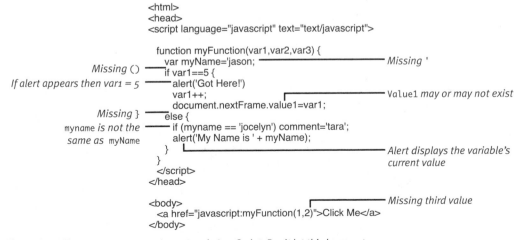

Figure 21.10 These errors commonly crop up in JavaScript. Don't let this happen to you.

If you have an error, check the following

Look for these common problems:

- **Do you have matching curly brackets ({}) for every instance?** If either end is left out, the script will fail.

- **Do you have matching quotes (' ') for every instance?** If you don't close a quote string, the script will fail.

- **Have all referenced objects and variables loaded before being referenced?** This situation is called a "timing problem." If a page in one frame attempts to reference a nonexistent object or an object that simply hasn't finished loading yet, the script will fail. One way around this problem is to test for the existence of the object or variable before trying to perform an action on it, as follows:

```
if (document.nextFrame.value1)
→ { document.nextFrame.value1 = x}
```

- **Have you used a reserved word for a variable?** Certain words, such as *new*, have a special meaning for JavaScript and cannot be used for variables. You can use derivations of these words, such as *newObject*; you just can't use the exact word. See Appendix B for a list of reserved words.

- **Do your variable names match?** A typo in a variable name may cause a function to fail or act unpredictably, but JavaScript is also case-sensitive, so even a difference in a letter's case will cause the function to think that it is dealing with different variables. The variable noWhere, for example, is completely different from nowhere.

♦ **Have you placed all the necessary values in the function call, and are they in the right order?** If not, your JavaScript may fail or act unpredictably. You wouldn't believe how many hours I've wasted debugging code only to realize that I simply placed my variables in the wrong order when I referenced the function.

♦ **Do your `if` statements have parentheses around their arguments?** I forget the parentheses all the time. Your `if` statements need to have the following structure:

```
if (argument) doThis;
```

♦ **Is your JavaScript running the correct code?** Sometimes code that you expect to run doesn't run for some reason. The best way to test this situation is to put alerts in strategic places in the code to show what's running (and what is not). Place the following line in your code where you think the code might not be running.

```
alert ('Got Here!');
```

If the code is running, the alert should appear.

♦ **Are your variables getting the right values?** Your variables may not get the values you expect them to get. Place an alert immediately after a variable to test its value, as follows:

```
alert ('My Name is ' + myVariable);
```

♦ **Is your logic sound?** Simply stated, you need to make sure that what you've programmed makes sense. If actions occur out of order for the desired effect, things will go wrong. Trace through your code as though you were the computer running it, keeping track of what variables have what values at a given time and whether the correct actions are executed at the correct time.

✔ Tips

■ Although you can use double quotes ("") or single quotes ('') in your JavaScript and HTML, I recommend sticking with single quotes for JavaScript and double quotes for HTML. This practice will help prevent a lot of confusion. I make fewer programming errors if I stick to this simple rule.

■ Although you don't have to use it, JavaScript has an accepted way of creating variable names, often referred to as "JavaScript notation." Simply put, if you have multiple words in a variable, the first word is lowercase, and the first letter of each subsequent word is uppercase, with other letters in lowercase. So my last name—Cranford Teague—would be `cranfordTeague` in JavaScript notation.

The PNH Developer Toolbar

If you're developing Web pages for Mozilla browsers, such as Firebird or Netscape 6+, the PNH Developer Toolbar from Placenamehere.com is indispensable (www.placenamehere.com/ pnhtoolbar/). This easy-to-install widget adds a list of drop-down menus underneath your Bookmarks toolbar (**Figure 21.11**), and includes the following:

◆ **W3C Docs:** Links to all of the most relevant W3C standards documents (HTML, XHTML, CSS, DOM, and so forth).

◆ **Page Tests:** Links where you can submit the currently displayed page for CSS or HTML validation (bypassing the forms) or to a link checker to ensure that all of the page's links are active.

◆ **Layout Tools:** Commands that allow you to change or turn on and off the style sheets used on the currently displayed page: show borders for block elements, replace elements and table data cells (great for checking layout), remove images, and precisely size the browser window for checking how designs fit in different resolutions.

◆ **Other Tools:** Commands that show the form element details or cookies used in the currently displayed page.

◆ **View Source:** Quick link for showing the HTML code for the currently displayed Web page in a new tab.

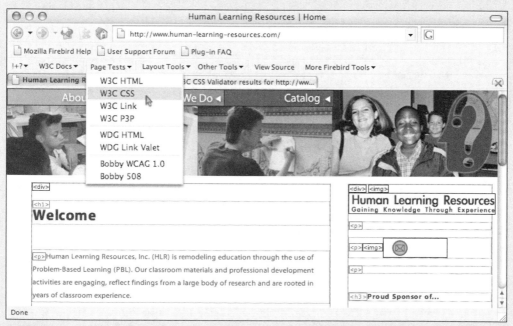

Figure 21.11 The PNH Toolbar in action. The displayed page has its block elements outlined, and also shows the tags used to create the block element while a new tab is running CSS validation.

Cross-Browser Conundrums

Figure 21.12 In Internet Explorer for Windows (top), the header looks fine with the line-height set to normal. However, in the Mac version (bottom), the lines of

HTML, CSS, JavaScript, and the Document Object Model are all referred to as *interpreted code*. That is, every browser that can understand these technologies follows a set of rules to help it translate and display the code you set up. Unfortunately, these translations can vary slightly or enormously from browser to browser.

A friend of mine was experimenting with CSS in his Web site, and the line-height was set to normal in every rule (see "Adjusting Text Spacing" in Chapter 4). Although this setup looked perfectly fine in Internet Explorer 5 for Windows, in Internet Explorer 5 for the Mac, the headlines (which were multiple lines of large text) overlapped. Why? Apparently, when Microsoft programmers created Internet Explorer for Windows, they interpreted normal to mean that the browser should apply the current font size being used at that point in the page. Conversely, the Mac development team interpreted normal as meaning the default font size for the page. Thus, in Windows, the line-height would have to be the same as the font size of the text being presented. But in the Mac version, the line-height would more than likely be around 12 points, causing the 36-point text lines to overlap (**Figure 21.12**).

continues on the next page

I run across these problems all the time. Many of them aren't really bugs—they're just slightly different ways that one browser interprets HTML, CSS, or JavaScript compared with other browsers, in much the same way that words (even in the same language) may mean different things in different countries (see the sidebar "A Matter of Interpretation: The Case of Pants or Trousers?"). Although this situation usually isn't life-threatening, it can be confusing, not to mention annoying. You can't do much to fix these problems—unless you reprogram the browsers and then install them on the computers of all the people who will be viewing your site. But you *can* work around the problems.

Cross-browser workarounds:

◆ **Adjust your code.** In my friend's case, he didn't need the `line-height: normal` definition, so he took it out. The layout then looked fine in both browsers.

◆ **Tailor your code to the OS, the browser, or both.** I showed you how to do this in "Customizing Styles for the OS or Browser" in Chapter 16.

◆ **Rethink the method you're using to create the page.** Because Netscape 6 has difficulty displaying backgrounds and borders for nested CSS layers, if you require nested layers, you may have to forego border colors.

◆ **Live with it.** Some problems are just not worth the effort of fixing them. If a problem is small—for instance, one browser puts a few extra line breaks after an `<h1>` header, while another browser does not—you can be doing far better things with your time than trying to offset the problem in both browsers.

A Matter of Interpretation: The Case of Pants or Trousers?

While I was a student living in London, I frequented a local pub (one of about six within a five-minute walk of my flat) on the banks of the Thames River. On one occasion, I was talking to some friends, and a drunken rugby player who was standing next to us sloshed lager on me. After the third time this happened, I stood up and started yelling at him, "Hey, do you want to clean my pants?" Unfortunately, I forgot that to a Brit, the word *pants* means *underwear*, whereas to a "Yank," it means *trousers*. He and his six mates, who were not familiar with this little linguistic twist, proceeded to try to throw me into the Thames. Make no mistake about it—misinterpreting a word can mean the difference between life and death.

CSS
QUICK REFERENCE

Chapters 2 through 8 present in detail the CSS properties and values and how to use them. In this appendix, those properties are presented in a more concise format, with their possible values and browser compatibility. In addition, these tables include information about the applicability of each property in the various types of HTML tags. Each property is described in terms of what it can be used with, whether the property is inherited by its child elements, and whether the property is supported by various browsers and operating systems.

- ◆ **Table A.1**: CSS Basics (Chapter 2)

- ◆ **Table A.2:** Pseudo-classes and pseudo-Elements (Chapter 2)

- ◆ **Table A.3:** Font Controls (Chapter 3)

- ◆ **Table A.4:** Text Controls (Chapter 4)

- ◆ **Table A.5:** Element Controls (Chapter 5)

- ◆ **Table A.6:** Element Positioning Controls (Chapter 6)

- ◆ **Table A.7:** Element Visibility Controls (Chapter 7)

- ◆ **Table A.8:** List, Table, and Interface Controls (Chapter 8)

Browsers Legend

N   Netscape

IE   Internet Explorer

S   Safari

O   Opera

In addition to the browsers listed, remember that Netscape 6 and above is based on the Gecko rendering engine. Therefore, generally speaking, Mozilla 1 will have the same compatibility as Netscape 6. Mozilla 1.3 and 1.5, Firebird, and Camino will have roughly the same compatibility as Netscape 7.

Keep in mind that each browser has several versions, even within a single version number. There is not a single Netscape 4, for example, but several versions (4.06, 4.5, and 4.7), with slight differences among them. The information presented in this appendix is generally correct, but if you want to test the CSS capabilities of your own browser, check out the W3C's test suite at www.w3c.org/Style/CSS/Test

This utility will help you confirm which properties work in your browser.

Compatibility Legend

■   Mac and Windows

○   Neither

W   Windows only

M   Mac only

P   Problems

All   Property can be applied to any HTML tag

Block Property can be applied only to block-level tags

Inline Property can be applied only to inline tags

Boldface Indicates the default value for that property

Properties marked with a **P** in the browser columns are partially implemented or buggy in one or both operating systems. I generally recommend avoiding these properties.

Table A.1

CSS Basics

Name	N4	N6	N7	IE4	IE5	IE6	S1	O7
<style>	■	■	■	■	■	■	■	■
<link>	■	■	■	■	■	■	■	■
@import	○	■	■	■	■	■	■	■
@media	○	■	■	○	■*	■	■	■
Inheritance	■	■	■	■	■	■	■	■
Contextual	■	■	■	■	■	■	■	■
Comments	■	■	■	■	■	■	■	■
!important	P	■	■	P	■	■	■	■
Media: Print	○	■	■	○	■	■	■	■

IE5.5 for Windows

Table A.2

Pseudo-Classes and Pseudo-Elements

Name	Value	Applies to	Inherited	N4	N6	N7	IE4	IE5	IE6	S1	O7
:link	—	Anchor	Yes	■	■	■	■	■	■	■	■
:active	—	Anchor	Yes	○	■	■	■	■	■	■	■
:visited	—	Anchor	Yes	○	■	■	■	■	■	■	■
:hover	—	All*	Yes	○	■	■	■	■	■	■	■
:first-line	—	Block	No	○	■	■	○	■**	■	■	■
:first-letter	—	Block	No	○	■	■	○	■**	■	■	■

* Applies only to Anchor tags in IE for Windows
** IE5.5 for Windows

Table A.3

Font Controls

Name	Value	Applies to	Inherited	N4	N6	N7	IE4	IE5	IE6	S1	O7
font-family	<family-name>	All	Yes	■	■	■	■	■	■	■	■
	serif			■	■	■	■	■	■	■	■
	sans-serif			■	■	■	■	■	■	■	■
	cursive			M	■	■	■	■	■	■	■
	fantasy			M	■	■	■	■	■	■	■
	monospace			■	■	■	■	■	■	■	■
font-style	**normal**	All	Yes	■	■	■	■	■	■	■	■
	italic			■	■	■	■	■	■	■	■
	oblique			○	■	■	■	■	■	■	■
font-variant	**normal**	All	Yes	○	■	■	■	■	■	■	■
	small-caps			○	■	■	P	■	■	■	■
font-weight	**normal**	All	Yes	■	■	■	■	■	■	■	■
	bold			■	■	■	■	■	■	■	■
	bolder			W	■	■	■	■	■	■	■
	lighter			○	■	■	■	■	■	■	■
	100-900*			■	■	■	■	■	■	■	■
font-size	<length>	All	Yes	■	■	■	■	■	■	■	■
	<percentage>			■	■	■	■	■	■	■	■
	smaller			■	■	■	P	■	■	■	■
	larger			■	■	■	P	■	■	■	■
	xx-small			■	■	■	P	■	■	■	■
	x-small			■	■	■	P	■	■	■	■
	small			■	■	■	P	■	■	■	■
	medium			■	■	■	P	■	■	■	■
	large			■	■	■	P	■	■	■	■
	x-large			■	■	■	P	■	■	■	■
	xx-large			■	■	■	P	■	■	■	■
font	<font-style>	All	Yes	■	■	■	■	■	■	■	■
	<font-variant>			○	■	■	P	■	■	■	■
	<font-weight>			■	■	■	■	■	■	■	■
	<font-size>/<lineheight>			■	■	■	P	■	■	■	■
	<font-family>			■	■	■	■	■	■	■	■

Requires the visitor's computer to have display-weighted fonts available

Table A.4

Text Controls

Name	Value	Applies to	Inherited	N4	N6	N7	IE4	IE5	IE6	S1	O7
color	<color>	All	Yes	■	■	■	■	■	■	■	■
word-spacing	**normal**	All	Yes	○	■	■	M	M	■	■	■
	<length>			○	■	■	M	M	■	■	■
letter-spacing	**normal**	All	Yes	○	■	■	■	■	■	■	■
	<length>			○	■	■	■	■	■	■	■
vertical-align	**baseline**	Inline	No	○	■	■	■	■	■	■	■
	<percentage>			○	■	■	○	M	■	■	P
	sub			○	■	■	■	■	■	■	■
	super			○	■	■	■	■	■	■	■
	top			○	■	■	○	M**	■	■	■
	text-top			○	■	■	○	M**	■	■	■
	middle			○	■	■	○	M**	■	■	■
	bottom			○	■	■	○	M**	■	■	■
	text-bottom			○	■	■	○	M**	■	■	■
line-height	**normal**	All	Yes	■	■	■	■	■	■	■	■
	<number>			■	■	■	■	■	■	■	■
	<length>			P	■	■	■	■	■	■	■
	<percentage>			P	■	■	■	■	■	■	■
text-decoration	**none**	All	No	■	■	■	■	■	■	■	■
	underline			■	■	■	■	■	■	■	■
	overline			○	■	■	■	■	■	■	■
	line-through			■	■	■	■	■	■	■	■
	blink***			■	■	■	○	○	○	○	■
text-transform	**none**	All	Yes	■	■	■	■	■	■	■	■
	capitalize			P	■	■	■	■	■	■	■
	uppercase			■	■	■	■	■	■	■	■
	lowercase			■	■	■	■	■	■	■	■
text-align	**left**	Block	Yes	■	■	■	■	■	■	■	■
	right			■	■	■	■	■	■	■	■
	center			■	■	■	■	■	■	■	■
	justify			P	■	■	W	■	■	■	■
text-indent	<length>	Block	Yes	■	■	■	■	■	■	■	■
	<percentage>			■	■	■	■	■	■	■	■
direction	**rtl**	All	Yes	○	■	■	○	W	■	■	○
	ltr			○	■	■	○	W	■	■	○
unicode-bidi	bidi-override	All	Yes	○	■	■	○	W	■	■	○
	embed			○	■	■	○	W	■	■	○
	normal			○	■	■	○	W	■	■	○
page-break-before, page-break-after	always	All	No	○	○	■	■	■	■	■	■
	auto										
white-space	**normal**	Block	Yes	■	■	■	○	■**	■	■	■
	pre			■	■	■	○	■	■	■	■
	nowrap			○	■	■	○	■**	■	■	P

*** IE5.5 for Windows*
*** Because it can be highly annoying, many browsers do not support blink, or allow users to turn it off.*

Table A.5

Element Controls											
Name	**Value**	**Applies to**	**Inherited**	N4	N6	N7	IE4	IE5	IE6	S1	O7
margin-top, -right, -bottom, -left	<length>	All	No	P	■	■	P	■	■	■	■
	<percentage>			P	■	■	P	■	■	■	■
	auto			P	■	■	P	■	■	■	■
margin	<length>	All	No	■	■	■	○	■	■	■	■
	<percentage>			■	■	■	○	■	■	■	■
	auto			○	■	■	○	■*	■	■	■
padding-top, -right, -bottom, -left	<length>	All	No	P	■	■	P	■	■	■	■
	<percentage>			P	■	■	P	■	■	■	■
padding	<length>	All	No	P	■	■	P	■	■	■	■
	<percentage>			P	■	■	P	■	■	■	■
border-color	<color>	All	No	P	■	■	■	■	■	■	■
	transparent			P	■	■	■	■	■	■	■
	inherit			P	■	■	■	■	■	■	■
border-style	**none**	All	No	■	■	■	■	■	■	■	■
	dotted			○	■	■	M	■*	■	■	■
	dashed			○	■	■	M	■*	■	■	■
	solid			■	■	■	■	■	■	■	■
	double			■	■	■	■	■	■	■	■
	groove			■	■	■	■	■	■	■	■
	ridge			■	■	■	■	■	■	■	■
	inset			■	■	■	■	■	■	■	■
	outset			■	■	■	■	■	■	■	■
border-top, -right, -bottom, left-width	medium	All	No	■	■	■	P	■	■	■	■
	<length>			■	■	■	P	■	■	■	■
	thin			■	■	■	P	■	■	■	■
	thick			■	■	■	P	■	■	■	■
border-width	medium	All	No	■	■	■	P	■	■	■	■
	<length>			■	■	■	P	■	■	■	■
	thin			■	■	■	P	■	■	■	■
	thick			■	■	■	P	■	■	■	■
border-top, -right, -bottom, -left	<border-width>	All	No	○	■	■	P	■	■	■	■
	<border-style>			○	■	■	P	■	■	■	■
	<color>			○	■	■	P	■	■	■	■
border	<border-width>	All	No	P	■	■	P	■	■	■	■
	<border-style>			P	■	■	P	■	■	■	■
	<color>			■	■	■	P	■	■	■	■
-moz-border-radius, -bottomleft, -bottomright, -topleft, -topright,	<length>	Block	No	○	■	■	○	○	○	○	○
	<percentage>			○	■	■	○	○	○	○	○
width	**auto**	Block	No	P	■	■	P	■	■	■	■
	<length>			P	■	■	P	■	■	■	■
	<percentage>			P	■	■	P	■	■	■	■

(table continues on next page)

Table A.5 *continued*

Element Controls

Name	Value	Applies to	Inherited	N4	N6	N7	IE4	IE5	IE6	S1	O7
height	**auto**	Block	No	○	■	■	P	■	■	■	■
	<length>			○	■	■	P	■	■	■	■
max-width, min-width, max-height, max-width	<length>	All	No	○	■	■	○	○	○	■	■
	<percentage>			○	■	■	○	○	○	■	■
	auto			○	■	■	○	○	○	■	■
float	**none**	All	No	■	■	■	■	■	■	■	■
	left			P	■	■	P	■	■	■	■
	right			P	■	■	P	■	■	■	■
clear	**none**	All	No	■	■	■	■	■	■	■	■
	left			P	■	■	M	■	■	■	■
	right			P	■	■	M	■	■	■	■
	both			■	■	■	■	■	■	■	■
display	block	All	No	P	■	■	■	■	■	■	■
	inline			○	■	■	W	■	■	■	■
	list-item			P	■	■	M	M	■	■	■
	table			○	■	■	○	M	○	■	■
	table-cell			○	■	■	○	M	○	■	■
	table-footer-group			○	■	■	○	M	○	■	■
	table-row			○	■	■	○	M	○	■	■
	table-row-group			○	■	■	○	M	○	■	■
	none			■	■	■	■	■	■	■	■
background-color	<color>	All	No	■	■	■	■	■	■	■	■
	transparent			■	■	■	■	■	■	■	■
background-image	**none**	All	No	■	■	■	■	■	■	■	■
	url(<url>)			■	■	■	■	■	■	■	■
background-repeat	**repeat**	All	No	■	■	■	■	■	■	■	■
	repeat-x			P	■	■	■	■	■	■	■
	repeat-y			P	■	■	■	■	■	■	■
	no-repeat			■	■	■	■	■	■	■	■
background-attachment	**scroll**	All	No	○	■	■	■	■	■	■	■
	fixed			○	■	■	■	■	■	■	■
background-position	<percentage>	Block	No	○	P	P	P	■	■	■	■
	<length>			○	■	■	■	■	■	■	■
	top			○	P	P	■	■	■	■	■
	center (vertical)			○	P	P	■	■	■	■	■
	bottom			○	P	P	■	■	■	■	■
	left			○	P	P	■	■	■	■	■
	center (horizontal)			○	P	P	■	■	■	■	■
	right			○	P	P	■	■	■	■	■
background	<background-color>	All	No	■	■	■	■	■	■	■	■
	<background-image>			■	■	■	■	■	■	■	■
	<background-repeat>			■	■	■	■	■	■	■	■
	<background-attachment>			○	■	■	■	■	■	■	■
	<background-position>			○	■	■	■	■	■	■	■

*IE5.5 for Windows

Table A.6

Element Positioning Controls

NAME	VALUE	APPLIES TO	INHERITED	N4	N6	N7	IE4	IE5	IE6	S1	O7
position	**static**	All	No	■	■	■	■	■	■	■	■
	absolute			■	■	■	■	■	■	■	■
	relative			■	■	■	■	■	■	■	■
	fixed			○	○	■	○	M	○	■	■
left	**auto**	All**	No	■	■	■	■	■	■	■	■
	<length>			■	■	■	■	■	■	■	■
	<percentage>			■	■	■	■	■	■	■	■
top	**auto**	All**	No	■	■	■	■	■	■	■	■
	<length>			■	■	■	■	■	■	■	■
	<percentage>			■	■	■	■	■	■	■	■
bottom	**auto**	All**	No	○	■	■	○	■	■	■	■
	<length>			○	■	■	○	■	■	■	■
	<percentage>			○	■	■	○	■	■	■	■
right	**auto**	All**	No	○	■	■	○	■	■	■	■
	<length>			○	■	■	○	■	■	■	■
	<percentage>			○	■	■	○	■	■	■	■
z-index	**auto**	All	No	■	■	■	■	■	■	■	■
	number			■	■	■	■	■	■	■	■

** *The* position *property for the element must also be set to* absolute *or* relative.

Table A.7

Element Visibility Controls

NAME	VALUE	APPLIES TO	INHERITED	N4	N6	N7	IE4	IE5	IE6	S1	O7
clip	**auto**	All*	No	■	■	■	○	■	■	■	■
	<shape>			■	■	■	○	■	■	■	■
overflow	visible	All*	No	■	■	■	○	■	■	■	■
	hidden			■	■	■	○	■	■	■	■
	scroll			■	■	■	○	■	■	■	■
	auto			■	■	■	○	■	■	■	■
visibility	**inherit**	All	Yes**	■	■	■	■	■	■	■	■
	visible			■	■	■	■	■	■	■	■
	hidden			■	■	■	■	■	■	■	■
	hide			■	○	○	○	○	○	○	○
	show			■	○	○	○	○	○	○	○
-moz--opacity	<0.0ñ1.0>			○	■	■	○	○	○	○	○

* *The* position *property for the element must also be set to* absolute *or* relative.
** *If* visibility *is set to* inherit.

Table A.8

List, Table, and Interface Controls

Name	Value	Applies to	Inherited	N4	N6	N7	IE4	IE5	IE6	S1	O7
list-style-type	disc	All*	Yes	■	■	■	■	■	■	■	■
	circle			■	■	■	■	■	■	■	■
	square			■	■	■	■	■	■	■	■
	decimal			■	■	■	■	■	■	■	■
	lower-roman			■	■	■	■	■	■	■	■
	upper-roman			■	■	■	■	■	■	■	■
	lower-alpha			■	■	■	■	■	■	■	■
	upper-alpha			■	■	■	■	■	■	■	■
	none			■	■	■	■	■	■	■	■
list-style-image	**none**	All*	Yes	○	■	■	■	■	■	■	■
	url(<url>)			○	■	■	■	■	■	■	■
list-style-position	**outside**	All*	Yes	○	■	■	■	■	■	■	■
	inside			○	■	■	■	■	■	■	■
list-style	<list-style-type>	All*	Yes	■	■	■	■	■	■	■	■
	<list-style-position>			■	■	■	■	■	■	■	■
	<list-style-image>			○	■	■	■	■	■	■	■
border-collapse	collapse	All*	No	○	○	■	○	M***	■	■	■
	separate			○	○	■	○	M***	■	■	■
caption-side	**top**	Table	No	○	■	■	○	M	M	■	■
	left			○	○	○	○	○	○	○	○
	bottom			○	■	■	○	M	M	■	■
	right			○	○	○	○	○	○	○	○
cursor	**auto**	All	Yes	○	■	■	■	M***	■	■	■
	crosshair			○	■	■	■	M***	■	■	■
	hand**			○	○	○	■	M***	■	○	○
	pointer			○	■	■	■	M***	■	■	■
	move			○	■	■	■	M***	■	■	■
	n-resize			○	■	■	■	M***	■	■	■
	ne-resize			○	■	■	■	M***	■	■	■
	e-resize			○	■	■	■	M***	■	■	■
	se-resize			○	■	■	■	M***	■	■	■
	s-resize			○	■	■	■	M***	■	■	■
	sw-resize			○	■	■	■	M***	■	■	■
	w-resize			○	■	■	■	M***	■	■	■
	nw-resize			○	■	■	■	M***	■	■	■
	text			○	■	■	■	M***	■	■	■
	wait			○	■	■	■	M***	■	■	■
	help			○	■	■	■	M***	■	■	■

* In Netscape 4 & 6 and IE 4 & 5, applies only to the <list> tag. In standard CSS, these properties can be applied only to tags that include display: list-item; in the definition.
** IE only. Same as pointer. *** IE 5.5 for Windows

DHTML QUICK REFERENCE

Chapters 10–13 present in detail how to find information about the different parts of your Web environment. The tables in this appendix present that information in a form that you can read quickly. If there is more than one method to find a particular property, the preferred method will be **bold**.

In addition, this appendix includes a list of reserved words and other words that you should avoid using for ID names, class names, or JavaScript variables.

- **Table B.1:** Common Event Handlers (Chapter 10)

- **Table B.2**: Finding Objects (Chapter 10)

- **Table B.3:** System Properties (Chapter 11)

- **Table B.4:** Browser Properties (Chapter 11)

- **Table B.5:** Page Properties (Chapter 11)

- **Table B.6:** Object Properties (Chapter 12)

- **Table B.7:** Event Properties (Chapter 13)

Table B.1

Common Event Handlers

NAME	WHEN IT HAPPENS	APPLIES TO
onload	After an object is loaded	Documents and images
onunload	After the object is no longer loaded	Documents and images
onfocus	When an element is selected	Documents and forms
onblur	When an element is deselected	Documents and forms
onmouseover	When the mouse pointer passes over an area	All*
onmouseout	When the mouse pointer passes out of an area	All*
onclick	When the mouse button is clicked over an area	All*
onmousedown	While the mouse button is pressed	All*
onmouseup	When the mouse button is released	All*
onmousemove	As the mouse is moved	Document
onkeydown	While a keyboard key is pressed	Forms and document
onkeyup	When a keyboard key is released	Forms and document
onkeypress	When a keyboard key is pressed and immediately released	Forms and document
onresize**	When the browser window or a frame is resized	Document
onmove	When the browser window is moved	Document

Available only for anchor links and images in Netscape 4
**Not supported by Internet Explorer 4*

Table B.2

Finding Objects

TO FIND	METHOD	COMPATIBILITY
Object	document.getElementById(objectID)	IE4, N6, S1, O5
	document.all[*objectID*]	IE4, O5
	document.layers[objectID]	N4 (Only)

Table B.3

System Properties

TO FIND	METHOD	VALUE TYPE	COMPATIBILITY
Operating system	navigator.appVersion	<string>	IE3, N2, S1, O5
Screen width (total)	screen.width	<pixels>	IE4, N4, S1, O5
Screen height (total)	screen.height	< pixels>	IE4, N4, S1, O5
Screen width (live)	screen.availWidth	< pixels>	IE4, N4, S1, O5
Screen height (live)	screen.availHeight	< pixels>	IE4, N4, S1, O5
Number of colors	screen.colorDepth	<number>	IE4, N4, S1, O5

Table B.4

Browser Properties

To Find	Method	Value Type	Compatibility
Browser name	navigator.appName	<string>	IE3, N2, S1, O5
Browser version	parseInt(navigator.appVersion)	<number>	IE3, N2, S1, O5
Browser window width	window.outerWidth	<pixels>	N4, S1, O5
Browser window height	window.outerHeight	<pixels>	N4, S1, O5

Table B.5

Page Properties

To Find	Method	Value Type	Compatibility
URL	self.location	<string>	IE3, N2, S1, O5
Title	document.title	<string>	IE3, N2*, S1, O5
Visible width	window.innerWidth	<pixels>	N4, S1, O5
	document.body.clientWidth	<pixels>	IE4, N7, S1, O5
Visible weight	window.innerHeight	<pixels>	N4, S1, O5
	document.body.clientHeight	<pixels>	IE4, N7, S1, O5
Scroll position left	window.pageXOffset	<pixels>	N4, S1, O5
	document.body.scrollLeft	<pixels>	IE4, N7, S1, O5
Scroll position top	window.pageYOffset	<pixels>	N4, S1, O5
	document.body.scrollTop	<pixels>	IE4, N7, S1, O5

Buggy in Mac version of Netscape 4; returns file name instead of title.

Table B.6

Object Properties

To Find	Method	Value Type	Compatibility
Object ID	evt.target.id	<string>	N4, S1, O5
	evt.srcElement.id	<string>	IE4, O5
Width	**offsetWidth**	<length>	IE4, N6, S1, O5
	style.width*	<length>	IE4, N4, S1, O5
Height	**offsetHeight**	<length>	IE4, N6, S1, O5
	style.height*	<length>	IE4, N4, S1, O5
Left position	**offsetLeft**	<length>	N6, S1, O5
	pixelLeft	<length>	IE4, N6, S1, O5
	style.left*	<length>	IE4, N4, S1, O5
Top position	**offsetTop**	<length>	N6, S1, O5
	pixelTop	<length>	IE4, N6, S1, O5
	style.top*	<length>	IE4, N4, S1, O5
Z-index	style.zIndex*	<number>	IE4, N4, S1, O5
Visibility	style.visibility*	visible	IE4, N4, S1, O5
		hidden	IE4, N4, S1, O5
		show	N4 (only)
		hide	N4 (only)
Clip area	**style.clip[]****	<array>	IE4, N6, S1, O5
	style.clipBottom	<length>	IE4 (Win)
	style.clipLeft	<length>	IE4 (Win)
	style.clipRight	<length>	IE4 (Win)
	style.clipTop	<length>	IE4 (Win)

Requires that value be set using JavaScript before it can be read.
** The most reliable way to find the clip area is by querying the clip array as discussed in "Detrmining an Object's Visible Area" in Chapter 12.

Table B.7

Event Properties

To Find	Method	Value Type	Compatibility
Event type	evt.type	<string>	IE4, N4, S1, O5
Key pressed	evt.charCode	<number>	N4
	evt.keyCode	<number>	IE4, N6
Shift key	evt.shiftKey	<boolean>	IE4, N6, O5, S1
Control key	evt.ctrlKey	<boolean>	IE4, N6, O5, S1
Alt/Option key	evt.altKey	<boolean>	IE4, N6, O5, S1
Command key	evt.metaKey	<boolean>	N6
Mouse button pressed	evt.button	<string>	IE4, N6, S1, O5
Left mouse position (screen)	evt.screenX	<length>	IE4, N4, S1, O5
Top mouse position (screen)	evt.screenY	<length>	IE4, N4, S1, O5
Left mouse position (window)	evt.clientX	<length>	IE4, N6, S1, O5
Left mouse position (screen)	evt.clientY	<length>	IE4, N6, S1, O5

Reserved Words

When you are creating names for a CSS class, CSS ID, or JavaScript variable, keep in mind that the browser has dibs on certain words. I recommend not using these.

That said, it's OK to combine different words to form compound words, even if both words are on the reserved list. For example, although `new` and `label` would not make good variable names, `newLabel` would be fine.

JavaScript and Java reserved words

The following words are part of the JavaScript or Java language and should be avoided at all costs:

abstract	false	private
boolean	final	protected
break	finally	public
byte	float	return
case	for	short
catch	function	static
char	goto	super
class	if	switch
comment	implements	synchronized
const	import	this
continue	in	throw
debugger	instanceOf	throws
default	int	transient
delete	interface	true
do	label	try
double	long	typeof
else	native	var
enum	new	void
export	null	while
extends	package	with

Other words to avoid

Although not officially on the reserved list, these words are used by JavaScript and will cause problems if you use them.

Remember that Netscape is case-sensitive, so capital letters make a difference. For example, history is not the same as History.

alert	event	length	outerHeight	Select
Anchor	evt	Link	outerWidth	self
Area	FileUpload	location	Packages	setInterval
arguments	find	Location	pageXoffset	setTimeout
Array	focus	locationbar	pageYoffset	status
assign	Form	Math	parent	statusbar
blur	Frame	menubar	parseFloat	stop
Boolean	frames	MimeType	parseInt	String
Button	Function	moveBy	Password	Submit
callee	getClass	moveTo	personalbar	sun
caller	Hidden	name	Plugin	taint
captureEvents	hide	NaN	print	Text
Checkbox	history	navigate	prompt	Textarea
clearInterval	History	navigator	prototype	toolbar
clearTimeout	home	Navigator	Radio	top
close	Image	netscape	ref	toString
closed	Infinity	Number	RegExp	unescape
confirm	innerHeight	Object	releaseEvents	untaint
constructor	innerWidth	onblur	Reset	unwatch
Date	isFinite	onerror	resizeBy	valueOf
defaultStatus	isNaN	onfocus	resizeTo	watch
document	java	onload	routeEvent	window
Document	JavaArray	onunload	scroll	Window
Element	JavaClass	open	scrollBars	
escape	JavaObject	opener	scrollBy	
eval	JavaPackage	Option	scrollTo	

RESERVED WORDS

THE DHTML AND CSS BROWSERS

The browser wars are over. That is, most everyone cruising the Web is using either Microsoft Internet Explorer 5.5 or 6. So we can all just code for Internet Explorer, right? No. There are still a significant number of browsers that are not coming from Microsoft. The good news is that, due to the convergence of standards and the dominance of a single browser, it is getting easier to code once and use it everywhere. Still, it's important that you understand not only the different browsers that your viewing audience might be using to visit your Web site, but also all of the different standards out there for you to contend with.

In this appendix you'll find a brief overview of the main Web standards and how they fit with the top browsers.

The Browser Standards

For a browser to be considered DHTML- and CSS-capable, it must support the following technologies to some degree. The browsers discussed in this appendix all meet (or exceed) these criteria.

HTML/XHTML

HTML is the foundation of all DHTML. The most recent version of the Hypertext Markup Language is version 4.01, but the W3C has "recast" this workhorse of Web design as XHTML, combining it with XML. The "4" browsers were created long before XHTML, but most modern browsers support XHTML, while remaining backward-compatible with HTML.

JavaScript

If HTML is the foundation, JavaScript is the keystone of DHTML. However, JavaScript goes by many names.

◆ **JavaScript 1.5:** The Netscape/Mozilla flavor, originally created by Netscape. The first DHTML browsers used version 1.2, but modern DHTML browsers use version 1.5.

◆ **JScript 5:** The Microsoft flavor of JavaScript. Although extremely similar to JavaScript, JScript has slightly different syntax for some methods. DHTML browsers first used JScript 3, but are currently using JScript 5.

◆ **ECMAScript 262:** ECMAScript is the official standardized version of JavaScript, used by Safari and Opera.

Although they're roughly equivalent, there are important differences that are noted throughout this book and in Appendix B.

CSS

Cascading Style Sheets provide the form for HTML's structure. CSS has evolved over the years.

◆ **CSS Level 1:** CSS1 provided much-needed style controls for Web layout, as well as the ability to define elements as objects on the screen.

◆ **CSS Positioning:** CSS-P introduced the ability to move and change objects, however, the browser must support the positioning controls in the early CSS-P standard—which was later integrated into CSS Level 2.

◆ **CSS Level 2:** CSS2 combines and expands on the abilities of CSS1 and CSS-P. Most modern browsers support CSS2.

The W3C released a slight revision to the Level 2 standard (2.1), which corrects some errors and adds some of the most popular features that will eventually find their way into the long-delayed Level 3 specification. However, since browsers can take years to update, don't expect to see any of these changes implemented anytime soon.

DOM

The browser must use some form of the Document Object Model in order to locate and change objects rendered by the browser. Modern browsers all use the W3C standard DOM, but older versions of Netscape and Internet Explorer used their own proprietary DOMs.

- **W3C DOM 1 or 2** standardizes the object model for Web pages, allowing Web designers (for the most part) to code once for dynamic scripts. However, differences in the type of JavaScript used by the browser may require differences in syntax. The W3C DOM is currently at Level 2, but most browsers still only support Level 1, while a few are already looking to the forthcoming Level 3, still only in the proposal stage.

- **All DOM** was introduced in Internet Explorer 4, and although it is still available in Internet Explorer 5 and 6, it's generally not used, in favor of the W3C DOM.

- **Layers DOM** was only ever available in Netscape 4, and was replaced by the W3C DOM in later browser versions.

Table C.1

Internet Explorer 4 Specs	
TECHNOLOGY	VERSION
HTML	HTML 4
JavaScript	JScript 3
CSS	CSS1, CSS-P
DOM	All DOM

Table C.2

Internet Explorer 5 & 6 (Win) Specs	
TECHNOLOGY	VERSION
HTML	HTML 4 (partial), XHTML 1 (partial)
JavaScript	JScript 5
CSS	CSS1 (partial), CSS2 (partial)
DOM	W3C DOM 1 (partial), All DOM

Internet Explorer for Windows and the Web Standards Project

There is little doubt that Internet Explorer 6 is a huge step forward in standards compliance, especially when compared with version 4. But even Internet Explorer 6's implementations of CSS and the DOM are far from complete.

By integrating the browser further into the operating system, Microsoft managed to increase the divide between users of the Windows version of Internet Explorer and users of all other browsers, even Internet Explorer 5 for the Mac (discussed later in this appendix). In fact, Microsoft has only backhandedly implemented some of the most important standards, such as the W3C DOM and HTML 4, and has already drawn the ire of many developers, including the Web Standards Project (www.webstandards.org/wfw/ieah.html).

Internet Explorer

www.microsoft.com

Microsoft's Internet Explorer has become the dominant browser on the Web, garnering the lion's share of Web traffic around the world. Although I recommend creating Web sites that are compatible across browsers and are as standards-compliant as possible, most of the people viewing your Web site are likely to be using some version of Internet Explorer.

Internet Explorer 4

Internet Explorer 4 has almost all but disappeared, as most private and business users have upgraded to the more standards-compliant Internet Explorer 5.5 and 6. Version 4 was Microsoft's first serious contender as a Web browser, and despite the legal debates about its integration in the Windows operating system, Internet Explorer is the browser that began to turn the tide on the once-dominant Netscape browser.

Internet Explorer 4 adopted many of the W3C's standards. Although it wasn't perfect, it was the first browser to build its DHTML capabilities around those standards.

Internet Explorer 5 & 6 (Windows)

Internet Explorer has now been strategically integrated into the Windows operating system and dominates the Web-browser market. It's estimated that as much as 85 percent of the browsing market uses it and it has been widely adopted by the corporate world.

Internet Explorer 6 will be the last major upgrade to the browser until at least 2006 when the new Microsoft Windows operating system is released (code-named "Longhorn"), so we're stuck designing to these limitations until then.

INTERNET EXPLORER

Internet Explorer 5 (Mac)

www.microsoft.com/mac

Aside from the fact that they were both made by Microsoft, the Mac and Windows versions of Internet Explorer 5 have only two things in common: They are both Web browsers, and they are both called Microsoft Internet Explorer 5. Beyond that, Internet Explorer 5 for the Mac is as different from the Windows version as the Mac OS is from Windows.

Although it was the most popular browser on the Mac for several years, Microsoft decided in early 2003 to stop development in deference to the new Safari browser created by Apple. Although Safari will be the default browser for all newer Macs, Internet Explorer will still hold on in the Mac market for a while as older machines are gradually phased out.

Table C.3

Internet Explorer 5 (Mac) Specs

TECHNOLOGY	VERSION
HTML	HTML 4, XHTML 1
JavaScript	JScript 5
CSS	CSS1, CSS2 (partial)
DOM	W3C DOM 1, All DOM

Table C.4

Netscape 4 Specs	
TECHNOLOGY	VERSION
HTML	HTML 4
JavaScript	JavaScript 1.2 (4.0–4.05), JavaScript 1.3 (4.06+)
CSS	CSS1 (partial), CSS-P (partial)
DOM	Layers DOM

Netscape and Mozilla

http://channels.netscape.com/ns/browsers

Netscape (the company) has undergone significant changes in the last several years, as it has moved from producing the premier Web browser to being a portal service, and now an Internet service provider. With Netscape 6, the Netscape browser itself is no longer developed by Netscape, but by the Mozilla organization. Both Netscape and Mozilla share the same core technology, called "Gecko," to create their Web pages. In theory, this means that all browsers using Gecko (Netscape 6+, Mozilla, Firebird, and Camino) should render Web pages more or less alike.

Throughout this book I refer to Netscape 6+ or Mozilla-compatible browsers to mean roughly the same thing. If a particular attribute, value, or method works in Netscape 6, then you can assume it will work in any of the Mozilla-compatible browsers.

Netscape 4

Netscape 4 lasted for more than four years as Netscape's flagship Web product and became the workhorse browser for many Web designers, despite its shaky and incomplete support of Web standards. To be fair, however, many of the standards used today either did not exist or were in nascent form when Netscape 4 appeared on the scene.

Netscape 4 introduced its own flavor of DHTML that relied on the `<layer>` tag. This technique never caught on, though, and Netscape has since abandoned it in favor of the standards set forth by the W3C.

Netscape 4 is now all but gone from the World Wide Web, making up, at best, less than 1 percent of the market. Unless you know that your audience is likely to be using this browser I don't recommend coding for it any longer.

Netscape 6 & 7

Netscape 6 (yes, 6, not 5 which was never released to the public) was built around the Gecko rendering engine, which was created to comply with the latest Web standards. This news was welcome to the Web-development community, which had suffered for years trying to make incompatible browsers play nicely on Web sites.

Netscape 7 makes some speed and interface enhancements over the previous version and also adds greater compatibility with Internet Explorer.

Both versions include much more than a Web browser, adding features such as email, address book, HTML editor, and instant messaging.

Mozilla, Firebird, Camino

www.mozilla.org

Mozilla.org has created three different browsers based on the Gecko rendering engine.

◆ **Mozilla** (Mac/Win): Although similar to Netscape, the Mozilla interfaces are paired down. Mozilla includes all of the same features as Netscape, including email, chat, address book, and HTML editing tools.

◆ **Firebird** (Mac/Win): Unlike Mozilla, Firebird is just a browser. No bells and whistles. This makes it extremely fast and easy to use. Many Web designers rely on this as their primary browser.

◆ **Camino** (Mac): Like Firebird, Camino is just a basic browser, but it has been built specifically for the Mac OS X operating system, taking advantage of its GUI elements.

Table C.5

Netscape 6 & 7 Specs	
TECHNOLOGY	VERSION
HTML	HTML 4, XHTML 1
JavaScript	JavaScript 1.5, JScript 1.5 (partial)
CSS	CSS1, CSS2
DOM	W3C DOM 1

Table C.6

Mozilla Specs	
TECHNOLOGY	VERSION
HTML	HTML 4, XHTML 1
JavaScript	JavaScript 1.5
CSS	CSS1, CSS2
DOM	W3C DOM 1

Table C.7

Safari Specs	
TECHNOLOGY	VERSION
HTML	HTML 4, XHTML 1.0
JavaScript	ECMA Script 262
CSS	CSS1, CSS2 (partial)
DOM	W3C DOM 2, W3C DOM 3 (partial)

Safari (Mac)

www.apple.com/safari

Possibly realizing that it couldn't depend on Microsoft forever to deliver a Web browser for its operating system, Apple developed the Safari Web browser. Based on the open-source Konqueror browser, Safari was built specifically for Mac OS X and is rapidly becoming the browser of choice for Mac users.

Like Konqueror, Safari is extremely standards compliant. It is still being developed, though, and can be quirky at times, meaning that scripts that should work fine do not run at all.

Opera (Mac/Windows/Unix)

www.opera.com

Opera Software set out with a mission to create a completely standards-compliant browser. With Version 7 of the Opera browser, the company is closer than ever to hitting the moving target of Web standards. Although the browser is not perfect, Opera considers W3C standards as being not just a good idea, but the law.

It started as a Windows-only browser, but Opera has added several other platforms including EPOC, Linux, and Mac. Currently, The Mac version is 6 while the Windows version is 7, however, both versions work very much the same.

In addition to computer-based browsers, Opera is increasingly popular for Web delivery on other platforms, such as PDAs and mobile phones.

Table C.8

Opera Specs	
TECHNOLOGY	VERSION
HTML	HTML 4, XHTML
JavaScript	ECMA Script 262
CSS	CSS1, CSS2
DOM	W3C DOM 2

OPERA (MAC/WINDOWS/UNIX)

Table C.9

OmniWeb Specs	
TECHNOLOGY	VERSION
HTML	HTML 4, XHTML 1
JavaScript	ECMA Script 262
CSS	CSS1, CSS2 (partial)
DOM	W3C DOM 2, W3C DOM 3 (partial)

Table C.10

Konqueror Specs	
TECHNOLOGY	VERSION
HTML	HTML 4, XHTML 1
JavaScript	ECMA Script 262
CSS	CSS1, CSS2 (partial)
DOM	W3C DOM 2, W3C DOM 3 (partial)

Other Browsers

The browser wars may be over, but that doesn't stop developers from coming out with new and better browsers. Nowhere is this more apparent than in the alternative browsers being created by the open-source community and for the Mac.

OmniWeb (Mac)

www.omnigroup.com/applications/omniweb

OmniGroup is renowned in the Mac community for its excellent OS X software. The Web browser it developed, one of the first available for Mac OS X, is no exception. Although OmniWeb had some initial difficulties rendering DHTML in earlier versions, it has come a long way and now takes advantage of OS X's built-in Web capabilities, making it extremely standards compliant.

Konqueror (Open Source)

www.konqueror.org

Konqueror is not only an open-source browser, it also works as a file manager and viewing application. Although not a browser likely to be used by the general public because Safari is based on Konqueror, its development bears close watching.

iCab (Mac)

www.icab.de

iCab is small—a mere 900 KB download. It is fast, with pages seeming to appear as soon as you click a link. It adheres to the standards, following the W3C's recommendations to the letter. It does everything that a Web surfer needs it to do.

OTHER BROWSERS

BROWSER-SAFE FONTS

You can use the font-family attributes to specify the font(s) to be used with your Web page:

```
font-family: times, "times new roman",
→ serif;
```

Of course the fonts you can use are directly dependent on the fonts that are available on the visitor's machine. If they do not have the font installed, then the visitor will not see the design exactly as you intended it. To keep their designs as consistent as possible, many Web designers stick to using Times for their serif font, Arial/Helvetica for their sans-serif fonts, and Courier for their monospace font. Most machines are preinstalled with dozens of fonts, the trick is knowing which fonts are likely to be installed on which computers.

The following tables present the fonts that are preinstalled on Windows and Macintosh computers as they come out of the box, as well as the list of the Microsoft Core Web fonts which are installed by Internet Explorer. The list also includes the styles (bold, bold italic, or italic) that are available for the fonts, the generic family the font belongs to, and an example of the font.

continues on next page

To use these fonts, either pick a font available for both Mac and Windows, or choose similar fonts and list both of them in the font list. Remember that multi-word font names should be in quotes (example: "Andale Mono").

If you want a PDF version of this appendix to print out for quick-reference, visit the support Web site:

www.webbedenvironments.com/dhtml

Table D.1

Microsoft Core Web Fonts

NAME	WEIGHTS & STYLES	GENERIC FAMILY	EXAMPLE
Adobe Minion Web		Sans-serif	ABCDEFGHIJKLMNOPQRSTUVWXYZ abcdefghijklmnopqrstuvwxyz 1234567890
Andale Mono*		Monospace	ABCDEFGHIJKLMNOPQRSTUVWXYZ abcdefghijklmnopqrstuvwxyz 1234567890
Arial	bold, italic, bold italic	Sans-serif	ABCDEFGHIJKLMNOPQRSTUVWXYZ abcdefghijklmnopqrstuvwxyz 1234567890
Arial Black		sans-serif	**ABCDEFGHIJKLMNOPQRSTUVWXYZ abcdefghijklmnopqrstuvwxyz 1234567890**
Comic Sans MS	bold	Cursive	ABCDEFGHIJKLMNOPQRSTUVWXYZ abcdefghijklmnopqrstuvwxyz 1234567890
Courier New	bold, italic, bold italic	Monospace	ABCDEFGHIJKLMNOPQRSTUVWXYZ abcdefghijklmnopqrstuvwxyz 1234567890
Georgia	bold, italic, bold italic	Serif	ABCDEFGHIJKLMNOPQRSTUVWXYZ abcdefghijklmnopqrstuvwxyz 1234567890
Impact		sans-serif	**ABCDEFGHIJKLMNOPQRSTUVWXYZ abcdefghijklmnopqrstuvwxyz 1234567890**
Times New Roman	bold, italic, bold italic	Serif	ABCDEFGHIJKLMNOPQRSTUVWXYZ abcdefghijklmnopqrstuvwxyz 1234567890
Trebuchet MS*	bold, italic, bold italic	sans-serif	ABCDEFGHIJKLMNOPQRSTUVWXYZ abcdefghijklmnopqrstuvwxyz 1234567890
Verdana	bold, italic, bold italic	sans-serif	ABCDEFGHIJKLMNOPQRSTUVWXYZ abcdefghijklmnopqrstuvwxyz 1234567890
Webdings		Fantasy	

* Previously named Monotype.com

Table D.2

Mac OS			
NAME	WEIGHTS & STYLES	GENERIC FAMILY	EXAMPLE
American Typewriter*	bold	Monospace	ABCDEFGHIJKLMNOPQRSTUVWXYZ abcdefghijklmnopqrstuvwxyz 1234567890
Andale Mono**		Monospace	ABCDEFGHIJKLMNOPQRSTUVWXYZ abcdefghijklmnopqrstuvwxyz 1234567890
Apple Chancery		Cursive	ABCDEFGHIJKLMNOPQRSTUVWXYZ abcdefghijklmnopqrstuvwxyz 1234567890
Apple Symbols*		Fantasy	ABΧΔΕΦΓΗΙϑΚΛΜΝΟΠΘΡΣΤΥςΩΞΨΖ αβχδεφγηιφκλμνοπθρστυϖωξψζ 1234567890
Arial	bold, italic, bold italic	Sans-serif	ABCDEFGHIJKLMNOPQRSTUVWXYZ abcdefghijklmnopqrstuvwxyz 1234567890
Arial Black		Sans-serif	**ABCDEFGHIJKLMNOPQRSTUVWXYZ abcdefghijklmnopqrstuvwxyz 1234567890**
Arial Narrow*	bold, italic, bold italic	Sans-serif	ABCDEFGHIJKLMNOPQRSTUVWXYZ abcdefghijklmnopqrstuvwxyz 1234567890
Arial Rounded MT Bold*		Sans-serif	**ABCDEFGHIJKLMNOPQRSTUVWXYZ abcdefghijklmnopqrstuvwxyz 1234567890**
Baskerville*	bold, italic, bold italic	Serif	ABCDEFGHIJKLMNOPQRSTUVWXYZ abcdefghijklmnopqrstuvwxyz 1234567890
Big Caslon*		Serif	ABCDEFGHIJKLMNOPQRSTUVWXYZ abcdefghijklmnopqrstuvwxyz 1234567890
Brush Script MT*		Cursive	ABCDEFGHIJKLMNOPQRSTUVWXYZ abcdefghijklmnopqrstuvwxyz 1234567890
Capitals**		Sans-serif	ABCDEFGHIJKLMNOPQRSTUVWXYZ ABCDEFGHIJKLMNOPQRSTUVWXYZ 1234567890
Charcoal**		Sans-serif	**ABCDEFGHIJKLMNOPQRSTUVWXYZ abcdefghijklmnopqrstuvwxyz 1234567890**
Chicago**		Sans-serif	ABCDEFGHIJKLMNOPQRSTUVWXYZ abcdefghijklmnopqrstuvwxyz 1234567890
Cochin*	bold, italic, bold italic	Serif	ABCDEFGHIJKLMNOPQRSTUVWXYZ abcdefghijklmnopqrstuvwxyz 1234567890
Comic Sans MS	bold	Cursive	ABCDEFGHIJKLMNOPQRSTUVWXYZ abcdefghijklmnopqrstuvwxyz 1234567890
Copperplate*	bold	Sans-serif	ABCDEFGHIJKLMNOPQRSTUVWXYZ ABCDEFGHIJKLMNOPQRSTUVWXYZ 1234567890
Courier**	bold, oblique, bold oblique	Monospace	ABCDEFGHIJKLMNOPQRSTUVWXYZ abcdefghijklmnopqrstuvwxyz 1234567890
Courier New	bold, italic, bold italic	Monospace	ABCDEFGHIJKLMNOPQRSTUVWXYZ abcdefghijklmnopqrstuvwxyz 1234567890
Didot*	bold, italic	Sans-serif	ABCDEFGHIJKLMNOPQRSTUVWXYZ abcdefghijklmnopqrstuvwxyz 1234567890
Futura*	Sans-serif	Serif	ABCDEFGHIJKLMNOPQRSTUVWXYZ abcdefghijklmnopqrstuvwxyz 1234567890
Gadget**		Sans-serif	**ABCDEFGHIJKLMNOPQRSTUVWXYZ abcdefghijklmnopqrstuvwxyz 1234567890**
Geneva		Sans-serif	ABCDEFGHIJKLMNOPQRSTUVWXYZ abcdefghijklmnopqrstuvwxyz 1234567890
Georgia	bold, italic, bold italic	Serif	ABCDEFGHIJKLMNOPQRSTUVWXYZ abcdefghijklmnopqrstuvwxyz 1234567890
Gill Sans*	bold, italic, bold italic	Sans-serif	ABCDEFGHIJKLMNOPQRSTUVWXYZ abcdefghijklmnopqrstuvwxyz 1234567890

(table continues on next page)

Table D.2 *continued*

Mac OS			
NAME	WEIGHTS & STYLES	GENERIC FAMILY	EXAMPLE
Helvetica	bold, oblique, bold oblique	Sans-serif	ABCDEFGHIJKLMNOPQRSTUVWXYZ abcdefghijklmnopqrstuvwxyz 1234567890
Helvetica Neue*	bold, italic, bold italic	Sans-serif	ABCDEFGHIJKLMNOPQRSTUVWXYZ abcdefghijklmnopqrstuvwxyz 1234567890
Herculanum*		Cursive	ABCDEFGHIJKLMNOPQRSTUVWXYZ ABCDEFGHIJKLMNOPQRSTUVWXYZ 1234567890
Hoefler Text	bold, italic, bold italic	Serif	ABCDEFGHIJKLMNOPQRSTUVWXYZ abcdefghijklmnopqrstuvwxyz 1234567890
Impact		Serif	ABCDEFGHIJKLMNOPQRSTUVWXYZ abcdefghijklmnopqrstuvwxyz 1234567890
Marker Felt*		Fantasy	ABCDEFGHIJKLMNOPQRSTUVWXYZ abcdefghijklmnopqrstuvwxyz 1234567890
Monaco		Monospace	ABCDEFGHIJKLMNOPQRSTUVWXYZ abcdefghijklmnopqrstuvwxyz 1234567890
New York**		Serif	ABCDEFGHIJKLMNOPQRSTUVWXYZ abcdefghijklmnopqrstuvwxyz 1234567890
Optima*	bold, italic, bold italic	Sans-serif	ABCDEFGHIJKLMNOPQRSTUVWXYZ abcdefghijklmnopqrstuvwxyz 1234567890
Palatino**	bold, italic, bold italic	Serif	ABCDEFGHIJKLMNOPQRSTUVWXYZ abcdefghijklmnopqrstuvwxyz 1234567890
Papyrus*		Cursive	ABCDEFGHIJKLMNOPQRSTUVWXYZ abcdefghijklmnopqrstuvwxyz 1234567890
Sand**		Fantasy	ABCDEFGHIJKLMNOPQRSTUVWXYZ abcdefghijklmnopqrstuvwxyz 1234567890
Skia		Sans-serif	ABCDEFGHIJKLMNOPQRSTUVWXYZ abcdefghijklmnopqrstuvwxyz 1234567890
Symbol		Fantasy	ABXΔEΦΓHIθKΛMNOΠΘPΣTYςΩΞΨZ αβχδεφγηιφκλμνοπθρστυπωξψζ 1234567890
Techno**		Fantasy	ABCDEFGHIJKLMNOPQRSTUVWXYZ abcdefghijklmnopqrstuvwxyz 1234567890
Textile**		Cursive	ABCDEFGHIJKLMNOPQRSTUVWXYZ abcdefghijklmnopqrstuvwxyz 1234567890
Times	bold, italic, bold italic	Serif	ABCDEFGHIJKLMNOPQRSTUVWXYZ abcdefghijklmnopqrstuvwxyz 1234567890
Times New Roman	bold, italic, bold italic	Serif	ABCDEFGHIJKLMNOPQRSTUVWXYZ abcdefghijklmnopqrstuvwxyz 1234567890
Trebuchet MS	bold, italic, bold italic	Sans-serif	ABCDEFGHIJKLMNOPQRSTUVWXYZ abcdefghijklmnopqrstuvwxyz 1234567890
Verdana*	bold, italic, bold italic	Sans-serif	ABCDEFGHIJKLMNOPQRSTUVWXYZ abcdefghijklmnopqrstuvwxyz 1234567890
Webdings**		Fantasy	
Zapf Dingbats*		Fantasy	
Zapfino*		Cursive	ABCDEFGHIJKLMNOPQRSTUVWXYZ abcdefghijklmnopqrstuvwxyz 1234567890

* = as of OS X; ** Only installed in OS X if Classic is installed
* As of Mac OS 8.5

Table D.3

Windows OS

NAME	WEIGHTS & STYLES	GENERIC FAMILY	EXAMPLE
Arial	bold, italic, bold italic	Serif	ABCDEFGHIJKLMNOPQRSTUVWXYZ abcdefghijklmnopqrstuvwxyz 1234567890
Arial Black		Serif	**ABCDEFGHIJKLMNOPQRSTUVWXYZ abcdefghijklmnopqrstuvwxyz 1234567890**
Comic Sans MS	bold	Cursive	ABCDEFGHIJKLMNOPQRSTUVWXYZ abcdefghijklmnopqrstuvwxyz 1234567890
Courier New	bold, bold italic, italic	Monospace	ABCDEFGHIJKLMNOPQRSTUVWXYZ abcdefghijklmnopqrstuvwxyz 1234567890
Franklin Gothic Medium*	italic	Sans-serif	**ABCDEFGHIJKLMNOPQRSTUVWXYZ abcdefghijklmnopqrstuvwxyz 1234567890**
Georgia	bold, bold italic, italic	Serif	ABCDEFGHIJKLMNOPQRSTUVWXYZ abcdefghijklmnopqrstuvwxyz 1234567890
Impact		Sans-serif	**ABCDEFGHIJKLMNOPQRSTUVWXYZ abcdefghijklmnopqrstuvwxyz 1234567890**
Lucid Console		Serif	ABCDEFGHIJKLMNOPQRSTUVWXYZ abcdefghijklmnopqrstuvwxyz 1234567890
Lucida Sans Unicode		Sans-serif	ABCDEFGHIJKLMNOPQRSTUVWXYZ abcdefghijklmnopqrstuvwxyz 1234567890
Marlett		Serif	[symbol font example]
Microsoft Sans Serif*		Sans-serif	ABCDEFGHIJKLMNOPQRSTUVWXYZ abcdefghijklmnopqrstuvwxyz 1234567890
Palatino Linotype	bold, bold italic, italic	Serif	ABCDEFGHIJKLMNOPQRSTUVWXYZ abcdefghijklmnopqrstuvwxyz 1234567890
Symbol		Fantasy	ΑΒΧΔΕΦΓΗΙϑΚΛΜΝΟΠΘΡΣΤΥςΩΞΨΖ αβχδεφγηιφκλμνοπθρστυϖξψζ 1234567890
Tahoma	bold	Sans-serif	ABCDEFGHIJKLMNOPQRSTUVWXYZ abcdefghijklmnopqrstuvwxyz 1234567890
Times New Roman	bold, bold italic, italic	Serif	ABCDEFGHIJKLMNOPQRSTUVWXYZ abcdefghijklmnopqrstuvwxyz 1234567890
Trebuchet MS	bold, bold italic, italic	Sans-serif	ABCDEFGHIJKLMNOPQRSTUVWXYZ abcdefghijklmnopqrstuvwxyz 1234567890
Verdana	bold, bold italic, italic	Sans-serif	ABCDEFGHIJKLMNOPQRSTUVWXYZ abcdefghijklmnopqrstuvwxyz 1234567890
Webdings		Fantasy	[symbol font example]
Wingdings		Fantasy	[symbol font example]

* = as of Windows XP

KEYBOARD CHARACTER VALUES

Whenever a visitor to your site presses a key, it generates a keyboard event that includes a numeric value for the key that has been pressed.

The following tables list the values generated by a standard U.S. English keyboard and detected using either the **onkeyup** or **onkeydown** event handlers. To learn more about using keyboard characters, see "Detecting Which Key was Pressed" in Chapter 13.

Note: Another method for visitor interaction using the keyboard (without resorting to JavaScript) is the **accesskey** attribute discussed in the sidebar "Using Access Keys to Improve Accessibility" in Chapter 18.

Table E.1

Letters

CHARACTER	VALUE
A	65
B	66
C	67
D	68
E	69
F	70
G	71
H	72
I	73
J	74
K	75
L	76
M	77
N	78
O	79
P	80
Q	81
R	82
S	83
T	84
U	85
V	86
W	87
X	88
Y	89
Z	90

Table E.2

Numbers

CHARACTER	VALUE
0	48
1	49
2	50
3	51
4	52
5	53
6	54
7	55
8	56
9	57

Table E.3

Punctuation & Numeric

CHARACTER	VALUE
;	59
=	61
, (comma)	188
.	190
/	191
`	192
[	219
\	220
]	221
'	222

Table E.4

Number Pad	
CHARACTER	VALUE
0	96
1	97
2	98
3	99
4	100
5	101
6	102
7	103
8	104
9	105
-	109
*	106
.	110
/	111
+	107

Table E.5

Control	
CHARACTER	VALUE
Backspace*	8
Tab	9
Num Lock	12
Enter/Return	13
Caps Lock	20
Esc	27
Spacebar	32
Page Up	33
Page Down	34
End	35
Home	36
Arrow Left	37
Arrow Up	38
Arrow Right	39
Arrow Down	40
Insert	45
Delete	46
F1	112
F2	113
F3	114
F4	115
F5	116
F6	117
F7	118
F8	119
F9	120
F10	121
F11	122
F12	123

*Delete on Mac

KEYBOARD CHARACTER VALUES

Tools & Resources

I hope this book has opened your eyes to the possibilities of DHTML and CSS, and given you the foundation you need to get started creating your own Web pages. But this book is finite, and the Web is, well, maybe not infinite but about as close as we can contemplate. This appendix will help you explore the resources available to you on the Web.

In addition to these resources, I use lots of tools for Web design—not only the high-end stuff like FreeHand, Photoshop, Dreamweaver, and GoLive, but also smaller programs that make my life much easier. Some are freeware or shareware programs; others are Web sites. Here are a few of my favorites.

Software Tools

One of the greatest features that the Web offers is the ability to download software quickly and easily. This has led to an explosion of programs that have too small an audience to make it onto the shelves of your local store, but are nonetheless indispensable for Web designers.

Screen Ruler (Mac OS 9/Win) Free Ruler (Mac OS X)

www.kagi.com/microfox

www.pascal.com/software/freeruler/

Some ideas are so obvious, so simple, and yet so brain-bitingly useful that you kick yourself every time you use them for not having thought them up yourself. Screen Ruler and Free Ruler (**Figure F.1**) are just such an invention. Both programs place a ruler (in the form of a long yellow graphic) on your screen, which you can use anywhere and at any time, independent of other programs being run. These rulers are indispensable for figuring out positioning in your browser window, from how far over you need to nudge a graphic to make it fit to how wide a table needs to be to accommodate your text.

Art Directors Toolkit (Mac/Win)

www.code-line.com/software/
→ artdirectorstoolkit.html

Art Director's Toolkit is the Swiss Army knife of design. Whether you're working on Web or print design, this simple-to-use program can save you lots of time and effort. One of its many useful features is that you can select any pixel on the screen, and it will show you that pixel's color in hex, RGB, and CMYK values (**Figure F.2**).

Figure F.1 Screen Ruler.

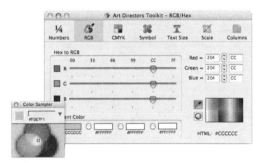

Figure F.2 Art Directors Toolkit.

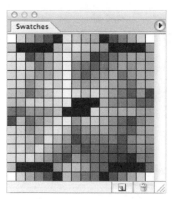

Figure F.3
VisiBone's CLUT.

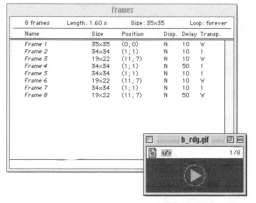

Figure F.4 GIFBuilder

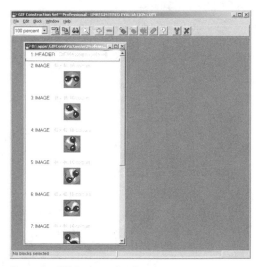

Figure F.5 GIF Construction Set.

Browser-safe color palettes (Mac/Win)

www.visibone.com/swatches/

If you're working in almost any graphics program to design your Web page, I recommend using the VisiBone swatch collection, which presents the colors in a user-friendly format (**Figure F.3**).

You can use these color-lookup tables (CLUT, for short) with your graphics software to ensure that you always have quick and easy access to the safe colors.

GIFBuilder (Mac) and GIF Construction Set (Win)

www.mac.org/graphics/gifbuilder/

www.mindworkshop.com/
→ alchemy/gifcon.html

Although far more complex and sophisticated programs for creating animated GIFs are on the market, you can't beat GIFBuilder (**Figure F.4**) and GIF Construction Set (**Figure F.5**) for pulling together a nice quick animation straight out of Photoshop. One of GIFBuilder's lesser known but choicest features is the ability to take a layered Photoshop file and make each layer an animation frame. On top of all that, these programs are free.

GraphicConverter (Mac) and LView Pro (Win)

www.lemkesoft.de/en/index.htm

www.lview.com

Although the program is not nearly as sophisticated as Photoshop in terms of graphics editing, I have used GraphicConverter (**Figure F.6**) to open files in odd formats and strangely encoded file types that sent its more sophisticated rival fleeing in panic. In addition, GraphicConverter can batch-convert any number of graphic files from one file format to another with great control.

StyleMaster (Mac/Win)

www.westciv.com/style_master/

If you're tired of hand-coding all of your CSS, but need a less expensive and less complex alternative than Dreamweaver or GoLive, StyleMaster is the program you seek. It allows you to code by hand or use convenient menus and buttons, and it always checks your code for browser compatibility (**Figure F.7**).

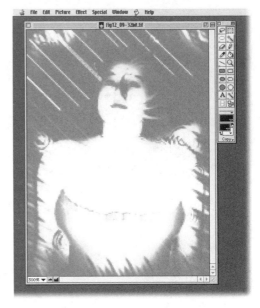

Figure F.6 GraphicConverter.

Figure F.7 StyleMaster.

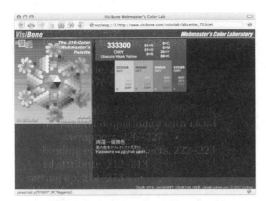

Figure F.8 Webmaster's Color Lab.

Figure F.9 W3C's CSS1 Test Suite.

Online Tools

In addition to offering software that you can download, plenty of Web sites provide functions and services that you can use to improve your own Web site.

Webmaster's Color Lab

www.visibone.com/colorlab/

How do you define the color palette for your Web site? It helps to place colors next to each other and see how they work together. VisiBone has created a very useful tool called Webmaster's Color Lab to help you do just that (**Figure F.8**). In one frame, you have a well-organized color wheel that contains all the browser-safe colors. Clicking a color causes a swatch of that color to appear in an adjacent frame. As you click more colors, they appear next to the previous swatch. Even better, though, an example of all of the previous colors appears in the swatch for comparison.

CSS1 Test Suite

www.w3.org/Style/CSS/Test

How do you know what CSS capabilities your favorite browser supports? Run it through the W3C's CSS1 Test Suite (**Figure F.9**). Every CSS attribute is represented. This tool is especially useful if you're creating a site with CSS or DHTML and need to make sure the CSS you want to use will actually work before you go to all the trouble of creating the Web site.

Technology and Standards

As complete as I tried to make this book, there is always more to know. These sites should help guide you to everything you could want to know about DHTML and CSS.

World Wide Web Consortium

www.w3.org

If you're looking for the source of all standards, this site is the place to go. Whether you need information on the most recent work being done to update the Document Object Model or the final recommendations for CSS Level 1, this site is the alpha and omega (**Figure F.10**). Here are some of the highlights:

◆ Cascading Style Sheets
www.w3.org/Style/CSS/

◆ Document Object Model
www.w3.org/DOM/

CSS: A Guide for the Unglued

www.thenoodleincident.com/tutorials/css/

This Web site presents a fast resource for designers wanting to learn more about developing Web sites with CSS (**Figure F.11**).

HTML Help by the Web Design Group

www.htmlhelp.com

This site is where I first learned CSS myself. After I slogged my way through the W3C's turgid specifications, HTML Help made some sense of it all. This site may not be the most attractive one on the Web, but don't be fooled—it's stocked with some of the clearest explanations of Web standards available (**Figure F.12**).

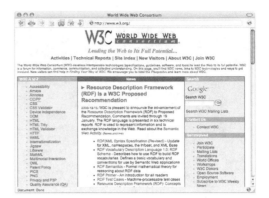

Figure F.10 The World Wide Web Consortium.

Figure F.11 CSS: A Guide for the Unglued.

Figure F.12 HTML Help.

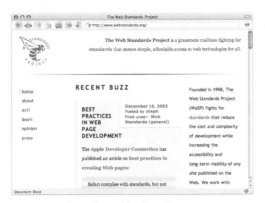

Figure F.13 The Web Standards Project.

Figure F.14 WebReference.com.

Figure F.15 Apple Developer Connection – Internet Developer.

The Web Standards Project

www.webstandards.org

This watchdog group does not set the standards; it watches the browser manufacturers and agitates when they go astray. The Web Standards Project does more than just complain, however. The group has started a browser-upgrade campaign to help designers stick to the standards (**Figure F.13**).

WebReference

www.webreference.com

WebReference concentrates on the nuts and bolts of front-end Web design, providing in-depth articles on the practical use of DHTML, CSS, and other technologies (**Figure F.14**).

Apple Developer Connection— Internet Developer

http://developer.apple.com/internet

Although slanted toward Web designers who use the Mac, the ADC site includes information that any Web designer can apply, written by some of the best minds in the industry (**Figure F.15**).

DHTML Frequently Asked Questions

www.faqts.com/knowledge_base/
→ index.phtml/fid/128

This site is one of my favorites. If you have a question about DHTML (or CSS or JavaScript, for that matter), it probably will be listed here, along with the answer (**Figure F.16**).

BrainJar.com

www.brainjar.com

Find everything from basic tutorials to advanced scripts all using the strictest CSS standards. The site is well written and the interface is easy to use (**Figure F.17**).

DHTML and CSS for the World Wide Web

www.webbedenvironments.com/dhtml

The support site for this book includes all the code presented in the book; you can view the code online and download it. In addition, I'll place updates and corrections on this site (**Figure F.18**).

Figure F.16 DHTML FAQ.

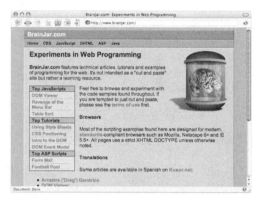

Figure F.17 BrainJar.com.

Figure F.18 DHTML and CSS for the World Wide Web (3rd Edition).

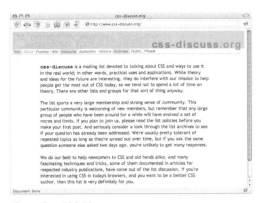

Figure F.19 CSS Discuss.

Figure F.20 Glass Dog.

Figure F.21 A List Apart.

Design and Theory

Creating an effective Web site takes more than just knowing how the code works. You also have to understand how to put the pieces together in a user-friendly design.

CSS Discuss

www.css-discuss.org

If you have a question about CSS, this is the place to get it answered. Join in the discussion, ask questions, and even answer a few (**Figure F.19**).

GlassDog

www.glassdog.com/design-o-rama

This site is a smart yet entertaining place to learn about Web-site design. GlassDog talks to you as though you are an intelligent human being, rather than a mindless drone, and still manages to slip in all the raw information you need (**Figure F.20**).

A List Apart

www.alistapart.com/

A List Apart is an online-only magazine with articles covering design, development, and Web content. It focuses on techniques that use Web standards (**Figure F.21**).

DESIGN AND THEORY

Scott McCloud

www.scottmccloud.com

Scott is an accidental Web guru. A renowned comic-book artist (*ZOT!* is a must-read), his book *Understanding Comics* became an instant classic in the burgeoning Web-design industry in the mid-1990s. Although his Web site concentrates primarily on Web-based comics, its message is relevant to anyone who wants to learn more about design for the Web (**Figure F.22**).

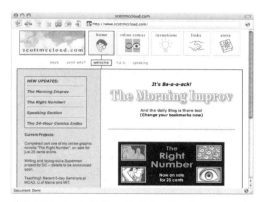

Figure F.22 Scott McCloud's Online Comics.

Glish CSS Layout Techniques

www.glish.com/css

This Web site focuses on using CSS to replace table-based Web designs, including several excellent techniques for scalable multicolumn designs (**Figure F.23**).

Figure F.23 Glish CSS Layout Techniques.

Useit.com

www.useit.com

Jakob Nielsen's Useit.com site provides articles that help readers make better Web sites through usability theory. Although I don't always agree with the conclusions Nielsen draws from his own theories, his ideas usually are intriguing (**Figure F.24**).

Figure F.24 Jakob Nielsen's Useit.com.

Figure F.25 Web Page Design for Designers.

Figure F.26 webbedENVIRONMENTS.

Web Page Design for Designers

www.wpdfd.com

Joe Gillespie is a designer's designer, and his site is chock-full of articles to help designers make the transition from print to the Web. Even seasoned veterans of the Web wars will find much to read here (**Figure F.25**).

webbedENVIRONMENTS

www.webbedenvironments.com

This is my own Web site, where I write about the intersection of technology and culture, concentrating on how the Web is shaping the way we think. Oh, and I occasionally share some new Web techniques I'm developing (**Figure F.26**).

Examples

The number of sites using DHTML to create their interfaces is growing every day. Here are a few that I recommend reviewing.

Panic Software

www.panic.com

Panic makes some of the best software available for Mac OS X, but its home page also has an impressive DHTML interface that allows you to drag and drop icons for download (**Figure F.27**).

Figure F.27 Panic Software.

International Herald Tribune

www.iht.com

Not only is this one of the best newspapers on the Internet, it's one of the best designed, with an elegant and extremely user-friendly interface created using DHTML. Some nice touches include the dynamic Clippings menu and the ability to change between single- and three-column viewing modes without having to reload the page. If you're serious about DHTML interfaces, study this site closely (**Figure F.28**).

Figure F.28 *International Herald Tribune.*

Sandman Film

www.sandmanfilm.org/film.html

I created this site for an independent film by my brother David, using DHTML scrolling techniques. The site has a "zoetropic" effect in which two frames slide horizontally back and forth, depending on which section you want to view (**Figure F.29**).

Figure F.29 *The Sandman.*

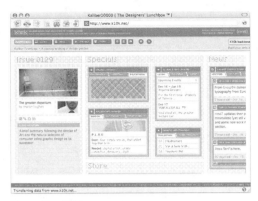

Figure F.30 Kaliber 10000.

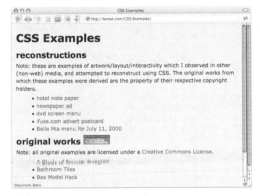

Figure F.31 Tantek CSS Examples.

Kaliber 10000

www.k10k.net

Kaliber 10000, also known as K10K, is a popular destination for Web designers looking for cutting-edge Web design ideas that work. This site is a great place to pick up ideas for integrating DHTML into your site's interface (**Figure F.30**).

Tantek CSS Examples

http://tantek.com/CSS/Examples

This site showcases some great and simple uses of CSS to inspire you and get the creative juices flowing (**Figure F.31**).

Books, Magazines, and Other Publications

Although the Web happens on the screen, many great print publications can help you as well.

Visual Explanations

Although words seem to dominate our lives, it's surprising how much more information we derive from visual cues than from letters. Edward Tufte's book *Visual Explanations: Images and Quantities, Evidence and Narrative* (Graphics Press) deals with the complexities of conveying information through a visual medium and the important role that visual communication plays in our lives.

Understanding Comics

I mentioned Scott McCloud's excellent Web site earlier in this appendix; his book *Understanding Comics* (Kitchen Sink Press) is also worthy of mention. Although ostensibly about comic books, the book is really about visual communication. If you're looking for a captivating introduction to the wonders of sharing information through images rather than letters, I highly recommend this book.

Invisible Computer

The basic message in Donald A. Norman's book *Invisible Computer: Why Good Products Can Fail, the Personal Computer Is So Complex and Information Appliances Are the Solution* (MIT Press) is that people don't want to use computers; they want to get things done. We tend to forget about that when we think of all the things a computer can do. *Invisible Computer* is a great book about the philosophy of creating products to be distributed through the computer medium.

BOOKS, MAGAZINES, AND OTHER PUBLICATIONS

Figure F.32 Computer Arts Web site.

Figure F.33 VisiBone's HTML and CSS Reference Card Web site.

Computer Arts

www.computerarts.co.uk

Each month, this magazine is full to the spine with tips and step-by-step instructions, as well as articles examining a range of issues that are important to designers of all stripes. Although *Computer Arts* is published in the United Kingdom, I've found it in many bookstores in the United States as well as online (**Figure F.32**).

VisiBone HTML and CSS Card

www.visibone.com/html

VisiBone HTML and CSS Card is the perfect cheat-sheet for anyone who creates code for the Web. These four pages contain virtually everything you need to know about HTML tags and CSS properties, including attributes, values, browser compatibility, bugs, and special characters. This card is a must-have for all Web designers (**Figure F.33**).

INDEX

INDEX

INDEX